P9-CMY-977

Toward the
Visualization of History

Toward the Visualization of History

The Past as Image

Mark Moss

LEXINGTON BOOKS

A division of
ROWMAN & LITTLEFIELD PUBLISHERS, INC.
Lanham • Boulder • New York • Toronto • Plymouth, UK

LEXINGTON BOOKS

A division of Rowman & Littlefield Publishers, Inc.
A wholly owned subsidary of The Rowman & Littlefield Publishing Group, Inc.
4501 Forbes Boulevard, Suite 200
Lanham, MD 20706

Estover Road
Plymouth PL6 7PY
United Kingdom

Copyright © 2008 by Lexington Books
First paperback edition 2010

All rights reserved. No part of this publication may be reproduced, stored
in a retrieval system, or transmitted in any form or by any means, electronic,
mechanical, photocopying, recording, or otherwise, without the prior permission
of the publisher.

British Library Cataloguing in Publication Information Available

Library of Congress Cataloging-in-Publication Data

Moss, Mark Howard, 1962–
  Toward the visualization of history: the past as image / Mark Moss.
     p. cm.
  Includes bibliographical references and index.
  1. Mass media and history. I. Title.
  P96.H55M68 2008
  901'.9—dc22

2008010162

  ISBN: 978-0-7391-2437-6 (cloth: alk. paper)
  ISBN: 978-0-7391-2438-3 (pbk: alk. paper)
  ISBN: 978-0-7391-4434-3 (electronic)

Printed in the United States of America

∞™ The paper used in this publication meets the minimum requirements of
American National Standard for Information Sciences—Permanence of Paper
for Printed Library Materials, ANSI/NISO Z39.48-1992.

This book is dedicated to my mother, Phyllis and my two children, Jesse and Becca.

Contents

Preface

W hen I first began to think about the subject that eventually became this work, I was concerned with my initial assumptions. Having just spent a few years pondering the connection between mass culture and fascism, I was convinced that students, who derived the bulk of their historical knowledge from the products of mass culture, would not be able to make the enlightened decisions necessary for the continued functioning of a liberal democracy. They would in fact, leave themselves and their offspring open to the machinations of totalitarianism or of "friendly fascism." Then, in 1994 I received the opportunity to teach at a college in Toronto. I was asked to step in and continue a class on war and social change.

Many of the students I had the pleasure to teach brought with them keen insights regarding the nature of history. They asked provocative questions and pursued acute lines of thought. After some probing, I was informed that the majority of their inquiries and most of their foundations of historical knowledge were derived from film and television. The odd student even mentioned a photograph of some historical event—although they could rarely recall the photographer's name. What this suggested to me was that far from destroying their capacity to understand and process historical knowledge, the mass media, and specifically, the visual media at their disposal, was eminently capable of provoking intellectual discussion on matters related to the past. As well, in revelatory fashion, the singular source of historical awareness that they possessed was the media. Over the past ten years, I have seen this process grow and to an important extent, mature or at least evolve, to a point where I can confidently state that most of the students in high school and college receive most of their historical knowledge from television, film, photography, and new media. This being said, what I have tried to do as a professor, is to build upon this established "fact" within the classroom.

If this is the case, why not use this form of knowledge as a starting point, a base, to work from? If they are coming to the classroom or lecture hall with a sense of visual history firmly put in place by the visual media, rather than dismissing it as trite or mindless, I felt that it was necessary to use the language that they already possess as a way to get them to appreciate and understand the more established and traditional forms of historical discourse and historiography.

When I began to discuss this idea with some of my colleagues, most of them were uncomfortable with the concept of validating visual forms of mass culture, especially within the confines of traditional academic environments. Most have come around and have acknowledged that it would be a wise move to credit the culture of youth with something—provided certain standards are upheld. The remaining reluctant voices are too petrified to move in this direction. They see this validation as a sell out to the interests of corporatism. By validation, I mean that the products of mass culture can bridge gaps between teachers and learners and can provide for a wonderful introduction to a complex topic. By validation, I also suggest that this visual youth culture comes to the classroom, the tutorial and to the lecture hall, and should not be dismissed simply because it is different from traditional modes of intellectual endeavor.

What is presented in the following pages is not a plea to recognize the usefulness of visual history, but rather an acknowledgment that it is here and will not be going away. I offer sketches and surveys, comparisons and contrasts, anecdotes and facts that trace the growth in importance of this varied method of communicating history. I do this reluctantly. I am not a huge fan of technology in the classroom. I am a traditionalist. Yet I recognize that this is a significant part of the culture of today's student and that visual culture and all that it entails is key to unlocking the appeal of the past.

Many people have read portions of this book and deserve to be acknowledged for their contributions. These have come in suggestions, revisions, sources, and queries. Maria Vasilodimitrakis read the manuscript with an exacting eye and offered many original and positive criticisms. To her I owe a special debt. Peter Meehan provided support and encouragement. Ourania Kourakis, Rhonda Roth, Gail Strachan, Joy Muller, and Kelly Donaldson provided their time and energy in purveying books and articles for me. Henry Decock, Dave Phillips, Brian Nakata, Doug Hunt, Naomi Herman, Tracy Pogue, Paula Gouveia, Jennipher Yebuga, and Jim Moran also provided assistance, reassurance, and motivation. My former dissertation advisor David Levine, as well as a number of anonymous readers at various institutions, also deserves acknowledgment. Emily Andrew was an early champion of this idea and her efforts on my behalf are greatly appreciated. Joseph Parry at Lexington books and the staff at Rowman and Littlefield justifiably deserve my praise. Shelly Hornstein of York University's Faculty of Fine Arts was instrumental in many ways and a special thanks goes to her.

A version of Chapter 3 appeared in the *College Quarterly*, Summer 2004 and a version of Chapter 7 appeared in the *College Quarterly*, Fall 2005.

Parts of this work were first given at a number of conferences held over the past few years. Parts of Chapter 2 as "The Gutenberg Revolution," Plenary Address, presented at CALL (College Association of Language and Literacy) 2000, Orillia, Ontario, June 5–7, 2000; Chapter 6, as "Modern Visual Literacy and Film," at the same conference. Elements found in the introduction were first presented as "Visualizing the Past: History as Image," presented at *100 Years of American Mass Culture*, Carnegie Mellon University, Pittsburgh, Pennsylvania, September 29–October 1, 2000. Significant portions of Chapter 2 were first discussed as "The Past and Future of the Book," presented at New Perspectives on Popular Culture, Technology and Society, Seneca College, June 23, 2003. And finally, a substantial portion of the final chapter was talked about as "Visualizing History; Computer Technology and the Graphic Presentation of the Past," presented at The Teaching, Learning and Technology Conference, Ryerson University, November 23–24, 2003.

Introduction

This book is about recognizing the culture of students who are currently in schools, colleges and universities. It is about the "net generation," "millennial learners," and their perspectives and mindsets. Young people today enter the classroom with a visual component within their psyche that people over the age of thirty simply do not possess. If they are not completely immersed in the world of the keyboard, than they are extremely comfortable with the television screen as a source of information, the movie theater as a lecture hall, the magazine as a teacher. As one authority has written:

> Most students entering our colleges and universities today are younger than the microcomputer, are more comfortable working on a keyboard than writing in a spiral notebook, and are happier reading from a computer screen than from paper in hand.[1]

This book is also about sending a message to educators and teachers who are in the class room, the lecture hall or administrative offices. This varied group must be aware of the culture of the learner. They bring to the classroom a mentality that is as different as anything ever experienced in education. They are, for all intents and purposes, a different generation. They are not completely at home with books and with listening. Anyone who has lectured recently knows that after sixty minutes, students grow bored. This is the recognition that I am moving towards.

Yet within education today and within the teaching of history, one must not and cannot lose site of the importance of the written and printed word. One should also never buy into the fact that the traditional ways of instruction are completely redundant and that lectures and tutorials are superfluous. What is needed is a compromise that benefits both parties and that recognizes the essential aspects of traditional curriculum delivery with an emphasis on the visual nature of society.

One example of this balance in favor of traditional forms of history education comes from Edward Ayers. Ayers suggests that "history is everywhere." There are thousands of websites, visits to historical places, and even numerous history channels on television.[2] There has also been a plethora of movies devoted to historical subjects and hundreds of games that use history as their base. Yet Ayers (and others) reminds us that poll after poll suggests that young people do not know their history—in this case American—not to mention the history of other nations.[3] This is confirmed in Canada by the Dominion Institute as well as through testing and examination of the curriculum.[4] There is a disconnect from the amount of history available and the fact that students are not learning it— or not learning it properly. Ayers remarks that the human connection between teachers and students is where we can succeed:

> In that classroom we can create communities of trust that do not exist in the outside world. We can sustain conversations across weeks and months. We can ask questions that cannot be answered in the span of an hour-long documentary. We can offer coherence and proportion. We can show the importance of sequence and context. We can embody the excitement that engagement with the past can bring.[5]

Professor Ayers writes that "we have no choice but to engage the history pouring in on them."[6] And this is the point. To utilize what they bring to the classroom, to harness what exists in their world, within the realms of good teaching.

The book begins with a wide-ranging analysis of visual culture and its various manifestations. Everything about contemporary society has a visual component and thus, it does and will affect historical awareness or historical consciousness. From subtle to profound, these changes have enormous pedagogic importance. Chapter 2 discusses how history has evolved to accommodate the visual nature of society. Central to this idea is the fact that individuals gravitate towards the narrative structure of history—the storytelling component of the visual—just as often as popular historians frame history in these terms. The notion of narrative and the concept of the storyteller come primarily from Hayden White and Walter Benjamin, respectively. Chapter 3 involves an in-depth analysis of the past and future and of print culture. It begins by discussing how written culture affected classic oral culture and then continues to describe the way in which the printing press affected reading. A concise historical dialogue moves into an examination of new technologies and their impact on print culture, libraries and reading. The starting point in any discussion of history inevitably leads to the subject of archival/written documentation. The place of print culture in the future of historical interpretation is thus, extremely relevant and even essential as a foundation for understanding the future of history in the visual world. In Chapter 4 the photograph as a conveyor of historical meaning is illustrated. There is a juxtaposition of photography with painting, as well as a rumination on how the war photograph has become a staple of historical knowledge and a definitive visual conveyor of history. The importance of film is discussed in Chapter 5. Discussion here ranges from documentaries to Hollywood feature films. The following chapter deals with the pervasiveness of television and its role as key disseminator of historical ideas and knowledge in numerous forms. These range from the TV movie of the week, to news and information programs, to the constant appearance of historical tropes in popular entertainment formats. Chapter 7 explores the application of film, photography and televised versions of history to a case study—the Holocaust. Important here is the recognition that these three media have impacted the commemorative forms of history in very significant and unique ways, which force museums and monuments to respond to the visual nature of mediated history. The final chapter delves into the "new media" as purveyors of historical knowledge. With each passing day, the Internet and other forms of computer mediated information, from Web Sites that are interactive to CD-ROMs, devote more and more data to historical renderings. Some of these products are indeed fatuous but many, like the best historical films, can not be dismissed as irrelevant. Some, in fact, must be recognized as having both validity and merit as historical offerings.

NOTES

1. Jason L. Frand, "The Information-Age Mindset: Changes in Students and Implications for Higher Education," *EDUCAUSE Review*, September/October, 2000, p. 15.

2. Edward L. Ayers, "History in the Air," *Magazine of History*, Vol. 18, No. 4, July 2004, p. 61.

3. Edward L. Ayers, "History in the Air," p. 61.

4. See Peter Mansbridge, "2004 Canada Post Lecture: Do the Media Reflect Canada's History?" *Tabaret: The Magazine of the University of Ottawa*, Spring 2005, p. 4.

5. Edward L. Ayers, "History in the Air," pp. 61–62.

6. Edward L. Ayers, "History in the Air," p. 62.

1

Visual Cultural and Historical Consciousness

Ours is the age of the picture. Pictures abound in our newspapers and magazines, in storybooks and on the glossy pages of instruction manuals. We find them on billboards and postage stamps, on the television screen and in the cinema. And in all of these cases pictures inform us: they explain, they clarify, they elucidate—and at times, too, they entertain and delight us. Images on the television screen have all but replaced the printed word as a source of information about the world; and nowadays, too, picture books and comic strips are consulted much more readily, and with much less intellectual effort, than the printed word. There can be little doubt but that pictures have come to play a very important role in communication.

—David Novitz, *Pictures and Their Use in Communication*, xi

Seeing comes before words. The child looks and recognises before it can speak.

—John Berger, *Ways of Seeing*, 7

We see naturally. We look without effort. We are born to gaze.[1] The above quotes and ideas encapsulate the argument that many have articulated for some time, but that only recently, has come to the fore as a feature of life; that individuals access images more readily than words.[2] Seeing is a central feature of modern society and as Mitchell Stevens cogently puts it, "Moving images use our senses more effectively than do black lines of type stacked on white pages."[3] The image, to use contemporary parlance, is "where it's at."[4] The image has not only matured to an unheard of level of sophistication,[5] it has challenged, and in many cases surpassed the culture of print. This point is succinctly put in the standard text on the subject of visual culture:

> The world we inhabit is filled with visual images. They are central to how we represent, make meaning, and communicate in the world around us. In many ways, our culture is an increasingly visual one.[6]

The supremacy of the image is a definitive modern and an iconic post-modern feature of society. By the middle of the nineteenth century, the move towards a graphic based culture was well on its way to eroding the culture of print. Images, ocularity and seeing were everywhere, from department store windows to magazines, to small portable cameras. Not only was the dominance of the visual a quantified fact, but it had an impact on how the individual began to sense his or her environs.[7] As Martin Heidegger recognized in his essay, "The Age of the World Picture," technology, modernism and society have conflated to put an overriding emphasis on the visual. To perceive of the world in modern society, means, according to Heidegger, that the world has become a picture.[8] The visual nature of society biases the ocular and favors it above all else. It becomes our *lingua franca*, as illustrated in the way that both music videos and much advertising are easily absorbed and digested across boundaries, without much emphasis on words.[9] The image, whether the photograph or the television picture, has the ability to summarize, condense, and in turn render comprehensible the difficulties of history.

In this work the conception of the past is often intertwined with history—the academic rendering of previous events—and it also merges with aspects of collective memory to form a cornucopia-like recipe that can be described as "historical consciousness,"[10] public commemoration, or popular history. The last appellation is the most all encompassing for it integrates and recognizes the vitality of visual forms of communication at their most powerful.

Brian Plane has made the argument that the technology that brings history to so many, in on-line formats, is simply "inconceivable without the democratization of images." Plane writes, "The Internet's efficiency as a reference tool lies in its ability to transmit information in image form as easily as text." Plane goes on to remark that the plethora of images contained in contemporary textbooks is astonishing. "A 1,000 page textbook," he observes, "usually contains over one hundred historical maps, and over four hundred historical illustrations, not to mention tables, timelines, and text boxes, which bring colorful images to virtually every textbook page."[11] The similarities between the contemporary textbook and many Web-based products are quite pronounced. Where Web-based formats have the edge is in accessibility and fluidity.

To some this is problematic and dangerous, to others this is reality.[12] In harmony with mass culture, the visualized emphasis of society becomes the currency by which to express thought. Even more to the point, for many people, most of what they perceive of as life, as history, as society, is in some way or form, a derivative of the image.[13] Even in his or her most intimate thoughts, what an individual understands to be wholly their own, are in fact some composite of image drenched society. Human understanding has come to be defined in the form of visuals.[14] The visuals are all around us, and even within us, and thus it is not so much the pictures themselves but "the modern tendency to picture or visualize existence."[15] History is often perceived of as a visual composition, one that involves the digestion of myriad visual accoutrements that have been "archived" and are retrievable, and that are capable of being consumed and played over and over again.[16]

Beyond the confines of what goes on in the classroom or in the lecture hall, the subject of history, in its visual, postmodern manifestations, is extremely popular.[17] Historical presentations are highly valued and eagerly watched. Robert Burgoyne feels that many people wish to almost touch history. Burgoyne notes that in Walter Benjamin's originative essay, "The Work of Art in the Age of Mechanical Reproduction," Benjamin suggests that there is a desire for people to "bring things close" and in particular, artifacts or images from the past that possess a patina of culture which imbues them with an aura of veneration. He feels that often this material desire to connect, has an "analogous" parallel today with history, which comes out in numerous historical variations:

> In my view, the contemporary desire to re-experience history in a sensuous way speaks to an analogous desire to dispel the aura of the past as object of professional historical contemplation and to restore it to the realm of affective experience in a form that is comparable to sensual memory.[18]

Burgoyne is suggesting that we desire and consume history in a variety of ways, which can range from Civil War recreations in full historical costume, to antique collecting, because it is both more satisfying and significant if it is something palatable and even tangible.

What we have is the convergence of popular history with public history. History in the nineteenth century was often a discourse for the public. The average person in Europe and in parts of North America, who was literate, read history. History was not divisive yet it could be interpreted differently depending on who was writing and when. Significant in this arena was the fact that simply put, history was history. By the 1970s, history had been carved up into numerous disciplines. On the one end was consensus or establishment history while on the other rested the "new" history which spoke about women, minorities and the marginalized. As well, a strong element of social was present in the later, with emphasis on crafts and workers. By extension, focus was given not just to the grand and the great but towards the ephemeral and the unique, the small and the obscure. Writers and teachers that moved in this direction were often the most creative of a new generation and who sought to break new ground by shedding light on unique aspects of society and their institutions, those that had rarely been discussed. Joining in this blossoming of historical interpretation were popular purveyors of the past, such as journalists and novelists, as well as those trained in history but not teaching in a postsecondary environment and increasingly, those working for government agencies such as museums or battlefields, charged with interpreting the past for and to the public. Thus there were now popular historians and public historians. By the 1980s, what was once the preserve of folklorists has now become another variant of historical methodology, the oral historian, who sought with a tape recorder or video camera to capture someone's voice and someone's story? Buttressing all of this were the film makers and the television producers and writers, who with photographers also stepped in to capture variations of the past.[19]

A corollary to the above is the increasing use of audio/visual/computer technology to talk about the past, to engage the viewer/receiver with elements and aspects of historical discourse that are often absent from education. Two developments stand out in these cases. The first is the creation of an abundance of museums devoted to the study of the mass media; radio and television institutions now have buildings devoted to their industry. Within the confines of these structures, the research and library facilities have been turned inside out. People can go and watch famous broadcasts and listen to tapes of live performances. The second version of this has been the related creation of archives devoted to the preservation and recognition of the audio/visual record. In some cases these have been sanctioned by a government body, such as the Library of Congress, while in other cases, universities have been the main agencies devoted to this kind of sanctioning. These steps have served to legitimize radio, television, film, and other forms of nontraditional history, and pushed them to the forefront of historical usefulness.[20] As if to confirm this form of legitimization, one scholar has written of the liberation-effect involved. "Today's historical scholars have the opportunity to 'go beyond the printed descriptions to the primary source material of our age.'"[21]

With the recent millennium celebrations and the constant pressure of postmodern industrial society, many people have taken solace in history. There has been a constant attempt to reconnect with the past, from obsessions with Druidic cults to the never ending fascination with Atlantis and ancient Egypt. Historical attachments of this kind are often symptoms of a "deeply felt need" in the way that they allow people to feel more se-cure.[22] History, as events in the Middle East, the former Yugoslavia and elsewhere have shown, is still with us and still very powerful. People are willing to go to war over incidents that occurred hundreds or thousands of years ago.[23]

From one perspective, the current emphasis on presentism may be said to have eroded the necessity of historical enquiry and possibly, may have contributed to the fact that teaching history to students is no longer seen as vital. At the same time, one can surmise that this has created an envi-ronment where there is a great deal of hostility directed towards history and all its related disciplines. Young people are often bored with history and are often exposed to history in ways that are, to put it mildly, unimag-inative and irrelevant. Given the fact that students often approach history as a chore rather than as an area of excitement and relevance, there is not, in the words of Ken Osborne, "an automatic and inherent love of the past," among the current student body.[24] Yet there is a great paradox in-herent in discussions of the past and its contemporary place. As James B. M. Schick has found, "people like history."[25] But it is a specific presen-tation of history that people gravitate towards; this history involves tele-vision miniseries, movies, popular fiction, and theme park or "public his-tory" which runs the gamut from recreations of battles to the kind of history presented at Disneyland.[26]

Vital to this appeal is both the spectacle and the visual. In an almost tan-gible way, this orientation of the presentation is more real and more ac-cessible to many who would not normally receive historical information. This is an important point to consider. As Mike Wallace recognized, "it's possible that Walt Disney has taught people more history, in a more mem-orable way, than they ever learned in school."[27] Marketers know this bet-ter than most. History is often harnessed as a commodity and sold to peo-ple. The reason why this is so successful a format is that most people group perceptions of society around historical themes.[28] Merchandising history as well as the presentation of historical knowledge in a commod-ified format can result in the most careless of descriptions, often found in the "synthetic nostalgia" produced in Medieval Times-like restaurants.[29]

At the same time, it must be recognized that this move towards the pres-entation of history, this popularization of historicisms, has precedents. Television and film, as well as photography and new technologies *present* history. To some extent, these media do modify what history is, in new ways, comparatively to older established forms, but they do constitute forms of historical discourse which demand acceptance.[30] History is not dead and it is certainly not over. John Cook has taken Francis Fukuyama to task on this point. Cook feels that Fukuyama jumped the gun in declar-ing "the end of history." With September 11 and the more recent Gulf War, it is apparent that history "never ends." Quite the contrary is occurring. Cook proposes that given the numerous historical events "there is enormous media interest in all things historical."[31]

These aspects of historical interpretation are all in line with Frederick Jameson's key characteristics of postmodernism.[32] These include the "disappearance of depth," in particular, meaning that "only surfaces matter" and that "only images are real"; the notion of "pastiche," which allows for the merging of many styles and elements all present in one place; the "schizophrenic" or fragmented nature of culture, which in turn allows for incoherence; and the increasing reduction of history to "nostalgia."[33] Concomitant to this, what often occurs is the full-fledged eruption of Jean Baudrillard's concept of "simulacrum." Baudrillard remarks that in the postmodern world, "the difference between and image (or code) and reality is no longer important." For many people, image is the reality.[34]

Perhaps influenced by the conflation of visual with shallow or surface presentations, critics and thinkers on the subject of visual culture and visualized history are often terribly uncomfortable with the acknowledgement that historical discourse is so dominated by the image. From their perspective, that of the written word, anything that seeks to erode the supremacy of that medium, is suspect. There is a tendency to dismiss the visual as "trivial," and anything that moves the focus away from print or the written word is negated. As one commentator has remarked, the conservative nature of the historian, who prizes the written or print culture above all else, makes the equation of visual as trivial "self-fulfilling."[35]

For more than one hundred years, the image has been ascendant. This has not so much been the American century, but rather the visual century, the "movies century," where film, photography, video and the television have come to challenge and in some cases make superfluous, print, books, and writing. The visual attributes of culture have come to be the means by which we communicate, understand and amuse.[36] Beginning around 1910, groups of educators, film producers and government officials in the United States pushed for visual education, which sought to use visual artifacts, in particular film, as a way "to stimulate and enlighten students while making far-flung technological worlds seem concrete and knowable." Some were aware of the "anesthetizing and corrupting effects of motion picture," but the attempt was to socialize and educate a wide array of viewers to a "visually oriented world."[37]

While visual media made an impact, general notions of history have undergone a significant and radical change from those in place in the nineteenth century and even earlier. The concept of what constitutes history (historical evidence, accepted historical "reality," etc.) has made a move from a firm anchoring in print to one dominated and defined by the image.[38] Key to this shift has been the growth of a mass culture industry which has intentionally and unintentionally caused this reorientation.

During the last half of the nineteenth century, the "visual" began to assert itself in immeasurable ways. Not only in quantity, but in impact, did the "multiplication of images" have an enormous effect.[39] By the last third of the nineteenth century, the visual accoutrements of mass culture had made an impingement in most urban environments in the west. At the same time, this move towards visualizing culture not only influenced the public sphere, but also, the private one. Within the home, the vestiges of visual culture—whether in the form of Victorian chintz or sepia toned photographs—caused the image to be seen as a definitive barometer of culture and taste. "Homes," according to Todd Gitlin, "turned into private shrines of visual icons."[40] At the same time as electronic diversions, "collective spectacles," newly minted grand public amusements and commercialized leisure began to overtake the mass spectacle of entertainment, a premium was being placed upon increased powers of concentration and the ability to pay attention for long periods of time.[41] The opera, the ballet, the symphony and the culture of the museum dictated that quiet, sustained focus and prolonged attention were, among money and nice clothes, something that one absolutely had to possess in order to succeed in the participation of these cultural endeavors. The nickelodeons, dancehalls, saloons, and other, more democratic environments, not to mention the street, and all its offerings, were more anti-focus in their orientation. The modern, urbanized city suggested noise, and stimulation, in particular visual stimulation. As Todd Gitlin has observed, "the high arts demanded sustained attention."[42] Not being rapt in one's focus and devoted in one's thoughtfulness was increasingly deemed problematic. Gitlin suggests that it was at the end of the nineteenth century and the beginning of the twentieth century that "psychologists began to treat inattention as a flaw."[43]

Individuals were forced, whether they wanted to, to pay more attention especially in certain venues. Yet, paradoxically, there was too much going on—in the street, in the sky, on the sides of buildings—everywhere there were neon lights, noises, signs, and traffic. Crossing the street required one, to at least, temporarily devote one's attentions to a specific task. Eventually, the dictates of modernism[44] and mass culture forced one to begin to selectively examine, to scan, to "eyeball," rather than to plunge headlong and completely into something. The latter became the reserve of the intellectual/academic elite. The more pervasive former became the ingredients for our image-saturated culture.[45]

Although photography had been around since 1839, it was in the 1880s that the photograph or the picture, found its way into the minds of the masses. During this period, high quality photo-line illustrations came into being in the daily press. Very quickly, these visual depictions of events as well as their imaginative renderings came to be seen as key pieces of information, which in certain environments rapidly surpassed the written word. As pictures in general came to occupy key places in the dissemination of information, any kind of visual image quickly challenged the supremacy of the written word. This occurred with the comic strip as much as it did with the modern advertisement. In a society that was composed of immigrants who did not share a common heritage, the picture was (and still is) extremely effective. More and more did the visual image take on an important and vital role.[46]

Hand in hand with the growth of mass culture has come the sophisticated and omniscient presentation of history as image. History in pictures, if you will, has been around for quite some time. Ancient Greece was as much a visual culture as it was an oral one. The visual imagery that surrounded the citizens of city states like Athens was constant and varied. It ranged from monuments and carvings on statues to the pervasive painted vases.[47] Roman buildings contained frescoes depicting key historical events. Roman statuary in particular was a very important form of communication.[48] During the Middle Ages, stained glass and sculpture and the tapestry were used to convey what then passed for historical knowledge.[49] The importance of Medieval Cathedrals and the images that they contained in wood, stone and bronze was also recognized.[50] For the Renaissance and in general, the early modern period, images retained an enormous potency of power. There were periodic backlashes against the image, as in the more extreme Calvinist regions of Europe, but for the most part the reign of the image remained unchallenged. In fact, this was reaffirmed during the Council of Trent, held during the mid-sixteenth century, which stated the importance of images in defining and worshipping God. This unique form of image reaffirmation was designed to counter the word-based transmission of information that was so much a part of the Lutheran Reformation.[51]

Paintings have always used historical scenes as subject matter and reached a level of sophistication during the French Revolution that still has potency today. Yet veracity and access have always been problems. Only small numbers of people could view these images.[52] And therein lies one of the major distinctions between visual history then, and the kind of visual history that began in the early twentieth century.

The photographs taken by Mathew Brady and others (and used extensively and effectively in Ken Burns' documentary) during the Civil War marked a major move to mechanically encapsulate or artificially document a significant historical event. Just a few years earlier, depictions of the war in the Crimea had been sketched. Within a few decades, the merging of history and photojournalism would be complete with just about every major event being photographed[53] and thus pass on to future generations a level of accuracy (even though staging was common) that previous generations only had to access via an artist's vision. The still picture that glares at you every morning in the front page of your newspaper is archived and recycled to provide a visual historical record.

One only has to think of any major historical event of the last 100 years—Potsdam, Vietnam, the Holocaust, the Kennedy years, the Depression, WWI, the atom bomb, the earth as seen from the moon, and chances are that you have thought of it in some kind of visual terms. A photograph, a grainy newsreel, early color TV footage, or a Hollywood film—all of these provide visual evidence of history and in many cases jump to prominence in our mind's eye.

By the early decades of this century, films were being used to either capture and record major events, or to restage history in the form of a narrative story. Film quickly came to stand for, record, or to tell the historical tales that professional historians had so long held a monopoly on. Yet film, at first silent film, being a medium of moving pictures, was embraced by so many because it provided information that most could absorb; in essence, unlike learning to read, one could simply watch it.[54]

As film matured, it was capable of capturing a variety of historical figures and situations and conveying them in a palatable manner to large audiences, thereby exposing millions to history. Critics have always harped on this problem of content versus audience. At its best, visual history was capable of translating to many the complexities of history. Yet, it was someone's often-distorted version of history. The power of the film to dictate history reached an apex during the late 1960s and early 1970s, moving a vast distance from the Hollywood biopic, to the revisionist history which captured social history in a way that paralleled developments in academic history.[55]

Mass culture, as Walter Benjamin recognized with regard to the work of art, brings to many what had previously been available to only a few. Mass culture exposes, enlightens, teaches and tells. But, like the concept of aura in the work of art in the age of mechanical reproduction, something is lost. Complexities are often boiled down, disparities are conveniently erased and troublesome questions run the risk of being banished. Yet despite these concerns, it is vital to recognize that television products and historical films reach numbers that academic historians can only dream of. As is the natural tendency of mass or popular culture, the needs of action, adventure and romance often obscure the staid realities of print versions. This is exactly why a film maker like Ken Burns is troubling to many historians working in traditional methodologies. The appeal of his television films is so fast that they have effectively challenged the dominance of written history. In an almost single-handed manner, the work of

Burns' has come to define historical discourse for the general public.[56] According to Gary R. Edgerton,

> *The Civil War* asserts in one fell swoop that history is no longer the principal domain of specialists, as it had been for nearly a half-century, but now is relevant and compelling for everyone—only this time on TV.[57]

The early development of television illustrated very quickly that television could provide a take on history that was unique, and often, quite accurate, given the constraints and the nature of the medium. Yet the 1950s television shows that some have marked as the golden age of television, quickly gave way to westerns, situation comedy's and other entertainment fare that handled history in both bizarre and inaccurate ways. At the same time this evolution was occurring, television news stepped in to compensate, at least for a while, with accurate, original and riveting reports. From Edward R. Murrow's *See It Now*, to the Cronkite broadcasts of Kennedy's funeral, television news filled a much needed gap. The problem now became that what was now not shown on TV, not filmed, was to be banished from the new historical record.

The watershed of television as "purveyor" of history came about with two significant 1990s events: the Gulf War and the airing of Ken Burns' *The Civil War*. Over 14 million people watched the Civil War in its initial broadcast[58] and this points to a significant fact: that history for most people today is being presented through the media.[59] History is what they see on TV. According to Jim Cullen, this documentary "probably reached more people than that of any contemporary academic . . ."[60] The 1990 Gulf War happened in real time; and this removed the barrier time for digestion that was once a process of decision making and deliberation. As Johanna Neuman has observed, "Governments watched history with their publics, losing the luxury of time to deliberate in private before the imperative to *do something* stood on their doorsteps."[61] Not only was history being presented before one's eyes, and not only were government officials seeing it at the same time as the public, thanks to CNN, the traditional gatekeepers, the popular historians, the print journalists were shut out of their role as well. "Never before," recalls Howard Kurtz, "had newspaper people felt so utterly obsolete as during the first days of the Persian Gulf War. It was a CNN war and we all knew it. The story was changing by the hour and we came out only once a day."[62] While Kurtz may be correct on many levels, one must also keep in mind that the pictorial spreads that newspapers put out in the days after the attacks, along with commentary and opinion, revitalized the newspaper industry in a number of significant ways. Still photographs in particular became very effective at conveying or reconveying news and information through traditional outlets.[63] The Internet also 'came alive' during this crisis and matured to a point where it was capable of playing with the more established conveyors of news—at least for a time.[64]

Over a significant period of time, the products of mass culture moved away from leisure, play, amusement, and somehow found a way to convey what had been the preserve of the representatives of high culture. Profit motives, entertainment values, and the marketing industry all served to shape mass culture in various ways, yet seriousness, art, and knowledge—not just information, was also present. To simply dismiss the "massification" of culture as carnivorous or parasitic[65] is today, an elitist assumption. The days of the Frankfurt School's rejection of mass culture as pure entertainment no longer exist. Passivity and acceptance of the status quo aren't necessarily part of the mass culture recipe today.[66] Alternate voices and view points—independent film, guerrilla TV, and the Internet provide quality and provocative products. The "500 channel universe" gives the viewer access to environmental, political and social viewpoints that would have been seen as heresy during the 1950s. The viewpoints of Clement Greenberg and Dwight Macdonald, among others, also seem somewhat hysterical from today's perspective. The 1950s fears have not been realized—at least not in the way many theorists expected. The fact remains the most North Americans discern historical knowledge and access information about the past through television, film, photography, and, increasingly, Internet and CD ROM sources.[67]

Mass culture as provider of history is not without traces of some of these notions, yet it has grown into an area that is far richer and far more diverse than mid-century commentators had foreseen. Not to realize that most people receive their notions of history from television and film is to agree with the erroneous generalization that mass culture is used by the 'uncultured' majority.[68] The distinctions that were used are no longer (as) relevant or can no longer be maintained.[69]

In harmony with many of the ideas voiced by the 1950s critics of mass culture, Daniel Bell wrote eloquently on alienation, consumption and of course, the middlebrow aesthetic. In the 1960s and 1970s, he was as convincing as the earlier models. Yet Bell, in *The Cultural Contradictions of Capitalism*, realized that "the dominant outlook," culturally speaking was/is "visual." He wrote that "in a mass society it could not be otherwise."[70] The notion of the visual dominating in a mass society is an interesting concept, especially when one starts to investigate in the area of etymology. The word "idea" incidentally happens to come from the Greek verb meaning 'to see.' According to Chris Jenks, whose concept this is, "the way we think about the way we think in Western culture is guided by a visual paradigm. Looking, seeing, and knowing have become perilously intertwined."[71] It must be recognized that in harmony with mass culture's ascendency, a significant feature of modernity, according to Martin Jay, is the "privileging of 'sight.'" The respect given to the visual as a primary means of communication suggests that the modern world is very much a 'seen' phenomenon.[72]

To see means to know, to understand. Our culture; our history; our sense of society, are all dominated by sight. The image, as brought to us by mass culture has moved into a position of prominence. The image of history has, in the words of Mitchell Stephens, "gained the upper hand over words."[73] Not to recognize this or not to believe this is intensely problematic. To be part of history today, to "witness history" is to be in front of the television. We rush to the set or to see the latest YouTube images as soon as possible. To contemplate history, at least for most of the people in the West, is to conceive the past in images. We can't imagine the JFK assassination without the Zapruder film.[74] We can't recall the moon landing without seeing the grainy images of Neil Armstrong stepping down from the lunar module.[75] If you watched the recent Olympics, no doubt you heard Bob Costas or some other commentator, say, "this is a historical moment" or "she's making history," implying, that by watching, you are there, you are involved, your are, in essence viewing live history.

What this all may suggest is that history, as an academic subject, may be perceived to be redundant as would be history teachers and professors.[76] It is not taught in the schools and if it is taught in the universities or colleges, it is the kind of history that is so neutralized, so as not to offend anyone, that it is without any essence whatsoever.[77] It used to be said that history was essential for the making of citizens; history as a school subject instilled knowledge of the past to inculcate loyalty. As well, and importantly, most people probably used to have some kind of understanding of what history was. Many people could relate to, if not accept some kind of dominant narrative of the past that became a part of their heritage. But today, a fragmentation has occurred, splitting up historical knowledge into myriad explanations.[78] If it can be argued that television and film are now doing the job that the schools previously undertook, and are, perhaps doing it better, then is history no longer a subject fit for the schools?[79] Both the intent and the effect of the Heritage Minutes and the CBC's *Canada: A People's History* fall into line with this line of thinking. They originated in order to compensate for the paucity of historical knowledge that Canadian's possess as well as to rectify the canard that Canadian history is boring. And they have both been extraordinarily successful in these goals, which in turn accentuates the argument that the media can often do a better job than the schools.[80]

As mass mediated popular and commercial culture makes larger inroads into the structure and fabric of societies, they likewise assume newer roles and perform duties that involve the production of historical messages. Michael Kammen argues that this came to be of central importance in the 1980s with the centennial of the Statue of Liberty. He singles out Disney culture, theme parks and as well "second-rate action films," as taking the past and parading around "as a colorful pastiche of patriotic pap."[81] This process is also pronounced within the commodity sphere.

One finds the packaging and presentation of history virtually everywhere. Commercials utilize historical motifs ad nauseam, with everything from breakfast cereal (Quaker Oats)[82] to impersonators playing presidents getting in on the act, to image-based marketing that provokes questions regarding historical furniture styles and whole clothing lines.[83] Given the fact that students are not getting access to history in the curriculum, one newspaper even went so far as to praise a comic book on Canadian history that was being distributed by McDonald's.[84] A trip to the local furniture store, where historical motifs, tropes and accents blend from room (era) to room doesn't do much to disrupt the consumer's perception of humanistic historical linearity but rather, displays a postmodern "simultaneity of multiple historical reactivations" all presented at the same time, that most people are quite comfortable with.[85] Some of this is obviously low brow, but some, perhaps a lot, is not. Has the presentation of history via the translations of mass culture reached a point where a definition of what history is must be rethought?

The overall thesis of this work is that students today are exposed to history—ideas, knowledge, culture—from film and television far more than from print versions. Further, what this suggests is that traditional notions of history—textbook, academic, footnoted—must be reevaluated to factor in the impact of the visual nature of contemporary history. What has occurred over the last few years has been, to use the name of a book by Mitchell Stephens, *The Rise of the Image and the Fall of the Word.*

With the recent exception of *Harry Potter*, most students do not read books. That is a complaint that is often voiced around the coffee room or in the corridors of educational institutions. And this complaint does in fact have merit. From a very young age children are either watching television or listening to an IPOD or MP3 player. Their leisure—waking time—is rounded out by watching DVDs or playing video games or surfing the net. It is thus not surprising that they would therefore receive most of those historical pieces of information from the above listed formats. It is part of their media ecology.[86]

Print[87] has been the dominant medium since the invention of the printing press until the mid-twentieth century when it began television usurped its place as a source of knowledge and information. Film, photography and radio have, arguably aided in the erosion of print over the last one hundred years, but it was not until the late 1960s and early 1970s that a real challenge was noticeable. In the last ten years computer technology has increased in sophistication to such a point that it is itself starting to challenge the primacy of television. Gauging the decline of readership in daily newspapers is a depressing path to embark. Many young people today do not read a newspaper at all.[88]

Teachers and Professors have been using film as a potent way to interest students in a variety of disciplines for many years. Students however, prefer a different sort of film to the ones teachers traditionally use. Most often, and this is by no means backed up by a scientific survey, the films chosen by the instructor resemble a play. There is an emphasis on dialogue not action. But, given the fact that there are now so many movies and television choices, this has begun to change. Many more choices today certainly appeal to children or young adults who have grown up with television and film as constant sources of both entertainment and information.[89]

This in itself is problematic. If television and film are both entertainment oriented then students react to these media in a way that is not necessarily conducive to learning. We all know that it is increasingly difficult for even bright youngsters to sit still and listen to a talk for any longer than, say, forty minutes. Some lectures leave students with headaches and exhaustion. Yet the exact opposite is at work when they are viewing something. The process of absorbing ideas from a visual source is much less taxing on the mind than from an aural/verbal source.

Significant here is the fact that they—the students—have grown up with television and film as entertainment sources and thus, react to them in a way that is fundamentally different than when a professor is talking or writing on the blackboard. If you grew up watching *Sesame Street*, a noble educational experiment, you expect constant changes in the scenes in front of you. You expect steady modification and a quick pace; the dynamics of a TV ad! By altering education into entertainment, there was the expectation of fun. *Sesame Street*, with its "skits, songs, jokes, cartoons, puppets, commercials, and hyperkinetic tempo . . . all designed to stimulate even the most incurious and apathetic preschooler." This in turn would give rise to shows such as *Grammar Rock* and would eventually result into turning learning into a game—as in the world of computer software.[90] Visual media often means entertainment. And this is a meaningful obstacle that must be overcome. The collective body posture of the class seems to shift to a more relaxed position when the DVD cart is wheeled in. From slides to films on 16mm to video cassettes, a peculiar kind of process is at work. Here is how the American writer Paul Auster, remembers the situation "movies in the classroom":

> I was hired by the subdivision of a publishing company to write material for educational filmstrips. I had been subjected to a barrage of "audiovisual aids" during my childhood, and I remembered the intense boredom they in-

variably produced in me and my friends. It was always a pleasure to sit in the dark for twenty or thirty minutes (just like going to the movies!), but the clunky images on screen, the monotone voice of the narrator and the intermittent 'ping' that told the teacher when to push the button and move on to the next picture soon took their toll on us. Before long, the room was abuzz with whispered conversations and frantic, half-suppressed giggles. A minute or two later, the spitballs would begin to fly.[91]

Given the certainty that students have grown up in an environment where and when visual information is dominant, active and kinetic—anything that does not fit this description seems boring and quickly leaves them restless. Not only does the instructor have to be aware or up-to-date regarding what will appeal to them, but one has to ensure it contains all the right triggers to keep them focused, lest spitball fights result. In his remarkable book, *Silicon Snake Oil*, Clifford Stoll, himself a computer expert, asks the reader to name any kind of multimedia experience that was actually inspiring. Then he writes, "name three teachers that made a difference in your life." What Stoll is suggesting is that there is no substitute for the motivated teacher and the inspiring lecturer. The ability of a human being to impart knowledge is unsurpassed. The bias against the visual as a distraction from good teaching is no substitute. Stoll goes on to voice a similar scenario to the one sketched out by Auster:

> I do remember that whenever I saw an educational film in high school, it meant fun for everyone. The teacher got time off, we were entertained, and nobody had to learn anything.[92]

Now granted, both Stoll and Auster are reminiscing about dated audio-visual tools. More impact is generated with a Hollywood blockbuster than some sixty-year old documentary about the history of the forest produced by a pulp and paper conglomerate. Research confirms that certain presentations of history in visual formats, such as CD-ROM, greatly accentuate the absorption of historical knowledge.[93] Yet, a key problem is, as Stoll has recognized elsewhere, the fact that "Most learning isn't fun. Learning takes work. Discipline. Commitment, from both teacher and student."[94] Professor Kevin Mattson reaches a similar conclusion in more contemporary terms. After worrying about whether or not the students even get the subtext, ideology or universalism of an older film, such as *Dr. Strangelove* [1964] he pins the problem on entertainment:

> The problem was that the students were having a difficult time extricating themselves from the silky power of entertainment. Over and over I saw this played out: once the film started to roll in class, the pens went down, and the students' eyes glazed over.[95]

Like Stoll, Mattson feels that a lot of what passes for entertainment is simply not capable of being transported into the classroom. The comfort of watching a movie and even discussing it afterward simply do not compare to the rigors of learning.

A number of factors are at work here. At its best, the use of film as a historical document may provoke the student to investigate the subject further. He or she may be inspired to research the topic on his or her own. Most often, the print versions of history are superior to the filmed one. There may be dozens of perspectives given in print to a particular time in history but usually just one filmed version. And this in itself is interesting and problematic. *The* filmed version of history becomes an actual historical document. It takes on a life of its own and comes to stand for that past moment in a way that a book cannot. The movie version reaches many more people than the print versions and it is far easier for many in today's society to digest.

This last point is also extremely crucial. What is meant here is the fact that for many students, the time required to absorb a massive and potentially dry historical text is time they simply do not have. But it is not just the time. They often do not have the patience and endurance to tackle a difficult book of history. And it is not just history. Unlike in previous generations historical knowledge does not come primarily from the teacher/professor or through books. For those over 35, most forms of knowledge were derived from either a print source or from dialogues with others. This is certainly not the case today. The stability and permanence of print; the dominance and ubiquitousness of the book has now given way to a constantly changing influx of technologies. The screen, the image, the visual now supersedes print sources—not necessarily totally displacing them, but certainly gaining ground.[96]

The once dominant reading public is eroding. Yes, one can argue that book sales are booming, but what is being sold? Look at any mainstream bestseller list and one will see a plethora of how-to guides, cook books, *Idiots* manuals, light mystery, romance, and get-rich quick lessons. Statistically, one could guess that the quantity of quality readers as far as students are concerned has decreased enormously—although with the success of the *Harry Potter* books, that may change.[97] The competition for readers is daunting: music, TV, videos, electronic games, cell phones, all dwarf the lowly book. The earlier allusion to the fast pace of technology returns here to complicate things. Young people today are accustomed to such a hurried tempo of information absorption and in their lives in general, that it is truly daunting to teach some—especially in traditional ways.[98] Being able to process information from a variety of sources, to "multiprocess," has a number of advocates who will remark that it is a part of millennial culture. Yet one must ask, are they really absorbing information? Is it possible to learn difficult concepts from these sources? John Seely Brown for one, proposes that multiprocessing does not necessarily mean the student/viewer is not concentrating.[99] But, is this true learning?

As far as literature is concerned, in *The Gutenberg Elegies*, Sven Birkerts intimates the opposite. Students have difficulty slowing down enough to concentrate on prose of any density; they have problems with allusions, diction, vocabulary, indirect references, and deviations from straight plot. Now sure, Birkerts agrees, what they lack in the above list, they make up for in their electronic literacy, but he worries about a larger problem: "Our entire collective subjective history—the soul of our societal body—is encoded in print." Everything that is anything, from subtle to profound rests in books. And, he feels, "if a person turns from print—finding it too slow, too hard, too irrelevant to the excitements of the present—then what happens to that person's sense of culture and continuity?"[100]

The dominance of visual culture also pervades the culture of print. Look at the flashy images in newspapers today. Years ago, a standard type face dominated, but today, we see both larger, easier to read characters, and more images; more color, more graphs, and graphics in the newspaper. This was a process initiated by *USA Today*, to capture more readers, and it seems to have permeated the whole newspaper industry in a desperate desire to capture new readers—rather than to appeal to aging readers who need larger characters. According to David Marc, "*USA Today*, with its tiny blocks of print set among large splashes of color, shape, and narrative image might hardly be recognizable as a newspaper to a nineteenth-century reader."[101] Like so much of today's culture, *USA Today*, with its brief stories and ever-present maps resembles television. This is a "paper to watch, not to read."[102] This was a deliberate attempt to demonstrate that *USA Today* was a paper for viewers of television, comfortable with television aesthetics.[103]

The attributes of visual culture can be found virtually anywhere one chooses. And they are not confined to impacting on print. Go to a museum block buster show. It is no longer sufficient to look at paintings or antiquities; one must purchase those headsets that tell you what you are seeing. One used to go to a gallery or museum not just to see art or artifacts, but to contemplate it. Next time you go, count how long a young person stares at a picture. Museums have had to adapt to the changing nature of information absorption. Specifically in the post-World War II period, architecture and design began to incorporate new public attitudes and the concerns of the museum directors themselves regarding the increased emphasis of visual culture. The most obvious example of the new type of museum/gallery was the Guggenheim, designed by Frank Lloyd Wright, which became the definitive spectator museum. Here, the spectator, no longer the discerning art patron, is "never lost and can see where he has been and where he is going."[104]

Sven Birkerts, Neil Postman, Marshall McLuhan, and many other commentators have defended the importance of print culture to the maintenance of cherished values and institutions democracy to civility. It seems almost like a well-worn cliché to constantly cite this yet, when one examines what is at work with a book, one must be concerned. Print possesses certain attributes and characteristics that both allow and force the individual to expand beyond a certain place. The attention necessary to read a book leads to an increase in patience and comprehension. The act of reading is certainly much more active than watching TV or viewing a film.

What is often at work with film, television, video, and the like, is quite the opposite. We all know how easy it is to watch TV, in comparison to reading, especially when we are tired. And there are even different levels to this process of visualization. My students—or at least those who I have asked— will not watch a black and white film. Only the diehard—pardon the pun—film buffs will. Why?

Print culture requires the reader to "crack the code." In order to do so, a certain set of skills have to be mastered. With electronic—especially visual culture, this is not necessarily the case. The television viewer, who could be an infant, has virtually no code at all to "crack." The images are simply present and available to be absorbed. For some this is quite democratic, but for others it is viewed as scary.[105] Why? In his famous work *Ways of Seeing*, John Berger stated that to see, to look, to recognize, was a process that came before speech, as far as the child was concerned.[106] Learning to read takes time. We do not necessarily have to learn to see. It is an innate attribute. The time and effort required to master reading affects us is many ways. Viewing means instant gratification. The viewer expects to be titillated, entertained, and does not have to work for the information. And do not confuse viewing with prolonged observation. Watching a TV for information is not the same as studying a painting. Both use the eyes yet two totally different processes are at work.

It is often difficult for those set in their ways and comfortable with the way things are to understand another's propensity for doing things in a specific manner and at a certain pace. When I was growing up, we did not think of having the TV on while we were doing our homework. Yet young people today seem quite comfortable with doing many different things at the same time. Whether they do them well is open to debate. In her book, *Joystick Nation: How Videogames ate our Quarters, Won Our Hearts and Rewired our Minds*, J. C. Hertz defends this ability to simultaneously deal with the phone, television, fax, pager, e-mail, music, and the Internet, as a 'natural' component of today's youth culture. Life is akin to an arcade experience, where you "have to process all of this at once." And to do it "fast."[107] This last point, the ability to do it "fast," has permeated society today in an almost epidemic kind of way. The speed at which images bombard us and at which we must absorb them is something that younger people are quite comfortable with.

There are countless examples of how society is moving much quicker than it used to. On television, you must get your message across in a sound bite format,[108] otherwise it will not air or someone will change the channel. Movies must move at a quicker pace in order to "keep the viewer in his seat" and they are increasingly shorter in overall length, about ninety to one hundred minutes, lest the viewer get bored.[109] And just as J. C. Hertz suggests, James Gleick also feels that this is a situation that is quite common. It is a new "visual language made up of images and movements instead of words and syllables. It has its own grammar, abbreviations, clichés, lies, puns, and famous quotations." And we are very good at this new hyper-visual literacy; we can take it in "with true virtuosity."[110] Many of us do not have the slightest problem with it; it seems to many almost natural.

An absolute determinant here is the notion of time. Building on Gleick's ideas, one gets the sense that in some way, time has speeded up. This poses an interesting contradiction with regard to reading. The general assumption is that the attributes and characteristics of visual, digital culture revolve around speed.[111] In contrast, the Innisian bias of space kicks in when one discusses books. Books slow things down. Quantities of information are also weighted in this equation. Books take time and the information is, arguably, finite. A visual screen with news, weather, stock quotes and a talking head provides much more varied information, faster. The bias to books is much more reflective and much more oriented around absorbing thought. The distinction between information and knowledge is also applicable here.[112] This argument always ends up focusing on the idea that books, because of the reflective capacity they inspire, are oriented firmly around substance. The visual world seems to pale in comparison, according to this line of thinking.[113] But one must be wary of making too forceful a distinction here. The arguments that Postman, Birkerts and others advance suggests a bias towards elitism. Given the changes that YouTube, the iPOD, abbreviated text messaging, and the Internet in general have fostered, the resulting cultures differ significantly from many aspects of previously dominant information and knowledge-based culture.

The anthropologist Marc Auge has suggested that not only has time speeded up but so has history. The "acceleration of history" or what becomes history morphs into history once it has been lived. The pace of events that fall into history have to be put into a context. Auge feels that there is a pressing need to give "meaning" to these events but there is an excessive amount to contextualize. He intimates that as people live longer

and as more information is available about what happens, "collective, genealogical and historical memory" merge and reproduce "the occasions on
which an individual can feel his own history intersecting with History."[114]

How much substance is in fact lost?[115] One simply cannot convey a
complex problem in two sound bites.[116] Much of what is happening with
local TV news reflects this. Look at Toronto's CITY-TV and their newscast.
There is movement of people and brevity of information to such an extent
that you have absolutely no real knowledge of what is going on. Even
pseudo-intellectual programming is progressing in this direction. In-
depth interviews are giving way to quickie brushes with the camera. And
the camera doesn't stay still, it moves in a documentary style in order to
compensate for the fact that someone is trying to speak. On most public
affairs/current events shows, out of, for example, three guests, two are
most probably polished media professionals, while the third is usually a
representative (token) of some organization. The professionals know to
make short snappy statements—right to the point—the "amateur" will
drone on and on so much so that he/she will seem both unprofessional
and unpolished.

The belief that television's main purpose is to entertain rather than to
inform or educate may explain why it is so difficult to convey certain
kinds of information.[117] Television is a wonderful medium for disseminating specific kinds of information. It can excel in many areas: dramas,
the shows on the learning channels, the comedies, the cartoons, the sports
and the news. Yet for the most part it is a business that is increasingly
competitive and fragmented. The competition for audiences means simply that slow-paced, intellectually challenging programs do not last. But,
given the fact that there are now so many options, there is hope that quality shows, educationally informative shows will survive and thrive. Over
the years there have been wonderful attempts to inform and educate on
television. Look at Ken Burns' *Civil War* series which aired on PBS a few
years ago. Not only did it reach more people than any academic treatment
of the War, but it was provocative, intelligent and dependent on still photographs and voiceovers. This series illustrates the observation that when
television is good, it can be very good.

Historical films—whether documentaries, docudramas, or fiction—
have the power to "shape the thinking of millions." One could effectively
make the case that those behind the camera are now performing the role
of the historian.[118] This gives them an audience that the average historian
simply will never have. This also gives them the potential to convey a version of history that can have enormous ramifications. This is, of course,
not a new phenomenon. Since the advent of film/cinema, this has been an
established fact. Think of D. W. Griffith's *Birth of a Nation*, or even *Gone
With the Wind*. But directors who deal with historical subjects are effec-

tively competing with traditional tellers of history; "the school teacher, the college professor, and the history book author."[119] Youngsters and others may be forced to choose. Governments may be happy with this situation and feel that history in the classroom is no longer necessary.[120]

In the introduction to his book, *Screening History*, Gore Vidal comments on this process: "It is possible that even when working from memory, I saw the world in movie terms, as who did not or, indeed, who does not?"[121] Vidal himself was often inspired by movies to be more aware of historical periods and historical people. He would seek out books on topics that he had seen in films.[122] For him, viewing a film was a ritualistic experience. This was before the days of the VCR or DVD. A VCR or a DVD not only allows multiple viewings, but also the possibility of owning the film. The technology of recording allows one to back up, pause, and play again. Vidal writes that seeing a film once at a screening was like a "return to that oral tradition where one acquired a Homeric song through aural memory." One saw the movie once and it was nearly impossible that you would get to see it again. As a consequence, Vidal implies, you really had to pay attention. "Since we knew," he writes, "that we would have only one encounter, we learned how to concentrate totally."[123]

This last point suggests that we do not watch films or television for that matter, with the same level of concentration as Vidal and his contemporaries did.[124] Vidal grew up in a culture that was dominated by print. The focus, concentration, and effort that one puts into reading were probably put into viewing. By contrast, children today skim everything, sample, channel surf. How is it possible for them to apply themselves to one thing in good effort, with everything happening at the same time?

Movies—whether seen on TV, on DVD, downloaded from the Net, or in the Cineplex—have always been enormously powerful in their influence on everything from history to attitudes to behavior. We look towards movies for meanings both profound and trivial. Movies teach us—of that there is no question—and they show us worlds to which we cannot travel. For some it is about style and dress, for others it is how to kiss, how to smoke.[125] For numerous viewers, movies expose us to issues that we may have never been interested in or even cared about.

Films have always provided information to a variety of audiences. In some cases, films have served as the primary means of informing individuals about the culture in which they live. In the early part of the twentieth century, silent films, in nickelodeons and in early cinemas, provided the appropriate mix of "fun and social education" for many new immigrants. Andrew Heinze describes the fact that silent films were particularly appealing to those who could not understand English, yet provided a forum where they could grasp the basics of American habits and values, simply by viewing these short films.[126] Stories conveying basic human situations were transferable to viewers who had little or no knowledge of English. The working class immigrants of major urban centers flocked to the Nickelodeon and the cinema for an evening's education and entertainment. The strong visual nature of films had great appeal to those wishing to learn as much as possible about their new home.[127]

Because a subject or a historical detail is on film, it is more palatable. Then again, there are varying degrees of what is digestible. How are we to get an accurate historical message or at least an intelligent treatment of history if action adventure, the quick pace, strong narrative characteristics, and the general properties of visual media increasingly encroach in place of traditional forms of history? This is one of the reasons why Stephen Spielberg's *Schindler's List* has become such an important (visual) document for understanding the Holocaust. It reached a large audience in the theatres and when it was shown on television, an estimated 65 million American viewers saw it. By utilizing established conventions of mass mediated storytelling, Spielberg was capable of telling the history or a history to a vast group of people. Regardless if it bows to conventions and ideas that traditional historians abhor, the film has become the definitive vision of the Holocaust for most people.[128] But this still provokes the question of what to do with this new body of historical information.

Certainly ignoring it is not the answer. In fact that would be almost destructive. History presented on film is not going away—in fact, it is proliferating with the History Channel, The Learning Channel, Public Television offerings, CD-ROMs, Internet Access and the made for TV series like *The 70s* or the cable offering *Rome*. Pierre Sorlin feels that the difference between this new visual history, exemplified by him with the "World at War" series and traditional forms of history is the fact that visual history is oriented around a desire "to strike by its evidence and through immediate contact, instead of convincing through reason and deduction."[129] When one is reading a book, one can pause and think about what one has just read. When one is listening to a lecture, one can make mental notes to challenge the argument. But when one is listening to and watching a visual presentation, there is more of a level of acceptance based upon the appeal to the visual, which is increasingly fast paced and contrapuntal to reason. Films can enlighten, provoke and inspire; television can be thoughtful and informative, yet and this is a big yet, when we depend too much for our sense of history or education for that matter on the visual, we can run into huge problems.

The dynamics and the constraints of television news provide an illustration. What is ignored is lost to history. And what is often ignored is usually a story that has no visual evidence; no "film at eleven." If producers choose not to discuss a story because they have no film, one gets the sense that the topic is not important—not newsworthy—or else, in the long term, one starts to question if it in fact even ever existed.[130] The dependence on the visual means, if something has not been filmed, photographed, or recorded then it is assumed to never have existed. If one has watched those millennium or century ending survey shows, a great significance was attached to events occurring after the invention of film.

What we know of the past is not static; it is an ongoing process that in order to be meaningful, must be shaped.[131] Writing history is a complex open-ended process that involves research and extreme diligence. Filmed history denies this complexity in favor of a straight story and a disregard for alternatives. If, according to Robert Rosenstone, the main source of historical knowledge is from the visual media, we have to pay much more attention to what, how and why certain subjects come to be historicized by the media.[132] As the visualization of society increases we must be aware of how it artificially constructs a reality for us that, to paraphrase Leo Braudy, can only be viewed in certain set ways. We know that it has captured our imaginations when we say things like "I felt like I was in a movie" or we see places and think "this is like a film set."[133] And just another example of how potent the media can be. Have you ever judged the realism of TV shows like *Grey's Anatomy* or *Chicago Hope* not against your knowledge of actually being in a hospital or an emergency room, but against another medical drama—like *St. Elsewhere*, or *Ben Casey*? If so, an interesting process is at work. We are admitting a literacy with TV genres in a way we might not initially acknowledge.[134]

Why so many of us have a certain historical awareness of specific historical periods, such as the cowboy period—1865–1880 only fifteen short years, also known as *Westward expansion*—or World War II, no doubt comes from the fact that film makers have chosen to emphasize those periods and they have in turn, entered our collective popular culture as history.[135] An important coda to keep in mind regarding popular history is that for many people it often serves as a bridge from vague notions of historical data to comprehension of and familiarity with historical knowledge. It fills in gaps and allows for the construction of a form of social or cultural bonding, which in turn allows viewers to make sense of history, and importantly, contemporary society.[136]

An interesting definition of history is given by Arthur Marwick in his book, *The Nature of History*. He wrote, "History, then, is an interpretation of the past, one which a serious effort has been made to filter out myth and fable."[137] Perhaps that is just too boring and the myth and fable are the interesting parts. Perhaps filmmakers, television producers, photographers and game designers recognize just how important a role these features play in most societies. This is a key distinction to make and one which permeates this work. According to Gary R. Edgerton, it was in *Culture as History* that Warren Susman made the important, "intimate" connection about the close relationship between myth and history. Edgerton, commenting on Susman, writes, "One supplies the drama; the other, the understanding. The popular heritage holds the potential to connect people passionately to their pasts; the scholarly camp maps out the processes for comprehending what actually happened with richness and depth."[138]

The fact is, the way historical knowledge and information is being transmitted today and has been for some time, has more in common with myth, fable, and narrative than the seemingly objective, scientific notions associated with academic history. The history presented on television, through film, created in photographs and depicted in video games and CD-ROMs is a popular history that is structured around the rules of storytelling and is firmly in line with mythologised history. Whereas this interpretation of historical knowledge was dismissed by academic historians as being "artistic" and "ceremonial," as opposed to "empiricist," and "objective," these boundaries are increasingly being crossed.[139]

As consumers of history through the lenses of the media, we are conditioned to see the drama in everyday life. We look for the trappings of drama and expect to be rewarded by their offerings. Roles, actors, scripts; beginnings, middles and ends; high-points, resolutions, and a variety of special effects are what the current consumer of history is expecting. On some levels this is a return to earlier epochs when drama was a staple of culture.[140] The reason why history presented through images is so popular is because it conforms to the way people have not only been taught to see but the way in which they see society.

What must be appreciated in this work and in general, is the simple fact that students today receive their ideas of history primarily through exposure to mass media. That is a "given" that permeates this work. How, why and what to do with this idea, are questions that this work seeks to discuss, and not necessarily answer. It is vital for historians and educators, media professionals and those concerned with the transmission of knowledge to grant this as an established paradigm. To bemoan this fact and not to recognize it is indeed, problematic.

NOTES

1. It is important to recognize, as Martin Jay does, the debate between vision and seeing that is "natural" and vision or seeing that is "cultural." This is acutely problematic when one recognizes that visualization is very much linked to verbal and written processes of information digestion. For the most part here, what this work is concerned with is the cultural recognition of visualizing which when merged with the concept and word 'image' can include references to "graphic, optical, perceptual, mental" and "verbal" media. Martin Jay, *Downcast Eyes: The Den-*

igration of Vision in Twentieth-Century French Thought, (Berkeley, CA: University of California Press, 1994), pp. 3–9.

2. Frits Gierstberg and Warna Oosterbaan, "Introduction: The Image Society," *The Image Society: Essays on Visual Culture*, eds. Frits Gierstberg and Warna Oosterbaan, (Rotterdam: Netherlands Foto Institut, Nai Publishers, 2002), p. 7.

3. Mitchell Stevens, *The Rise of the Image: The Fall of the Word*, (New York: Oxford University Press, 1998), p. xi.

4. According to Vicki Goldberg, *The Power of Photography: How Photographs Changed Our Lives*, (New York: Abbeville Publishing Group, 1991), p. 135: "Civilization uses, even requires, visual symbols—the cross, the swastika—for shorthand communication of complex groups of ideas. As international trade, easy travel, instant world-wide transmission of visual data, and vast movements of people from country to country have complicated the problem of spoken communication, visual signs have taken over: there are corporate logos everywhere and simplified figures that indicate men's room, women's room, deer crossing, no smoking, poison."

5. One must be aware of the changing nature of visual reality, even though, this notion is beyond the scope of this work. In *Techniques of the Observer: On Vision and Modernity in the Nineteenth Century*, (Cambridge, MA: MIT Press, 1992), Jonathan Crary, p. 1., writes, "The rapid development in little more than a decade of a vast array of computer graphics techniques is part of a sweeping reconfiguration of relations between an observing subject and modes of representation that effectively nullifies most of the culturally established meanings of the terms *observer* and *representation*."

6. Marita Sturken and Lisa Cartwright, *Practices of Looking: An Introduction to Visual Culture*, (New York: Oxford University Press, 2005), p. 1.

7. Daniel J. Boorstin, *The Image: A Guide to Pseudo-Events in America*, (New York: Atheneum, 1961/1987), pp. 197–98, and Neil Gabler, *Life: The Movie, How Entertainment Conquered Reality*, (New York: Vintage Books, 1998), pp. 53–55.

8. Martin Heidegger, "The Age of the World Picture," in *The Question Concerning Technology and Other Essays*, translated and with an introduction by William Lovitt, (New York: Harper Colophon Books, 1977), p. 129, cited in Rey Chow, "The Age of the World Target: On the Fiftieth Anniversary of the Dropping of the Atomic Bomb," in Peter Gibian, ed. *Mass Culture and Everyday Life*, (New York: Routledge, 1997), p. 94.

9. James B. Twitchell, *Carnival Culture: The Trashing of Taste in America*, (New York: Columbia University Press, 1992), p. 256.

10. Peter Seixas, "Introduction," in *Theorizing Historical Consciousness*, Ed. Peter Seixas, (Toronto: University of Toronto Press, 2006), pp. 3–9.

11. Brian Plane, "Computer-Generated Graphics and the Demise of the History Textbook," in Dennis A. Trinkle and Scott A. Merriman, Eds., *History.edu: Essays on Teaching with Technology*, (Armonk, NY: M. E. Sharpe, 2001), p. 73.

12. Vicki Goldberg, *The Power of Photography*, p. 135.

13. Neil Postman, *Technopoly: The Surrender of Culture to Technology*, (New York: Knopf, 1993), p. 68, and James W. Carey, *Communication as Culture: Essays on Media and Society*, (Boston: Unwin Hyman, 1989), p. 2.

14. Lawrence Grossberg, Ellen Wartella, and D. Charles Whitney, *MediaMaking: Mass Media In A Popular Culture*, (Thousand Oaks/London: Sage Publications, 1998), p. 1.

15. Nicholas Mirzoeff, *An Introduction to Visual Culture*, (New York: Routlege, 1999), pp. 1, 5.

16. David Harvey, *The Condition of Postmodernity*, (Cambridge, MA: Blackwell, 1990/1995), p. 85.

17. David Lowenthal, *The Past is a Foreign Country*, (Cambridge: Cambridge University Press, 1985), p. xv.

18. Robert Burgoyne, *Film Nation: Hollywood Looks at U.S. History*, (Minneapolis: University of Minnesota Press, 1997), p. 105.

19. Peter Charles Hoffer, *Past Imperfect*, (New York: Public Affairs, 2004), pp. 114–16.

20. Donald G. Godfrey, "Broadcast Archives for Historical Research: Revisiting the Historical Method," *Journal of Broadcasting and Electronic Media*, vol. 46, no. 3, September 2002, p. 493.

21. Cited in Donald G. Godfrey, "Broadcast Archives for Historical Research: Revisiting the Historical Method," p. 493.

22. Alexander Stille, *The Future of the Past*, (New York: Farrar, Straus and Giroux, 2002), p. xiv.

23. Alexander Stille, *The Future of the Past*, p. 311.

24. Ken Osborne, *In Defense of History: Teaching the Past and the Meaning of Democratic Citizenship*, (Toronto: Our Schools/Our Selves Educational Foundation, 1995), p. 1.

25. James B. M. Schick, "What Do Students Really Think of History?," *The History Teacher*, vol. 24, no. 3, May 1991, p. 340.

26. James B. M. Schick, "What Do Students Really Think of History?," p. 340.

27. Mike Wallace, "Mickey Mouse History: Portraying the Past at Disney World," *Radical History Review* 32, 1985, p. 33.

28. Mark Gottdiener, *The Theming of America: Dreams, Visions and Commercial Spaces*, (Boulder, CO: Westview Press, 1997), pp. 144–51.

29. John Heskett, *Toothpicks & Logos: Design in Everyday Life*, (New York: Oxford University Press, 2002), p. 121.

30. Marc Ferro, *Cinema and History*, translated by Naomi Green, (Detroit, MI: Wayne State University Press, 1988), p. 158.

31. John R. Cook, "History-Makers," Review Essay, *Historical Journal of Film, Radio and Television*, vol. 22, no. 3, 2002, p. 375. Interestingly, Cook writes that the highest paid performer on British television is a historian, Dr. David Starkey.

32. Frederick Jameson, *Postmodernism or the cultural logic of late capitalism*, (Durham, NC: Duke University Press, 1991).

33. Lawrence Grossberg, Ellen Wartella, and D. Charles Whitney, *MediaMaking: Mass Media In A Popular Culture*, p. 54.

34. Lawrence Grossberg, Ellen Wartella, and D. Charles Whitney, *MediaMaking: Mass Media In A Popular Culture*, p. 55.

35. Michael L. Wilson, "Visual Culture: A Useful Category of Historical Analysis?" Vanessa R. Schwartz and Jeannene M. Przyblysk, eds., *The Nineteenth-Century Visual Culture Reader*, (New York: Routledge, 2004), p. 30.

36. Benjamin Barber, *Jihad Vs. McWorld*, (New York: Times Books/Random House, 1995), p. 88,

37. Elizabeth Wiatr, "Between Word, Image, and the Machine: Visual Education and Films of Industrial Process," *Historical Journal of Film, Radio and Television*, vol. 22, no. 3, 2002, p. 333.

38. Hayden White's distinctions of "historiophoty—the representation of history and our thought about it in visual images and filmic discourse" and "historiography—the representation of history in visual images and written discourse" are useful here. See Hayden White, "Historiography and Historiophoty," *American Historical Review*, Forum, December 1988, vol. 93, no. 5, p. 1193.

39. Jean-Louis Comolli, "Machines of the Visible," in Timothy Druckrey, Editor, *Electronic Culture: Technology and Visual Representation*, (New York: Aperture, 1996), p. 109.

40. Todd Gitlin, *Media Unlimited: How the Torrent of Images and Sounds Overwhelms Our Lives*, (New York: Henry Holt/Metropolitan Books, 2001), pp. 49–50.

41. Todd Gitlin, *Media Unlimited*, p. 65.

42. Todd Gitlin, *Media Unlimited*, p. 66.

43. Jonathan Crary, *Suspensions of Perception: Attention, Spectacle and Modern Culture*, (Cambridge, MA: MIT Press, 1999), pp. 1–79, cited in Gitlin, *Media Unlimited*, p. 66.

44. Norman Cantor, *The American Century: Varieties of Culture in Modern Times*, (New York: HarperCollins Publishers, 1997) for a concise list of the seminal characteristics of modernism.

45. Todd Gitlin, *Media Unlimited*, pp. 66–67.

46. Gunther Barth, *City People: The Rise of Modern City Culture in Nineteenth-Century America*, (New York: Oxford University Press, 1980), pp. 92–93, 105.

47. N. Keith Rutter and Brian A Sparkes, "Introduction," to *Word and Image In Ancient Greece*, eds. by N. Keith Rutter and Brian A. Sparkes, (Edinburgh: Edinburgh University Press, 2000), p. 1.

48. Asa Briggs and Peter Burke, *A Social History of the Media: From Gutenberg to the Internet*, (Cambridge, MA: Polity Press, 2002), p. 8.

49. Martin Jay, *Downcast Eyes*, p. 41. Jay, p. 50, cites, Norman Bryson, *Word and Image: French Painting of the Ancien Regime* (Cambridge: Cambridge University Press, 1981), p. 1 on the importance of stained-glass in the service of narrative.

50. Asa Briggs and Peter Burke, *A Social History of the Media*, p. 9.

51. Peter Burke, *Eyewitnessing: The Uses of Images as Historical Evidence*, (Ithaca, NY: Cornell University Press, 2001), p. 57.

52. John Berger, *Ways of Seeing*, (London: Penguin, 1972), p. 106, and Stuart Ewen, *All Consuming Images: The Politics of Style in Contemporary Culture*, (New York: Basic Books, Inc., 1988), p. 38.

53. In Susan Sontag's *On Photography* (New York: Farrar, Straus and Giroux, 1978), Sontag writes, "The inventory started in 1839 and since then just about everything had been photographed, or so it seems." p. 3. Elsewhere, she comments that it is the photograph "which now provides most of the knowledge people have about the look of the past and the reach of the present." p. 4.

54. It is important to note here, that there is a western bias at work on the visual nature of modern society. As McLuhan points out, in certain cultures, the ability to

simply "just see" is problematic, and gives rise, as numerous anthropologists have noted, to misunderstandings and misinterpretations of what is being shown and what has just been seen. Marshall McLuhan, *The Gutenberg Galaxy*, (Toronto: University of Toronto Press, 1986), pp. 36–39.

55. George F. Custen, *Bio/Pics: How Hollywood Constructed Public History*, (New Brunswick, NJ: Rutgers University Press, 1992).

56. Gary R. Edgerton, *Ken Burns's America*, (New York: Palgrave/St. Martin's Press, 2001), pp. 2–3.

57. Gary R. Edgerton, *Ken Burns's America*, p. 4.

58. JoAnna Baldwin Mallory, "Introduction," *Telling The Story: The Media, The Public, and American History*, ed. Sean B. Dolon, (New England Foundation for the Humanities, 1994), p. vii.

59. Robert Rosenstone, "Historians and Their Audience," in *Telling The Story*, p. 7.

60. Jim Cullen, *The Civil War In Popular Culture: A Reusable Past*, (Washington: Smithsonian Institution Press, 1995), p. 2. Cullen writes, "Indeed, some of the most respected historians in the field contributed to the project, a sign of an increased willingness on the part of professionals to participate in the making of public culture." p. 11.

61. Johanna Neuman, *Lights, Camera, War: Is Media Technology Driving International Politics*, (New York: St. Martin's Press, 1996), p. 3.

62. Howard Kurtz, *Media Circus: The Trouble With America's Newspapers*, (New York: Times Books, 1993), p. 223.

63. Barbie Zelizer and Stuart Allan, editors, *Journalism After September 11*, (New York/London: Routledge, 2002).

64. See the essays in Barbie Zelizer and Stuart Allan, eds., *Journalism After September 11*, (New York/London: Routledge, 2002) and *Afterwords: Stories and Reports from 9/11 and Beyond*, Compiled by the Editors of Salon.com, Forward by David Talbot, (New York: Washington Square Press, 2002). David Talbot writes "The Web allows for an immediate, intimate, and reflective type of journalism not easily replicated by other media. This was the first major war in which Americans used the Web to follow the news as it happened, logging on from work during the day instead of waiting for the evening TV news." p. x.

65. Dwight Macdonald, "A Theory of Mass Culture," in *Mass Culture*, eds. B. Rosenberg and D. Manning White, (London: Collier-Macmillan, 1957), p. 59.

66. Max Horkheimer and Theodore Adorno, *Dialectic of Enlightenment*, (New York: Continuum, 1972), Max Horkheimer, *Critique of Instrumental Reason*, (New York: Continuum, 1974), Leo Lowenthal, *Literature, Popular Culture and Society*, (Palo Alto, CA: Pacific Books, 1968), and Martin Jay, *The Dialectical Imagination*, (Boston: Little Brown and Co., 1973).

67. This last point is particularly interesting, and will be covered in the final chapter. The 1996–1997 *Voyager* CD-ROM catalogue is particularly telling about where new technologies were going.

68. Herbert J. Gans, *Popular Culture and High Culture*, (New York: Basic Books, 1974), p. 10.

69. Chandra Mukerji and Michael Schudson, "Rethinking Popular Culture," in *Rethinking Popular Culture: Contemporary Perspective in Cultural Studies*, Eds. Chan-

dra Mukerji and Michael Schudson, (Berkeley, CA: University of California Press, 1991), p. 35.

70. Daniel Bell, *The Cultural Contradictions of Capitalism*, (New York: Basic Books, 1976), p. 105.

71. Chris Jenks, "The Centrality of the Eye In Western Culture—An Introduction," in *Visual Culture*, ed. Chris Jenks, (London/New York: Routledge, 1995), p. 1.

72. Martin Jay, *Downcast Eyes*, cited in Chris Jenks, "The Centrality of the Eye in Western Culture," p. 2.

73. Mitchell Stephens, *The Rise of the Image, The Fall of the Word*, p. 5.

74. Marita Sturken, *Tangled Memories: The Vietnam War, The Aids Epidemic, and The Politics of Remembering*, (Berkeley, CA: University of California Press, 1997), pp. 25, 29. Novelist and popular culture observer Douglas Coupland, in "J.F.K. Remembered, Even for Those Who Don't," *The New York Times*, Sunday November 14, 1993, p. 34h, asks, "What if there had never been a Zapruder film? Consider *that*. Without the Zapruder film, there would never have been the visual touchstone for three decades of questions about what really happened." "Without the assassination—more importantly, without its subsequent showings on television and the photo spreads in Life magazine, without the endless relooping of the Zapruder film in the collective brain—the Kennedy Administration would today be considered in the same calm tones reserved for the Johnson Administration."

75. Vicki Goldberg, *The Power of Photography*, pp. 54–57, and Michael L. Smith, "Selling The Moon: The U.S. Manned Space Program and the Triumph of Commodity Scientism," in Richard Wightman Fox and T. J. Jackson Lears, eds., *The Culture of Consumption: Critical Essays in American History, 1880–1980*, (New York: Pantheon Books, 1983), p. 175–80.

76. This is not meant as a statement of fact, but rather to draw attention to the idea that perhaps the role of the history instructor is going to change. In the introduction to a textbook on instructional media and learning, the authors write: "The roles of instructor and learner are clearly changing because of the influence of media and technology in the classroom. No longer are teachers and textbooks the sources of all knowledge. The teacher becomes the director of the knowledge access process. Along the continuum of instructional strategies, sometimes the teacher will elect to provide direct instructional experience for students. At other times, with a few keystrokes students can explore the world, gaining access to libraries, other teachers and students, and a host of resources to obtain the knowledge they seek." "The teacher," write the authors, "makes the difference in the integration of media and technology in this process." Robert Heinich, Michael Molenda, James D. Russell, Sharon E. Smaldino, *Instructional Media and Technologies for Learning*, Seventh Edition, (Upper Saddle River, NJ: Merrill/Prentice Hall, 2002), p. 6. With ideas like that circulating, especially at the post-secondary level, the definition of what a teacher does in the classroom/lecture hall is open for debate. One of the consequences is that a premium may be put on the professor as teacher or even as entertainer, rather than as researcher. The academic who can engage students in a way that is not often rewarded in the academy may find herself as coveted as the research superstar. See the arguments on this topic articulated in Tom Pocklington and Allan Tupper,

No Place to Learn: Why Universities Aren't Working, (Vancouver, BC: University of British Columbia Press, 2002).

77. Jack L. Granatstein, *Who Killed Canadian History?,* (Toronto: HarperCollins, 1998).

78. Joyce Appleby, Lynn Hunt, Margaret Jacob, "Telling the truth about history," in Keith Jenkins, ed., *The Postmodern History Reader,* (New York: Routledge, 1997), p. 209.

79. Bob Davis, *Whatever Happened To High School History? Burying The Political Memory of Youth, Ontario: 1945–1995,* (Toronto: OS/OS/James Lorimer & Co., 1995), pp. 2, 9, 14.

80. Emily West, "Selling Canada to Canadians: Collective Memory, National Identity and Popular Culture," *Critical Studies in Media Communication,* June 2002, pp. 212–29. For Canadians, there is also the lurking problem of globalization and the enormous American influence. One main reason to support Canada's artistic and cultural institutions is to preserve and to differentiate them from the hugely successful American products. According to some critics, this is an essential process to maintain if a distinct Canada is to be preserved. See Tom Henighan, *The Presumption of Culture: Structure, Strategy, and Survival in the Canadian Cultural Landscape,* (Vancouver: Raincoast Books, 1996), pp. 3–4.

81. Michael Kammen, *American Culture American Tastes: Social Change and the 20th Century,* (New York: Knopf, 1999), p. 194.

82. Leila Zenderland, "Introduction," *Recycling the Past: Popular Uses of American History,* ed. Leila Zenderland, (Philadelphia: University of Pennsylvania Press, 1978), p. ix.

83. See Mark Moss, "Dressing History: Nostalgia and Class in the Worlds of Ralph Lauren," *Popular Culture Review,* vol. xiv, no. 2, Summer 2003, and Michael Frisch, "The Memory of History," in Susan Porter Benson, Stephen Brier and Roy Rosenzweig, eds., *Presenting The Past: Essays on History and The Public,* (Philadelphia: Temple University Press, 1986), pp. 5–17.

84. "Sir John A. McDonald's," *Ottawa Citizen,* 26 February, 1997, p. A14, cited in Heather-Jane Robertson, *No More Teachers, No More Books: The Commericalization of Canada's Schools,* (Toronto: McClelland and Stewart, 1998), p. 58. The editorial stated: "Meagre as they are, these tiny morsels of the past will be as filling as the thin history gruel our multibillion dollar school systems are serving to students."

85. Jim Collins, "No (Popular) Place Like Home?" in Jim Collins, ed., *High-Pop: Making Culture into Popular Entertainment,* (Boston: Blackwell Publishers, 2002), p. 189.

86. On this topic, see Neil Postman's concerns in *The End of Education: Redefining the Value of School,* (New York: Knopf, 1995), p. 167.

87. Not a week goes by without some article in a newspaper or a journal or a new volume discussing the decline of reading and dire effects on printing. See Caleb Crain, "Twilight of the Books," *The New Yorker,* December 24, 31, 2007, pp. 134, 135 and Jeff Gomez, *Print is Dead: Books in Our Digital Age,* (New York: Macmillan, 2008).

88. David T. Z. Mindich, *Tuned Out: Why Americans Under 40 Don't Follow the News,* (New York: Oxford University Press, 2005), p. 3.

89. Quite often over the last few years, whenever I lecture on or discuss a certain historical topic to or with a class, a student will come up to me and ask me if I've seen a particular movie that bears a slight resemblance to the topic just mentioned. For example, If I have just finished talking about ancient Egypt, a student will ask me if I've seen *The Mummy*—which I have not seen. They will then go on to list a few of the key points of the movie, that usually have nothing to do with the lecture. The best case scenario is one where the movie has some actual historical relevance, is grounded in a more accurate sense of history, and deals with its subject matter in an intelligent manner. Regardless of the topic there are numerous examples: *Gladiator, Schindler's List, Glory, The Return of Martin Guerre*.

90. Neil Gabler, *Life: The Movie*, p. 138.

91. Paul Auster, *Hand to Mouth: A Chronicle of Early Failure*, (New York: Henry Holt, 1997), p. 24.

92. Clifford Stoll, *Silicon Snake Oil: Second Thoughts on the Information Highway*, (New York: Doubleday, 1995), p. 117.

93. Konrad Morgan, Madeleine Morgan, and John Hall, "Psychological Developments in High Technology Teaching and Learning Environments," *British Journal of Educational Technology*, vol. 31, no. 1, January 2000, pp. 71–79. In *Zero Tolerance: Hot Button Politics In Canada's Universities*, (Toronto: Penguin Books, 1996), p. 187, Peter C. Emberley a traditionalist in the sense of culture, books, and the established university based on liberal arts, makes the following point: "Alternative delivery mechanisms also bring their benefits. While Luddites question all use of advanced technologies, conveniently forgetting that the Gutenberg press spawned print culture and revolutionized communication, it is questionable whether the new technologies will actually cause a sea change in the scholarly culture. Unless one has acquaintance with videoconferencing, the Internet, interactive CD-ROM technology and electronic mail, one has little qualification to speak, as some do, of the end of teaching and learning. The Internet for example is, as some faculty fear, filled with much frivolous diversion and indiscriminate information. But it also contains hard-to-find documents of the Carolingian period, rare commentaries of St. Basil and reports of recent breakthroughs in understanding atomic particles–and it hosts rich international roundtables on topics as diverse as Renaissance iconography and enzymes. There is among many faculty a great reluctance to experiment with the new technologies, a reluctance reinforced by institutional inertia, which, once moralized, results in stubborn resistance to new opportunities."

94. Clifford Stoll, *HighTech Heretic*, (New York: Doubleday, 1999), p. 12.

95. Kevin Mattson, "Movies as History," *The Common Review*, Summer 2007, vol. 6, no. 1, p. 11.

96. See Sven Birkerts, *The Gutenberg Elegies: The Fate of Reading In An Electronic Age*, (Boston: Faber and Faber, 1994), p. 3.

97. Judy Stoffman, "Taking Fancy to Fantasy: How Harry Potter changed Children's Literature Forever," *The Toronto Star*, November 9, 2002, p. J15. Stoffman writes that the Potter books have sold more than 6 million copies in Canada alone and over 170 million worldwide. What is particularly fascinating is that the volumes are quite large—640 pages—in some cases.

98. Steven Levy, *The Perfect Thing: How the iPOD Shuffles Commerce, Culture, and Coolness*, (New York: Simon & Schuster, 2006), p. 4 and Frances Jacobson Harris, *I Found It On the Internet: Coming of Age Online*, (Chicago: American Library Association, 2005), p. viii.

99. John Seely Brown, "Growing Up Digital: How the Web Changes Work, Education, and the Ways People Learn," *USDLA Journal*, vol. 16, no. 2, February 2002.

100. Sven Birkerts, *The Gutenberg Elegies*, p. 20.

101. David Marc, *Bonfire of the Humanities: Television, Subliteracy, and Long-Term Memory Loss*, (Syracuse, NY: Syracuse University Press, 1995), p. 27.

102. Neil Gabler, *Life: The Movie*, p. 88.

103. Paul Martin Lester, *Visual Communication: Images with Messages*, Second Edition, (Belmont, CA: Wadsworth/Thomson Learning, 2000), p. 73.

104. J. C. Taylor, "The Art Museum in the United States," in Sherman Lee, editor, *Understanding Art Museums*, (Upper Saddle River, NJ: Prentice Hall, 1975), p. 50.

105. Joshua Meyrowitz, *No Sense of Place: The Impact of Electronic Media on Social Behavior*, (New York: Oxford University Press, 1985), pp. 75, 79.

106. John Berger, *Ways of Seeing*, p. 7.

107. J. C. Hertz, *Joystick Nation: How Videogames Ate Our Quarters, Won Our Hearts and Rewired Our Minds*, (Boston: Little Brown & Co., 1997), pp. 2, 3.

108. According to David Shenk, *Data Smog: Surviving The Information Glut*, (New York: HarperCollins 1997), p. 29, from 1965 to 1995, "the average TV news 'soundbite' shrunk from 42.3 seconds to 8.3 seconds."

109. James Gleick, *Faster: The Acceleration of Just About Everything*, (New York: Pantheon, 1999), pp. 98, 176.

110. James Gleick, *Faster*, pp. 177–178.

111. On this point, Todd Gitlin, in *Media Unlimited*, p. 88, writes, "Look through any video archive. Pre-MTV rock concert footage seems to sleepwalk. Jump cuts were the preserve of avante-garde cinema, not de riguer in commercials for spectators younger than thirty. Look back fifty years, and it is hard to resist the impression that the movies were slower, newspaper and magazine articles longer, sentences longer and more complex, advertising text drawn out."

112. Marilyn Gell Mason, "The Yin and Yang of Knowing," *DAEDALUS—Books, Bricks and Bytes*, Fall 1996, vol. 125, no. 4, p. 167.

113. In her analysis of children's picture books, *Inside Picture Books*, (New Haven, CT: Yale University Press, 1999), pp. 29–30, psychologist Ellen Handler Spitz makes the following observation regarding the classic *Goodnight Moon*:

Two clocks in the bunny's room are set at seven when *Goodnight Moon* begins. As measured by the hands on these clocks, the time has progressed to ten past eight by the time the last page is reached; thus, an entire imaginary hour has elapsed between the book's first and final moments. This slowing down is exquisitely appropriate to its final theme: the transition between day and night, activity and repose.

This prolongation of time in *Goodnight Moon* symbolizes and concretizes an antidote for conditions even more poignant today than when the book was originally published some fifty years ago. Today's American children are, of necessity, clamped squirming in the vise of our rapidly paced, technologically driven culture. Paradoxically, they are being held down while being speeded up at an ever-accelerating rate. Given little space for the growth of their own imaginations and little time for the gradual acquisition of mastery, today's children are bombarded with prefabricated stimuli—images, sensations, impressions that occur fast and furiously. As the media disseminate *information* in visual terms and pictures fly past, we understand little about the long- or short-term effects of the speed and volume of communication.

114. Marc Auge, *Non-Places: Introduction to an Anthropology of Supermodernity*, Translated by John Howe, (New York: Verso, 1995), pp. 26–30.

115. Marilyn Gell Mason writes: "Books are different from digital documents, and for that reason they are unlikely to disappear. Books have substance. They take up space. They present us with a past, a present, and a future." "The Yin and Yang of Knowing," p. 167.

116. But one does get comfortable with an easily digestible and quick accounting of the days events. This also leads to questions of convenience and time allotment.

117. Knowlton Nash, *Trivia Pursuit: How Showbiz Values are Corrupting the News*, (Toronto: McClelland & Stewart, 1998), pp. 9–10.

118. Robert Brent Toplin, *History By Hollywood: The Use and Abuse of the American Past*, (Urbana, IL: University of Illinois Press, 1996), pp. vii–viii.

119. Robert Brent Toplin, *History By Hollywood*, p. ix.

120. And it is not just the person. Whole scenes within movies become for individuals, a mediated version of history, supplanting the past in the glowing color of a celluloid dream. And of course this extends beyond history into the realm of memory. Was I there? Did I remember a particular event from being in a specific place in time or has the media implanted this memory within me. The fact that "flashbulb memory" is even a psychological concept buttresses this idea. Robert A. Baron, Bruce Earhard, Marcia Ozier, *Psychology* (Scarborough, ON: Allyn & Bacon Canada, 1995), p. 252.

121. Gore Vidal, *Screening History*, (Cambridge, MA: Harvard University Press, 1992), p. 11.

122. Gore Vidal, *Screening History*, p. 49.

123. Gore Vidal, *Screening History*, p. 16.

124. My mother and my uncle still prefer the movie theatre; going out to a film, as opposed to watching it at home. They also, as the cliche goes, can't change the time on the VCR—but that is another matter—(they also don't use the ATM). This generalization should be qualified by stating that "Senior citizens are also proving adept at learning to use computers and are currently the second-fastest group of customers (after kids) for computer manufacturers." John Seely Brown and Paul Duguid, *The Social Life of Information*, (Boston, Mass.: Harvard Business School Press, 2002), p. 89.

125. Susan J. Douglas, *Where the Girls Are: Growing Up Female With the Mass Media*, (New York: Random House, 1994), p. 13, Peter Biskind, *Seeing is Believing: How Hollywood Taught Us To Stop Worrying and Love the Fifties*, (New York: Pantheon Books, 1983), p. 2, and Garth Jowett and James M. Linton, *Movies as Mass Communication*, (Beverly Hills, CA: Sage Publications, 1980), p. 110.

126. Andrew R. Heinze, *Adapting to Abundance: Jewish Immigrants, Mass Consumption, and the Search for American Identity*, (New York: Columbia University Press, 1990), p. 119.

127. Larry May, *Screening Out The Past: The Birth of Mass Culture and The Motion Picture Industry*, (Chicago: University of Chicago Press, 1983), p. 101 and Elizabeth and Stuart Ewen, *Channels of Desire*, (New York: McGraw-Hill, 1979), p. 81.

128. Tim Cole, *Selling The Holocaust: From Auschwitz to Schindler—How History is Bought, Packaged, and Sold*, (New York: Routledge, 2000), p. 74.

129. Pierre Sorlin, *The Film in History: Restaging the Past*, (Oxford: Basil Blackwell, 1980), p. 4.

130. Pierre Sorlin, *The Film in History*, p. 16.

131. Natalie Zemon Davis, "'Any Resemblance to Persons Living or Dead": film and the challenge of authenticity', *Historical Journal of Film, Radio and Television*, vol. 8, no. 3, 1988, p. 270.

132. Robert A. Rosenstone, "History in Images/History in Words: Reflections on the Possibility of Really Putting History onto Film," *American Historical Review*, 'Forum,' vol. 93, no. 5, December, 1988, pp. 1174–75.

133. Leo Braudy, *The World in a Frame: What We See in Films*, (Chicago: The University of Chicago Press, 1984), p. 22.

134. Alexander Nehamas, "Serious Watching," *The South Atlantic Quarterly*, vol. 89, no. 1, Winter 1990, p. 166, and Michael Dunne, *Metapop: Self-Referentiality in Contemporary American Popular Culture*, (Jackson, MS: University Press of Mississippi, 1992).

135. Garth Jowett and James M. Linton, *Movies as Mass Communication*, p. 111.

136. Robert Burgoyne, *Film Nation: Hollywood Looks at U.S. History*, p. 6.

137. Arthur Marwick, *The Nature of History*, third edition, (London: Macmillan, 1989), p. 3.

138. Gary R. Edgerton, "Introduction: Television as Historian: A Different Kind Of History Altogether," p. 6, in Gary R. Edgerton and Peter C. Rollins, eds., *Television Histories: Shaping Collective Memory in the Media Age*, (Lexington, KY: The University of Kentucky Press 2001).

139. Gary R. Edgerton, "Introduction: Television as Historian: A Different Kind Of History Altogether," p. 8 and Steve Anderson, "History TV and Popular Memory," p. 20, in Gary R. Edgerton and Peter C. Rollins, eds., *Television Histories: Shapping Collective Memory in the Media Age*.

140. Raymond Williams, "Drama in a Dramatised Society," in Alan O'Connor, ed., *Raymond Williams On Television*, (Toronto: Between The Lines Press, 1989), pp. 3–5.

2

Media, Memory, and History

Why is it that different ages and different nations have represented the visible world in such different ways?

—E. H. Gombrich, *Art and Illusion*, 3

The notion of what history is has undergone significant changes in the last 100 years. As discussed earlier, mass culture and in particular, visual media representations of the past introduced a significant trend to fragmenting the definition of history. Historical images come at us from a variety of different sources; television, advertising, film, photography, newspapers, museums, magazines, popular fiction, Web Sites, and Internet channels. In contemporary parlance these versions of the past are known as popular history and at times, the more selective versions, such as museum displays and former battlefields are described as public history. All of these formats present versions of history to a public that receives these historical sources in an almost constant stream.[1] This process started in earnest at the turn of the century but did not truly affect academic notions of history and the interpretations that they foster until the 1970s. It is at this point in time, that established historical discourse or consensus history started to give way to the "new" history, which was a form of social history that sought to incorporate the voices of the marginalized, from women and minorities to workers and those not in the pantheon of the "great men."[2]

One of the features that has always made history interesting to so many, and continuously popular to a variety of diverse audiences, has been the fact that from its consensus history origins, the notion of a moving narrative has come to dominate the telling of the tale. The concept of "narrative" is particularly attractive as a way to understand, comprehend, and unite historical discourse because of its elasticity, universalism and ability to bond the diverse elements which constitute historical discourse.[3] While some may simply dismiss narrative structure as banal storytelling, it has survived as a complex and appealing vehicle for the transmission of ideas and knowledge for thousands of years.

Added to the view of history as grand story is the important fact that for many readers and viewers of history, the historical discourse is much more than a description of events that occurred long ago. In many national histories, history was designed to educate, and later to entertain, but it was also meant to inform citizens. History for much of time was certainly something contrived to "inspire and delight,"[4] but it was meant to move people, to provoke and strike with patriotic awe. One of the reasons why popular consensus history continues to be extremely representative and is embraced by so many is that it serves the dual functions informing and inspiring in the collective consciousness of nationalism. The works of writers such as Pierre Burton in Canada or Stephen Ambrose in the United States transcend the specialized focus of academic historians and reach out to a much larger audience. Those who are actively engaged in producing visual forms of history are intensely aware of why this is so.

The key theme that runs throughout this work is the fact that people, and in particular students, receive historical information and gain historical knowledge from visual sources primarily rather than from traditional print sources.[5] If, as David Thelen has stated, "the challenge of history is to recover the past and introduce it to the present,"[6] then, the visual media are gaining ground over the traditional delivery systems of historical knowledge. This recognition was given academic focus in 1980, in the forward to an important selection of essays on contemporary historical discourse. John Hope Franklin wrote that the Bicentennial celebrations in the United States had an enormous impact in conveying popular historical interpretations to the public at large. Consequently, visual presentations of historical events reached huge audiences and, remade how history was perceived. In turn, Hope Franklin acknowledged that "the average person's awareness of his own history and the history of the United States has come from a number of influences and has intensified in the last two decades." This situation, remarked Hope Franklin, was forcing the professional historical community, who regarded themselves as the "custodians of the nation's past," to recognize this development. Historical discourse and historical knowledge from visual and popular formats has had a "considerable" influence.[7]

Peter Charles Hoffer puts much of the blame for this evolution firmly on the heads of the new historians. To a great extent, Hoffer implies that the group, composed of those with political agendas as much as with a desire to see a change from the history of diplomacy and great battles, sought to reassert their versions of historical discourse, without regard for the audience. More and more, suggests Hoffer, the new history moved from clear and concise writing towards jargon filled inaccessible writing, often with interpretations borrowed from literary theory or the social sciences. As a consequence, many felt that historians were writing to each other and for each other, rather than for an audience beyond the university. As Hoffer remarks:

> The result was a widening gap between what gained applause as popular history, often the work of journalists or historians who had left the classroom, and minutely detailed, methodologically involuted professional monographs that few outside of the academy read. In short, historians were so busy inventing newer kinds of history and trying to master newer methods that they did not see how far they had strayed.[8]

One could suggest that the void that was left was filled by popular historians and increasingly, producers, writers, photographers, directors, and others who sought to recapture the popularity and accessibility of traditional consensus history. Those, including many from the academy, who began to incorporate the wonders of the visual into historical discussions, were regarded with skepticism if not outright hostility by both representatives who practiced academic consensus history and those engaged in the various forms of new history. These pioneers, coming to the fore in the late 1970s, began to utilize the plethora of visual sources in creative and remarkable ways.

Historians and those who use historical resources are fatigued by the constant and consistent "reminders" to "take seriously the pictorial traces of the past."[9] It is no secret that regardless of what they are searching for, images and visuals are present. In the classroom, the use of power point and down-loaded images are employed, on a seemingly growing basis, to reach out towards a society that sees as much as it reads. But as Michael Wilson has observed, coming from a logocentric universe does not make the job any easier for historians. To many historians, images are merely supplements; accents that are designed to round out a linguistic thesis.[10] To some extent, not being media savvy has left the historian without the tools to connect to his or her audience. Thus, the preserve of history is no longer confined to academics, teachers, and instructors. A host of other players have stepped in to define, confront, and depict the past.

Historical awareness and specifically, historical knowledge is no longer the sole preserve of the professional academic historian, or even the journalist/writer as popular historian.[11] In fact, the "poststructuralist" argument regarding history, defined as a series of "socially constructed narratives" presented to audiences who "endlessly refashion them in changing contexts," provokes one to question the continuing necessity of the professional historian.[12] Increasingly an array of other agents as well as other media have stepped in to carve out territory which, besides the practitioners within the mass media, include the viewers and consumers of mediated images who are being empowered to process and deal with historical nuances without the confines of structures.[13]

In the preface to the second edition of his important text, *The Varieties of History*, Fritz Stern acknowledges that "times have changed"—referring to the twenty years from the mid-1950s until the mid-1970s since his work had come out. Stern wrote that the place of history "no longer commands the kind of automatic acceptance that it once did." He proposes that historians are now less confident and perhaps more tentative about what they do as a consequence of the changing definitions of historical thought and historiography.[14] Stern's text provides selections of the great historian's work (since the Renaissance) until the late 1960s. In the excerpt from Lewis Namier, "History and Political Culture," Stern has chosen a most stimulating offering. Namier writes that to "popularize usually means to oversimplify." Namier's point is that this is the standard equation with regard to forms of history that are academic, scholarly, and traditional. Yet Namier, refreshingly and importantly, recognizes that in order for history to have any bearing or effect upon the everyday lives of people—to be relevant in other words—it must pander to the emotions and passions of the masses, "projecting them through a distorted mythical past." Returning to this emotive form of history, by attempting to capture hearts rather than minds, two things are accomplished. History reaches into the fabric of society in ways that esoteric history can never do, and secondly, according to Namier, the historian is utilizing imagination and "fervour," along the lines of the novelist, more so than "accurate perception and critical understanding."[15] What gives this popular history more value and depth than shallowness, despite Namier's conclusions, is the fact that it often employs the cultural capital of the narrative. Most established history is framed in a structured narrative and is presented from the viewpoint of the historian's bias.[16] Beginning with *Metahistory* and accentuated with other works, Hayden White has posited that historians are in essence storytellers and bring to bear, in their work, a novelist's appreciation of the narrative.[17]

This is something that was a part of history from classical antiquity and was revitalized by the Humanists during the Renaissance. This is also something that the great French Encyclopaedists and Philosophes understood. According to Arthur Marwick, what Voltaire and his contemporaries were doing was "not so much at the beginning of a new historical tradition, but at the highest point of an old one." It is only with Ranke and his German contemporaries in the nineteenth century that the disciplined, scientific, and academic thrust of history begins.[18] Ranke and his German and British disciples attempted to factualize history and to literally "show" how the past "really was." This positivist approach, which focused on factual evidence, attempted to employ forms of scientific objectivity.[19]

As E. H. Carr has summarized, "first ascertain the facts, then draw your conclusions from them." This was fully in line, according to Carr, with the British empiricist tradition which situated a "complete separation between subject and object." This "common sense" view of history suggested that all one needed was the facts and then one's interpretation would be authoritative. As long as one had the "right" facts, one had the "backbone" of history. Key to this equation was accuracy of facts. Carr though, is quick to make the point that "to praise a historian for his accuracy is like praising an architect for using well-seasoned timber or properly mixed concrete in his building." To supplement this, Carr states that the historian has to rely on supplements—archaeology and numismatics—to buttress factual arguments. In turn, what people preserved or thought worthy of preserving has to be considered in the form of a conscious decision. This last point, reminds us that history cannot in fact be pure and fully objective but at some juncture has been tinkered with or made visible to present day historians because of a subjective decision. Carr writes, ". . . the facts of history never come to us pure, since they do not and cannot exist in a pure form: they are always refracted through the mind of the reader. It follows that when we take up a work of history, our first concern should be not with the facts which it contains but with the historian who wrote it." Later in his discourse Carr reiterates this point by interpreting history as a "process of interaction between the historian and his facts, an unending dialogue between the present and the past." It is thus almost vital to remember that from multiple facts comes a subjective interpretation, bounded by the historian's place in time and guided by contemporary obligations and current fashions.[20] Historians have always utilized such devices and desires in their interpretations of history even when they do not acknowledge that is what they are doing.

The work of Macaulay was considered popular because of the British historian's aptitude in using the power of narrative. He could, as Robert Fulford notes, "recreate historic events as powerful narratives." Fulford remarks that Macaulay had the ability to stimulate a visual impression of history that was extraordinarily powerful by combining "the qualities of playwright and set designer."[21] What Fulford is suggesting is a process that is occurring with online Web-based versions of history. The notion of the hypertext narrative allows for students and scholars of history to move around with much more fluidity and to seek historical data in a manner that is harmonious with the open-ended narratives and possibilities of the past. In the age of MTV and instant text/image messaging, capturing a historical narrative by appropriating the language of the visual media has, according to Margaret E. Newell, "significant pedagogical pluses." In her investigation and research into multimedia and history, Professor Newell highlights serious obstacles to approaching history from the traditional vantage point. In particular, she states that students raised in a predominantly visual culture "find it difficult to garner information from reading and listening alone." Newell also feels that the lack of the ability to take notes is also extremely problematic. Without sacrificing content, digitized presentations allow the professor to "respond to" the "conditions" facing young students and to reach the students.[22]

A significant stream within historical discourse today is the pervasiveness of contemporary themes and concerns being presented through the lenses of history.[23] Political and social concepts that are firmly contemporary are often worked into the framework of historical discourse. In the beginning of the nineteenth century, the definition of history began to evolve, in the words of Robert Hanke, "in response to modernity." It was at this juncture, that the emphasis on presentism came into being. As Hanke implies, historians attempted to "reconnect the present to the past at the very moment that new media—the telegraph and the daily newspaper—began to dissolve previous barriers of space and time."[24]

After the Second World War, the narrative approach to structured history gained acceptance, in fact, "enjoyed scholarly status and wide popular acclaim" in the works of Samuel Eliot Morison and Arthur Schlesinger, Jr. According to Warren Susman, there was a break from a focus on politically charged tracts, an "escape from ideology," and "a return to the mythic and the dramatic."[25] It is not outlandish—or even inaccurate to perceive of historical information in dramatic terms—in categories that are often applied to fiction and which possess the attributes of narrative. In fact, most of "recorded" or documented history is framed in the above ways; ones that usually apply to the dictates of film and TV. The earliest historians, from Homer to the Hebrews to Herodotus employed the techniques found in narrative and focused on myth and drama. Children perceive of history in "mythic structure and mythic time."[26] This is in fact the reason why this history, the "popular history tradition" was so effective and is so remembered. According to Gary Edgerton,

> The master narrative was typically populated by heroes and villains, who allegorically personified certain virtues and vices in the national character that most members of the general population recognized and responded to immediately. Television as popular history still adopts facets of this strategy at its most rudimentary level.[27]

The work of Homer illuminates some of the similarities between history as narrative mythology as presented on television and, as well, provides an interesting parallel with some of the current concerns. Both the *Iliad* and the *Odyssey* are heroic poems. The hero or more accurately, a hero, is one, who behaves in certain ways, pursuing specified goals through personal courage and bravery. However, it should be emphasized that the hero lives in and is molded by a social system and a culture, and his actions are intelligible only in reference to them. The *Odyssey* is one of the most popular epics in Western culture and has been remade and reworked time and again. It has all the ingredients of a best seller: pathos, sexuality, violence, a strong hero who braves many dangers—in fact some have called it the greatest of all adventure stories. In the *Odyssey*, the Gods are directly involved; Athena leads Odysseus and Telemachus step to step; in the *Iliad* the gods interfere occasionally. The *Iliad* is filled with the action of heroes; that is the focus. The *Odyssey* focuses on the action of one hero, Odysseus.[28]

According to Robert B. Kebric, most classical Greeks viewed Homer's poems as accurate accounts of the Trojan War. They were an important part of the common heritage of Greece, and their content was not to be doubted. In the fifth century BC, for example, the historians Herodotus and Thucydides felt no reason to question the Homeric version of events at Troy. Later, Alexander the Great traced his ancestry to Achilles, modeled himself on his exploits, and carried a copy of the "Iliad" with him on campaign. Greek children were nurtured on the stories and many were made namesakes of the godlike heroes. These epic poems were continually combed for suitable parallels and instructional material to fit contemporary situations.[29]

Greek culture and society cherished legends of the Mycenaean kings, legends of the past, and most of all, stories of heroes. The heroic ideal embodied a notion of what men should be and how they should act. The notion of a heroic world, when gods walked the earth as the friends of men, when heroes indulged in noble deeds, was something the Greeks cherished as one of their most precious possessions. Honor and the notions of respect and dignity became supreme characteristics.[30]

The poetry that had been passed down, orally, from generation to generation, contained all that was notable. Its authentic spirit was codified in the poems of Homer which became the cornerstone of Greek education. The Homeric ideals encouraged a conception of manhood in which personal worth held pride of place. The city-state system in turn, encouraged an individualistic attitude, and colored both the beliefs and behavior of its male citizens.[31]

The essence of the heroic outlook, relates C. M. Bowra, "is the pursuit of honor through action. The great man is the one who, endowed with superior qualities of body and mind, uses them to the utmost and wins the applause of his fellows, because he spares no effort and shirks no risk in his desire to make the most of his gifts and to surpass other men in his exercise of them." At the core of his being is honor—any affront to it calls for immediate amends.[32]

The classic Greek hero gladly looks for danger. Why? This gives him the best opportunity of showing of what stuff he is made. And success in thwarting danger gives him not only an enlarged sense of personality and well-being, but also fame! Fame also leads back to honor, which the hero seeks before anything else. This outlook runs through Greek history from Homer's Achilles to Alexander the Great.[33]

An educated Greek would probably be able to recite most of the *Iliad* and the *Odyssey* by heart. Like the Bible or the Koran, it was a seminal text. These epic poems were not only key educational texts, but key nationalistic myths. They would be recited at rituals, at festivals, and the men who listened to them would live vicariously through them. Today, our notion of myth means fantasy. To the Greeks, this was history. They believed the narrative implicitly. They believed it once happened. Not only did they never doubt the existence of mythological heroes, they also knew all about them: their names, their genealogies, and their exploits. Homer was their most authoritative source of information, but by no means the only one—Hesiod is also cited often.[34]

One of the themes of the work of Homer that has timeless relevance is the fact that this kind of history is ripe with emotional content. It fires the imagination and provokes people to action. Like the catch phrase sayings "Remember the Alamo" or "Je me souviens," individuals make an emotional connection to history when it carries this resonance.[35] Problematic here is the fact that this can be manipulated in the form of propaganda. Classic totalitarian propaganda employs images and often replaces words. Because images and non-textual formats such as music appeal to emotion, often at the cost of reason, there is the ability to prey upon emotions in a much more potent way.[36] This creates a grand danger. What memories turn into history have been "chronicled" in some way, most often by being written down. The choice to write down is evidence of "significance" and importance.[37] Societies, cultures, nations, and countries seek to select and choose what it is they wish to remember and what it is they wish to become part of their respective history. This can occur in what are postmodern, mass cultural forms, such as a T-shirt inscription or poster or in the form of films such as *Pearl Harbor* not to mention traditional academic history. According to Roger Simon, these

> historical representations are practices that deliberately attempt to shape social memory. Such practices seek to either maintain or re-interpret dominant narratives, revive marginal ones, or bring to light those formerly suppressed, unheard or unarticulated. Historical representations are provocations aimed at altering our on-going process of collective remembrance.[38]

The belief or understanding that historical knowledge should come from the lecture hall, the professor, and the footnoted history book stems from the antipathy that most serious students of history possess for the mass media. There is an expansive form of suspicion directed toward history present on film or television, photographs and CD-ROMs that fails to acknowledge let alone to take into account the fact that most people in the West derive historical knowledge from the various forms of mass media. To simply dismiss the often very "creative" and persuasive forms of popular history found in the visual technologies is to close one's eyes to the realities of modern society.[39] History and historical knowledge are not simply confined to traditional academic history. History can be processed and consumed, witnessed and absorbed in many ways. The success of the Canadian Broadcasting Corporation's production, *Canada: A People's History*, illustrates this point. As historian Margaret Conrad has remarked,

> While the series could scarcely be expected to add significant academic knowledge in the narrow sense, it has made a major contribution to our understanding of the past by forcing film producers, academic historians, archivists, and critics to think about how best to render our past in a visual way. Everyone involved in producing and reviewing the series—and there were many—no doubt learned something about the challenges of producing history on film. In an age when visual representation is rapidly overtaking the printed word, the series serves as a major marker in this shift.[40]

Conrad states that for Canadians, the series was epochal as a "major marker" because of the realization that this production was a conscious attempt to mould collective memory and deliver it as a form of public history. A key distinction between traditional academic history and public history, notes Conrad, is both how the material is presented and to whom. Most often, (although there is tremendous and increasing synergy) public history is created by those working outside of the academy—journalists, documentary film makers—and offered to a wide cross section of individuals in a more relaxed viewing environment.[41] The producer of this series, Mark Starowicz, was conscious of these demands and paradoxes while making the series. The development of multimedia accoutrements necessary for the production emerged as a significant concern. These included bilingual Web sites, the production of a companion book, DVD and video sets, not to mention the advertising and promotion that was necessary to publicize the project.[42] As well there was the notion that this project was more than just history and more than traditional history. The diversity of style involved in the project was testament to history's new role.

On the one hand this is harmonious with the post-modern conception of history that takes into account the work of Hayden White. What this suggests is that history can be all around us, in various manifestations and styles, bombarding the viewer from all angles and in many different contexts. The distinctions between what was once thought of as factual and real in contrast to the mythologized and the imaginary, no longer hold up in this view. These distinctions no longer matter as much given the fact that they can no longer be deciphered. According to Hayden White, this was something that was once understood—he cites the reader of the nineteenth-century novel as an example of someone who could make the distinction—but now, "everything is presented as if it were on the same ontological order."[43]

Significantly within this framework is the fact that history can straddle both ends of the same spectrum; it can be a pastiche and at the same time, be governed by the dramatic structures of the narrative.[44] Vital to comprehending historiographer Hayden White is an understanding of his theory of "emplotment."

Putting history into a narrative structure, whether mediated history or academic history, allows for ease of comprehension. From this perspective, history with narrative is defined as a way to understand and process the real which in turn gives this history meaning.[45] When the historian uses emplotment, he or she is crafting history in a way that allows people within a culture to understand this history. To some extent, what is happening is a reduction of superfluous interpretations and a return to the process of history that Herodotus and Homer employed. What is occurring is that one is moving towards a structure that is natural and in White's interpretation, "inevitable."[46] What White suggests is that history is and must be framed or fashioned by utilizing familiar narratives and a common literary structure. It is about solving the problem of how to convey or "how to translate knowing into telling."[47] The way to convey is to access what White calls the "meta-code," which are the human universals of storytelling.[48] Narrative not only gives structure to events, and to their interpretation but it is also capable of closure; it provides boundaries to organize experiences, events and their transformation into history.[49] An example of this is the Oliver Stone film, *JFK*, which not only "blurs the distinction between fact and fiction" but utilizes this device to stretch the bounds of the story of history.[50]

A significant reason for the ability to do this, now, is that over the past century there has been the conflation of memory, experience and the awareness of historical events. This most certainly is derived from the ubiquitous presence of the mass media, but also, according to White, is the germinal fact that the twentieth century has been one of the most violent. This violence has also been recorded, explained, and analyzed in contrast to the violence of previous centuries. A definitive benchmark for the past century has been the catastrophic levels of violence or, the holocaustal events, which are so epochal, that they cannot be processed in a way that they might have been two or three centuries ago.[51] This merges, very neatly, with Walter Benjamin's observation about channeling the forces of memory into history at the time of their eruption. Benjamin, manipulating Ranke, suggests that it is not just about "the way it really was," but rather more so, to "articulate the past historically . . . means to seize hold of a memory as it flashes up at a moment of danger."[52]

Violent, action-oriented events become consciousness touchstones that not only cannot be forgotten—they are, according to White, too large for that—but at the same time, they cannot be adequately remembered. An ongoing negotiation for their meaning must take place in order to give them coherence.[53] What allows them to survive in time, is the fact that, harmonious with the essential features of modernity, is their interpretation in narrative structures. As White suggests:

> these kinds of events do not lend themselves to explanation in terms of categories underwritten by traditional humanistic historiography, in which human *agents* are conceived to be in some way fully conscious and morally responsible for their actions and capable of discriminating between the causes of historical events and their effects over the long as well as the short run in relatively common-sensical ways—in other words, agents who are presumed to understand *history* in much the same way as professional historians do.[54]

There of course must be relevance to contemporary society, but the key here is the fact that most historical indicators in the postmodernist interpretation must be observable. If it was not or if it is not, it must be made to be processed in this way, or recreated in this observable form. Accordingly, White celebrates Stone's *JFK* because it falls back onto the notion of history as narrative mythology.[55]

What White is touting is that one very significant way to master history, to give it substance, staying power, and accessibility, not to mention contemporary relevance and intellectual parameters, is through the use of narrative structure. As has been stated, this is proven and is as old as western history. It also takes into account a significant and inveterate aspect of humanity. Janet Staiger cites psychologist Jerome Bruner's "The Narrative Construction of Reality," as an essential benchmark. Bruner, according to Steiger, intimates that the narrative is one of the principal ways in which knowledge is "transferred" from culture to culture. Bruner states that humans structure experience and memory primarily in the form of stories and myths. Not only is this done for management reasons but also, is essential for the process of integrating these structures into the larger social order. Bruner feels that very much related to this is the importance of dramatization, in particular, the dramatization of history, which allows for interpretation and understanding.[56]

One of the reasons why the holiness of the documentary has been reinterpreted or perhaps, according to some, blasphemed, has to do with the above. At the extreme, mixing the purity of the documentary film vision, with aspects of the docudrama, can be defended by utilizing White and Bruner. Yet it is also a way to reach the audience without the handcuffing that may be part of the traditional, established process. Yes it may confuse the viewer[57], but in the post-modern vision of history, that is something to be left to the individual. When a weighty documentarian like Leslie Woodhead begins to use fiction in his work, he justifies it by arguing that in order to tell the story, one that would be impossible in the conventional formats, he must resort to this mixing. But, this is done with strict accuracy, or at least the intention to keep to the facts. The end result is that you get more of a journalistic result than full-fledged fiction.[58]

The old boundaries, or rather the nineteenth-century boundaries for historical interpretation are no longer held up to the same rigor. The influence and accessibility of the narrative structure is simply too strong of an attraction. Fictional techniques, such as those employed by Simon Schama, and autobiographical characteristics such as those found on The History Channel, make the dividing line between traditional history and narrative storytelling very porous indeed.[59] To juxtapose popular mediated history with what used to pass for established academic history, in a strict comparison, is often to suggest the former is fully accurate and definitive while the latter is instead, shallow and mere entertainment. As Steve Anderson puts it,

> history does not end with the production of documents, narratives, or analyses. People consume and process written, filmed, or televised histories within a web of individual and cultural forces that influence their reception and the uses to which they are put.[60]

If one was to look at the textbooks offered up as history over the last one hundred years in Canada and the United States, one would see that from today's vantage point, this history may have been masquerading as objective, while the truth today, has changed. In her famous study of American high school history textbooks, Frances Fitzgerald suggested that what we read as history—as students—is in fact, not necessarily the most accurate account. Fitzgerald relates that as a child, she felt that the American history textbooks were viewed as the definitive truth because there was a seriousness about them that other books lacked. This notion was reinforced by the fact that her teachers "treated them with respect." These works dealt with the past in a way that was free from all the unpleasantness of American history. As with British textbooks, the 1950s American books presented America "as perfect: the greatest nation in the world, and the embodiment of democracy, freedom, and technological progress." The texts stayed along the same trajectory, "remaining constant from the time of the American Revolution." Importantly, Fitzgerald suggests that what they presented was historical truth; "reality," "a permanent expression of mass culture in America."[61] And this is exactly the point of one of the major themes of this work. What has in the past constituted history must be regarded as suspect—and perhaps, just as problematic as mediated versions of history.

One of the most significant issues affecting and effecting discussions and definitions of history centers on "whose" history should be taught, shown, and examined.[62] In a country such as Canada, and to a lesser extent, the United States, traditional conceptualizations of history are being challenged by a plethora of diverse interests who desire, and in many cases, have legitimate claims, to have their (versions of) history taught. The traditional narratives of history, the ones that have been taught for decades, the ones that Fitzgerald discusses, are now, not only subject to revisions and exclusions by the visual media, but are increasingly challenged by the demands of a multicultural public. It is no longer just about history, but, as Jack Granatstein has asked, "Whose history would we teach"? Granatstein implies that with so many "histories" challenging the dominant set of historical narratives, school boards and professional historians alike feel that perhaps it is safer and "better" to teach none at all. This, he feels, will erode the national fabric and the concept of what it means to be a Canadian.[63] By loosening the bonds on the cloth of the national narrative, the whole thing starts to come undone. In the place of traditional, structured, rigorous history, come the multiple manifestations of public and popular history.

The notion of objectivity in written or traditional history has been debated for years. The notion of objectivity and in particular, of authenticity is more appropriate for discussions of visual history. As Hayden White has remarked, "Demands for a verisimilitude in film that is impossible in any medium of representation, including that of written history, stem from the confusion of historical individuals with the kinds of characterization of them required for discursive purposes, whether in verbal or in visual media."[64] In other words, White is suggesting that the visual media of film, photography or television can be interpreted as something fundamentally different than the textual version. This can be linked up with the importance of the narrative. As Robert A. Rosenstone has observed, "In a medium where visual evidence is crucial to understanding, [such] pervasive fictions are major contributors to the meaning of the film, including its historical meaning."[65] Just as a historical film is a "construction of a past," so too is a history book. Rosenstone is referring to the replication of events to approximate a history by employing images that someone obviously had to create. As well, filmed history must condense the story and resorts to symbolization in order to shrink unmanageable amounts of data to a manageable format.[66] These qualifications can be applied to written history as well.

The multiplicity of definitions for explaining exactly what history is to-day suggests that one must be wary of dismissing the more popular forms of history and as well one must be careful of engaging in hypocrisy when criticizing popular forms of history. This is extremely "frustrating" to academic historians who have seen the rebirth of history's appeal, unfortunately within the confines of popular culture. Signs of this popularity include the explosion of historical societies, the mass appeal of genealogical sites and the increased sales of popular history books—vastly outnumbering academic works, which encompass historical literature.[67] History, it seems, can be found everywhere. Public history is usually defined as the historical associations most people grasp from the many offerings of mass culture. According to George F. Custen, public history "also conveys the idea that mass-media texts, and not other forms of historical narrative, are significant sources of history for large segments of the American population."[68] To some extent, one must distinguish between traditional forms of historical learning and the comparison to mediated, popular history. On the other hand, the new versions of history are more readily accepted as parallels to the old and even create streams that are capable of standing alone. Films as texts perform many of the same functions as books; they "interpret and comment on significant past events" which in turn places them within "a context of historiography and enables them to have an impact on the public that often exceeds that of scholarship in range and influence."[69]

The preeminent role that film has assumed in today's culture as a conveyor of historical knowledge is problematic. When historical films challenge accepted historical reality—or what passes for established historical discourse—a quandary arises for historians and keepers of the dominant narrative which is firmly oriented to the popularity of the filmed product. The fact that they garner so much attention and capture such a large audience suggests that they are going to be scrutinized in a way that books are not. This process is often undertaken by historians and authorities who are threatened by the power and access that the filmed version has.[70] This can be problematic when boundaries are crossed. A famous photographic still from Sergei Eisenstein's *Battleship Potemkin* is often used in history text books to stand for the iconic statement of the Revolution of 1905. This only accentuates the fact that for many, the visual and even the actual historical memorialization of the Revolution is Eisenstein's film.[71] Perhaps it is necessary to equate film as a legitimate historical source or even to refer to films in the same way as diaries and letters, as objects "to be studied and analysed."[72]

When a major documentary film is to be shown on PBS—*Baseball, New York, The Civil War, The War*—there is often if not always a tie-in book, a beautiful hardcover coffee-table book that is promoted very heavily in the media. Although this is somewhat removed from the narrow audience of pure academic history, these books are often given a blessing by established academics. To say that this is a nefarious commercialization is once again, to miss the point. In a widely read article on the connection between historical commemoration and corporate sponsorship (focusing on the centennial of the Statue of Liberty) Susan G. Davis argued that the close relationship between corporations and historical commemorations led to the privatization of public historical memory.[73] While that can be accurate on some levels, it censures most forms of public commemorization, such as the showing of many PBS, CBC, and assorted series that depend on corporate funding. This is particularly problematic when private organizations and foundations see it as their business to attempt to compensate for the paucity of history in the school curriculum. The "corporate agenda" has long been a phrase that has bothered academics and the worry that this will "infect" the sanctity of the historical discipline is something that has been debated for years. The fact that the CRB Foundation and McDonalds are involved in the production of Canadian history through films and comic books immediately invokes this reaction. As historian Del Muise was quoted as saying, "any time a big multinational gets involved in deciding what's worth transmitting," there is something to be concerned about.[74]

The Heritage Project, an ambitious visual history undertaking, sponsored by the Montreal-based CRB foundation, produces short "vignettes" on various aspects of Canadian history.[75] These brief and compelling commercial-like narratives are wonderfully constructed and very effective in conveying certain aspects of Canadian history. These Minutes, which air on television—often on the Canadian History Channel and in movie theatres, are very potent mini-narratives on relatively well-known topics. The goal behind the Minutes is to give "Canadians a greater feel for the color and accomplishments of their past."[76] Like the True North comic books that were distributed by McDonalds and were based on selected Heritage Minutes, these popular historical offerings attempt to inform the public on aspects of Canadian history as well as to capture interesting episodes of Canadian history for popular consumption. More than sixty-one Heritage Minutes have been produced.[77] These topics range from the Halifax Explosion, to the story of the building of the National Railway to the arrival of U.S. slaves to Canada through the Underground Railway. More are currently underway. Some of these, such as the adoption of the first hockey mask by Jacques Plante to the first woman doctor, fall fully in line with the expectations of popular visual history, while others, such as the story of Laura Secord's heroism indulge in a pseudo-patriotic embrace of national icons. What is significant is the fact that both the Minutes and the Comics speak to the language of youngsters.

It is *their* media that conveys the information—not the textbook and not the teacher. In attempting to reach young people through the media that they consume and by framing history in dramatic, narrative terms, both the comic books and the films are not necessarily guilty of trivializing history—which is always an understandable concern—but, attempting to make history accessible in a way that it very rarely is. According to one of the executive producers of the Heritage Minutes, Robert Scully, "History gains life and relevance through these productions."[78] Canadian history "comes to life" and speaks to the viewers in an accessible and interesting way which is often contrary to the traditional viewpoint of Canadian history. One of the common complaints often directed towards Canadian history is the fact that, unlike its American, British, and French counterparts, it is considered boring and dull. In pursuing this strategy the editor of the comic book series is attempting to do something quite different,[79] as do the Heritage Minutes.

It is critical to keep in mind that as changes to the curriculum marginalize history and push it to the back-burner, other agents have stepped into fill the role previously played by education, teachers and the government. As Desmond Morton has written, "these have been interesting times in the history trade."[80] What makes the Heritage Minutes and other forms of popular visual history so controversial is the fact that they are doing what was once the preserve of the educational system. According to figures compiled by the Dominion Institute and cited by Morton, the level of ignorance in the general population regarding the most fundamental aspects of Canadian history is astounding. This is a situation not very different from similar surveys conducted in the United States regarding American history.[81] Part of the problem is one that Granatstein has suggested: what history should be taught?[82] The other part could be that the government cannot afford to teach history in the school systems from a financial point of view as well as a politically correct one. Although debate often rages on the paucity of history in the classroom, the simple fact is that history is rarely taught and when it is, post junior high school, it is "subsumed" under the rubric of social studies to give it more "contemporary relevance."[83] The fact that students today can graduate without studying history in high school, most certainly leaves the door open for the influence of popular visual history. Related to this is the companion piece that is often discussed with the Heritage Minutes, the 30 hour, *Canada: A People's History*, televised on CBC and produced with an accompanying book. Once again, one of the most popular representations of history has been visualized.

Like the Heritage Minutes, the CBC-produced, *Canada: A People's History*, was designed to rectify popular notions of the Canadian past and to discredit the above perception and replace it with something more exciting, or dramatic. The 30 hour documentary which began airing in October 2000, at a cost of $25 million, was hugely popular with Canadian audiences and as a form of educational television,[84] succeeded in its goals, in the same way that Ken Burns' documentaries did south of the border. Where this production flourished was—as with the Heritage Minutes—in dispelling the traditional notion of Canadian history and replacing it with an exciting story, a narrative of action that proved to be of interest to many. This was accomplished—and is still being processed, by taking into account audience demands and using features of popular narrative traditions. In contrast to the stereotypical blandness that has characterized the perception of traditional Canadian history, both historical sources have "restored" Canadian history, complete with all the color, vibrancy and drama that had been missing.[85] In essence, by incorporating aspects of popular culture, and adopting narrative techniques, *finally* there is a perspective of Canadian history that is truly interesting and capable of reaching a huge audience. As with the Heritage Minutes, there was a deliberate attempt to steer away from the ingredients of traditional history and to focus on drama and action in order to engage the viewer.[86] Central to this process was instilling within Canadians a knowledge of their past that encourages them to understand "the present" as well to "make informed decisions about the future," although gauging this is quite difficult.[87] At the heart of these two historical offerings was the implication that a key motivating factor was the vibrancy of collective memory. And this raises the following question: all this has problematic consequences for the impact of national heritage and the intertwining of individual memory. Another way of saying this is given the impact of visual history, what is the place of memory?

A significant bias that has defined the difference between memory and history is the certainty that for many the simple, yet powerful fact is, that history *is* put down on paper or recorded. In doing this, the writer, historian, or the producer of history frames the past in a logical and admittedly coherent fashion. This process is often in contrapuntal relationship to both oral culture and specifically, to memory. History may be derived by or from memory, but by recording it—by putting it down on paper or by filming and recording, photographing or physically registering the past, one gets a tangible and repeatable version of the past that can be referred to over and over. The vagaries of memory lead one to conclude that it is just the opposite—at least originally—that it is "unreliable."[88] Yet, for many, memory is often where history begins.

Memory plays a vital role in the interpretation of history. According to Andrew Hoskins, in contemporary culture, memory is particularly important especially where historical factors are concerned.[89] Collective or social memory, as first interpreted by Maurice Halbwachs,[90] become important because these are memories "that a group shares and by which it defines itself." Our identity as people and nations, as cultures and ethnic groups, is defined by memory.[91] Collective memory is a very powerful aspect of how people engage with, interpret and understand history. Michael Frisch conducted research on memory and history and found that education (or lack of it) may not be as important in honing historical memory, as certain "collective cultural mechanisms." These "structures" suggest that within a culture, in this case, American culture, a combination of "shared beliefs, myths, 'meaning systems' and historical images" come together to form a "civil religion."[92] This is both interesting and important because it means that the static idea of history as a dispassionate look at the past is just one of many contributing features to one's collective historical memory. Frisch's research also buttresses what Halbwachs wrote: "Don't we believe that we relive the past more fully because we no longer represent it alone, because we see it now as we saw it then, but through the eyes of another as well"?[93] In other words, so much of what we define as the culture of our memory is based upon the visual information put in place by the mass media. History, in this case, is according to Thomas Elsaesser, not what's past, "but what is being passed on," through the media. Elsaesser makes the point in terms cast by White with the following: "Do you remember the day Kennedy was shot?" really means "Do you remember the day you watched Kennedy being shot all day on television."[94]

So important, if not vital for this discussion is the correlation between media, memory and history. Significantly, the memories experienced by viewing film and other mediated versions of the past are often as vivid for those watching as with those who have in fact participated in the event. Alison Landsberg terms this process "prosthetic memory," by which she suggests that even though one did not go through the process or the historical episode, one can nonetheless experience a very profound kinship in the form of shared memory. She feels that the viewer can experience a relationship as significant as anyone else even though the viewer did not go through the approach.[95]

Television has had an enormous influence on what individuals remember and recall as history. What has occurred is that the divisions between history and memory have merged on television. Television news in particular is often substituted for "primary source accounts of historical events, much in the same way that journals, diaries, and newspaper articles provide students and budding scholars with evidence for their latest high school research paper or tenure-anxiety-driven historical tome."[96] The mediation of memory—and history—often suggests that what is construed as collective memory or mediated history, is something that is manufactured for the viewer. This is certainly true of most television events as it is for one's comprehension of war. But Andrew Hoskins raises an interesting point regarding this. Many people have been filming their personal memories with great gusto over the last few years thanks to small, hand-held recording devices and computers.[97] Do these versions mean less because of their electronic format? It is fundamental to recognize that the photograph quickly became a robust way of maintaining history and memory. The photograph remains one of the most potent and ubiquitous memory/history formats, often supplanting the mind. And one certainly cannot forget "home movies" which were shot on 8mm or Super8 mm. These were and remain a staple of family and other memory/history triggers.[98]

One can suggest, as does David Lowenthal (and others), that what history is to memory is its extension. "History," according to Lowenthal, "extends and elaborates memory by interpreting relics and synthesizing reports from past eyewitnesses."[99] A key distinction is to be cognizant that history is often considered to be more about documentation and evidence, while memory is oriented more around the "premise of knowledge."[100] History is about giving memory's ideas, words, and images concrete expression. Collective memory can also be defined or thought of as "history in motion" a kind of history that occupies a different kind of space and that move at a "different pace and rate than traditional history." This resonates when the idea of presentism is particularly pronounced.[101]

The postmodern definition of reality and of seeing the world increasingly utilize the visual image; the cinema, photography, television and electronic imagery to evidence and define historical events. As Frank P. Tomasulo states:

> Our concepts of historical referentiality (what happened), epistemology (how we know what happened), and historical memory (how we interpret it and what it means to us) are now determined primarily by media imagery.[102]

We must have a sense of literacy to understand history as defined by image as opposed to the history that was once determined by words. This means that in order not to be passive but active and critical, a new form of distance has and will inevitably come into being. It is also important to be aware of the fact that images are "polysemic," meaning that a photograph or news footage can generate multiple meanings. From the where to the when can have enormous ramifications. Labeling a photograph and framing it a specific way can give it both unintended and intended cultural consequences. A news photo done up as art means something quite different in its new setting. This can affect the perception of history and can also alter meaning.[103]

The photograph as a historical touchstone has been recognized by Barbie Zelizer, as "one of the least understood dimensions of photography."

Central here is the fact that the photograph is an essential conduit for individuals to grasp the idea of the past, to understand it and most importantly, to remember it. The photograph becomes "a filter on the past" because it is so often relied upon. Yet the context in which the photograph is used has ramifications for the understanding of historical memory. In particular, photographs which have been elevated to a supreme status of defining history are not neutral. They can and do create specific memories and importantly, affect how history is remembered as well as how significant a role memory plays in defining history.[104]

The employment of images to define and stand for history and public memory lead them, especially when they are "decontextualized" to be defined and interpreted within the guidelines of narrative and mythology.[105] It is our Western bias to group images in this way and in turn, to interpret images in this manner. The "conventions of storytelling" are the way in which the realism of the documentary photograph makes its presence felt as a form of history.[106]

Marshall McLuhan, for all his pronouncements about the future of technology, was trained at Cambridge and received a doctorate in English Literature.[107] Like many of his generation, his preference tilted towards the book as a repository of knowledge. Yet he was very aware about the impact that technology had upon print culture as the established discourse of knowledge. In the 1960s he published his ground breaking *Understanding Media*. In this book, he wrote "Our Western values, built on the written word, have already been considerably affected by the electric media of telephone, radio and TV."[108] McLuhan intimated that studying the alphabet for clues to what makes culture tick, may be a case of too little, too late. Nonetheless, the search went on and continues.

According to Joshua Meyrowitz, Harold Innis felt that "different media have different potentialities for control." Media that were heavily regulated and required special skills to decode were usually the preserve of "an elite" that could control it. Media that were automatically accessible, with virtually no controls, were and are quickly adopted by the majority of people.[109] This concept has ramifications for mediated history. On the one hand, presenting history through images makes the process much more accessible to more people. On the other hand, media are, by and large products of corporations. Control of television and film as well as computers rests within the confines of these entities. The Internet, though, provides myriad opportunities to those who can access the computer. Steven Lubar has observed, that "information technology can be a strong centrifugal force, giving power to the individual." The democratic potential of these technologies can "let people in" to mainstream information culture.[110] Lubar, and others, cite the importance of information technology in liberating people from oppression—as in the importance of the Xerox in the heydays of communism, but also in allowing them to *simply* participate within.

The historian working within the archives of radio tapes, television programs, films and digitized photographs has to be more scrupulous in annotation and citation procedures than her counterpart, working with traditional textual material. The bias against these documents is still quite fierce and the characteristics that are often applied to them leave the scholar open to numerous attacks. Given the fact that "the primary purpose of broadcasting is not history"[111] the historian must be meticulous. While broadcast artifacts were not necessarily constructed for history, and presented along the lines of conventional historiography, they are also burdened by their character. This means that the bias against them—their possible novelty and their probable superficiality—is compounded by ephemerality and alienness. Most historians, while exceedingly comfortable with the written word and the protocols of print research, are often ill at ease when dealing with the vagaries of electronic and visual documentation. Many of these historians "lack sufficient technical and media-process knowledge to utilize mediated material as a primary source of evidence."[112]

Until courses on media awareness and media research as well as visual literacy become common, the natural and academic comfort level of print will serve as an obstacle in allowing historians who access online and electronic sources, to be as comfortable and confident as they are with the former. The citation process related to broadcast/electronic sources will have to be much more elaborate in order to justify using these documents. At the core is again the "validity" of the source.[113]

Closely related to the validity situation is the emerging series of questions surrounding the "authenticity" of the documents and data preserved in a digital format. The whole notion of the original and the authentic—as Walter Benjamin recognized with photography, becomes even more problematic within the digital universe. In comparison with the culture of print, the quandaries facing the historian with regard to verification of historical documents on the Internet are quite large. Whereas print has had over five-hundred years to establish a variety of mechanisms which attempt to guarantee authenticity, the vagaries of Cyberspace challenge these traditional notions.[114] Related to this are the tricky concerns of ownership and preservation. Libraries literally own books and old manuscripts, and are bequeathed letters and documents. In the digital age, licensing of technology and software pose hitherto unthought-of problems. The maintenance of digital archives by libraries is one way around this but, as Roy Rosenzweig has remarked, digitized documents can "undercut" the authority of ownership. In turn, the responsibility to preserve the originals, once the duty of the library/research institution, is left up in the air. Rosenzweig cites the hypothetical example of a large concern, perhaps Microsoft, not liking a particular document and subsequently, their refusing to allow a computer database to issue it. The corporate world has traditionally left preservation to the libraries and unless a profit motive can be generated for this very expensive undertaking this may prove to have very problematic consequences for historical research.[115] This is exactly what is going on with the numerous attempts to capture and digitize entire collections and to make them accessible. Copyright issues and publishers lawsuits both hamper and protect ownership and access. Nationalist concerns factor into all of this as do language issues and accusations of cultural imperialism. The issue gets further bogged down in terms of formatting.[116] Despite these concerns, there is one very positive development.

Perhaps the most often talked about positive result of the digitization of historical documents is the fact that in many ways it is both liberating and democratic. Those who enthusiastically support this process say that it is a boon to researchers and in general, to those who have traditionally not been able to access what was in an archive. With what has been going on with the Library of Congress, this has now changed. Citing Prelinger Kahle, Roy Rosenzweig implies that digitization has finally fulfilled the democratic vision of access as it relates to the public library, national archives, and the research library:

> Previously, few had the opportunity to come to Washington to watch early Thomas Edison films at the Library of Congress. And the library could not have served them if they had. Democratic access is the real payoff in electronic records and materials.[117]

What is occurring is simply that more and more people have access to historical sources, archives and documents, which increases and stimulates interest in history. This is liberating and to some, revolutionary. Sociologist Mike Featherstone suggests that this kind of access will lead to a "new culture of memory" which has almost unlimited access. Featherstone indicates the demise of "hierarchical controls" and "direct access" could "lead to a decline in intellectual and academic power." This in turn could result in the relaxing of the barrier between the historian and history.[118]

It is important to accept the fact that individual's selecting and suggesting alternate forms of history, via the mass media, are often those who have been traditionally shutoff from telling their story. This role has been played in contrast to custodians of traditional historiography which suggest that specific rules must be followed. The hostility and dismissal of other voices through alternate formats has prevented the acceptance of popular historical manifestations from being legitimized. This has been a very significant reality of historical film. As Robert Burgoyne has implied, film has been there to challenge traditional narratives, especially the dominant themes in American history. Importantly, Burgoyne suggests that the Hollywood historical product is not governed by any national or academic bodies, but is thus relatively free to pursue historical versions without constraints. Certain films produced by Hollywood offer competing or differing notions of the past—alternatives to what has usually been the case. Movies such as *Born on the Fourth of July*, *Glory*, and *JFK*, strongly "suggest that there are potentially many histories that may be plural and conflicting, and that require different constructions of the national past."[119]

The intention to reach a wider audience than the academy is also a motivating factor in presenting visual history. Established historians have moved in this direction with the intention of bringing history to a larger audience, as much as have journalists and film makers, such as Ken Burns. Natalie Zemon Davis has advocated film as a means to achieving the above. There is no reason why films cannot be as rigorously researched as the traditional printed text.[120] As will be illustrated in a later chapter, filmed versions of historical topics and people carry enormous weight.

One solution to the problems of doing visual history—the main problem being the criticisms from academic historians—that is often voiced and frequently incorporated, is to have practitioners of traditional forms of history collaborate with the practitioner of mediated, visual history. This has been done successfully many times and has resulted in both wonderful and exacting creations as well as the complete opposite, problematic and superficial products.[121] There is still a great deal of suspicion, on behalf of both camps, be they video designers or directors of film, and academic historians. In an ambitious project attempted during the 1920s, Yale University Press took their popular book series, *The Chronicles of America*, and translated them into films. Historian Donald J. Mattheisen makes the point that the Yale historians and academics felt that their prestige would give the project "an air of authority that would impress the educational film market."[122] Yet the project was a dismal failure and part of the reason, according to Mattheisen, was the imposition of a heavy-handed level of scholarship into an unfamiliar arena.[123] As with contemporary issues that surround the problems of translation from print to other formats, the *Chronicles* situation was plagued by the assumption, that just because something works in one version or media, it should therefore work in another. During the end of the second decade of the nineteenth century and into the 1920s, the idea of using film as a form of visual education was being discussed as a very viable idea.[124] It seemed like a wonderful idea, to translate a popular series of books into an accessible film series, yet the project increasingly got bogged down in a variety of problems. Paramount of these seems to have been "professorial meddling" to such an extent that the project was repeatedly sidetracked and delayed. As detailed by Mattheisen, scriptwriters and producers locked horns with historians on issues that ranged from content to substance. What the producers, directors and film people recognized, was that a theatrical/artistic shape was intrinsic to the success, indeed, the competence of the films.[125] Consequently, this came to conflict with historicism and pedagogical concerns. The films, despite their noble goals, became mired in melodrama and shallowness. The significance of their legacy suggests a number of things.

One must keep in mind that today's audience is much more visually sophisticated and not as historically literate. During the 1920s, the exact opposite, one could claim, was true. As a barometer, *The Chronicles* series suggests that despite over eighty years of time elapsing, many of the same concerns and issues still plague attempts at visual history. The example of the *Chronicles* has numerous contemporary parallels to how contemporary technology has been employed. James Ettema studied the production of an educational television series which was produced with the input of educators, researchers, and traditional television producers. In his research, Ettema found that the television professionals gained the upper hand over the other two groups by constantly utilizing the experience of what makes "good TV"—something that the other groups were lacking in their knowledge base.[126] Larry Cuban has suggested that as each new technology was brought into the classroom and after a period of time, was discarded, the educators were often blamed for not using it properly. What is significant in this parallel is that outsiders have dictated and demanded this utilization, rarely consulting with the teachers. Yet today, a tremendous amount of teacher input is involved—in many cases, though not all—with utilizing technology and the classroom. More teachers and professors today have familiarity with electronic visual technology than in the past.[127]

The influence of television, and in general, the visual nature of society on the presentation of history has manifested itself in numerous ways. The impact of the visual has been great. In two rather somber museums, the Holocaust Memorial Museum in Washington, D.C., and the Beit Hashoah/Museum of Tolerance in Los Angeles, the presence of television and video is pronounced. According to Jeffrey Shandler,

> Like many other museums, these two employ video displays in part as a response to ongoing concerns within museology. Increasingly, as museums have pursued a range of alternatives to the traditional exhibition of material artifacts, the use of video displays has become more common. Their functions within museum display have grown more complex, ranging from presenting vintage footage as historical artifact to offering viewers curatorial interpretation in the form of short documentaries or interactive video displays.[128]

The hundreds of monitors and screens that dot both museums are suggestive of the importance of the visual and the televisual in contemporary society. The utilization of the screen within the confines of the museum illustrates how vital this process is in reaching visitors wholly accustomed to constantly viewing. [129]

The dominance of the visual image in imagining, constructing and defining history gets more refined as every year passes. The visual conceptualizations of what war is are now totally dominated by the scenes shown on television. Both Gulf Wars and the Yugoslavian situation of the late nineties are illustrations of this state. Michael Ignatieff writes that while the bombing of Serbia was "as real . . . as war can be" for those living through NATO air strikes, for those living outside, "the war was virtual." The effect on Europeans and Americans was as watchers; as spectators."[130] This in turn has enormous ramifications, according to Ignatieff, for democracy and national interest. What he means is that "Wars whose consequences are visible are unsustainable in the long term."[131] Support will quickly erode once the horror and the cost becomes a staple of the nightly news. At the same time, the distance and lack of necessary sacrifice on behalf of the civilian population, who most probably aren't going to be inconvenienced, renders the post-modern war, virtual.[132]

A final way that the visual nature of society is affecting the definition of historical knowledge is, interestingly, in a traditional format. Scanning the periodicals devoted to history, one sees an increasing number of articles and reviews devoted to the interaction between technology and history.[133] This plethora of articles and essays is indicative of the fact that computer based digital technology has to be reckoned with as a force for the future of historians, historical discourse, historical analysis, and historiography.

It is important to keep in mind that historical scholarship and study has gone through a variety of cycles. At different moments and at different times in recent evaluation, the concept of history has been determined by different factors which suggest that it is much more than simply "about the past." This being the case, what was thought appropriate for historical discourse at one time, for example nineteenth-century patriotic nationalism, is not currently appropriate. The rise of sub-groupings within history and the move towards segmentation—social history, women's history—in the early nineteen sixties, fragmented the definitions of history even further. Now, one must also consider the myriad definitions for visual history. To conclude and to put this into further perspective, one must be as leery of dismissing visual history as invalid as one would be of dismissing some of the more recent forms of history, which have their origins in the political and social movements of the 1960s. The countless schools of history and the varied forms of historical discourse that permeate discussion today serve to remind one that the constitutive notion of what history is, is subject to evolutions and trends. By widening the boundaries the visual must be included,[134] and must factor in the past and future of print.

NOTES

1. Susan Porter Benson, Stephen Brier and Roy Rosenzweig, eds., "Introduction," *Presenting the Past: Essays on History and The Public*, (Philadelphia, PA: Temple University Press, 1986), pp. xvi–xvii.

2. Peter Charles Hoffer, *Past Imperfect*, (New York: Public Affairs, 2004), p. 91.

3. James V. Wertsch, "Specific Narratives and Schematic Narrative Templates," in Peter Seixas, Editor, *Theorizing Historical Consciousness*, (Toronto: University of Toronto Press, 2005), p. 49.

4. Peter Charles Hoffer, *Past Imperfect*, p. 91.

5. In a review of the television series, *Band of Brothers*, Nancy Franklin writes: "The enormous surge of interest in the Second World War that has taken place over the past ten years was to some extent inevitable; the early nineties saw the beginning of a succession of fiftieth anniversaries related to the war and it seems to be human nature to let no fiftieth anniversary go unobserved. Formerly reticent veterans, then in their seventies, began telling their stories, and reading newspaper articles and books about their experiences (and seeing them on the History Channel, which is so wrapped up in the Second World War that it is sometimes referred to by its devotees as the Hitler Channel) provided the education about the war that many of us never got in school, or—even if we had family members who fought in the war—at home." *The New Yorker*, September 17, 2001, p. 163.

6. David Thelen, "Memory and American History," *The Journal of American History*, March 1989, vol. 75, no. 4, p. 1117.

7. John Hope Franklin, "Foreword," to *The Past Before Us: Contemporary Historical Writing in the United States*, Edited by Michael Kammen, (Ithaca, NY: Cornell University Press, 1980), pp. 14–15.

8. Peter Charles Hoffer, *Past Imperfect*, p. 94.

9. Michael L. Wilson, "Visual Culture: A Useful Category of Historical Analysis," *The Nineteenth-Century Visual Culture Reader*, Edited by Vanessa R. Schwartz and Jeannene M. Przyblysk, (New York: Routlege, 2004), p. 26.

10. Michael L. Wilson, "Visual Culture: A Useful Category of Historical Analysis," pp. 27, 29.

11. In the late 1960s John Lukacs published *Historical Consciousness: The Remembered Past*, (New Brunswick, NJ: Transaction Publishers, 1968/1985), where he set forth the notion of a tangible historical awareness or consciousness that many people possess. Lukacs recognized the important role that popular history plays, as well as the considerations of history as both literature and science. See the comment by Christian Laville, in "Historical Consciousness and Historical Education: What to Expect from the First for the Second," in Peter Seixas, ed., *Theorizing Historical Consciousness*, (Toronto: University of Toronto Press, 2005), pp. 168–69.

12. Barbara Abrash and Daniel J. Walkowitz, "Sub/versions of History: a Mediation on Film and Historical Narrative," *History Workshop Journal*, Issue 38, 1994, p. 203.

13. In "Why History? Thinking About the Uses of the Past," *The History Teacher* vol. 25, no. 3, May 1992, pp. 293–312, Frank Stricker suggested that there are three key questions or issues that are important to the practice of history. These are the objectivity/truth issue, how to reach nonspecialist audiences and what Stricker calls the "utility question"; why does one study history. The article focuses on the last of these questions and Stricker offers a number of answers including: that "history is fun"; it is "a great tradition and a storehouse of great ideas"; "the past is a bulwark against contemporary confusion and overload"; "history is the story of noble deeds, noble person, moral examples." All of these categories or answers are applied to formal academic history but can just as easily be applied to visual history.

14. Fritz Stern, ed., *The Varieties of History: From Voltaire to the Present*, (New York: Vintage Books, 1973), p. 9.

15. Lewis Namier, "History and Political Culture," in Fritz Stern, ed., *The Varieties of History*, p. 376.

16. Lewis Namier, "History and Political Culture," p. 379.

17. W. Warren Wagar, "Past and Future," *American Behavioral Scientist*, vol. 42, no. 3, Nov./Dec., 1998, p. 366.

18. Arthur Marwick, *The Nature of History*, (Third Edition), (London: Macmillan, 1989), p. 28.

19. Peter Novick, in *That Noble Dream: The "Objectivity Question" and the American Historical Profession*, (Cambridge: Cambridge University Press 1988/1999), p. 1, writes: "At the very center of the professional historical venture is the idea and ideal of 'objectivity.' It was the rock on which the venture was constituted, its continuing raison d'etre. It has been the quality which the profession has prized and praised above all others—whether in historians or in their works. It has been the key term in defining progress in historical scholarship: moving ever closer to the objective truth about the past. Anyone interested in what professional historians are up to—what they think they are doing, or ought to be doing, when they write history—might well begin by considering the 'objectivity question.'"

20. E. H. Carr, *What Is History*, (London: Penguin, 1961/1990), pp. 8–13, 22, 30, 105, 134.

21. Robert Fulford, *The Triumph of Narrative: Storytelling in the Age of Mass Culture*, (Toronto: House of Anansi Press Limited, 1999), p. 48.

22. Margaret E. Newell, "Subterranean Electronic Blues; or, How a Former Technophobe Learned to Stop Worrying and Love Multimedia," *The Journal of American History*, March 1997, vol. 83, no. 4, p. 1347.

23. See E. H. Carr, *What Is History*, p. 134, and Gary R. Edgerton, "Introduction: Television as Historian: A Different Kind of History Altogether," in Gary R. Edgerton and Peter C. Rollins, eds., *Television Histories: Shaping Collective Memory in the Media Age*, p. 3.

24. Robert Hanke, "Quantum Leap: The Postmodern Challenge of Television as History," in Gary R. Edgerton and Peter C. Rollins, editors, *Television Histories: Shaping Collective Memory in the Media Age*, p. 61.

25. Warren Susman, *Culture as History*, (New York: Pantheon, 1984), p. 24, cited in Daniel Marcus, "Profiles in Courage: Televisual History on the New Frontier," in Gary R. Edgerton and Peter C. Rollins, eds., *Television Histories: Shaping Collective Memory in the Media Age*, pp. 81–82.

26. Susan Buck-Morss, "Benjamin's Passagen-Werk: Redeeming Mass Culture for the Revolution," *New German Critique*, 29, 1983, p. 217, cited in Shelton Waldrep, "Story Time," in *Inside The Mouse: Work and Play at Disney World*, The Project on Disney, (Durham, NC: Duke University Press, 1995), pp. 88–89.

27. Gary R. Edgerton, "Introduction: Television as Historian: A Different Kind of History Altogether," in Gary R. Edgerton and Peter C. Rollins, eds., *Television Histories: Shaping Collective Memory in the Media Age*, p. 8.

28. Moses I. Finley, *The World of Odysseus*, revised edition, (London: Penguin, 1979), pp. 74.

29. Robert B. Kebric, *Greek People*, (Mountain View, California: Mayfield Publishing, 1989), pp. 1–6.

30. C. M. Bowra, *The Greek Experience*, (London: Weidenfeld and Nicolson, 1957), p. 20.

31. C. M. Bowra, *The Greek Experience*, p. 20.

32. C. M. Bowra, *The Greek Experience*, p. 21.

33. C. M. Bowra, *The Greek Experience*, p. 21.

34. Moses I. Finley, *The World of Odysseus*, pp. 21–27.

35. Michael Schudson, *Watergate in American Memory: How We Remember, Forget, and Reconstruct the Past*, (New York: Basic Books, 1992) p. 127.

36. John Ralston Saul, *The Unconscious Civilization*, (Toronto: House of Anansi Press, 1995) pp. 61–63.

37. Barry Schwartz, Yael Zerubavel, Bernice Barnett, "The Recovery of Masada: A Study in Collective Memory," *The Sociological Quarterly*, vol. 27, no. 2, 1986, p. 148.

38. Roger I. Simon, "Forms of Insurgency In the Production of Popular Memories: The Columbus Quincentenary and the Pedagogy of Counter-Commemoration," p. 6. Draft Chapter.

39. Steve Anderson, "History TV and Popular Memory," in Gary R. Edgerton and Peter C. Rollins, *Television Histories: Shaping Collective Memory in the Media Age*, (Lexington, KY: The University of Kentucky Press, 2001), p. 20.

40. Margaret Conrad, "My Canada Includes the Atlantic Provinces," Round Table, *Histoire sociale/Social History*, vol. XXXIV, no. 68, November 2001, p. 399.

41. Margaret Conrad, "My Canada Includes the Atlantic Provinces," p. 399.

42. Mark Starowicz, *Making History*, (Toronto: McClelland & Stewart, 2003), p. 237.

43. Hayden White, "The Modernist Event," in Vivian Sobchack, ed., *The Persistence of History: Cinema, Television, And The Modern Event*, (New York: Routledge, 1996), pp. 18–19.

44. See Steve Anderson, "History TV and Popular Memory," p. 19.

45. Hayden White, *Tropics of Discourse*, (Baltimore: The Johns Hopkins University Press, 1978), p. 61.

46. Hayden White, *The Content of the Form: Narrative Discourse and Historical Representation*, (Baltimore: The Johns Hopkins University Press, 1987), p. x.

47. Hayden White, *The Content of the Form*, p. x, and *Tropics of Discourse*, p. 61.

48. Hayden White, *The Content of the Form*, p. 1. On this point and applied primarily to literature, Robert D. Newman in *Transgressions of Reading: Narrative Engagement as Exile and Return*, (Durham, NC: Duke University Press, 1993), p. ix, writes: "One important way to structure our experiences is by composing stories, shaped according to the demands culture places on us and we place on ourselves."

49. Susan Stewart, *On Longing: Narratives of the Miniature, the Gigantic, the Souvenir, the Collection*, (Durham, NC: Duke University Press, 1993), p. 22.

50. Hayden White, "The Modernist Event," p. 18.

51. Hayden White, "The Modernist Event," pp. 19–20.

52. Walter Benjamin, "Theses on the Philosophy of History," in *Illuminations*, Edited with an Introduction by Hannah Arendt, translated by Harry Zohn, (New York: Schocken Books, 1968), p. 255.

53. Hayden White, "The Modernist Event," pp. 20–21.

54. Hayden White, "The Modernist Event," pp. 21–22.

55. Hayden White, "The Modernist Event," p. 22.

56. Jerome Bruner, "The Narrative Construction of Reality," *Critical Inquiry*, 18, no. 1 (Autumn 1991), p. 4, cited in Janet Staiger, "Cinematic Shots: The Narration of Violence," in Vivian Sobchack, editor, *The Persistance of History*, pp. 40–41.

57. Janet Staiger, "Cinematic Shots: The Narration of Violence," in Vivian Sobchack, editor, *The Persistance of History*, pp. 43–44.

58. Alan Rosenthal, "Introduction: Part I," in Alan Rosenthal, editor, *New Challenges for Documentary*, (Berkeley: University of California Press, 1988), p. 17.

59. Efraim Sicher, "The Future of the Past: Countermemory and Postmemory in Contemporary American Post-Holocaust Narratives," *History and Memory*, Fall 2000, vol. 12, no. 2, p. 70. Sicher writes, "All narratives of past events require emplotment to tell their story and therefore are subject to interpretive judgement of their truth value. No historical moment can be recorded in a pure perception of the unadulterated 'event' devoid of interpretive perspectives of 'after'; the historical experience is invariably filtered through the prism of the narrator's psychological, cultural, linguistic, and social constructions which may also change over time."

60. Steve Anderson, "History TV and Popular Memory," p. 20.

61. Frances Fitzgerald, *America Revised: History Schoolbooks in the Twentieth Century*, (Boston: Little Brown, 1979), pp. 7–10. Somewhat in contrast to Fitzgerald's conclusions, Michael Schudson writes in *Watergate In American Memory*, p. 143, "The nature of textbook writing is a good reminder that different versions of the past coexist not only because different people have different interpretations of what happened but because people have different purposes for recalling the past and have different audiences they address. The textbook version of history self-consciously seeks to teach lessons out of a presumably consensual version of the past rather than to seek to establish a preferred view among contested versions of the past."

62. Heather-Jane Robertson, *No More Teachers, No More Books: The Commercialization of Canada's Schools*, (Toronto: McClelland and Stewart, 1998), p. 51.

63. Jack L. Granatstein, *Who Killed Canadian History*, (Toronto: HarperCollins, 1998), p. xi.

64. Hayden White, "Historiography and Historiophoty," *American Historical Review*, 93, no. 5, December 1988, pp. 1193–99.

65. Robert A. Rosenstone, "*JFK*: Historical Fact/Historical Film," in Alan Rosenthal, ed., *Why Docudrama? Fact-Fiction on Film and TV*, (Carbondale, IL, 1999), p. 337.

66. Robert A. Rosenstone, "*JFK*: Historical Fact/Historical Film," p. 337.

67. Harvey J. Kay, *The Powers of the Past: Reflections on the Crisis and the Promise of History*, (London: Harvester Wheatsheaf, 1991), p. 18.

68. George F. Custen, "Clio in Hollywood," in Alan Rosenthal, ed., *Why Docudrama? Fact-Fiction on Film and TV*, p. 28.

69. Leger Grindon, *Shadows of the Past: Studies in the Historical Fiction Film*, (Philadelphia: Temple University Press, 1994), p. 2.

70. Robert Burgoyne, *Film Nation: Hollywood Looks at U.S. History*, (Minneapolis: University of Minnesota Press, 1997), pp. 3–5.

71. Yosefa Loshitzky, "Introduction," *Spielberg's Holocaust: Critical Perspectives on Schindler's List*, ed. Yosefa Loshitzky, (Bloomington, IN: Indiana University Press, 1997), p. 1.

72. Bruce Chadwick, *The Reel Civil War: Mythmaking in American Film*, (New York: Knopf, 2001), p. 12.

73. Susan G. Davis, "'Set Your Mood To Patriotic': History as Televised Special Event," *Radical History Review*, 42, 1988, p. 128.

74. Quoted in Janice Kennedy, "Take-Out History: Canada's past served up with Big Mac," *The Calgary Herald*, February 16, 1997, p. C16. For an interesting view on the increasing influence of the business world in higher education, see Lawrence C. Soley, *Leasing The Ivory Tower: The Corporate Takeover of Academia*, (Boston: South End Press, 1995). It is important to recognize that in order to appeal to what Gary R. Edgerton has termed the, "varying segments" of the mass audience, multiple representations of one historical topic and have an enormous impact. Edgerton cites Ken Burns's *Empire of the Air* (1992) which first appeared "as a book, then as a major television special, and finally as a radio play." Gary R. Edgerton, *Ken Burns's America*, (New York: Palgrave/St. Martin's Press, 2001), p. vii.

75. See Tom Axworthy, "Memories Shape the Way We See Ourselves," *The Toronto Star*, September 26, 1997, p. A28.

76. Janice Kennedy, "Take-Out History," p. C16.

77. Janice Kennedy, "Take-Out History," p. C16 and Emily West, "Selling Canada to Canadians: Collective memory, national identity and popular culture," *Critical Studies in Communication*, June 2002, p. 212.

78. Robert Scully, "Heritage as Sound Bites," in Thomas H. B. Symons, ed., *The Place of History: Commemorating Canada's Past*. Proceedings of the National Symposium held on the Occasion of the 75th Anniversary of the Historic Sites and Monuments Board of Canada, 26–28, November 1994. The Royal Society of Canada, 1997, p. 191.

79. Janice Kennedy, "Take-Out History," p. C16.

80. Desmond Morton, "A Shared Past is a Nation's Compass," *The Toronto Star*, September 26, 1997, p. A28.

81. See Kenneth T. Jackson and Barbara B. Jackson, "Why the Time Is Right to Reform the History Curriculum," in Paul Gagnon, ed., *Historical Literacy: The Case*

for History in American Education, (Boston: Houghton Mifflin 1989), pp. 5–7. On pages 7–8, the authors write: "By 1980 it was clear that history no longer held the prominence it had earlier in the century. Its place in the curriculum had been weakened not only by the newer social sciences but also by ineffective teaching of the subject. Both political and ideological trends outside the classroom had contributed to the decline, but the key issue of the continuing debate over history's rightful place in the curriculum was the value of history itself."

82. Desmond Morton, "A Shared Past is a Nation's Compass," p. A28.

83. Ken Osborne, "Teaching Heritage in the Classroom," in Thomas H. B. Symons, ed.,*The Place of History*, pp. 164–65.

84. Emily West, "Selling Canada to Canadians: Collective memory, national identity and popular culture," *Critical Studies in Communication*, June 2002, p. 212.

85. Emily West, "Selling Canada to Canadians: Collective memory, national identity and popular culture," pp. 214–15.

86. Emily West, "Selling Canada to Canadians: Collective memory, national identity and popular culture," p. 215.

87. Margaret Conrad, "My Canada Includes the Atlantic Provinces," pp. 401–02.

88. Paul A. Cantor, *Gilligan Unbound: Pop Culture in the Age of Globalization*, (Lanham, MD: Rowman and Littlefield Publishers, Inc., 2001) p. 159.

89. Andrew Hoskins, "New Memory: Mediating History," *Historical Journal of Film, Radio and Television*, vol. 21, no. 4, 2001, p. 333.

90. Maurice Halbwachs, *The Collective Memory*, (New York: Harper Colophon Books, 1980).

91. Gary Taylor, *Cultural Selection: Why Some Achievements Survive the Test of Time—And Others Don't*, (New York: Basic Books, 1996), p. 15. Important to the discussion of visual history is Taylor's following remarks: "within the mind itself there seems to be a difference between the way we remember what we are told and the way we remember what we experience directly. The psychologist Endel Tulving calls the first kind of memory 'semantic,' and the second, stronger kind 'episodic.' My children have only a semantic memory of the Vietnam War; it is something they have heard about, but it ended before they were born, and they acquired information about it in circumstances and on occasions that were not in themselves remarkable. They know, without remembering when they learned what they know. By contrast, they have an episodic memory of the Vietnam Veterans Memorial because visits to it have been episodes in their own lives. If you have been to the memorial itself, the episodic memory you already have of it will be triggered by these words; if you have not been there, my words can create only a semantic memory or remind you of something you have heard or read." p. 35.

92. Michael Frisch, "American History and the Structures of Collective Memory: A Modest Exercise in Empirical Iconography," *The Journal of American History*, March 1989, vol. 75, no. 4, p. 1132.

93. Maurice Halbwachs, *The Collective Memory*, p. 23.

94. Thomas Elsaesser, "Subject Positions, Speaking Positions: From *Holocaust, Our Hitler* and *Heimat* to *Shoah* and *Schindler's List*," in Vivian Sobchack, ed., *The Persistence of History*, pp. 145–46.

95. Alison Landsberg, "Prosthetic Memory: *Total Recall* and *Blade Runner*," *Body and Society*, 1, nos. 3–4, 1995, p. 180.

96. Brad L. Duren, "NBC's *The 60s*: Incense, Politics, and the Power of Nostalgia," A Paper Presented at the AC/PCA Conference, New Orleans, LA, June 2000, p. 2.

97. Andrew Hoskins, "New Memory: Mediated History," p. 336.

98. Richard Chalfen, "Home Movies as Cultural Documents," in Sari Thomas, ed., *Film/Culture: Explorations of Cinema in its Social Context*, (Metuchen, NJ: The Scarecrow Press, 1982), pp. 126–38.

99. David Lowenthal, *The Past as a Foreign Country*, (Cambridge: Cambridge University Press, 1985), p. 210.

100. David Lowenthal, *The Past as a Foreign Country*, p. 212.

101. Barbie Zelizer, "From the Image of Record to the Image of Memory: Holocaust Photography, Then and Now," in *Picturing the Past: Media, History and Photography*, ed. by Bonnie Brennen and Hanno Hardt, (Urbana: University of Illinois Press, 1999), p. 99.

102. Frank P. Tomasulo, "I'll See It When I Believe It: Rodney King and the Prison-House of Video," in Vivan Sobchack, ed., *The Persistance of History*, p. 70.

103. Jay Ruby, "The Ethics of Imagemaking," in Alan Rosenthal, ed., *New Challenges for Documentary*, (Berkeley, CA: University of California Press, 1988), p. 311. In *Truth Needs No Ally: Inside Photojournalism*, (Columbia: University of Missouri Press, 1994), p. 1, Howard Chapnick writes, "The photograph does not exist in a vacuum. It almost always needs amplification with words and graphics."

104. Barbie Zelizer, "From the Image of Record to the Image of Memory: Holocaust Photography, Then and Now," in *Picturing the Past: Media, History and Photography*, p. 98

105. Michael Kammen, "Some Patterns and Meanings of Memory Distortion in American History," in *Memory Distortion: How Minds, Brains, and Societies Reconstruct the Past*, ed., Daniel L. Schacter, (Cambridge, MA: Harvard University Press, 1995), pp. 329–45.

106. John Taylor, *War Photography: Realism in The British Press*, (New York: Routledge, 1991), p. 159.

107. Phillip Marchand, *Marshall McLuhan: The Medium and the Messenger*, (Toronto: Random House, 1989).

108. Marshall McLuhan, *Understanding Media: The Extensions of Man*, (Cambridge, MA: The MIT Press, (1964, 1998), p. 82.

109. Joshua Meyrowitz, *No Sense of Place: The Impact of Electronic Media on Social Behavior*, (New York: Oxford University Press, 1985), p. 16.

110. Steven Lubar, *InfoCulture*, (Boston: Houghton Mifflin Company, 1993), p. 10.

111. Donald G. Godfrey, "Broadcast Archives for Historical Research: Revisiting the Historical Method," *Journal of Broadcasting and Electronic Media*, vol. 46, no. 3, September 2002, p. 494.

112. Donald G. Godfrey, "Broadcast Archives for Historical Research: Revisiting the Historical Method," p. 494.

113. Donald G. Godfrey, "Broadcast Archives for Historical Research: Revisiting the Historical Method," p. 498.

114. Roy Rosenzweig, "Scarcity or Abundance? Preserving the Past in a Digital Era," *The American Historical Review*, vol. 108, issue 3, p. 6, July 2003: www.history coop.org /journals/ahr/108.3/rosenzweig.html.

115. Roy Rosenzweig, "Scarcity or Abundance? Preserving the Past in a Digital Era," pp. 6–7.

116. Jean-Noel Jeanneney, *Google and the Myth of Universal Knowledge,* (Chicago: University of Chicago Press, 2006). Over the 2007 period, numerous magazines and journals, from *The New Yorker* to the *Queen's Quarterly* have run essays on this topic.

117. Roy Rosenzweig, "Scarcity or Abundance? Preserving the Past in a Digital Era," p. 13.

118. Mike Featherstone, "Archiving Cultures," *British Journal of Sociology,* 51, no. 1, January 2000, pp. 178, 166, cited in Roy Rosenzweig, "Scarcity or Abundance? Preserving the Past in a Digital Era," p. 13.

119. Robert Burgoyne, *Film Nation,* pp. 6, 10.

120. "Natalie Zemon Davis," interview, in Roger Adelson, ed., *Speaking of History: Conversations With Historians,* (East Lansing, MI: Michigan State University Press, 1997), pp. 54–55.

121. Donald J. Mattheisen, "Filming U.S. History During The 1920s: The Chronicles of America Photoplays," *The Historian,* vol. 54, no. 4, Summer 1992, p. 627.

122. Donald J. Mattheisen, "Filming U.S. History During The 1920s: The Chronicles of America Photoplays," p. 627.

123. Donald J. Mattheisen, "Filming U.S. History During The 1920s: The Chronicles of America Photoplays," p. 627.

124. Donald J. Mattheisen, "Filming U.S. History During The 1920s: The Chronicles of America Photoplays," p. 628.

125. Donald J. Mattheisen, "Filming U.S. History During The 1920s: The Chronicles of America Photoplays," pp. 630–31.

126. Cited in Lawrence Grossberg, Ellen Wartella and D. Charles Whitney, *MediaMaking: Mass Media In A Popular Culture,* (London: Sage Publications, 1998), p. 69.

127. Larry Cuban, *Teachers and Machines: The Classroom Use of Technology,* (New York: The Teachers College Press, 1986).

128. Jeffrey Shandler, *While America Watches: Televising the Holocaust,* (New York: Oxford University Press, 1999), p. 231.

129. Jeffrey Shandler, *While America Watches: Televising the Holocaust,* pp. 231–35.

130. Michael Ignatieff, *Virtual War: Kosovo and Beyond,* (Toronto: Viking, 2000), p. 3.

131. Michael Ignatieff, *Virtual War: Kosovo and Beyond,* p. 187.

132. Michael Ignatieff, *Virtual War: Kosovo and Beyond,* pp. 190–91.

133. Daniel Ringrose, "Beyond Amusement: Reflections on Multimedia, Pedagogy, and Digital Literacy in the History Seminar," *The History Teacher,* vol. 34, no. 2, February 2001, p. 1, www.historycooperative.or/journals/ht/34.2ringrose .html.

134. Lawrence W. Levine, *The Unpredictabble Past: Explorations in American Cultural History,* (New York: Oxford University Press, 1993), p. 8.

3

The Future and
Past of Print Culture

The emergence of new ways of knowing . . . stood in sharp contrast with
old ways of knowing available in the book and the printed word. It was
a significant break for a culture that had taken form under Bible and dictionary.

—Warren Susman, Culture as History, 111

Up until forty or so years ago, print culture, the definitive medium of
the last four-hundred years, was still the dominant form of information gathering in society. Most people formed their core ideas and knowledge from the book, the magazine, the newspaper. The linear world of
print reigned supreme until the late 1950s, early 1960s, when television began to usurp its role.[1] There are a number of factors that helped the visual
model erode the linear world of print, but before these can be discussed
and an analysis of the future of print undertaken, it is essential to gaze at
the history of the print world through the lens of the visualized one. One
reason for a discussion of print culture in such depth is, besides the obvious, the fact that "history as we understand it begins with writing."[2]

The written format, and more specifically the printed embodiment, is
the key feature of historical analysis and preservation and has been
since the time of Herodotus. As Alexander Stille has remarked, "The
modern progressive sense of history, the notion that each generation
builds upon the knowledge and achievements of the past, owes much to
the invention of print."[3] The idea of history and the practitioners of history have, traditionally, been oriented around the printed/written word.
In virtually everything that is done, print culture dominates. As David

J. Staley has observed, history is dominated by the culture of print and the written word. From research in archives to the publication of articles and monographs, from textbooks and the assignment of essays to students, history is firmly entrenched in the culture of the written/printed word. This "textual culture," he suggests, "provides the cognitive infrastructure to the discipline of history." Most often, continues Staley, historians use computers solely as a means to supplement this process, to "maintain this textual culture" in the form of typing and e-mail.[4] What happens when such an ingrained culture is challenge by a series of new developments?

A key conception to accept is the fact that whenever new communication mediums come into being they do not necessarily make their predecessors immediately obsolete.[5] Rather, what seems to occur historically is that the new technology has the effect of altering the previous one and forces it to change its character and possibly its main function.[6] Speaking, as Robert K. Logan observes, did not disappear with the written word, but rather, no longer served as the repository of a culture's traditions.[7] The fact that sermons could now be printed did not make the preacher obsolete, but accentuated the role of the speaker.[8]

According to Daniel Boorstin (and others), Plato's work bore the mark of a small community—Athens. Boorstin writes, "The Way of Dialogue was a special way of seeking," a style unique to a small community; speaking was what it was about! The spoken word in classical Greece was primary; writing secondary. To us, the thinker is writer, to them, the thinker was a speaker. To Plato and Socrates, the spoken word had a soul, while the written world is properly no more than an image.[9] According to Plato, Socrates feared writing as a tool that would make ideas and people dumb and incapable of intelligent arguments.[10]

It stands to reason according to Boorstin, that the thinking person must not take the written word too seriously. The written word was then seen "as a harmless pastime." But Plato worked and lived during a time when the written word was making grand inroads into the oral culture that had dominated for so long. Thinkers were talking, debating, and discussing the impact that the written word would have upon an oral culture, in much the same terms that people today, or intellectuals and academics discuss the merits of the written word in a time of transition. The worry and the bias focused on the loss of memory and the lack of skill that would come with writing.[11] In order for ideas and thoughts to be retained in an oral culture, it was necessary to constantly repeat the phrase or recite the idea. "Mnemonic formulas" were created to keep the thoughts alive. The mind had to constantly be trained in these devices in order to preserve the notion. Thus, the mind was not really free, as Walter Ong has suggested, to pursue more abstract thought—until the development and acceptability of written text.[12]

The culture of Athens was an oral one, where works of literature and history were meant to be recited and performed. Politics as well, were meant to be conducted in speaking terms. To understand the bias against the written word, one must be aware that they had no books as we know them, but cumbersome papyrus scrolls, which had to be unrolled. There was not the ease of finding passages because there was no index, no paragraphs, no spaces, and no punctuation. Government itself in Athens was not government by documents and bureaucrats creating miles of paper, but "a live assembly of citizens." The idea of representative government did not occur to them. Participation in Athenian democracy meant being physically present and saying your piece in your own voice. Since political wisdom was assumed to emerge from these encounters of the spoken word, it is not surprising that Athenians thought the fires of philosophic wisdom might be ignited in the same way.[13]

The point of Boorstin's remarks can be taken to suggest that new ways of thinking, recording and perceiving—in this case history—can at first be met with grand resistance, but in the long run, have a way of adapting and coexisting with established ways of intellectual activity. This is an important coda to bear in mind when discussing what historical literacy is in contemporary terms. New technologies that disrupt and alter ways of thinking—especially about the past, threaten those with a vested interest in maintaining the status quo. Writing had enormous potential to reorient communication as Harold Innis and Carl F. Kaestle and others have suggested. Concerns and effects range from the preservation of messages to the construction of an objectified sense of time.[14] Literacy, as Harvey Graff has implied, is primarily about communication.[15] Different forms of literacy have, historically speaking, altered and affected the dominant versions at specific times. There is no reason to think otherwise today. The fact is, as Kathleen Tyner indicates, "Just as oral traditions were both changed and incorporated by the printed word, electronic communication technologies seem to give with one hand and take with the other." There must be a recognition of this "ebb and flow" given the fact that new versions of literacy based on new technologies, "overlap, coexist, and change in symbiotic ways."[16] With the coming of the printing press, the same concerns regarding technology were voiced and it is instructive to look at that period.

Before the advent of the printing press and the changes it initiated, Western Europe was a relatively closed and static society during the High Middle ages. It was dominated by the church, the feudal system and above all, for the purposes of this topic, it was a society that possessed extremely low levels of literacy. Most of the readers were by and large members of the church. Literacy levels increased significantly beginning about 1200 and it was only then that we start to see significant levels of readership beyond the clerical sphere. Yet this is what all the "experts" tell us. We do not know for sure just how literate Europe was in the period from say 1200 on or even 1500 onwards. We can surmise though and that is exactly what most experts do. The problem of deciphering what literacy was during this period is compounded by the fact that just because someone could read and write—which is how I am defining literacy—does not necessarily mean that they did read—and did read books. Book ownership is one way to gauge literacy, as certain historians have done. But, as Elizabeth Eisenstein states in her masterful study on the printing press as an agent of changes we must be wary of "linking literacy and habitual book reading too closely."[17]

Prior to 1450, books, or more accurately, "manuscripts" were hand copied, predominantly by monks or scribes in scriptoriums located in monasteries. After approximately 1200, with the rise of universities, secular scribes started to compete with clerics in the copying trade. But until the twelfth century, "the monastery enjoyed an almost complete monopoly of book production and so of book culture. . . ."[18] Thus, for over seven hundred years there was no challenge to the monastic order's control over book culture.

Johann Gutenberg initiated challenges to this control and his invention brought the monopolies of knowledge to an end. He set out to make mirrors for souvenirs for the seven year pilgrimage to Aachen, not far from his hometown of Mainz. With the financial backing of some partners, he intended to mass produce these trinkets and reap a huge profit. As a consequence of some problems, namely a change of date and the return of the plague, Gutenberg moved toward an "alternate" investment idea, one that he had been thinking about for some time. This was the utilization of the press, combined with moveable type, to produce printed words on paper.[19] The timing of his invention could not have been better.

With the rise of the university, the rebirth of the city, and the increasing importance of commerce we start to see a change in the way both education and knowledge was structured. At the heart of this change is the fact that among the laity there was now both a desire and a need for education. This increasing mass of people throughout Europe now required access to books in quantities that was never before possible. From the early thirteenth century, it was the university that gave rise to this new reading public.[20] By the early fifteenth century, writing and reading had exploded beyond both the university and the monastery, and vernacular books, had started to reach larger audiences.[21] Another important factor that aided in the development of literacy and the demand for books is the fact that in the thirteenth century eyeglasses had been developed and by Gutenberg's time, they were in fairly common use, which meant an increase not only in the number of people physically able to read, but in the length of time one could devote to reading without strain.[22]

For the first time since the fall of Rome, Europe possessed a population that not only was increasing in size but no doubt, expanding in literacy. Specific figures are almost impossible to come by, but what becomes obvious from bookseller's records and later, printer's archives, is that more and more books were being produced and sold. Another factor of note which occurred between the twelfth and fifteenth centuries is the increasing use of vernacular languages as a method of communication. Latin still reigned supreme as the lingua franca, but steady inroads were being made with national languages. According to John Hale, by 1530, Latin had ceased to dominate and for a time Italian took precedence, jostling with Spanish and then, French began its rise to a position of dominance.[23]

Oral traditions still dominated European cultural life. In order to keep these alive, certain mechanisms were employed such as special mnemonic devices, for example, rhyme and cadence, in order to keep alive the oral ideals. With the advent of printing comes a severe reduction in the "art of memory."[24] Yet, the High Middle Ages still retained an oral tradition, literature was meant to be recited or read aloud to an audience. Until the fifteenth century, one could argue, as does Marcel Thomas, that the reading public was not large enough to warrant any other form of publication.[25] Being read to was sufficient. Hand copied books met the needs of those who could read. Yet, by the fifteenth century, this situation had changed. What was required was a way to produce volumes in a manner that had not been contemplated before, in order to meet the demands of a growing populace of literate individuals or at the very least, a populace who desired to own books.

Print technology had been invented by the Chinese and perfected by the Koreans. Yet, what was needed before the actual move into printing books were developments in what I would call basics. Paper, for example, had to reach a certain level of sophistication before it could become not just a common commodity but a cheap and durable one, ideal for printing pages. The first works to take advantage of the new developments in paper advancement were block prints that date from the late thirteenth century. Prints of religious pictures were produced on simple equipment, a block of wood and a knife. They were quite popular, given the importance of religious culture and the dominant position of the church, and the visual nature of the print, like the stained glass window image and the sculpted relief on the church, was quite potent in a culture that was predominantly oral.

The multiplication of images was seen as more important and necessary than words. These were portable as well, which allowed people the freedom to take them home; pictures of saints or stories of legends did not have to just rest on a church column. One could thus view a miracle scene at one's leisure. In the years before words began to be printed, this "simple visual resource" reached out to a wide variety of people who could not read.[26] It soon became obvious that a simple caption or short series of words could be added below the picture. They were inscribed by hand and then, engraved within the picture.[27] Coinciding with this was a move towards less theological themes and more secular ideas, such as animals, alphabets, and pictures of temporal rulers.[28] Very quickly it was discovered that if a larger sheet was divided and printed on all four sides, what resulted was a primitive book. These elementary, primarily illustrated woodcut quartos "were the first books that were within the reach of the mass of people. Those who could not read could at least grasp the sense of sequence of pictures, and those who had some rudimentary knowledge of reading could follow the texts much more easily because they were in the vernacular."[29]

According to Lucien Febvre and Henri-Jean Martin, "the technique of printing by hand can be reduced to three essentials: moveable type cast in metal; a fatty based ink; and the press."[30] Once these technological factors were mastered and perfected, the printing revolution occurred. The earliest books, or incunabula, looked exactly like manuscripts.[31] But they were different in a number of ways. One important way was the fact that they had been corrected or proofread in advance, which in turn, gave rise to the standard or uniform edition.[32] As well, it did not take long for printers to realize that the press could do other things that scribes could not. Well before 1500, footnotes, tables of contents, title pages and indexes came into being to set the new printed book apart from its hand-copied predecessor.[33]

Title pages gave the book "a feeling" and brought to it the qualities of an object that one could own and use, a fundamentally different relationship than one would have with ideas in an oral culture.[34] And, as more books came into being, their printed nature demystified them to the extent that they were less likely to be considered rare. Smaller formats allowed for more portability. People could carry them around, use them when they desired, instead of being dependent upon the monastery or library. People, in particular students and those from the upper classes, began to form personal libraries.[35] So too did a sizeable number of traders and merchants. Large scale books resided in libraries whereas small size works were being produced for the general public.[36]

Printing, although it did meet with some opposition, quickly caught on. "Venice had become the capital of printing [by 1482] because of its geographical position, its riches and its intellectual liveliness."[37] "By 1480, printing presses were in operation in more than 110 towns throughout Western Europe of which around fifty were in Italy, around thirty in Germany, five in Switzerland, two in Bohemia, nine in France, eight in Holland, five in Belgium, eight in Spain, one in Poland, and four in England. From that date it may be said of Europe that the printed book was in universal use."[38] According to Febvre and Martin, "About 20 million books were printed before 1500."[39]

Of the 100 million inhabitants, "only a minority could read."[40] We are assuming that there is an increase in literacy—the simple ability to read, not to write one's name—and this suggests that more people could read in the years after the introduction of print than could do so before. Historian Elizabeth Eisenstein contends that the initial shift to print had a very small impact on the overall population. Yet, she observes, within "this very small and largely urban population, a fairly wide social spectrum may have been involved. In fifteenth-century England, for example, mercers and scriveners engaged in a manuscript book trade were already catering to the needs of lowly bakers and merchants as well as to those of lawyers, aldermen, or knights."[41] In France, records cited by Febvre and Martin of book owners in the sixteenth century still suggest a predominance of clerics, followed by lawyers and merchants.[42]

Before 1500 the majority of books—approximately three quarters—were printed in Latin, and most were religious in content. Slowly though, literature began to be printed, including Dante and Boccaccio and other contemporary offerings. Law texts as well as scientific subjects also started to come off the presses.[43] Religious texts naturally had the largest; most literate audience; clerics—and printers were aware of this market.[44] Even though we have entered the Renaissance, the importance of religion did not simply disappear. In fact, to some extent it gained in importance especially after the Protestant Reformation. What is significant in the years after 1517 is that Luther's reformation made the printed bible a significant feature of Protestantism. And this had enormous ramifications. The Protestant Reformation exploited the potential of this mass medium in a truly significant way; the press was used as a propaganda mechanism against the established ideals of the Catholic Church.[45]

Key to the appeal of the Protestant reformation was the fact that the written word was wrenched from the control of an elite few—the priests—and allowed the individual to have a say, by reading it himself. Once the bible was translated into the vernacular and once the price fell, more and more individuals could have access.[46] The printing press liberated the word, freed literacy and allowed it to flourish. No longer chained and locked behind the scriptorium doors, any individual could, as Luther suggested, be his own priest.[47]

Economics also factors into the spread and to the appeal of printed books. Created first and foremost as a money-making enterprise, print benefited from the changing economic conditions in Europe. As John Hale has observed, "The broadened literacy of the age owed much to the cash available to produce, market and buy" books.[48] Printing was first and foremost a business. Printers and their backers, Gutenberg and Manutius, being the most famous, were interested in the printing of books as a profit making measure.[49] One could argue that they then had a vested interest in getting as many people as possible to learn to read and thus to buy books. But, failing that, they knew that they had a ready market in those inveterate book buyers who would not be able to resist another edition or a newer version of say, for example, the works of Aristotle. In a number of instances, they knew that a print run could take years to sell out but they were patient. That is why one sees print runs of upwards of 3,000 copies. "A book which was known in advance to be likely to have a guaranteed market, like Luther's German bible, was printed in a run of 4,000 even in its first edition." This attitude represented shrewd commercial understanding of consumer demand.[50] The bible itself, in both vernacular and Latin versions, was printed in order to make itself immediately accessible to a greater number of readers than ever before.[51]

While probably not well versed in the dynamics of market research, printers certainly knew who their buyers were. They supplied students and teachers at the universities with the major works of scholarship.[52] By the sixteenth century the sizes of textbook print runs (editions of one thousand or more) were quite large. This suggests that there was a confidence among printers that readers were out there and were going to buy more books—at least eventually.[53] "The reading public was extended by the sheer numbers of books which reached wider and wider audiences with increasing ease."[54] According to Febvre and Martin, "Some 150,000–200,000 different editions could have been printed between 1500 and 1600."[55]

Another significant feature of early printing is that it was possible to transmit many copies of an image. This had enormous ramifications for scientific and technical literature as well as how-to books, which were produced in enormous quantities.[56] The uniformity of multiple copies to convey information was truly unique.[57] This is interesting and vital according to this "story" cited by Lisa Jardine: In 1473, at the age of fourteen, Jakob Fugger was sent by his father to work in Venice in order to learn "Italian accounting"—double entry bookkeeping with Arabic numerals. "Within a generation, however, the printed book had made such trips largely unnecessary—an explosion in publication of manuals of technical commercial expertise—how-to books—had made it possible for merchants to learn their trade closer to home."[58]

With higher levels of literacy as well as relatively low cost writing materials, more people committed their private lives to paper in the form of journals and diaries. The private world suddenly went public with the ability to publish these works. As the popularity of journals and diaries increased, the ephemeral nature of the written work became more permanent with the printed one.[59] Whether for posterity or to titillate the imagination, more Europeans put their thoughts down with the eventuality that their work would be printed. John Hale writes that as a consequence of printing, people were encouraged to write more and to write with more care. Printing, according to Hale, fostered a more "alert literariness." More books meant more "imaginative stimuli" was received. As well, the increased quantities and the increased variety of book subjects caused writers and readers to be more aware of what others were doing and thinking. One could now select what one was interested in, in a much more satisfying way.[60]

As more books were published in indigenous or vernacular languages it became necessary to "relearn mother tongues when learning to read." This in turn fostered a movement toward the strengthening of national histories and memories.[61] According to Benedict Anderson, the foundations for national consciousness were laid with the rise and institutionalization of vernacular languages. Unified fields of exchange were created with the creation of a print form of language, allowing people to comprehend one another through print and paper. Add to this the permanence of the print form, and the infinite capacity to reproduce and one gets the recipe for the permanence of a nation.[62] Individuals began to demand that laws, for example, should be in their own language not in Latin.[63]

The reintroduction or rebirth of silent reading accompanied the development of printing. The Medieval period was still dominated by oral traditions but personalized reading systems and private ownership of books gave rise to silent reading as opposed to reading aloud. By the late-sixteenth century this was increasingly common.[64] McLuhan notes in the *Gutenberg Galaxy* that there was also a corresponding shift from the oral to the written/print in other areas. There was a move to replace sworn testimony with written documents, and a rhetorical style reminiscent of Rome and Greece gave way to a modern prose style. Legal practices moved towards written records and evidence examination, theological discussions came to depend on print. Heresy could now come from print form as well.[65]

All of these changes privileged print and in turn, had an impact on how society responded. One of the most significant was the allowance for privacy and the subsequent focus on the individual. Printing led to an increased emphasis on individualism for reading became a solitary activity. Novels also started to emphasize one key figure reinforcing that individualism. McLuhan speculated that reading in a sequential form from left to right produces an egocentric view of the world. We are inculcated with a single point of view, that of the reader. Rudy Volti suggests that this may have led to perspective in painting where the scene is also depicted from the perspective of the viewer—a fixed point in space.[66]

According to Lisa Jardine, "The printed book revolutionized the transmission of knowledge and permanently changed the attitudes of thinking
Europe." The printed book with its uniform pagination (each book copied
by hand probably had different page numbering) allowed two readers to
discuss a passage in a work they were both reading by referring to the
precise page on which it occurred. (As well, consistent pagination led to
the possibility of an index, "to which anyone collecting data on a particular topic could turn.") Why this is significant is that the "comparatively effortless production of multiple copies meant that printed books could disseminate knowledge much more rapidly, widely, and accurately than
their handwritten antecedents." Lower prices also made printed material
accessible for the first time to a "large, less privileged readership"[67]—yet
not really cheap until the nineteenth century.[68] The implications for this
were capacious. The printed book came to liberate the reader from the
here and now and to create a totally new world for the reader. This new
world meant that ideas could be retrieved 'later' and for education, the
notion of learning meant reading.[69]

Humanism, especially in Florence, but also the Northern Renaissance
version, embraced the reason of the classics with the new found prosper-
ity of an innovative society. Built on a reformed platform of education and
closely tied to the culture of books, humanism depended upon the
printed book. It was an intellectual and all-encompassing movement that
led intellectuals out of the cloistered life of the monastery into the secular
reality of culture, education, and politics. Humanism also had elements
within it that preceded the fifteenth century, (most conspicuously, the
work of Petrarch) but it matured as a multifaceted idea at this time. Historian Charles Nauert suggests that it is hard for us today to grasp what
was obvious to Italians of the Renaissance. In particular, education in humanistic subjects appeared practical while education of the medieval type
did not. Knowledge that allowed one to make wise choices was valued.[70]
Perhaps the printing press came at just the right time. As literacy levels
began to rise with the emergence of more universities and colleges, merchants and others demanded more books, and the printing press an-
swered the call in a practical and revolutionary way.[71]

Over the next two hundred years, books gradually made their way
into the fabric of everyday European[72] and eventually, American[73] society. It was during the seventeenth century that, according to Emmanuel
Le Roy Ladurie, literacy rates in the major cities of France began to
climb significantly. Compared to rural areas, the urban masses took to
reading in large numbers. This came as a result of both the profession-
alization of European society as well as the increasing emphasis on education. By the 1600s, vernacular language reading was enormous, ushering in a mania for books on virtually every topic. France led the way

and it took the German states until the beginning of the nineteenth century to catch up.[74]

By the eighteenth century, literacy rates were sufficiently high in France and England, and new forms of reading material evolved to meet the demand for new readers. The Enlightenment ushered in a new era for readers and publishers which has been termed a "publishing revolution." What had been available to the upper echelons of society now was accessible to many. As J. M. Golby and A. W. Purdue have observed, newspapers, essays in periodicals and the novel now came to the fore as cultural products.[75] Complete libraries could now be purchased by anyone who could afford them. Significant here was the fact that there was an attempt to synthesize and contain all the information available. Of course, the idea of what information was considerably different from what it is perceived as today. It had to be contained within a context—social, political, cultural—and to fit within a specific world view.[76] As a publishing event, the Enlightenment was an attempt to produce as much information as possible for the greatest possible good. The vast and ambitious Encyclopedia project attempted to codify and preserve, organize and rein in all the knowledge then available.[77]

When people spoke in the middle of the century of the 'philosophers,' they meant mainly the group of French writers who took part in the production of the "Great Encyclopedia" (35 Vols., 1751–1780). Diderot, Voltaire, and Montesquieu are just some of the more well-known thinkers associated with this project. This enterprise had begun as a design for a French edition of an English encyclopedia, but this had foundered because of disputes between the publisher and the editors. In 1746, publication was entrusted to Denis Diderot. Simply put, the plan was an attempt to collect and summarize all acquired knowledge and to dispel all superstitions imposed by ignorance and tradition. In Diderot the multivolume venture had found an extraordinarily versatile intellectual whose interests were truly catholic.[78] The first volume appeared on July 1, 1751 (titled as all subsequent volumes: Dictionary of the Sciences, Arts and Crafts) and was an instant success with virtually everyone but those in clerical circles, specifically the Jesuits, who fell upon this 'Satan's bible' and even attempted to have it banned. The ban had no more than a temporary effect, however, because leading politicians took the project under their wing. This volume revealed the influence of Locke, Bacon and others such as Pierre Bayle. In spite of a host of problems, it was completed after twenty-nine years in thirty-six volumes and became a work that was considered indispensable. It was much more comprehensive than previous works of reference and even included copious articles on grammar, synonyms, and gazetteer-like articles concerning countries and cities. The encyclopaedists attempted to explode superstitious errors of all kinds and to be as precise in definition as possible. An attempt was made to make exact technological explanations an accepted part of the language. Other intentions and characteristics include the suggestion of social reforms, a desire for greater civil liberties and careful criticism of religious dogma. All in all it was comprehensive, exacting, adventuresome, and bold. Selling almost five thousand sets of the original edition and more of later runs, a reader could be informed under competent guidance on any topic under the sun, in up-to-date rational and enlightened terms![79]

One can surmise that this was a great feat in publishing technology but what is singularly important is the fact that the Encyclopedia was a symbol of a new public philosophy. And this is fully harmonious with the appeal of the Enlightenment. If a distinguishing feature of Enlightenment philosophy was to cause change by questioning and challenging accepted dogmas, then confining knowledge to a handful of people would not do. Information on alternatives, on general understanding, would no doubt require the dissemination of ideas to as many people as possible. With a newly rising middle/merchant class in various parts of Europe, there was disposable income for the purchase of books. As well, a very significant feature of the social life of the Enlightenment was the rise of general academies and societies for economic or agricultural information exchange and these societies, acquired books for libraries. Popularizing knowledge and exchanging critical information was also channeled through informal meetings such as the Salons and through the curious phenomenon known as the coffee house. All these enlightenment institutions depended upon information and the access to information which was provided by the "philosophers," among others of the eighteenth century. Reading societies were especially important sources of the new knowledge exchange. They originated from the middle of the eighteenth century onwards to improve general knowledge in a public that was no longer interested simply in scholarship and literature. To this end the societies acquired libraries and organized discussions. Their comprehensive aim was to indoctrinate a broad readership with the ideas of the Enlightenment.[80]

Significant also is the economic and agricultural, scientific and mechanical societies that handled Enlightenment ideas. A general trend occurring here, which aided in the popularity of the Encyclopedia and other Enlightenment publications was that scientific and agricultural methods of doing business were changing. Information was needed to keep up-to-date and to provide resources should problems arise. Parallel encyclopedias and reference works were created, albeit on a much smaller scale which complemented and accentuated Diderot's work. The Enlightenment introduced a sense of unease into the stable world of religion, the monarchies and the social hierarchy. By popularizing the complex ideas of many of the most important thinkers of the century, it could be suggested, the Enlightenment paved the way for pure political action, culminating in the French Revolution.[81] It was during the early stages of the French Revolution that thousands upon thousands of visual-printed images were unleashed on the French populace. These included everything from political caricatures to scenes of contemporary events, which were literally applied to all forms of the media; from membership cards to calendars. All these "ephemera" were rich in images and illustrations reaffirming the importance of the visual. The attempt was to convince, in almost propagandistic ways, those not affected by traditional print formats. As James Leith sums up, "As heirs to the sensationalist psychology of the Enlightenment, the revolutionaries had great faith in the power of images to make a lasting impression on the minds of the citizenry. Above all, they believed images could arouse emotions in a way that printed words could not."[82]

The modern heyday of the printed word could be said to have occurred, in the west, and in the United States and Canada, between the start of Victorian period and the end of the First World War. According to Dan Lacy, "print played—as it never had before and never would again—a dominant and exclusive role." Print culture was omnipotent at this time, with film and photography only making slight inroads and not really having a major impact until the 1920s.[83] The reason for print being so effective as a medium at this time is that cultural forces such as compulsory education, the creation of libraries and mass literacy merged with technological ones, such as the steam driven press, to produce an enormous quantity of reading material that was voraciously consumed.[84] As Neil Gabler has observed about this period in the United States,

> Literacy among ordinary Americans was relatively high then, and nearly everyone seemed to love to read. Not only did the number of published books skyrocket in this period, thanks in part to less costly printing techniques, but between 1828 and 1860 the number of newspapers in the country rose from 852 to 4,051 with a combined annual circulation of nearly one billion. (The circulation of newspapers was to increase another 400 percent between 1870 and 1900 while the population increased only 95 percent.)[85]

It is also during the middle to late Victorian period that the full-fledged notion of a "historical consciousness" comes into being in a very potent manner. According to John Lukacs, along with compulsory education came the dissemination of "all kinds of historical information" as well as the rise of history as a distinct subject or separate discipline. Lukacs makes the point that as a consequence, individuals who had never been affected by literacy and in turn by historical literature were now overwhelmed by the historical information available. Thus, while their societies were being modernized and changed, while many of "their old and durable traditions, habits, and habitations," were being given up, they were being exposed to substantial manifestations of historical offerings.[86]

One of the key arguments that is always cited in distinguishing print culture from mediated visual culture is that print requires both understanding and time to unlock its code. There is a patience necessary for reading that does not come into play with watching. With certain kinds of watching, there is a patience factor involved—for example, with a foreign film, a documentary, a fifteenth century oil. One may argue, that looking at a Medieval cathedral or gazing at a stained glass window required the same effort that it does to see a "heavy" foreign film, which it probably did, but a key distinction is that there was not much else to look at then.[87] In a world such as ours, where one is exposed to thousands of images everyday, and perhaps millions over the years, the competition makes the playing field quite different. It is not just the quantity of images but their "ubiquity" that changes this equation.[88] They are everywhere today and this forces people to make split-second decisions on, for example, whether or not to read the print text in an ad, or just glance at the picture. This is the reason why modern art has to find a home in a museum. If it is left in the urban landscape it blends in the multitude of images already out there.[89]

When a society—the late middle ages and the Renaissance until the 1950s—is to be dominated by a particular media—print culture—a kind of hierarchy is created that excludes those who do not possess the skills necessary to interpret or use that media. As Joshua Meyrowitz has written, "Communication through writing and books is "automatically" restricted to those who know the required access code, and—even among those who have knowledge of the basic code—messages can be directed at different groups by varying the complexity of the coded message. Young children and illiterates, therefore, are excluded from all printed communication, and society is further divided into many distinct sets of information-systems on the basis of different levels of reading ability."[90] Put another way, one has to be trained to follow the rules in a text-based culture, which is in contrast to looking at a religious image or watching television where virtually no instruction is required.[91] This does not mean that there was no writing and reading before the printing press but it strongly suggests that the level of exclusion between literates and illiterates was significantly increased. Neil Postman argues in regard to this point that this is where and when we start to see modern notions of childhood coming into discussion. As well, the notions of social control *vis-à-vis* early modern society come into being at this time.[92]

Books are no longer the key repositories of knowledge that they once were. They are not capable of molding the "public imagination" in the way they once were.[93] Today's child or student has so much to choose from that making the choice to read can be a serious obstacle. Looking at picture books is not the same as reading. Mastering the alphabet is not the same as reading. Whereas one hundred years or so ago, the child had both no choice as well as few if any alternatives, today, the force of television poses a serious threat. There is no question that children who have grown up watching television visualize in a way that is quite different from earlier generations. As Stephanie B. Gibson has remarked,

> the introduction of television into culture brought an emphasis on the visual from which arbiters of literacy to this day have not yet recovered. Children learn quickly and from the medium itself how to become proficient at reading the cues in the texts of television. Meanwhile the part of the culture that was not television was also developing greater emphasis on the visual and the reading of visual texts became almost as significant, albeit tacitly, as the reading of verbal texts.[94]

Whatever constitutes literacy today,[95] according to Gibson has been impacted by the visual; and "is being pulled in [yet] another direction with the nonlinearity, nonsequentiality, and interactivity of several forms of hypertext."[96] Gibson goes on to restate Walter Ong's assumption that literacy, in the form of writing and print will be around because it is necessary to many in society. Yet there are instances which suggest that the differing dispositions and visual nature of hypertext is more suited to a postmodern society that values speed and instantaneous responses.[97] Richard A. Lanham is of the opinion that the dynamics of technology, as applied to reading, must be incorporated in order for the foundations of literacy to be maintained. "If the codex book is being revolutionized, surely we must ponder this process. We cannot preserve Western culture in a pickle. It must be recreated in the technologies of the present, especially if these technologies prove more condign to the oral and rhetorical part of it [literary study]."[98] "What has occurred in western culture as far as the impact of digital communication upon literacy is that there has been a conflation of many forms of communication—oral, written, print, and electronic— into one significant new hybrid. This hybrid has been described as a "malleable nugget(s) of data," which has the power to empower "diverse media to converge gracefully into a unified audiovisual schema."[99]

Reading requires a linear visual sequencing. Television watchers read as if they are watching television, by taking "quick looks." The process of taking in information has changed since the advent of television and relegates reading to a secondary stature.[100] If reading happens outside of school, it occurs less and less. According to one study, "by the time they reach Grade 12, less than 25 percent of kids read daily for pleasure."[101]

Even as "sacred" an environment as the library has undergone radical changes in order to accommodate the increasing influence of visualized media technology. What once was a bastion of print culture, quiet, and inviolable has come to resemble not "the conservation of literacy's history, the education of the heart, eye and mind" but a place of "amusement."[102] In the words of Sally Tisdale, the library is a "trendy, up-to-date, plugged" place. This in itself is not bad, for it is in keeping up with the times and thus must be both recognized and adhered to—to some extend—but with certain qualifications. Like museums, (more of later) the library is according to Tisdale, a place where there is everything but books. One can debate the merits of this but one runs up against the question, "so what"? As Tisdale observes, "you can now get movies there and Nintendo games, drink cappuccino, and surf cyberspace, go to a gift shop or a cafeteria, rent a sewing machine or a camera."[103] While Tisdale laments the passing of the quiet library which was devoted to solitary scholarship, she recognizes that the library "*is* made more popular by the addition of Internet stations and CD-ROM games."[104] Like the museum that struggles to bring in patrons, the library has to adapt. And like the movie that may provoke a child to go out in search of a book, the library brings in the potential readers with attractions that they can relate to. This is especially significant for university and college libraries which are now debating between the requirements necessary for the digital age and the importance and continuing relevance of the book as the standard source of knowledge. What is at the heart of this battle is the fact the books are often displaced in favor of fancy new technology that emphasizes the thrust towards computers. Books on shelves take up enormous amounts of space and given the pressures that institutions of higher education are under, they are quickly being removed, placed underground or in warehouses, away from the main building of the library or learning commons.[105]

The supreme example of this new form of library/information centre as a response to digital/visual culture is the five year old San Francisco Public Library. The building itself and the controversy surrounding its construction, purpose, and place in society is a lightening rod in the debate over book versus electronic visual culture. As Kathleen Tyner has stated, the library "is the site where the culture of books collides with the emerging digital culture of the late twentieth century."[106] The library was designed to be the "model" of the new digital culture. It was stocked with all the latest technology: satellite access, video conferencing capability, an electronic children's playground and hundreds of computer terminals, all of which had to displace numerous stacks of books.[107] And therein lies the major concern.

The problem is that where reading once a key feature of life, both sacred and fatuous, it is increasingly absent from these spectrums. Whereas once everyone read on the train today they are listening to their iPODs and playing online games. Whereas once individuals took the time to focus and concentrate on reading, they now prefer to be informed by numerous other methods.[108] This manifests itself in some very interesting ways. How do Sally Tisdale's comments, as well as those of J. C. Hertz and James Glieck merge together? When Sven Birkerts was attempting to teach literature to a group of college freshmen he ran into numerous obstacles in getting them to read. The main problem stemmed from the fact that

> they were not, with a few exceptions, readers—never had been; that they had always occupied themselves with music, TV, and videos; that they had difficulty slowing down enough to concentrate on prose of any density; that they had problems with what they thought of as archaic diction [James], with allusions, with vocabulary that seemed *pretensious*; that they were especially uncomfortable with indirect or interior passages, indeed with any deviations from straight plot; and they were put off by ironic tone because it flaunted superiority and made them feel that they were missing something. The list is partial.[109]

Birkerts provides the reasons for this severe issue; he puts the blame primarily upon the impact of electronic culture. He feels that this is not a "temporary generational disability,"[110] but the way things are. Like so many others commenting on this development, Birkerts is worried that because print culture dominated for so long and thus became the repository of history and culture—in the west—so much is going to be lost. With the dominance of electronic media as a purveyor of history and with the emphasis on the visual (and the aural), reading is no longer the main way in which our society is informed and is no longer the primary means by which history is conveyed.[111] Like Birkerts and Alvin Kernan, Ben Agger suggests that the demise of the written word in its print format leads to "the decline of discourse." He blames, not just the postmodern condition for this decline, but interestingly, the "academization" of writing that leads to an "obscurantism" that most cannot comprehend. Without "instant comprehension" the reader is forced to go elsewhere.[112] One could go on and on about how print was and is so fundamentally different from the visual—in the portrayal of history—but the fact remains that, for today's generation, history comes from images.

One barometer of the indication that the kind of reading that is going on has evolved is the fact that over the last sixty plus years, the length of the sentence in an analysis of bestsellers, has declined, as have the number of punctuation marks. The contemporary bestseller, according to Todd Gitlin, contains sentences that are "briefer, simpler, and closer to screenplays." Gitlin's survey takes into account the fact that over this chronological period, television has moved to the center of culture. Consequently, writers, in seeking an audience have had to change the way they write in order to appeal to people who are in need of simpler content, because of laziness or time constraints, and "popular fiction" for example, resembles television.[113] To a great extent, Gitlin is correct in his analysis. The most popular book "franchise"—the single most profitable series of the last fifteen years has been the *Star Wars* series, which has consistently appeared on the *New York Times* best-seller list.[114] The fact is, most bestsellers, have some key relationship with other media: film, photography, television, or the Internet.

This is not to say that reading will disappear. Surfing the net involves an inordinate amount of reading.[115] The problem is—for now—that it is more oriented around information than knowledge. This is significant for there is just so much information out there. Who, one might ask, has the time to read for knowledge? But perhaps, we are moving towards a scenario that encompasses speed and brevity in reading. We attempt to sift out the "extraneous" information and gravitate directly in our reading, toward what we need. This process, more akin to culling than reading, means that "the reading we practice seems more and more to involve short bursts or shallow attendings."[116] What this may also suggest is that reading is not the only way to acquire information. To some extent there is a form of convergence going on. As Peter Lyman writes, "the computer will not replace the book any more than the book has replaced electronic speech. Oral, print, and digital media are not alternatives; rather, it is the interrelationship of these modes of communication that is significant in shaping public knowledge."[117] The main problem is that to a great extent people and children in particular must want to read. Reading is threatened not so much by technology but by the fact that there is a general lack of will to read in North American culture. As Birkerts has lamented, others such as Donald Lamm are concerned that the reading that is done has been reduced to its lowest form; digest publications, executive summaries, abstracts, Cliff's notes and so on.[118] One can add the resurgence of icon or graphical shorthand to this mix, and even the decline of letter writing. By extension, even the way one writes has changed. The short forms of words that are a staple of e-mail, have now found their way into the mainstream of writing. It is now almost acceptable to use the most informal forms of address as well as to leave in typos. "Terseness" is key as is, in harmony with the emphasis on speed, the ubiquitous abbreviations. As Rachel Ross writes in an article celebrating thirty years of e-mail, "Writing out the full phrase 'by the way' was more labor-and-time-intensive than simply typing BTW."[119] On the positive side of this, what is perhaps warranted is the ability to intellectually multitask. According to Vassar English Professor Michael Joyce, "In an age like ours, a sustained attention span may be less useful than successive attendings."[120] The ability to grasp, quickly, the information from a variety of different textual sources may be seen to be just as relevant and may even supersede the necessity for prolonged focus and concentration. Viewed in this light, books and the book-oriented process of research may seem both archaic and cumbersome. As computer scientist David M. Levy puts it:

> Always in a rush, we want to liberate just the information we need, as quickly as possible: to find that client's phone number or e-mail address, to get the latest stock quotes for the companies we've invested in, or the weather report for the city we're about to fly to. The more efficiently and effectively we can do this, and the less we are distracted by, or beholden to, the physical embodiment of the physical materials before us, the better off we will be. No wonder that the technopile sees the physical properties of the book as an encumbrance, a restraint.[121]

As the first part of this argument goes, changes in the "material aspects of texts" and the "material containers" of where writing goes is just the beginning.[122] What this means is that whether one is talking about a papyrus scroll, a stone tablet, an illuminated manuscript, a printed book or hypertext,[123] these "material containers" alter the relationship of the reader to the reading. With the interactivity of the new media and in particular, hypertext, what happens is that the stationary physicality of the culture of print can evaporate and the once orderly world of the reader—and by extension, the writer—dissipates. The fixed roles of the reader and the writer (and the publisher) become fluid and blend together, in a way not too dissimilar from the early days of print.[124] "The reader," according to Richard A. Lanham, "can change it [the text], and become the writer."[125]

Another vital qualification in this context is the fact that the problem with a digital document or a digital material is that it is dependent upon electronics to give it life. Unlike pure paper documents, the digitized version requires an electronic tool to define itself. The paper book can stand alone while the digital document must have some other force to literally give it life. The primary, and most often cited difference between the new generation of E-Books and traditional paper based text, is this technological essence.[126] This gives computer and electronic based information resources a more dynamic and even powerful existence, but as has been recognized, is also confusing and schizophrenic.[127]

Related to this is the fact that there is more data available now than at any other time in history, but at the same time, more of it is being lost. Technologically driven data storage cannot keep pace with changing computer hardware and software. It would take centuries to constantly re-archive and reformat material that exists in a specific electronic format now and convert it to the latest format available. This in turn, gives rise to questions about what to keep and what to "discard" before a particular version becomes obsolete.[128] On the one hand, the digitized versions can offer historians a bounty of unprecedented quantity, but this is almost an unreachable plateau. "As the pace of technological change increases," writes Alexander Stille, "so does the speed at which each new generation of equipment supplants the last." Stille has found that while societies are saving tremendous amounts of information, the media used to "save" or preserve, is increasingly less and less durable.[129]

This last point has enormous ramifications for the structure and maintenance of historical knowledge and even more fundamentally, the process of doing history. Huge amounts of data have either been lost or are currently not retrievable. Roy Rosenzweig has termed this "the absolute nature of digital corrosion," and remarks that it is quite "sobering." Not only is this corrosion an epidemic problem, but the fact that accessing information technology from hardware/software systems which are only a few years old is even more of a problem. Rosenzweig writes that "acid-free paper and microfilm" can "last a hundred to five hundred years, whereas digital and magnetic media deteriorate in ten to thirty years." But the key point is, as Rosenzweig recognizes, that

> before most digital media degrade, they are likely to become unreadable because of changes in hardware (the disk or tape drives become obsolete) or software (the data are organized in a format destined for an application program that no longer works). The life expectancy of digital media may be as little as ten years, but very few hardware platforms or software programs last that long. Indeed, Microsoft only supports its software for about five years.[130]

This process has a significant track record. One only has to think of vinyl LPs, eight-tracks and cassettes in the recording realm to see how valid a factor this is. As well, inventions that are quite new such as the video cassette recorder have in twenty years, given way to DVD formats which in turn, will be obsolete. Beyond technology, there are also more personal concerns.

Nancy Kaplan suggests that one must be very aware of where reading is situated. One cannot divorce the act of deciphering or breaking the code from the contextualized situation. If one does do this, and she accuses Svend Birkerts of doing, than the often quoted generalizations crop up. With regard to reading on the screen, some of these criticisms include the discomfort factor, the fact that paper is tactile, and, consistently, the fact that you can not take a computer into the bath—yet.[131] The touch/smell sensory aspect of the book is one that comes up as a comparative concern over and over again. Some feel that it is nothing more "than the bibliophile's pleasure in handling his possessions."[132] Yet, with magnanimous written objects, from the Torah to a document like the Declaration of Independence, larger cultural and political concerns are at stake. What is interesting is the smaller, micro-objectification. We all have a tendency to get attached to material objects such as the calculator on your desk; thus, why should not the computer or 'e-book' take on the same kind of fetish appeal. Still, as Geoffrey Nunberg writes, we still have a long way to go before we can reproduce the tactile and sensory complexity of *Pat the Bunny*.[133]

Until these and other problems and characteristics can be worked out, the advantage remains in favor of the book. Even when computer software billionaire Bill Gates released his first book in the early nineties, it came with a CD-ROM![134] If Gates was not ready to abandon this functional and sacred object, then the future is still bright for the printed word. The traditional book is a relatively safe object; it is comforting to hold one and familiar to even a child. As Alison Armstrong and Charles Casement have commented,

> If we pick up a book, we know at a glance how long it is, and by turning to the table of contents we can see how the author approaches the subject and, often, by noting the emphasis give to certain topics, what is his or her point of view. Flipping through the pages, and stopping when our eye catches something of interest, can give us an idea of whether the book lives up to our initial expectations.[135]

Even with the E-Book and the Sony Reader, one must still abide by some restrictions to which the traditional book is not bound. And reading on a laptop or desktop is still much more restrictive than the book.[136] Research has shown that reading on traditional paper is much faster than in an electronic format.[137] While it is restrictive—on the one hand, it is dynamic on the other. Another key feature of hypertext is the fact that in contrast to "traditional print" there is the characteristic of motion. Movement is a central feature of the text—the hypertext—that gives it a "kinetic quality" which encourages a form of interactivity.[138] The problem here is that stationary print provokes reflection, but the dynamic provocations on the computer screen encourage the opposite. Images and movement force the receiver to act, rather than reflect.[139]

Nancy Kaplan, building on Robert Darnton's work, feels that if you look at the historical record, you would find the same biases directed toward every new reading development. For example, reading was difficult for most until the development of artificial lighting.[140] Printed books were met with hostility by those most threatened by the printing press: the monks in the scriptorium.[141] Perhaps though, it is best to perceive of the state of the book in the terms alluded to in the first paragraph of this chapter: "the passage of time rearranges their position in the order of daily life, sometimes pushing them from the center to the margins."[142]

The place and the future of the book in an age that is technologically driven and visually oriented appears safe if one looks at the number of books published and the revenues generated. In 1997, according to figures cited by Joseph and Phylis Bernt of Ohio University, over two billion books were sold generating 26 billion dollars in revenue, indicating that "despite assaults from exploding video offerings and computerization, print culture in the United States has maintained a surprising rate of growth. . . ."[143] The Bernt's go on to suggest that no matter what the category—even newspapers and libraries—print culture, in all its manifestations grew in the late nineties. The World Wide Web has been an aid to the culture of books, in particular, the used book market as well as for smaller stores. They conclude that the WWW "has established an international market, a community or culture of collectors, scholars, librarians, and everyday readers seeking specific titles."[144] Thus, in its most simplistic form, the move toward electronic technologies is no different from the impact of moveable type. Radical changes will occur in the way information is disseminated, yet people will still read. As publishing guru and pioneer Jason Epstein writes, "technologies change the world but human nature remains the same."[145] The fact is that people will read.

Robert Fulford has suggested that every predecessor of the printed book has gone on to become "technologically obsolete" after a period— even a very long period—of time. Yet, the antecedents of a previous information/reading technology can still live on and possess great power.[146] Fulford cites the Torah as an example of this and feels that despite the fact that the most convenient form will inevitably be adopted, "books will survive as art objects and icons."[147] One reason that they will survive, more so than just as curiosities, is the cost factor. They are, regardless of format, reasonably cheap. And they are much cheaper and more accessible than computers or 'e-book' alternatives. Both the hardware and software of digitization is extremely expensive and it is thus limiting in access.[148] Yet despite this potential, there are those who strongly feel that with the exception of a few antiquarians and those too stubborn to change, the book has no choice to but to step aside. By stepping aside, it is moving "to the margin of our literate culture." This Mcluhanesque observation is being made by an academic who studies classics. Jay Bolter contends that "the issue is not whether print technology will completely disappear; books may long continue to be printed for certain kinds of texts and for luxury consumption. But the idea and the ideal of the book will change: print will no longer define the organization and presentation of knowledge, as it has for the past five centuries." Instead, what will result will be new ways to write and new formats which supersede the book.[149] The most common version of publishing, a variation on the 'e-book' is pegged to be a form of a "kiosk" where one could go and download or transfer texts that in some cases are printed and bound in single copies.[150]

One of the few areas in which reading technology is making an impact is in the above area. The ability to download books has appeal to specific segments of society while at the same time, it ostracizes others. In his significant survey of the book industry, sociologist John Thompson suggests that after much hoopla surrounding books being replaced by a variety of technologies, corporations, and large publishers have pulled back from the mania that characterized the late 1990s. Thompson remarks that this period marked an "abrupt end" to the excitement and speculation that was rampant among technological enthusiasts. Simply put, despite major investments, most "electronic publishing initiatives" fell far short of what analysts predicted. In essence, the proposed e-book revolution "stalled."[151]

Even those ardent bibliophiles, those most enamored with the printed book are willing to concede that certain electronic alternatives do have merit, especially given space and environmental concerns.[152] Scientific journals which depend on timeliness more than works of history have been found to be more amenable to electronic formats, but until technology can make reading them as attractive as reading a 'hard copy' this development will likely have to wait.[153] The tons and tons of official government documents, which range from directories to census reports, as well as the mountains of books and printed material that come with every major technology, may be better off being produced in an electronic format. Accessing information from the last text version of the Encyclopaedia Britannica is a telling example of the situation. The set itself, last available in the early nineties costed about $1500.00 U.S. and weighed about 118 pounds. It took up more than four feet of shelving space as well. The electronic version or a comparable CD-ROM sold for no more than $100.00 and weighed less than an ounce.[154] As well, there are numerous interactive and dynamic supplements such as the ability to listen to music when clicking Beethoven or seeing a very colorful reproduction when accessing Edvard Munch.[155] Sarah Lyall makes a similar comparison with the hefty multivolume Oxford English Dictionary. She cites Donald Norman, who surmises that in the very near future, the electronic dictionary will be the definitive format, because "they offer ease of access and readability."[156]

It is essential to distinguish between high culture books and the more mundane technical and official writing that seems to grow larger and more cumbersome every year.[157] Included in this mix is the fact that electronic books seem more appropriate or conducive to low brow literature along the lines of best selling novelists. This rekindles the familiar hostility that copyists exhibited towards printed works. As was hinted at earlier, there was the assumption and expectation that the printed works were inferior and dangerous in comparison to the manuscript. This same

sentiment was voiced with regard to the paperbacks that came out in the
1930s and again in the 1950s.[158] Jacques Barzun insists that there is a grand
difference when one reads for information and when one reads to expand
one's mind or soul. Only the latter can be accessed through books.[159] So,
as we must distinguish between the two spheres of text—the literary and
the more prosaic, we must also distinguish from reading on a desktop or
even a laptop and the electronic versions of books such as the E-Book or
Sony Reader

Even the most loyal devotee of computer culture will no doubt have a
problem reading a full-length book on the average PC screen. As of 2007,
these devices were still in their infancy in terms of what will eventually
be available. Who knows how light, easy to see and how clear the screens
will become in the near future? These "tablets" have potential as recepta-
cles but, with access to virtually everything on the net, the limits seem un-
bounded.[160]

One example of how ambiguous people are to fully embrace substitutes
for the book in its traditional format can be found in the spring of 2000.
Best-selling author Stephen King put out an online novella, *Riding the Bul-
let*, which sold over half a million copies in a download format in less than
two days. The publishing world thought that the end was near and that
quite simply, the bound paper book was finished. Yet very quickly, interest in this novelty faded. Stephen King's follow-up novella, *The Plant*, in
the words of two information scholars, "failed to find a paying audience."
The capriciousness towards information technology must be considered
especially when cost and convenience are still large factors in consumer
selection.[161]

The *Rocket* E-Book, a device the size of a paperback, showed grand potential. The *Rocket* shows one page at a time and has a large selection of
texts that can be accessed. One can hold it with one hand—it is light, ad-
just the lighting, and the device even keeps your place.[162] As Jacob Weisberg writes,

> There is no reason to believe our culture will be poorer even in amorphous
> ways when people absorb them [novels] from screens as well. And in defi-
> nite and obvious ways, readers and writers alike will be richer for the access
> they will gain to an electronic version of Borges's infinite "Library of Babel."
> In the near future, books will cost little or nothing, never go out of print and
> remain eternally available throughout the wired world. Can anyone really be
> against that?[163]

From about 1998 until 2002, there was a lot of press devoted to the various new electronic books available—*RocketeBook*, *SoftBook*, and other
versions of the electronic book. These handheld devices can hold numerous books and can be constantly replenished from computer databases,

kiosks, or other central depots. Some come with leather coverings. What has held enthusiasts in thrall has been their infinite storage capacity. For example, the ability to hold all of semester one's textbooks in a single electronic tablet has been of great appeal. The ability, as has been mentioned, to access hyperlinks and to utilize built in dictionaries is also highly praised. The fact that titles will never go "out of print," and that more experimental and less commercially popular titles can be accessed is also highly touted. The lack of a uniform propriety system and the simple yet overwhelming bias in favor of traditional paper books seem to be huge obstacles. These concerns lead to copyright and ownership problems as well as an array of technological problems which often focus on display and resolution. In terms of overall appeal, certain sectors are favored markets for the electronic. These include students, industries and technical/legal consortiums, where information quantity is way above the norm. Until price and technology reach a happy medium, and until the important psychological considerations have been dealt with, electronic books will remain a segmented aspect of publishing.[164] From 2002 to 2007, talk of electronic books in the media virtually disappeared. The Sony Reader started to get some attention but once again, it is too soon to speculate. Given the popularity of Apple Computers iPhone and other personal electronic devices, the possibilities for a device that has mass appeal might be more acceptable.

What is often not taken into account is that in the wired world the orientation is not around permanence, but rather, is subject to the vagaries of technology, coolness and space. This means that older technologies prevent the reader from accessing information stored in a specific format because these models have become obsolete and have disappeared. Another way of putting this is that they no longer have the cool factor which is often associated with cutting edge electronic technology. And this is not just relevant to hardware; both content and software are also subject to fast changes. What appears on the web one day disappears the next. This "serendipity of cyberspace" means, or could mean, that we are not as concerned with the preservation of the past or of the present for that matter, as we once were.[165] To a great extent, this is a boon for the lover of the book. As technology continues to change the book remains accessible and virtually uneroded by the necessity of a display system.[166] But, inevitably, and especially for the historian who depends upon the printed word, the journal, the diary, and the letter, this has dire ramifications. The written word, and the traditional notion of the printed word, may no longer have the same currency. In its most extreme version, this could mean the end of what was considered traditional, established written history.[167] Consequently, either what history is will have to be rethought or else, retaught.

NOTES

1. Alvin Kernan, *The Death of Literature*, (New Haven, CT: Yale University Press, 1990), pp. 129–38, Marshall McLuhan, *Understanding Media: The Extensions of Man*, (New York: McGraw-Hill, 1964), pp. 308–37, and Alvin Toffler, *The Third Wave*, (New York: Bantam Books, 1981), pp. 156–65.

2. Alexander Stille, *The Future of The Past*, (New York: Farrar, Straus and Giroux, 2002), p. 314.

3. Alexander Stille, *The Future of The Past*, p. 319.

4. David J. Staley, *Computers, Visualization, and History: How New Technology Will Transform Our Understanding of the Past*, (Armonk, NY: M. E. Sharpe, 2003), p. 4.

5. In *Convergence Culture: Where Old and New Media Collide*, (New York: New York University Press, 2007), p. 13, Henry Jenkins writes, "Yet, history teaches us that old media never die—and they don't even necessarily fade away. What dies are the tools we use to access media content—the 8-track, the Beta tape. These are what media scholars call delivery technologies. Delivery technologies become obsolete and get replaced; media, on the other hand evolve. Recorded sound is the medium. CDs, MP3 files, and 8-track cassettes are delivery technologies."

6. Henry Jenkins, *Convergence Culture*, p. 14.

7. Robert K. Logan, *The Fifth Language: Learning a Living in the Computer Age*, (Toronto: Stoddart Publishing, 1995), p. 34.

8. Elizabeth Eisenstein, *The Printing Revolution in Early Modern Europe*, (Cambridge: Cambridge University Press, 1993), p. 92.

9. Daniel Boorstin, *The Seekers*, (New York: Random House, 1998), p. 33.

10. Nancy Kaplan, "Literacy Beyond Books: Reading When All the World's a Web," in Andrew Herman and Thomas Swiss, eds., *The World Wide Web and Contemporary Cultural Theory*, (New York: Routlege, 2000), p. 208.

11. Daniel Boorstin, *The Seekers*, p. 34.

12. Walter J. Ong, *Orality and Literacy: The Technologizing of the Word*, (London: Methuen, 1986), p. 24.

13. Daniel Boorstin, *The Seekers*, pp. 33–36, C. M. Bowra, *The Greek Experience*, (London: Weidenfeld and Nicolson, 1957), M. I. Finley, *The World of Odysseus*, (Revised Edition, London: Penguin, 1979), Robert B. Kebric, *Greek People*, (Mountain View, CA: Mayfield Publishing, 1989).

14. Carl F. Kaestle and others, *Literacy in the United States: Readers and Reading Since 1880*, (New Haven, CT: Yale University Press, 1991), pp. 8–9.

15. Harvey J. Graff, editor, *The Labyrinths of Literacy: Reflections on Literacy Past and Present*, (Pittsburgh, PA: University of Pittsburgh Press, 1995), p. 10, cited in Kathleen Tyner, *Literacy In A Digital World: Teaching and Learning in the Age of Information*, (New Jersey: Lawrence Erlbaum Associates, 1998), p. 13.

16. Kathleen Tyner, *Literacy In A Digital World*, p. 13.

17. Elizabeth L. Eisenstein, *The Printing Revolution In Early Modern Europe*, p. 34.

18. Marcel Thomas, "Manuscripts" in *The Coming of The Book: The Impact of Printing 1450–1800*, by Lucien Febvre and Henri-Jean Martin, (London: Verso, 1976), p. 15.

19. John Man, *The Gutenberg Revolution*, (London: Review, 2002), pp. 75–79, James Burke and Richard Ornstein, *The Axemaker's Gift*, (New York: Grosset/Putnam, 1995), pp. 122–123.

20. Marcel Thomas,"Manuscripts," p. 19.

21. John Man, *The Gutenberg Revolution*, p. 88.

22. Eric Burns, *The Joy of Books: Confession of a Lifelong Reader*, (Amherst, NY: Prometheus Books, 1995), p. 53.

23. John Hale, *The Civilization of Europe in the Renaissance*, (New York: Antheneum, 1994).

24. Elizabeth Eisenstein, *The Printing Revolution*, p. 35.

25. Marcel Thomas, "Manuscripts," p. 23.

26. Febvre and Martin, *The Coming of the Book*, pp. 30, 45–46. According to Anne Hollander, "By the end of the fifteenth century, print had made it possible for illustrated books to take over part of the function of public sculpture and wall painting, and to begin the almost infinite modern expansion of visual life for ordinary people. The way in which many people could see the same image was individualized—the picture could come to the public one person at a time. This in itself was the beginning of cinematic experience, whereby many people, may be gripped by something simultaneously, and yet quite privately." *Moving Pictures*, (New York: Alfred Knopf, 1989), p. 74.

27. It is interesting to contrast E. H. Gombrich's observations with Anne Hollander's: "Now the historian knows that the information pictures were expected to provide differed widely in different periods. Not only were images scarce in the past, but so were the public's opportunities to check their captions. How many people ever saw their ruler in the flesh as sufficiently close quarters to recognize his likeness? How many travelled widely enough to tell one city from another? It is hardly surprising, therefore, that pictures of people and places changed their captions with sovereign disregard for truth. The print sold on the market as a portrait of king would be altered to represent his successor or enemy." *Art and Illusion: A Study in the Psychology of Pictorial Representation*, (Princeton: Princeton University Press, 1960/1984), p. 68.

28. Febvre and Martin, p. 47.

29. Febvre and Martin, p. 47.

30. Febvre and Martin, p. 50.

31. Febvre and Martin, p. 77.

32. S. H. Steinberg, *Five Hundred Years of Printing*, (England: Penguin, 1961), p. 8.

33. Elizabeth L. Eisenstein, *The Printing Revolution In Early Modern Europe*, p. 22.

34. Walter Ong, *Orality and Literacy*, p. 125.

35. Febvre and Martin, p. 88.

36. Febvre and Martin, p. 89.

37. Febvre and Martin, p. 183.

38. Febvre and Martin, p. 182. Also see Steinberg, *Five Hundred Years of Printing*, p. 27.

39. Febvre and Martin, p. 248.

40. Febvre and Martin, p. 249.

41. Elizabeth Eisenstein, *The Printing Revolution*, p. 32.

42. Febvre and Martin, p. 263.

43. S. H. Steinberg, *Five Hundred Years of Printing*, p. 118, and Febvre and Martin, p. 249.

44. Febvre and Martin, p. 250.

45. Elizabeth Eisenstein, *The Printing Revolution*, p. 148.

46. Leonard Shlain, *The Alphabet Versus The Goddess: The Conflict Between Word and Image*, (New York: Viking, 1998), p. 326.

47. Leonard Shlain, *The Alphabet Versus The Goddess*, p. 325.

48. John Hale, *The Civilization of Europe*, p. 274.

49. William Dana Orcutt, "Aldus Manutius," in Harold Rabinowitz and Rob Kaplan, eds., *A Passion For Books*, (New York: Three Rivers Press, 1999), pp. 240–55.

50. Lisa Jardine, *Worldly Goods: A New History of the Renaissance*, (New York: Nan A. Talese/Doubleday, 1996) p. 161.

51. For more on the publishing history of bibles see Ben D. Zevin, "The Bible Through The Ages," in Harold Rabinowitz and Rob Kaplan, eds., *A Passion For Books*, pp. 228–32.

52. Febvre and Martin, p. 252.

53. Lisa Jardine, *Worldly Goods*, p. 156.

54. Febvre and Martin, p. 252.

55. Febvre and Martin, p. 262.

56. Elizabeth Eisenstein, *The Printing Revolution*, p. 64.

57. Walter Ong, *Orality and Literacy*, p. 126: "Once print had been fairly interiorized, a book, was sensed as a kind of object which *contained* information, scientific, fictional or other, rather than, as earlier, a recorded utterance. Each individual book in printed edition was physically the same as another, an identical object, as manuscript books were not, even when they presented the same text." This comment is relevant, as will be seen in the next chapter, to works of art in the age of mechanical reproduction.

58. Lisa Jardine, *Worldly Goods*, pp. 320–21.

59. Elizabeth Eisenstein, *The Printing Revolution*, pp. 84–85.

60. John Hale, *The Civilization of Europe*, p. 275.

61. Elizabeth Eisenstein, *The Printing Revolution*, p. 90.

62. Benedict Anderson, *Imagined Communities*, (London: Verso, 1991), pp. 36–37, 44.

63. Elizabeth Eisenstein, *The Printing Revolution*, p. 165.

64. Elizabeth Eisenstein, *The Printing Revolution*, p. 92, and Walter Ong, *Orality and Literacy*, p. 130.

65. David Olson, *The World on Paper*, (Cambridge: Cambridge University Press, 1994), pp. 58–60. On the dangers of the printed text, especially with regard to the Enyclopedia, Philipp Blom, *Encyclopedie: The Triumph of Reason in an Unreasonable Age*, (London: Fourth Estate, 2004).

66. Rudi Volti, *Society and Technological Change* (Third Edition), (New York: St. Martin's Press, 1995), p. 182.

67. Lisa Jardine, *Worldly Goods*, p. 177.

68. According to David Vincent, *Bread, Knowledge and Freedom: A Study of Nineteenth-Century Working Class Autobiography*, (London: Europa Publications Limited, 1981), p. 131: "The impact of the Industrial Revolution upon the pursuit of knowledge was far from straightforward. The innovations in printing and distribution transformed the volume and cost of literature and laid the foundation for the expansion in the number of readers and the range of their activities and organizations, but it was the continuing difficulties experienced by those who

sought book knowledge which threw them together and led to the growth of a distinct culture of self-improvement."

69. Lewis Mumford, *Technics and Civilization*, (New York: Harcourt, Brace & World, 1963), p. 136.

70. Charles Nauert, *Humanism and the Culture of Renaissance Europe*, (Cambridge: Cambridge University Press, 1995), and Jacques Barzun, *From Dawn to Decadence: 1500 to the Present*, (New York: Harper Collins, 2000), pp. 228, 600.

71. Euan Cameron, "The Power of the Word: Renaissance and Reformation," in *Early Modern Europe: An Oxford History*, Edited by Euan Cameron, (London: OUP, 1999), p. 65.

72. Roger Chartier's fascinating article, "Libraries Without Walls," *Representations*, 42 Spring 1993) p. 39.

73. Note Cathy Davidson's comments on the situation in early America: "The novel, I argue throughout this study, became the chapbook of the nineteenth century—that is, a cheap book accessible to those who were not educated at the prestigious men's colleges, who were outside the established literary tradition, and who . . . for the most part read few books besides novels. Given both the literary insularity of many novel readers and the increasing popularity of the novel, the new genre necessarily became a form of education especially for women. . . . *Revolution and the Word: The Rise of the Novel in America*, (New York: Oxford University Press, 1996), p. 10

74. Emmanuel Le Roy Ladurie, *The Ancien Regime: A History of France 1610–1774*, (Cambridge, MA: Basil Blackwell, 1996), p. 309, F. Furet and M. Ozouf, *Reading and Writing Literacy in France from Calvin to Jules Ferry*, (New York: Cambridge University Press, 1982), p. 160, and J. Merriman, *A History of Modern Europe: From the Renaissance to the Age of Napoleon*, (New York: W. W. Norton, 1996), p. 417.

75. J. M. Golby and A. W. Purdue, *The Civilisation of the Crowd: Popular Culture in England, 1750–1900*, (London: Batsford: 1984), p. 32.

76. Neil Postman, *Building a Bridge to the Eighteenth Century: How the Past Can Improve the Future*, (New York: Knopf, 1999), pp. 85–86.

77. Philipp Blom, *Encyclopedie: The Triumph of Reason in an Unreasonable Age*, (London: Fourth Estate, 2004) and Ulrich Im Hof, *The Enlightenment*, (Oxford: Basil Blackwell, 1994).

78. Norman Davies, *Europe: A History*, (New York: Oxford University Press, 1996), pp. 596–608, Jacques Barzun, *From Dawn to Decadence: 1500 to the Present*, pp. 368–83, Ulrich Im Hof, *The Enlightenment*, (Oxford: Basil Blackwell, 1994), Jackson L. Speilvogel, *Western Civilization*, (USA/Canada: Thomson/Wadsworth, 1999), John Garraty and Peter Gay, eds., *The Columbia History of the World*, (New York: Harper & Row 1972).

79. Norman Davies, *Europe: A History*, pp. 596–608, Jacques Barzun, *From Dawn to Decadence: 1500 to the Present*, pp. 368–83, Ulrich Im Hof, *The Enlightenment*, Jackson L. Speilvogel, *Western Civilization*, John Garraty and Peter Gay, eds., *The Columbia History of the World*.

80. Norman Davies, *Europe: A History*, pp. 596–608, Jacques Barzun, *From Dawn to Decadence: 1500 to the Present*, pp. 368–83, Ulrich Im Hof, *The Enlightenment*, Jackson L. Speilvogel, *Western Civilization*, John Garraty and Peter Gay, eds., *The Columbia History of the World*.

81. Norman Davies, *Europe: A History*, pp. 596–608, Jacques Barzun, *From Dawn to Decadence: 1500 to the Present*, pp. 368–83, Ulrich Im Hof, *The Enlightenment*, Jackson L. Speilvogel, *Western Civilization*, John Garraty and Peter Gay, eds., *The Columbia History of the World*.

82. James Leith, "Ephemera: Civic Education Though Images," in Robert Darnton and Daniel Roche, eds., *Revolution In Print: The Press in France, 1775–1800*, (Berkeley, CA: University of California Press/New York Public Library, 1989), pp. 270–71.

83. Dan Lacy, "Reading in an Audiovisual and Electronic Era," in *Books In Our Future: Perspectives and Proposals*, John Y. Cole, ed. (Washington, DC: Library of Congress, 1987), p. 118.

84. Naomi S. Baron, *Alphabet to Email: How Written English Evolved and Where It's Heading*, (London and New York: Routledge, 2000), p. 80, and Neil Postman, *Technopoly: The Surrender of Culture to Technology*, (New York: Knopf, 1993), p. 44.

85. Neil Gabler, *Life: The Movie, How Entertainment Conquered Reality*, (New York: Vintage Books, 1998), p. 29.

86. John Lukacs, *Historical Consciousness: The Remembered Past*, (New Brunswick, NJ: Transaction Publishers, 1968/1985), p. 18.

87. Even the obvious assumption that "they" looked at nature cannot be considered. The appreciation of the sublime landscapes that surrounded European communities did not come until the late 1700s and perhaps as late as the mid-nineteenth century. Kenneth Clark, *Civilization: A Personal View*, (New York: Harper & Row, 1969).

88. Jay David Bolter, "Ekphrasis, Virtual Reality, And the Future of Writing." In Geoffrey Nunberg, ed., *The Future of the Book*, (Berkeley: University of California Press, 1996), p. 263.

89. Robert Hughes, *The Shock of The New*, (New York: Knopf, 1981).

90. Joshua Meyrowitz, *No Sense of Place: The Impact of Electronic Media on Social Behavior*, (New York: Oxford University Press, 1985), p. 75.

91. Derrick De Kerckhove, *The Skin of Culture: Investigating the New Electronic Reality*, Christopher Dewdney, ed. (Toronto: Sommerville House Publishing, 1995), p. 16.

92. These concepts are discussed in my book, *Manliness and Militarism: Educating Young Boys in Ontario for War*, (Don Mills, Ontario: Oxford University Press, 2001), chapter 4.

93. Robert Fulford, "The Ideology of the Book," *Queen's Quarterly*, 101, 3, Winter 1994, p. 803.

94. Stephanie B. Gibson, "Literacy, Paradigm, and Paradox: An Introduction," in Stephanie B. Gibson and Ollie O. Oviedo, eds., *The Emerging Cyberculture: Literacy, Paradigm, and Paradox*, (Cresskill, NJ: Hampton Press, Inc., 2000), p. 7.

95. Kathleen Tyner, in *Literacy In A Digital World*, p. 13, writes: "historical shifts in the tools of literacy change conceptions about what it means to be literate—a much more vexing and complicated question."

96. Stephanie B. Gibson, "Literacy, Paradigm, and Paradox: An Introduction," p. 7. On this point Richard A. Lanham, in *The Electronic World: Democracy, Technology and the Arts*, (Chicago: University of Chicago Press, 1993) writes that the "electronic screen" is now firmly, an "alternative to the printed page." It is thus, ac-

cording to Lanham, capable of a much richer ability to present images and sounds, which brings it closer to the Italian Futurists' dream of a more dynamic medium for communication, pp. ix, x, xi.

97. Stephanie B. Gibson, "Literacy, Paradigm, and Paradox: An Introduction," pp. 8–9.

98. Richard A. Lanham, *The Electronic World*, p. 17.

99. Kathleen Tyner, in *Literacy In A Digital World*, p. 13

100. This information is based on the work of Herbert Krugman, who published his findings in the late seventies. Krugman feels that there is increased difficulty in learning to read when a child has been exposed to television from an early age. Herbert Krugman, "Memory Without Recall, Exposure Without Perception," *Journal of Advertising Research*, vol. 7, no. 4 (August 1977) p. 8, cited in De Kerchove, *The Skin of Culture: Investigating the New Electronic Reality*, Edited by Christopher Dewdney, (Toronto: Sommerville House Publishing, 1995), p. 16.

101. Dyanne Rivers, "Why Don't You Read Something Worthwhile?," *Home & School*, January 1995, p. 31.

102. William H. Gass, "In Defense of The Book," *Harper's*, November 1999, p. 48.

103. Sally Tisdale, "Silence Please: The Public Library as Entertainment Center," *Harper's*, March 1997, p. 86.

104. Tisdale, "Silence Please," pp. 67–68.

105. Scott Carlson, "Do Libraries Really need Books?" *The Chronicle of Higher Education*, July 12, 2002.

106. Kathleen Tyner, *Literacy In A Digital World*, p. 10.

107. Kathleen Tyner, *Literacy In A Digital World*, p. 10.

108. One must keep in mind that reading/literacy was a key feature of life in the last few hundred years and significant here is the fact that it was not just the privilege of the elite. Lawrence Levine, "William Shakespeare and the American People: A Study in Cultural Transformation," in Chandra Mukeji and Michael Schudson, eds., *Rethinking Popular Culture: Contemporary Perspectives in Cultural Studies*, (Berkeley: University of California Press, 1991), p. 161–87. Levine contends that it wasn't just books but the theatre as well, that served as a key cultural transmission site, comparing the theatre in the nineteenth century to the place of movies in the twentieth century.

109. Sven Birkerts, *The Gutenberg Elegies: The Fate of Reading In An Electronic Age*, (Boston: Faber and Faber, 1994), p. 19.

110. Birkerts, *The Gutenberg Elegies*, p. 20.

111. Alvin Kernan, *The Death of Literature*, pp. 140, 146.

112. Ben Agger, *The Decline of Discourse: Reading, Writing and Resistance in Postmodern Capitalism*, (Bristol/Philadelphia: The Falmer Press, 1990), pp. 25, 27, 30.

113. Todd Gitlin, *Media Unlimited: How the Torrent of Images and Sounds Overwhelms Our Lives*, (New York: Henry Holt/Metropoliton Books, 2001), pp. 99–101.

114. John Seabrook, *Nobrow: The Culture of Marketing, The Marketing of Culture*, (London: Methuen, 2000), p. 133.

115. In *Literacy In A Digital World*, p. 40, Kathleen Tyner writes: "The Internet borrows extensively from the conventions of alphabetic literacy and is extremely dependent on the printed word. Static Web pages look like billboards. Interactive

Web pages mimic radio, telephone, and line speech. The way that pictures and texts work together in multimedia interfaces is reminiscent of the visually stunning illustrations of Biblical texts seen in the illuminated manuscripts of medieval times. E-mail has revived letter writing. In some ways, digital media has the potential to revive and refresh oral and print communication forms, by making new juxtaposition of image, text, and sound possible."

116. David M. Levy, *Scrolling Forward: Making Sense of Documents in The Digital Age*, (New York: Arcade Publishing, 2001), p. 113.

117. Peter Lyman, "What is a Digital Library? Technology, Intellectual Property, and the Public Interest," *DAEDALUS: Books, Bricks and Bytes* (Fall 1996) vol. 125, no. 4, p. 4. Lyman also states: "Print is not a homogenous medium of communication; newspapers and books are significantly different kinds of knowledge artifacts, using different rhetorical forms and having very different social uses," p. 5.

118. Donald S. Lamm, "Libraries and Publishers: A Partnership at Risk," *DAEDALUS*, Fall 1996, p. 139.

119. Rachel Ross, "E-mail @ 30," *The Toronto Star*, October 8, 2001, p. E3. Ross lists some other versions of this lingo: FWIW—For what it's worth, IOW—In other words.

120. Cited in David M. Levy, *Scrolling Forward*, p. 114.

121. David M. Levy, *Scrolling Forward*, p. 114.

122. Nancy Kaplan, "Literacy Beyond Books," pp. 212–13.

123. New media prophet Nicholas Negroponte writes: "Hypermedia is an extension of hypertext, a term for highly interconnected narrative, or linked information. The idea came from early experiments at the Stanford Research Institute by Douglas Engelbart and derived its name from work at Brown University by Ted Nelson, circa 1965. In a printed book, sentences, paragraphs, pages, and chapters follow one another in an order determined not only by the author but also by the physical and sequential construct of the book itself. While a book may be randomly accessible and your eyes may browse quite haphazardly, it is nonetheless forever fixed by the confines of three physical dimensions." *Being Digital*, (New York: Alfred Knopf, 1995), p. 69.

124. Stephanie B. Gibson, "Literacy, Paradigm, and Paradox: An Introduction," p. 11.

125. Richard A. Lanham, *The Electronic World*, p. 31.

126. Subash Gandhi, "E-Books: The Future of Reading and Ultimate Book Publishing," *Journal of Educational Technological Systems*, vol. 29, no. 1, 2000–2001, pp. 49–66.

127. David M. Levy, *Scrolling Forward*, p. 138.

128. Alexander Stille, *The Future of The Past*, p. 300.

129. Alexander Stille, *The Future of The Past*, pp. 301–302.

130. Roy Rosenzweig, "Scarcity or Abundance? Preserving the Past in a Digital Era," *The American Historical Review*, vol. 108, issue 3, p. 5, July 2003: www.history coop.org/journals/ahr/108.3/rosenzweign.html.

131. Stephanie B. Gibson, "Literacy, Paradigm, and Paradox: An Introduction," p. 9.

132. Geoffrey Nunberg, "The Places of Books in the Age of Electronic Reproduction," *Representations*, 42 (Spring 1993) p. 17.

133. Geoffrey Nunberg, "The Places of Books in the Age of Electronic Reproduction," p. 17.

134. Sarah Lyall, "Are These Books, or What? CD-ROM and the Literary Industry," *The New York Times Books Review*, August 14, 1994, p. 3.

135. Alison Armstrong and Charles Casement, *The Child and The Machine: Why Computers Put Our Children's Education at Risk*, (Toronto: Key Porter Books, Limited, 1998), p. 90.

136. Gary Gumpert, *Talking Tombstones & Other Tales of the Media Age*, (New York: Oxford University Press, 1987), p. 154.

137. Subash Gandhi, "E-Books: The Future of Reading and Ultimate Book Publishing," p. 57.

138. Stephanie B. Gibson, "Literacy, Paradigm, and Paradox: An Introduction," p. 9.

139. Alison Armstrong and Charles Casement, *The Child and The Machine: Why Computers Put Our Children's Education at Risk*, p. 15.

140. Nancy Kaplan, "Literacy Beyond Books," p. 212, and Robert Darnton, "What is the History of Reading?," in Cathy Davidson, editor, *Reading in America: Literature and and Social History*, (Baltimore: Johns Hopkins University Press, 1989).

141. Robert K. Logan, *The Fifth Language*, p. 60.

142. Robert Fulford, "The Ideology of the Book," p. 803.

143. Joseph and Phyllis Bernt, "World Wide Web, E-Commerce, and the Rise of the Book: Survey of Online Booksellers Indicates Increasing Value of Used Books," A Paper Presented to the Electronic Communication & Culture Area, Popular Culture Association Conference, New Orleans, LA, April 20, 2000, p. 1.

144. Joseph and Phyllis Bernt, "World Wide Web, E-Commerce, and the Rise of the Book," pp. 2–3.

145. Jason Epstein, *Book Business: Publishing, Past, Present and Future*, (New York: W. W. Norton and Co., 2001), p. xiii.

146. Jonathan Rosen, in *The Talmud and the Internet: A Journey Between Worlds*, (New York: Farrar, Straus and Giroux, 2000), pp. 8–9, suggests that these older media/texts do not only possess great power, but also, parallel in some ways, new technology: "I have often thought, contemplating a page of Talmud, that it bears a certain uncanny resemblance to a home page of the Internet, where nothing is whole in itself but where icons and text boxes are doorways through which visitors pass into an infinity of cross-referenced texts and conversations."

147. Robert Fulford, "The Ideology of the Book," p. 804.

148. Robert Fulford, "The Ideology of the Book," p. 809–10.

149. Jay David Bolter, *Writing Spaces: The Computer, Hypertext, and the History of Writing*, (Hillsdale, NJ: Lawrence Erlbaum, 1991), pp. 2–3.

150. Jason Epstein, *Book Business*, p. xii.

151. John B. Thompson, *Books in the Digital Age*, (Cambridge, MA: Polity Press, 2005), pp. 310–11.

152. It should be mentioned, that in 1945, in the Atlantic, Vannevar Bush had written presciently, as it turned out of the idea of compressing a text such as the *Encyclopaedia Britannica* into a near microscopic format that could be accessible on

demand. See Vannevar Bush, "As We May Think," in Timory Druckrey, Editor, *Electronic Culture: Technology and Visual Representation*, (New York: Aperture, 1996), pp. 33–41.

153. Christine L. Borgman, *From Gutenberg To The Global Information Infrastructure: Access to Information In the Networked World*, (Cambridge, MA.: MIT Press, 2000), p. 90. On p. 92, Borgman writes, "Most of the activities of scholars, publishers, and libraries are likely to be conducted differently with the proliferation of information technologies, the availability of a broader array of formats, and the shifting economics of scholarly publishing. Librarians see advantages to electronic journals, as do other players. They can provide electronic journals on demand to their user communities, 24 hours per day, without incurring the costs of physical storage space on library shelves. Electronic journals are searchable in more ways than print journals, and they can be packaged in a variety of ways to provide new services. Though publishers and libraries may operate much differently a decade or two hence, they will continue to exist and to be essential."

154. Sarah Lyall, "Are These Books, or What? CD-ROM and the Literary Industry," p. 3.

155. Sarah Lyall, "Are These Books, or What? CD-ROM and the Literary Industry," p. 3.

156. Sarah Lyall, "Are These Books, or What? CD-ROM and the Literary Industry," pp. 3, 20.

157. Geoffrey Nunberg, "The Places of Books in the age of Electronic Reproduction," p. 14. Nunberg writes, "The printed documentation that accompanies the delivery of a single Boeing 747 weighs about 350 tons, only slightly less than the airplane itself. Who would have any reservations about putting texts like these into electronic form, if it will make the world a roomier and greener place?"

158. Alberto Manguel, *A History of Reading*, (Toronto: Alfred A. Knopf, 1996), pp. 133, 140–42, and Jacob Weisberg, "The Good E-Book," *The New York Times Magazine*, June 4, 2000, pp. 23–24.

159. Jacques Barzun, "The Future of Reading," in *Books In Our Future*, p. 141.

160. Gerry Blackwell, "Reinventing the 'book'," *The Toronto Star*, May 31, 2001, p. K6.

161. John Seely Brown and Paul Duguid, *The Social Life of Information*, (Boston: Harvard Business School Press, 2002), p. xx. This story is of course juxtaposed with the *Harry Potter* mania and the sale of over 30 million books in the United States.

162. Jacob Weisberg, "The Good E-Book," p. 24.

163. Jacob Weisberg, "The Good E-Book," p. 24.

164 . Subash Gandhi, "E-Books: The Future of Reading and Ultimate Book Publishing," pp. 49–66.

165. Stephanie B. Gibson, "Literacy, Paradigm, and Paradox: An Introduction," p. 10.

166. Fred Lerner, *The Story of Libraries: From the Invention of Writing to The Computer Age*, (New York: Continuum, 1999), p. 209.

167. Dale Spender, *Nattering on the Net: Women, Power and Cyberspace*, (Toronto: Garamond Press, 1995) p. 259.

4

Photographing History

Photographs have the kind of authority over imagination today, which the printed word had yesterday, and the spoken word before that. They seem utterly real. They come, we imagine, directly to us without human meddling, and they are the most effortless food for the mind conceivable.

—Walter Lippmann, *Public Opinion*, 61

In the age of photography, the memory of particular events became more and more closely associated with their visual images.

—Christian Meier, *From Athens to Auschwitz: The Uses of History*, 23

In a society that prides itself on speed of access, quickness of recall and timeliness of information, the photograph has become both a touchstone to the past and at the same time, a form of historical shorthand. Given the fact that academic history is often beyond the comprehension of most people and the interpretation of history is "less accessible" the photograph remains a key tool to unlocking the complexities of history.[1]

The photograph, despite being over 150 years old, continues to be both a potent source of fascination, capturing "real life" as well as being the all important visual historical text. The photograph, being a key component of visual synthesis, has the ability to shrink enormous complexity into a manageable and compressed form and in turn to stand for much more than is first apparent. Like the touchstones of visual culture, the photograph is direct and capsulated. The impact of the photograph is "instantaneous, visceral, and intense."[2] Often dismissed as irrelevant in the world of video and the Internet, it has shown a robust capacity to survive and thrive despite numerous "threats" to its role. It has held a fundamental place in the perception of reality since its invention, and despite being swamped by more sophisticated technological visualizations, it still carries persuasive weight as far as its ability to capture history.[3] In turn, certain images merge into memory. The potency of some images—the ones that stand out—have the capacity to "stop time," so to speak, and make us ponder the world and ourselves in truly unique ways.[4] As Susan Sontag has perceptively written, in a world governed by "non-stop imagery" the photograph retains a "deeper bite." This is particular to historical memory in that a kind of "freeze-framing" occurs. Sontag comments that:

> In an era of information overload, the photograph provides a quick way of apprehending something and a compact form of memorizing it. The photograph is like a quotation, or maxim or proverb. Each of us mentally stocks hundreds of photographs, subject to instant recall. Cite the most famous photograph taken during the Spanish Civil War, the Republican soldier "shot" by Robert Capa's camera at the same moment he is hit by an enemy bullet, and virtually everyone who has heard of that war can summon to mind the grainy black-and-white image of a man in a white shirt with rolled-up sleeves collapsing backward as his rifle leaves his grip—about to fall, dead, onto his own shadow.[5]

This list continues on and on. Most citizens of the West can instantly recall a number of key photographic images that stand as history: the young boy with his arms raised, outside the Warsaw ghetto, the young girl, screaming in horror, running naked, after a napalm attack. These images have become part of a "collective historical consciousness."[6] In many cases they were the work of a select group of photographers known as photojournalists. Howard Chapnick, involved with the famous Magnum and Black Star agencies, writes, that photojournalists "have provided us with a visual history unduplicated by images from any comparable period of human existence." Chapnick is of the very strong opinion that it is the photograph, created by the best photographers, that has given us the ability to document our time. "To ignore photojournalism," he concludes, "is to ignore history."[7]

A key attribute to photography and the photograph which parallels history is the importance of interpretation. What we see in the photograph and how we decipher the image carry important weight, especially in using the photograph as a historical device. The merging of interpretation with the actual photograph gives the photograph historical resonance and makes photography similar to historical data in that one must peruse it and select from it.[8]

Photographs are the best way to "visualize time in passage. They enhance, for us, the transient role of humans among relatively stable objects."[9] As Wright Morris has noted, the camera now affirms "the world around us" and puts it into a "coherent image." "When we think of the world," writes Wright, "do we not think of a photograph?"[10]

Upon entering the United States Holocaust Museum in Washington, the dominant image is of a large photograph showing "American soldiers standing around a pyre in which the remains of charred bodies are visible."[11] The selection of such a visual document—a powerful photograph—is a reminder of the continuing power of the photograph to convey the enormity, the actuality, and the complexity of history.[12] This is especially relevant in the news coverage of the 9/11 situation, where still photographs, either on or in magazines and newspapers, or within the pages of commemorative books, have come to play a key, if not definitive role, in the historicization of this tragic event. In a very short period of time, the photographs of 9/11 have achieved a level of status on par with other iconic images. In particular, the photograph taken of the three firemen raising the American flag stands out as a key piece of visual record. The flag raising of 9/11 instantly evokes the famous Iwo Jima record. It is this type of image, reproduced in many different formats and ingrained in historical consciousness that gives the photograph its ability to convey information and to tell a story.

According to Afsun Qureshi, Joe Rosenthal's flag raising at Iwo Jima and Eddie Adams' execution of a Viet Cong are two key historical icons that constantly pop-up in the mind's eye to sum up a historical epoch. Stan Honda's photographs of the World Trade Center tragedy will likely become part of the same powerful historical iconography.[13] Harmonious with visual culture and all its attributes, the photograph is a key historical indicator, one that people carry with them in a constant and effortless linkage to the past.

Extending the single snapshot into an image or refraction, the concept or the idea of the photograph has become "imperious."[14] It is the dominant aspect of visual culture. It is speeded up in film, captured for newspapers, displayed in the home and carried in wallets. It is part of modern human experience and so much so that for most in the west, culture, society, life, and history are not imaginable without it. During the heyday of photography, in the 1920s and the 1930s, the publisher Jean Prouvost remarked, "The image has become the queen of our age. We are no longer content to know—we must see."[15] Cultural observer James Twitchell suggests that the comment, "Did you see?" has replaced "Did you know?" as a phrase that is indicative of the way things are.[16] Visual proof, according to Vicki Goldberg is how we perceive of reality.[17]

The significance of the photograph as conveyor of knowledge, information, and history, made itself apparent in the early decades of the twentieth century. The photograph, along with the film, transformed the task of defining the past and "constructing reality" in such a forceful way that it provoked a fierce and defensive response from those who were oriented around the vigor of the word. Journalists, critics, writers, and those who depended upon the established impact of the word were often quite hostile to those who endeavored to convey information via the image.[18]

One of the supreme mediums of photographic messages of history has been *National Geographic* Magazine. It has, over the decades, acquired a reputation for its startling photographs of people, places, animals, and other events that take the visual to new heights. When the magazine was started, it focused on words, maps, and graphs to convey knowledge. In the early part of the twentieth century, under pressure from its printers to fill-up an issue, editor Bert Grosvenor stumbled upon a package from the Imperial Russian Geographical Society. Inside were photographs of Lhasa, the capital of Tibet—until then, never before seen by many people, especially westerners, and certainly not photographed. Grosvenor put the photographs into the January 1905 issue and almost overnight, changed the way stories were told. He understood that subscribers to the *Geographic* would be enamored with the visuals which shed light upon things that they had only been able to imagine. Within a few years, photographs would make up almost half of the monthly page total and quickly became a central feature of the magazine and its version of how events came to be told.[19]

The photograph as historical document and as testament to reality matured in the 1920s during the golden age of documentary. The documentary ideal ironically came out of the tabloid papers of the 1920s, which in turn came out of the penny press's of the turn of the century. The ideals of the documentary, in particular, the objective of the camera, were allowed to grow and form with the emphasis on the visual.[20] Increasingly, newspapers and magazines adapted their formats to contain more and more photographs. The cultural power of *Life* and *Look* in the United States and numerous other publications in Europe enhanced the impact of the photography as a definitive part of the visual landscape but importantly, as a key historical tool.[21] Photography spoke of the past to people in a fundamentally new way. Prior to 1839, people depended on stories and text or painting to comprehend, visually, the past that they were seeking. When the first photographers brought back their photographs of the Holy Land, of the sites in Italy, of the ruins in some distant part of the world, they contextualized the past in a fundamentally new way. From this point onward, a most potent source of defining history came from the photograph. In explaining history, in deciphering the past for us, the photograph and its offspring play an enormously important role.[22] One reason is that the photograph has always been associated with reality;[23] its literalness in recreating an image gives it a form of authenticity that painting did not and does not have. A photograph has the legitimacy of precision in recreating the visual.[24] Since the Scientific Revolution and the Enlightenment, this notion has grown in importance and to a substantial extent, is key in defining our association of seeing as believing.[25]

It is important to look at the photographic record in the same way one looks at the historical record. On the one hand, the photograph stands alone as a singular document, like an archive resource. It is present, in and of itself, and how it is interpreted or deciphered, how it is given meaning, without obscuring its original intention, is the secret to unlocking its power. A printed or hand-written archived resource is there to be made sense of, but so too is a photograph.[26] It exists to be interpreted and to be discussed, yet it carries the uniqueness of visual power. Not solely confined to the image, but rather, a conglomeration of image and interpretation, the photograph is more accessible to the untrained observer, to the amateur historian. This process of knowledge accumulates overtime and it is instructive to look toward the interaction between painting as a visual resource and photography.

When photography is juxtaposed with painting, one starts to see, not only the importance of visual culture in defining history, but the authenticity guaranteed the photograph. For a long time painting served as a way to reach people who were fundamentally illiterate. Visuals, especially in a nonliterate society, or an oral culture, are key features in transmitting ideas, and especially, a sense of the past. Memory reigned supreme in these cultures.[27] Painting, especially historical perspective painting, played a key role in telling the narratives of history, which are so vital to western notions of the past.[28] With the development of photography, the visual image and the use of memory began to change. And this change was epochal! From teaching us a new visual code, to use Susan Sontag's phrase, to allowing a portable and tangible means of acquiring an image, photography altered and transformed every aspect of society.[29] Walter Benjamin was one of the first to decode this. He stated that photography was so key in altering society because it allowed for "in unlimited quantities figures, landscapes, events that have either not been saleable at all or have been available only as pictures for single customers."[30] What Benjamin means here is that as with the printing press, many individuals could now benefit from the multiplicity of images, in essence have access to something that was once only the privilege of a few.

Many critics have felt that this was, to put it mildly, not a good thing. John Berger for example, asks, "What served in place of the photograph; before the camera's invention? The expected answer is the engraving, the drawing, the painting. The more revealing answer might be: memory. What photographs do out there in space was previously done within by reflection."[31] One was forced to use memory in order to reflect upon the past. What Berger intimates is that this process is now done for you by the literalness of the photograph. It is, he suggests, no longer important to recall when the photograph does that for you.

A significant end-result to this process has been that as images came to occupy more and more influence, the role as information purveyors evolved into something greater. Not just a document designed to explain, reflect, or illustrate by appearance, the photograph as an innovative part of the visual geography came to a crescendo in its impact. Suddenly, there was the "creation of a visual environment capable of transcending memory and reconstructing history." The photograph and later film and television came to take the place of memory and in many cases became the defining feature of historical awareness. In continual instances this has led to the manipulation of viewers and the distortion of reality. Yet, above all, this had led to the quick and effortless "acceptance" of the visual nature of society.[32]

In the introduction to this work, Gore Vidal remarked that one had to scan what one saw, frame by frame, in order to keep it.[33] With the photograph, and with the technological ramifications of say, video, anything, according to art critic Robert Hughes, "could be retrieved or reproduced." The "pretechnological eye was" according to Hughes, "obliged to scrutinize—one thing at a time. Objects could not, except at the cost of great labor be reproduced or multiplied."[34] One must remember that J. C. Hertz suggested that today, a different generation can indulge in a free-for-all of absorption, taking *in* many different things at the same time. But for anyone older, this procedure can be problematic.

Toward the middle of the last century everything changed as a consequence of the introduction of photography. Although, as Walter Benjamin stated, "a work of art has always been reproducible,"[35] it was done at enormous cost and great effort. Mass reproduction of art works because of the advent of photography was unlike anything ever before experienced. Mass reproduction of hitherto unseen images due to photography had ramifications in social, artistic, economic, political, and of course cultural arenas. Access to the image was no longer the privilege of a few. The rise of the middle classes, when for the first time, fairly large segments of the population attained political and economic power, resulted in an increased demand for goods of all sorts. Nearly everything had to be produced in greater quantities and as Gisele Freund remarks, the photograph in all its variations, was no exception.[36]

In a society emerging ready and willing to consume, amass, and acquire, photography was embraced with enormous fervor. It was the first unabashedly democratic "art" on many levels.[37] For example, it was easier to see or look at photography as opposed to studying a painting; little effort was required, a foreshadowing of what was to be with film and subsequently, with television. The incentive to work out a practical technique was stimulated by the unprecedented demand for pictures from the rising middle class. Reproductions in quantity were in order; lithography was invented and wood engraving revived, so that pictures could be almost endlessly duplicated. The new middle class wanted cheap portraits and in this new economy, what was demanded was quickly supplied. This also marked the simultaneous development of industry and technology and the growth of science to meet the needs of industrialization, which in turn required rational economic forms. This was to be of great importance later.

It is generally acknowledged that a work of art, be it a painting or a sculpture, was a creation for the rich or the powerful, confined to a single location and thus, accessible to a select few individuals. Photography radically altered this previous isolation of art. In a very significant sense, photography freed the work of art—a staple of historic illustration—from its stationary refuge and liberated it for the perusal and contemplation of the masses. Art and in this case, historical art, now could be seen by virtually everyone. What is particularly significant here is that art that hung in museums and the homes of the wealthy was now, through photography, accessible without the "mystique" of the "unique."[38]

The invention of photography created a grand paradox. It automatically brought art, for example, David's major works, out into the open, to the masses, but at the same time, the photographed work of art was "distorted,"—its uniqueness banished from its formerly undisturbed sanctuary. But as Gisele Freund has stated, "If photography can misrepresent a work of art by distorting its dimensions, it was immensely helpful in removing art from its isolation."[39] What this phenomenon triggered was a series of little 'domino effects.' When an image is presented as a work of art, the way people look at it is affected by a whole series of learned assumptions about art.[40] A photograph is a quick glimpse of something. A photograph of an art object is a quick glimpse at *culture*. "The more the photograph looked like a substitute for painting," observes Susan Sontag, "the more the uneducated public found it artistic."[41] Photographs taught the viewer a "new visual code," one that told the viewer what was "worth" looking at. By distorting what the viewer could observe, they become "an ethics of seeing."[42]

The whole complex act of seeing changed with the advent of photography. Objects and people became mirrored, imaginations corralled, and perhaps, a general sense of acceptance settled in with regard to viewing. Significant here is the impact that photography had not just upon art but upon history. Not only was the way paintings were looked at changed, but because historical paintings could now be reproduced over and over and divorced from their original context—the place where the painting resided—the uniqueness of the image was distorted. As a consequence of this distortion, the essence changed to allow for numerous interpretations.[43]

Less and less does a photographed work of art depend on being a "unique object," or even an object made by an individual artist.[44] The value of a work of art began to depend less upon the "workmanship, material quality, and rarity," and more and more value was derived from its financial worth and "the abstract and increasingly malleable factor of aesthetic appeal."[45] By reproducing a work of art, the whole becomes "dismembered." This fracturing allows the work to be sent out to a multitude of environments, and both changes the intent of the original while at the same time allows the copy to go places and inform people that the original could never penetrate. The paramount example of a work of art that has been reproduced and remade over and over is the Mona Lisa. For most people, the image of the Mona Lisa is one that they can perceive, yet this visual perception is one of the photograph, not of the original. The mass reproduction of an art image is the reason that the image has attained its place in the collective memory of most people.[46]

No longer confined to its original space, the place where it was supposed to have been seen—in context, the work of art that is photographed and reproduced on a massive scale, affects the distinction between the original and the reproduction, in that there is a blurring between the two. Robert Hughes, among others, suggests that by reproducing a work of art over and over, the uniqueness of the original is watered down into an easy-to-understand-sign, which is devoid of all nuance and ambiguity.[47] These attributes of art disappear when the original is reproduced, yet this liberates art from its former hibernetic isolation. Art is made accessible to many and in ways that were formerly unheard of.[48]

Harold Rosenberg, Robert Hughes, and John Berger are all expanding upon the notion that a certain something contained within a painting or any original work of art is lost when it is mass produced for a mass audience. This, sometimes elitist view, can be valid—in fact is—but avoids the access argument (more on which later). The intangible, almost ephemeral quality is Walter Benjamin's concept of "aura."

Walter Benjamin's concept of aura was developed in his major essay, "The Work of Art in the Age of Mechanical Reproduction." In this essay, written for the Institute for Social Research's journal, the idea of a work of art's aura is developed concomitantly with its erosion by technologically reproduced, mass art. All original, singular works of art—specifically painting and sculpture—but as well, music, drama, and to some extent, the novel, have or contain (an) aura. Simply put, aura is "their ritually or cultically induced halo of authenticity and uniqueness." This halo of authenticity and uniqueness is derived from a "singularity in time and space which is the hallmark of authenticity."[49] Because a work of art was tied to both a specific time and place, it retained aura. But mechanically reproducing this work of art and allowing it to be displayed virtually anywhere, served to sever the uniqueness of the work which largely depends on content.[50]

An unlimited number of copies of an original work of art produced from a photograph and then removed from the workplace's of origin has destroyed "the very basis for the production of auratic works of art—that singularity in time and space on which they depend for their claim to authority and authenticity."[51] By making a full color reproduction of a masterpiece and disseminating copies of it throughout the world, the original loses most of its authority."[52] By being reproduced, the work of art gives up a significant amount of its authority, and in the process, becomes part of the mass culture landscape.[53]

Jennifer Todd observes that Benjamin "argues that capitalism has destroyed the audience's ability to recognize an auratic artwork at the same time as it promotes forms of artistic production which do not lead to auratic artworks." Conversely, at the same time, Benjamin implies strongly that the new artistic techniques of photography and film have allowed for a vast expansion of the commodity market in art.[54] Photography had the effect of removing the aura of art by means of its endless reproducibility. To some extent, the uniqueness of the individual work of art was now controlled and could be reproduced en masse, not only removing the auratic aspect, but also making it a communal product as opposed to the work of a lone individual.[55]

A key development is the fact that reproduction enables the original to meet the beholder half way in situations which would be out of reach for the original itself. The audience does not have to be confined by the authority of the original.[56] In most museums—key visual history repositories—the viewer is seeing the work of art out of its original context, in a totally different environment. This changes the way the work of art was meant to be seen, but at the same time, makes the work of art more viewable in an environment that is composed of many free-floating images with no fixed ties to a place and time.[57] With editing and montage in film and television, by detaching an image from its original place and time, what can happen is that "totally new meanings" are constructed by mixing and merging a diverse array of images together.[58]

We have become quite comfortable seeing works of art in these new surroundings and we have become accustomed to the reproducibility factor. This democratization of the image has liberated works of art from their previous isolation and seems to fit quite well into the media saturated world of images.[59] Historically, many early photographs were resplendent

reproductions of paintings which had earlier been unseen by their now de-
mocratized audience. The main impetus for this freeing of the image was the
emerging consumer marketplace and the concomitant rise of mass culture.

This new development had revolutionary effects on how people acquired information. The picturing of history, while prominent with painting now came to the fore as dominant with the development of photography.[60] The definitive example of the massification of the image was the
cinema, but for about sixty years, the photograph or "picture" dominated.
Photographs began to appear in newspapers and magazines. Beginning
in 1897, with the "advent of the half-tone illustration as a regular feature
of journalism," the photograph became a significant part of the power of
the press to define through image, history, and reality.[61] This led to a level
of acceptance and familiarity that led the public to increasingly "expect
the latest news in photographic form."[62] This built upon the assumption
that the photograph was not only new, but perceived to be real or true.
This was employed not just in news reporting but also in advertising.[63]
This was also a key transforming principle in the analysis of history and,
to a great extent, reality. As Neil Postman has remarked:

> the image undermined traditional definitions of information, of news, and to
> a large extent of reality itself . . . the picture forced exposition into the back-
> ground, and in some cases, obliterated it all together. By the end of the nine-
> teenth century, advertisers and newspapermen had discovered that a picture
> was not only worth a thousand words, but, where sales were concerned, was
> better. For countless Americans, seeing, not reading became the basis for be-
> lieving.[64]

In little more than half a century, photography ingratiated itself with the
public; it moved from being an artistic medium to one with very democratic pretensions. Photography became "one of the most accessible and
accepted means of visual representation."[65] And, very quickly, people became competent at seeing things in mass produced form and quick studies at the new visual hieroglyphs of photographs (and film) with or without captions to explain. Often, as with new immigrants, only literate
enough to master the most basic demands and without the time do much
more, they welcomed the fare of the new visual mass culture. It was immediate and effortless to absorb, perfect for the tired or bored souls of the
city. They were wedded to the new products of mass culture: the exotic romance, the raw detective plot, the wealth, the opulence, the sorrow, and
fear that these products could stimulate. The vicariousness and titillation
of the latest serial, in either newspaper or film form, was hungrily antici-
pated and greedily devoured upon its release. Later, lurid photographs of
death and carnage, of accidents and murder, screamed across the pages of
dailies and marked *Life* Magazine as the visualizer of photographic his-

tory. From Margaret Bourke-White's grizzly pictures to Lee Miller's haunting concentration camp victims to Weegee's graphic photographs of the seedy side of life, there was a constant emphasis on the gory. As well, as the twentieth century progressed, legions of photographers began to capture the progress and the disillusionment of the times. Today, the photographs of Lewis Hine, Andre Kertesz, Eugene Atget, Bill Brandt, Walker Evans, Dorthea Lange, and others are the visual historical record.

Photography quickly took a place in the ability to render history in a more persuasive way than the etching or the report.[66] The documentary photograph, especially black-and-white photography, came to stand for the image of history in a way that painting or etching never could. The "realist" aspect of the documentary black and white added to the veracity of the picture.[67] By the second half of the nineteenth century, photography was having an impact on how history was being perceived. During the Crimean War (1853–1856) numerous artists set out to render the conflict in visual ways. Their drawing and paintings were sent to the newspapers which in turn, published these pictures. With the improvements in technology, the ease of transmitting the visual from the arena of conflict back to the centers of publishing became quick and efficient. The Crimean War was rendered visually for a visually hungry audience and from that point onward, war came to be seen, not just written about.[68] With that mind-set in place and with that set of expectations, the next major conflict would take the visual recording of an event—a history—to a whole new level. Coinciding with this were technological innovations which allowed photographs to be produced in large quantities and available virtually everywhere. As well, the public in the second half of the nineteenth century demanded visual information about whatever was going on.[69]

Mathew Brady's photographs of the American Civil War became and are for many, the record of that war. Beyond documentation, photography came to tell the story. According to Hubertus von Amelunxen, "Brady—marking the shift from writing to the visual medium—was able to call himself 'the eye of history.'"[70] For the first time it became possible to make a history out of images.[71] Brady seemed to think, as did most observers, that the Civil War would be brief and that there would be a "great popular demand for war photographs."[72] But he was also aware that his project was charged with an awareness of history, that what he was undertaking had significant historical value.[73]

Brady's photographs of the Civil War owed much to the historical paintings of the eras which had come before. In particular, the ways Brady and his associates framed many of the images, had much in common with paintings and sketches that were still a part of visual culture. Significant here is the fact that unlike what was to come in the area of the photojournalist, Brady's work is often characterized as having been

staged. The formal posing of the men who appear in his works is suggestive of an artful arrangement, yet at the same time, they retain auratic
appeal. Though, as Alan Trachtenberg has suggested: "However composed and staged, they bear witness to real events." Thus, as historical
accounts, they command enormous respect.[74]

Brady and others were aware that the ability to confuse and distort was
marked and defined. Encasing the photographs in a book gave them a formal cohesion and allowed them to retain their power as images and as
history because of the inherent meaning contained in this manner of presentation.[75]

The creation of the photojournalist, perhaps most defined by Robert
Capa, came of age at a time when people and industry were well aware
of the power of pictorialism. Almost from 1839, a key attraction of photography (and later, photojournalism) was war. As Fred Ritchin writes,
"Wars are, because of and in spite of their destructiveness, highly photogenic."[76] According to Ritchin, the development of smaller, portable cameras and more efficient film, facilitated, at least technologically, the explosion of war photography as did the plethora of mass-circulation
magazines that came to be defined by photographs.[77] The photographs of
the war dead that Mathew Brady and his assistants—Alexander Gardner
and Timothy O'Sullivan in particular—shot during the American Civil
War when exhibited in New York, were on the one hand described as "re-
pulsive, brutal," and "sickening," but at the same time, they attracted a
large audience.[78] What was at the heart of some of these photographs was
the true horror of war. The scale and the revulsion was unlike anything
ever seen. And it was seen, for the first time, in a way that had no comparison.[79] As Jonathan Marwil has recognized, "War was only one of
many subjects that lured early photographers, but it was one that prom-
ised a large audience, given its inherent appeal as spectacle and its habitual role in the shaping of national identities." What is significant about
the photograph of the theatre of war is that it was *as it were*, not someone's
idea or rendering.[80] For the first time, people saw the battlefield and the
place as if they were there. This, as far as history was concerned, was
epochal. From Brady's time onwards the camera became "the privileged
witness of events." The camera travelled with the army, the government,
and, increasingly, the journalist to tell the story. Every major event from
the building of massive projects such as the Suez Canal or a transnational
railway was photographed. "The world," writes Jean-Luc Daval, "was
brought before the eyes of all."[81]

Alan Trachtenberg has surmised that images become historicized when
they are used to explain the past. By moving from the simplicity of the
staid image to the more complex document, images "become history
when they are conceived as symbolic events in a shared culture."[82] A fun-

damental consideration here is that given their implicit or true visual ability, the photograph has come to be considered a form of "evidence." What we come to understand or to comprehend as history is often conveyed in the form of a photograph.[83]

Another feature in this process is that beyond recording history or historicizing the past, the photograph takes on the role of archival document. As certain historical sites begin to fade or disappear—in a literal way—a photograph takes on the role of evidentiary document. It then begins to stand as a signifier of what was once there and can be used as proof or as an example of comparison.

By the early days of the twentieth century, the photographer and the photojournalist had mastered war, and most of the major construction events of the time. They also turned their attention to social and natural phenomenon that in turn became the visual record or the visual history of the time. Photographs of labor strife, disasters brought on by fires and earthquakes quickly became staples of visual history, many of which we turn to today.[84] Since its inception, photography was employed to document the history of place. The Alinari brothers of Florence photographed not only their own city, but also the ruins of Rome and the monuments of Pisa and Sienna.[85] By the early part of the last century, the increasing importance of travel photography came into being. Although always a staple of historical discourse, it matured to a new level of sophistication.[86]

The idea or concept of taking a photograph of people or of a place gradually evolved into a stand-in for actually 'being there.' The photograph, with its sterile potency, its stark reality and its apparent verity, usurped reality and matured as a visual form of history in a very short period of time. The equating of photography and place and the photograph as evidence of history was well-enshrined by the middle of the nineteenth century. Although there were numerous scandals about veracity and pure objectivity, most observers accepted the photographs' offerings.

By the late 1920s and certainly by the 1930s, photographs were being recognized as a powerful way of documenting the culture that was being photographed. Even today, one often turns to the powerful and expressive work of Lewis Hine, Dorthea Lange or Ben Shahn to capture what life was like in the 1930s. The powerful images of industrialization, waste, and poverty still convey what their original intentions—often through the Roosevelt administration's New Deal programs—intended them to do.[87] They have become undisputed reminders of the past and in particular, of a specific era. These very weighty photographs carry the power and burden of history in a potent and authentic way. They become connections to that time in a manner that is literally unforgettable.[88] Dorthea Lange's "Migrant Mother" (1936) series of photographs became, according to Vicki Goldberg, "the canonical image of the Depression." Goldberg has written that photographs "easily acquire symbolic significance" because they "intensely and specifically represent their subjects." But they also transcend their subject and serve to "concentrate the hopes and fears of millions and provide an instant and effortless connection to some deeply meaningful moment in history."[89] If you want to understand what went on during the Great Depression, one only has to look at these photographs.

Along with the urban documentarians that trolled the cities of the early twentieth century—Hine, Steiglitz, Riis—the group of photographers employed by the Roosevelt administration's Farm Security Administration (FSA) project, headed by Roy Stryker, made unparalleled contributions to social welfare as well as to the capturing of a significant period of United States history. Beyond Dorthea Lange, Ben Shan, Arthur Rothstein, and importantly, Walker Evans created photographs that abound with historical resonance and which are overflowing with relevance in capturing the Depression and its consequences. Charged at first with the mission to capture workers "rather than the displaced poor," this group deviated from the established script and produced an unrivalled historical archive. Duplicating the work of the urban documentarians, these photographers created a potent story of rural strife, and disaffection.[90]

Robert Capa became synonymous with the idea of the photojournalist when his picture, "The Death of a Loyalist Soldier" was published in the October 1936 issue of the French picture magazine *Vu*.[91] This became an iconographic emblem for modern war and like Lange's "Migrant Mother" came to stand for the power of war as well as the power of photography to literally capture history. Michael Griffin has written that photographs become potent "markers of collective memory" because they connote in a concise format, "socially shared concepts or beliefs rather than present new or unfamiliar information."[92] This is an extremely important idea in the context of visual history. The photograph acts as a linkage between the private and public—historical—realms of memory. As well, photographs such as Capa's and others like the Vietnam photographs are such significant forms of history is that they become "mnemonic symbols," or "road signs" which prompt memory, encapsulate it as well as condense it.[93] To some extent, there is, as Umberto Eco has recognized, an element of self-referentiality to this process. This stems from the fact that images in some way or form refer back to something that one is familiar with.[94] Michael Griffin is adamant about this connection between memory and the images that we see. He feels that "we mark memories with relatively simple, predictable images." What makes this possible according to him is the dependence upon myths. Related to this, is the fact that photographs, press photographs and in particular, war photography, become "narrative emblems" which are dependent upon the myths of particular societies.[95]

The Vietnam War is often singled out as a moving image or television war. Yet, as Marianne Fulton has observed, "many of the most important images of the Vietnam War were single, often wire-service, photographs." She cites Nick Ut's photograph of the children running, the often reproduced Eddie Adams photograph of an execution, and John Filo's picture at Kent state.[96] What this suggests is that even in a period of time when speed and movement matter, the photograph carries, often, unparalleled historical resonance.

Specifically, what may matter most, is the innate human desire to slow things down, sometimes, "to take a closer look" to stop "the world at that moment of history" and to let us get on,[97] something seemingly contrary to the speed and movement of contemporary society. This intimates much about the continuing importance of the photograph.

The famous photo of Nixon and Khrushchev looking at an American kitchen in the middle of Moscow alleges a lot about the history of the cold war.[98] The image of Lee Harvey Oswald speaks volumes about the history of many things. And when we see them, twenty, thirty, or forty years after the fact we do not necessarily view them with the shock or surprise that we first brought to our first viewing. We see them through the lenses of our personal perspectives of history or else the filters of another. At the heart of the power of the photograph, from the 1940s until the early 1960s was *Life* magazine, which had, during its heyday, a circulation of twenty million. Until the American television networks expanded their news divisions, *Life*, according to Wendy Kozol, "was the main source of visual news for Americans," during this period. Kozol suggests that *Life*'s utilization of codes of realism merged neatly with Benedict Anderson's notion of "imagined communities" in that people were brought together and in turn, began to share a common sense of news and culture. *Life*'s photographs defined the post-war period and to a great extent still serve as the visual history of that era.[99]

As an historical messenger, the photograph has the power to alter, restore, reaffirm and even change the historical record. In the Fall 1991 issue of *American Photo*, the importance of photojournalism in the age of television is still emphasized. According to the editors, "The photographs on the pages that follow represent only the briefest instants of history. But the scenes they record . . . confront us with something unforgettable. Pictures like these hold the world up for us to view in wonder and in horror. The view can change us. To believe that photography possesses the power to make a difference is to believe in the power of truth."[100] In an Autumn 2002 issue of *American Photo*, the same themes are played out again. The cover commentary reiterates the relationship of photography to history.

To a capacious degree, the above is true. In the days following 9/11, one could make the argument that photography did in fact encapsulate history in a way it had only done periodically in the previous ten years. Photography even went beyond the traditional obligations of historical discourse in its role as a time stop medium. As Barbie Zelizer writes,

> Photography, it was widely claimed, rose to fill the space of chaos and confusion that journalism was expected to render orderly. Photographs in the popular press helped register—and counter—the disbelief in which people the world over found themselves lodged, and the frequent, systematic, and repetitive circulation of photographic images—in newspapers, news magazines, and eventually year-end reviews and commemorative volumes—created a place in which the public could see and continue to see the core visual representations of an event that seemed to buckle under existing interpretive schemes.[101]

Zelizer contends that photographic and, in general, visual discourse, was essential in allowing people to make sense of the catastrophic events, and allow them the luxury of space and pace necessary for healing contemplation. At the same time and perhaps paradoxically, the plethora of images unleashed in the aftermath of 9/11 and their incessant presence gave the impression of a photographic constant. Despite all the imagery, a few scenes seemed to stand out in photographic stillness. Whether this was the images frozen from television or video or the myriad visualizations from newspapers and magazines, their presence literally took hold of the moment.[102]

The issue of permanence and consistency, as well as access, is at the present, subject to a fair amount of discourse. Access to key historical photographs and contemporary interpretations of events is increasingly controlled by press agencies or image banks, such as Corbis and Getty. In order to reproduce the images within the control of these private corporations, permission and payment are in order. Many feel that this corporate control will lessen access as well as reduce attempts to seek out more experimental approaches.[103] The second issue, which has to do with permanence and consistency, is very similar to factors influencing the book and print culture.

In the not too recent past, photographers took rolls and rolls of film and shot multiple pictures. What was used was displayed, while the rest of the photographs, film, and negatives were kept in some form of archive. With the arrival of digital cameras, the higher the resolution, the less space available to take more photographs. Consequently not only are fewer pictures being taken but the technology allows for complete erasure of the non-used portions. Thus, little or no historical archive remains.[104]

The interplay between news and documentation also has to be recognized in the public's desire for photographs of the famous. Nothing is as popular as a magazine with pictures of a famous celebrity. The role that photography and photojournalism had been increasingly backed into was a traditional one which focused on individual's and the singular event. In particular, the plethora of magazines—*People, In Style, Vanity Fair*—that gave detailed exposure to famous people seemed to have become a substantial element of the role of photography.

This staple has since, made the transition from the cinema to TV. As Carlyle recognized in the nineteenth century and Leo Lowenthal and others have constantly restated and complained, the famous person, whether through biography or photograph, comes to stand for an historical epoch. The photograph resonates with clarity because of its potent stillness. The famous—Teddy Roosevelt, Freud, Albert Schweitzer, Churchill—are frozen into the consciousness of viewers in that pose.[105] The photograph triggers the memory of where and when, with whom and how. They become symbols or signs for the past. One of the ways that people see the past is through famous people. This notion quickly came to blur into celebrity.

NOTES

1. Christian Meier, *From Athens to Auschwitz: The Uses of History*, Translated by Deborah Lucas Schneider, (Cambridge, MA: Harvard University Press, 2005), p. 23.

2. Vicki Goldberg, *The Power of Photography: How Photographs Changed Our Lives*, (New York: Abbeville Publishing Group, 1991), p. 7.

3. Richard Bolton, "Introduction: The Contest of Meaning: Critical Histories of Photography," in Richard Bolton, ed., *The Contest of Meaning: Critical Histories of Photography*, (Boston: MIT Press, 1993), p. xiii.

4. Jessica Helfand, *Screen: Essays on Graphic Design, New Media, and Visual Culture*, (Princeton, NJ: Princeton Architectural Press, 2001), p. 132.

5. Susan Sontag, "Looking at War: Photography's View of Devastation and Death," *The New Yorker*, December 9, 2002, p. 87.

6. Hanno Hardt and Bonnie Brennen, "Newswork, History, And Photographic Evidence: A Visual Analysis of a 1930s Newsroom," in *Picturing the Past: Media, History and Photography*, edited by Bonnie Brennen and Hanno Hardt, (Urbana, IL: University of Illinois Press, 1999), p.15.

7. Howard Chapnick, "Foreword," to Marianne Fulton, *Eyes of Time: Photojournalism in America*, (Boston: Little Brown and Company, 1988), p. xii.

8. Alan Trachtenberg, *Reading American Photographs: Images as History— Mathew Brady to Walker Evans*, (New York: Hill and Wang/FSG, 1989), p. xiv.

9. Wright Morris, *Time Pieces: Photographs, Writing and Memory*, (New York: Aperture Foundation, Inc., 1989), p. 7.

10. Wright Morris, *Time Pieces: Photographs, Writing and Memory*, p. 17.

11. Alan Mintz, *Popular Culture and the Shaping of Holocaust Memory in America*, (Seattle: University of Washington Press, 2001), p. 30.

12. In Daniel Mendelsohn's *The Lost: A Search for Six of Six Million*, (New York: HarperCollins, 2006), he makes the point that we have a tendency to rely perhaps too heavily on the photograph: "How casually we rely on photographs, really; how lazy we have become because of them. What does your mother look like? Someone will want to know; and you'll say, Wait, I'll show you, and run to a drawer or an album and say, Here she is. But what if you had no photographs of your mother, or anyone in your family—indeed, even of yourself before a certain age? How would you explain what she, they, you, looked like?" p. 182.

13. Afsun Qureshi, "One Moment, Lasting Forever," *The Saturday Post*, December 29, 2001, pp. SP1, SP3.

14. Martin Lister, "Introductory Essay," in *The Photographic Image in Digital Culture*, Martin Lister, ed., (New York: Routledge, 1995), p. 4.

15. Cited in Vicki Goldberg, *The Power of Photography*, p. 34.

16. James B. Twitchell, *Lead Us Into Temptation: The Triumph of American Materialism*, (New York: Oxford University Press, 1999), p. 102.

17. Vicki Goldberg, *The Power of Photography*, p. 34.

18. Hanno Hardt and Bonnie Brennen, "Introduction," *Picturing the Past: Media, History and Photography*, eds., Bonnie Brennen and Hanno Hardt, p. 2.

19. Robert M. Poole, *Explorers House: National Geographic and the World it Made*, (New York: Penguin, 2004), pp. 66–67. For a dissenting view that suggests the *Geographic* was and is bound by conservative colonial objectives, see Catherine A. Lutz and Jane L. Collins, *Reading National Geographic*, (Chicago: University of Chicago Press, 1993).

20. Hanno Hardt and Bonnie Brennen, "Introduction," *Picturing the Past: Media, History and Photography*, p. 2.

21. Vicki Goldberg, *The Power of Photography*, p. 34.

22. Vicki Goldberg, *The Power of Photography*, p. 41. On p. 135, Goldberg writes, "The photograph is a highly efficient means of cultural communication; it has the advantages of credibility, easy mass distribution and instant convertibility into a symbol. Since visual imagery is more readily abstracted than sensations of touch, smell, sound, or taste, the mind is accustomed to using images as ideas (which is apparently what happens in dreams). People cherish photographs, and the culture relies ever more heavily on them, in part because they are so readily converted."

23. On the connections between the photograph, reality and "truth," see Andre Bazin, "The Ontology of the Photographic Image," in *What Is Cinema?*, Selected and Translated by Hugh Gray, (Berkeley, CA: University of California Press, 1967).

24. Don Stater, "Photography and Modern Vision: The Spectacle of 'Natural Magic'," in Chris Jenks, ed., *Visual Culture*, (New York: Taylor & Francis, 1995), pp. 219–20.

25. Steve Shapin, *The Scientific Revolution*, (Chicago: University of Chicago Press, 1996).

26. Alan Tractenberg, *Reading American Photographs*, p. xiv.

27. John Berger, "Problems in Socialist Art," in Lee Baxandall, ed., *Radical Perspectives in the Arts*, (London: Penguin, 1972), p. 218, and Robert Hughes, *The Shock of The New*, (New York: Knopf, 1981), p. 81.

28. Edgar Wind, "The Revolution of History Painting," in Harold Spencer, ed., *Readings in Art History*, Second Edition, vol. 2: The Renaissance to the Present,

(New York: Scribners, 1976), and Anne Hollander, *Moving Pictures*, (New York: Alfred Knopf, 1989).

29. Susan Sontag, *On Photography*, (New York: Farrar, Strauss, Giroux, 1978), p. 42.

30. Walter Benjamin, "The Work of Art in the Age of Mechanical Reproduction," in *Illuminations*, Hannah Arendt, ed., (New York: Schocken Books, 1969), p. 131.

31. John Berger, *About Looking*, (New York: Pantheon, 1980), p. 50.

32. Hanno Hardt and Bonnie Brennen, "Introduction," *Picturing the Past: Media, History and Photography*, pp. 4, 7.

33. Gore Vidal, *Screening History*, (Cambridge, MA.: Harvard University Press, 1994).

34. Robert Hughes, *The Shock of The New*, p. 325.

35. Walter Benjamim, "The Work of Art," in *Illuminations*, p. 220.

36. Gisele Freund, *Photography and Society*, (Boston: David R. Godine Publishers, 1980), p. 9.

37. Gary Gumpert, *Talking Tombstones & Other Tales of the Media Age*, (New York: Oxford University Press, 1987), p. 21.

38. Gisele Freund, *Photography and Society*, p. 95.

39. Gisele Freund, *Photography and Society*, pp. 95–96.

40. John Berger, *Ways of Seeing*, (London: Penguin/BBC, 1972), p. 11.

41. Susan Sontag, *On Photography*, p. 76.

42. Michael Langford, *The Story of Photography*, (London: Focal Press, 1980), p. 103.

43. John Berger, *Ways of Seeing*, p. 19.

44. Sontag, *On Photography*, p. 147.

45. Stuart Ewen, *All Consuming Images*, (New York: Basic Books, 1988), p. 75.

46. Harold Rosenberg, "The Mona Lisa Without the Mustache: Art in the Media Age," in Rosenberg, *Art & Other Serious Matters*, (Chicago: University of Chicago Press, 1985), pp. 3–4.

47. Hughes, *The Shock of The New*, p. 325.

48. Rosenberg, "The Mona Lisa," pp. 4–6.

49. Martin Jay, *Adorno*, (Cambridge, MA: Harvard University Press, 1984), pp. 123–24 and Richard Wolin, *An Aesthetic of Redemption*, (New York: Columbia University Press, 1984), p. 188.

50. Geoff Dyer, *Ways of Telling*, (London: Pluto Press, 1986), p. 95.

51. Richard Wolin, *An Aesthetic*, p. 188.

52. Joel Snyder, "Benjamin and Reproducibility and Aura," *The Philosophical Forum*, vol. XV, nos. 101–102, F/W, 1983–1984, p. 107.

53. Joel Snyder, "Benjamin and Reproducibility," p. 135.

54. Jennifer Todd, "Production, Reception, Criticism: Walter Benjamin and the Problem of Meaning in Art," *The Philosophical Forum*, vol. XV, nos. 101–102, F/W 1983–1984, pp. 107–08.

55. Pauline Johnson, *Marxist Aesthetics*, (London: Routledge and Kegan Paul, 1984), pp. 58–59, and Martin Jay, *Adorno*, p. 126.

56. Jennifer Todd, "Production, Reception, Criticism: Walter Benjamin and the Problem of Meaning in Art," pp. 107–08, and Walter Benjamin, "The Work of Art," in *Illuminations*, pp. 220–21.

57. Daniel Boorstin, *The Image: A Guide to Pseudo-Events in America*, (New York: Antheneum, 1971), pp. 10, Andrew Arato et al., *The Essential Frankfurt School Reader*, (New York: Urizen Books, 1978), p. 209, Robin Ridless, *Ideology and Art*, (New York: Peter Lang, 1984), pp. 4, 94.

58. John Walker, *Art in the Age of Mass Media*, (London: Pluto Press, 1983), p. 70.

59. Stuart Ewen, *All Consuming Images*, (New York: Basic Books, 1988), p. 38.

60. Graham Clarke, in *The Photograph* (New York: Oxford University Press, 1997), p. 12, writes, "The act of taking a photograph fixes time, but it also steals time, establishes a hold on the past in which history is sealed, so to speak, in a continuous present."

61. Hanno Hardt and Bonnie Brennen, "Newswork, History, And Photographic Evidence: A Visual Analysis of a 1930s Newsroom," in *Picturing the Past: Media, History and Photography*, p. 23.

62. Roland Marchand, *Advertising the American Dream: Making Way for Modernity, 1920–1940*, (Berkeley, CA: University of California Press, 1986), p. 150.

63. Roland Marchand, *Advertising the American Dream*, p. 150.

64. Neil Postman, *Amusing Ourselves to Death*, (New York: Penguin, 1985), p. 74.

65. Graham Clarke, *The Photograph*, p. 18. Clarke writes about the inexpensive cost of the pocket Kodak camera, which came out in 1895 and which in turn, facilitated the ready acceptance of picture taking and picture perceiving.

66. As Lewis Mumford writes in *Technics and Civilization*, p. 339: "The mission of the photograph is to clarify the object. This objectification, this clarification, are important developments in the mind itself: it is perhaps the prime psychological fact that emerges with our rational assimilation of the machine."

67. Graham Clarke, *The Photograph*, pp. 23, 28, 145–46.

68. Peter Burke, *Eyewitnessing*, p. 148.

69. William Stapp, "'Subjects of Strange . . . And of Fearful Interest': Photojournalism from Its Beginnings in 1839," in Marianne Fulton, *Eyes of Time: Photojournalism in America*, p. 15.

70. Hubertus von Amelunxen, "The Century's Memorial: Photography and the recording of history" in Michel Frizot, ed., *A New History of Photography*, (Cologne: Konemann, 1998), p. 143.

71. Richard Schickel, *Intimate Strangers: The Culture of Celebrity*, (New York: International Publishers, 1986), p. 70.

72. William Stapp, "'Subjects of Strange . . . And of Fearful Interest': Photojournalism from Its Beginnings in 1839," p. 16.

73. William Stapp, "'Subjects of Strange . . . And of Fearful Interest': Photojournalism from Its Beginnings in 1839," p. 16.

74. Alan Trachtenberg, *Reading American Photographs*, p. 73.

75. Alan Trachtenberg, *Reading American Photographs*, pp. 85–86.

76. Fred Ritchin, "Close Witnesses: The Involvement of the Photojournalist," in Frizot, ed., *A New History of Photography*, p. 591. Susan Sontag writes, "The ultra-familiar, ultra-celebrated image—of an agony, or ruin—is an unavoidable feature of our camera-mediated knowledge of war." "Looking At War," p. 87.

77. Fred Ritchin, "Close Witnesses," p. 591.

78. Jonathan Marwil, "Photography at War," *History Today*, vol. 50, no. 6, June 2000, p. 30.

79. William Stapp, "'Subjects of Strange . . . And of Fearful Interest': Photojournalism from Its Beginnings in 1839," p. 17.

80. Jonathan Marwil, "Photography at War," pp. 32–34.

81. Jean-Luc Daval, *Photography: History of an Art*, (New York: Rizzoli International Publications, 1982), p. 59.

82. Alan Tractenberg, *Reading American Photographs*, p. 6.

83. Derrick Price and Liz Wells, "Thinking About Photography," in Liz Wells, ed., *Photography: A Critical Introduction*, Second Edition, (London/New York: Routledge, 2000), p. 53.

84. Estelle Jussim, "'The Tyranny of the Pictorial': American Photojournalism from 1880 to 1920," in Marianne Fulton, *Eyes of Time: Photojournalism in America*, p. 58.

85. Arturo Carlo Quitavalle, *Fratelli Alinari, Photographers In Florence: 150 years of picturing the world, 1852–2002*, Guide to the Exhibition, Florence 2002, pp. 3–8.

86. Colin Osman and Sandra S. Phillips, "European Visions: Magazine Photography in Europe between the Wars," in Marianne Fulton, *Eyes of Time: Photojournalism in America*, p. 87.

87. Jean-Luc Daval, *Photography: History of an Art*, pp. 185–86.

88. Looking at the photographs of Hine and others from the 1930s is best explained, historically, by a passage from Leah Hager Cohen's *Glass, Paper, Beans: Revelations on the Nature and Value of Ordinary Things*, (New York: Doubleday/Currency, 1997), p. 68: "Even when history is two parts fancy, it carries the patina of being something real, and fixed, and weighty, in the way that things having occurred in the past seem naturally to heft about extra bulk. History lends force of gravity, knots one event to another, ensures connections, explanation, rationale.

89. Vicki Goldberg, *The Power of Photography*, pp. 135–36.

90. Derrick Price, "Surveyors and Surveyed," in *Photography: A Critical Introduction*, Second Edition, Ed., by Liz Wells, (New York: Routledge, 2000), pp. 94–97.

91. Michael Griffin, "The Great War Photographs: Constructing Myths of History and Photojournalism," in *Picturing the Past*, p. 137.

92. Michael Griffin, "The Great War Photographs: Constructing Myths of History and Photojournalism," in *Picturing the Past*, p. 147.

93. Michael Griffin, "The Great War Photographs: Constructing Myths of History and Photojournalism," in *Picturing the Past*, p. 147.

94. Umberto Eco, "A Photograph," in *Travels in Hyperreality*, 1986, p. 216, cited in Michael Griffin, "The Great War Photographs: Constructing Myths of History and Photojournalism," in *Picturing the Past*, p. 147.

95. Michael Griffin, "The Great War Photographs: Constructing Myths of History and Photojournalism," in *Picturing the Past*, pp. 147–48.

96. Marianne Fulton, "Changing Focus: The 1950s to the 1980s," in Marianne Fulton, *Eyes of Time*, pp. 213–19.

97. William Safire, "Standing History Still: A Prolegomenon," in Peter Galassi and Susan Kismaric, eds., *Pictures of the Times: A Century of Photography from The New York Times*, (New York: The Museum of Modern Art/Harry N. Abrams, Inc., 1996), p. 12.

98. Here is Stephen J. Whitfield's and Thomas Hine's observations on this "event," from *The Culture of the Cold War* (Baltimore: The Johns Hopkins University Press, 1991), p. 75, "The American journalists flocking around the exhibition did

not pause to analyze Khrushchev's anger at competition in both defense hardware and domestic software. It was much more photogenic to show the two politicians fiercely jabbing fingers at one another, and many Americans were reassured that the vice-president had stood tall against the Soviet ruler's bare-knuckle intimidation. With an election coming up, the news photos were raw meat hurled at Nixon's carnivorous constituents from one of the triumphant institutions of capitalism: the middle-class suburban home. 'The images that resulted were very powerful, largely because they seemed to confirm what many Americans believed,' Thomas Hine concluded. 'The way they lived, with their comforts and conveniences, was shown as an essential part of the American way of life. Not only was it worth defending, but it was a defense in itself because its richness challenged every other political system . . . to do the same for its citizenry.'"

99. Wendy Kozol, "'Good Americans': Nationalism and Domesticity in *LIFE* Magazine, 1945–1960," in John Bodnar, ed., *Bonds of Affection: Americans Define Their Patriotism*, (Princeton: Princeton University Press, 1996), pp. 232–33.

100. *American Photo*, September/October 1991, vol. II, no. 5, p. 49.

101. Barbie Zelizer, "Photography, Journalism and Trauma," in Barbie Zelizer and Stuart Allen, eds., *Journalism After September 11*, (New York: Routledge, 2002), p. 48.

102. Barbie Zelizer, "Photography, Journalism and Trauma," pp. 49–50.

103. Larry Gross, John Stuart Katz, and Jay Ruby, "Introduction: Image Ethics in the Digital Age," in Larry Gross, John Stuart Katz, and Jay Ruby, Editors, *Image Ethics in the Digital Age*, (Minneapolis: University of Minnesota Press, 2003), p. xix.

104. David D. Perlmutter, "The Internet: Big Pictures and Interactors," in Larry Gross, John Stuart Katz, and Jay Ruby, eds., *Image Ethics in the Digital Age*, (Minneapolis, MN: University of Minnesota Press, 2003), p. 18.

105. According to Clive James, *Fame in the 20th Century*, (New York: Random House, 1993), p. 29: "Teddy Roosevelt started his build up to the Presidency by gleefully cooperating with any printed organ which would run his photograph."

5

Visions of the Past:
Film and History

I think many historians come at filmmakers with attitude and hostility.
It is as though history is their territory, and we don't belong. We just
pervert the paradigm with emotion, sentimentality, and so on.

—Oliver Stone, *Past Imperfect: History According to The Movies*, 305

Besides making the large and tangible visions of the past available for movie goers, films have had the capacity to restructure how a viewer sees various portions of historical recreation and interpretation. As well, moving pictures that depict newsworthy scenes often become forms of very potent historical interpretation and access points in the way the past is seen. Film has the unique capacity to emphasize individuals as historical actors and bring the humanity of history to light, in other words to make history come alive. This is why so many viewers have blurred distinctions between the real Abraham Lincoln for example and a talented actor playing a role. The humanizing of historical discourse through the use of film has its origins in a number of developments. One of the most interesting is the rise of the individual film actor or personality.

The rise of celebrity is a consequence of the merging of cinema, photography, and photojournalism. It hinges on the creation of a cinematic invention, the close-up. Employed first by director D. W. Griffith as a means to change the pace of film narrative, the close-up became the primary method of conveying emotions by focusing on the face of the actor which in turn, raised enquiries about that person. The film going audience began to see that face repeatedly and instead of passing into oblivion, the actor's face became an obsession. People expressed interest in the person—the

125

face—acting in specific films. The photo magazines or fan magazines were launched to provide information about these actors. The actors were transformed into stars.[1]

A vicious circle or more aptly, a dialectic emerged. Stars played roles and their pictures circulated as stills and in movies. Since the advent of film, one of the most common ways of dealing with historical subject matter on film has been to resuscitate the Great Man/Person version of history. According to Robert Brent Toplin, using one person's achievements as shorthand for the historical process seems to be a way to both "strengthen audience interest in the story and to simplify the details of a complex situation."[2]

Biopics are well-suited to this approach. Hollywood produced many through the years and they have come back in fashion. It is easier for the audience to deal with history through the eyes of one individual, than to process it via the messy complexities of the past. This tactic, allows history to be reduced to a personal level. The viewer experiences history through the eyes of heroes, toward whom the audience is sympathetic.[3] There is a precedent for this. We might find its origins all the way back in the epics and dramas written and performed by the Greeks, but the staged historical biography matured and flowered during the heyday of the Elizabethan theatre. With the larger, outdoor arenas, the type of performance that brought in the crowds and that kept the people focused was oriented around action derived from historical figures such as "Tamburlaine, Faustus, and Hieronimo, the hero of The Spanish tragedy." These "powerful personalities" turned on action-oriented plots that spoke to the interests of the audience and entertained with a focus on war, which involved swordplay, drums, and noise.[4]

Hollywood has a particular "genius" for producing these heroic icons out of average or mundane individuals. And this is meant to apply both in the choice of heroic subject as well as the actor chosen to portray that individual.[5] When one "visualizes" in the mind's eye certain historical personages, we see the Hollywood actor chosen to stand in for that person: John Wayne as Genghis Khan or Charlton Heston as Moses. This reinforces the notion that knowledge of history comes from filmed versions, in this case, film biography.[6] The heyday of the biopic was the long stretch of time from the beginning of the motion picture until the early 1950s. The history and biography presented in these films—for example, *The Life of Emile Zola*, "played," according to George F. Custen, "a powerful part in creating and sustaining public history." The events and people depicted in these films "provided many viewers with the version of a life that they held to be the truth."[7]

Filmed versions of history or historical subjects developed as a result of the massive interest that film generated almost immediately from its inception. According to Bruce Chadwick, by the early years of the past century, Americans were seeing at least one film a week and by the Depression, many went to two. Chadwick feels that people saw history and believed it because many of the studios were marketing their films as rigorously researched documents. This ushered in and even cemented the notion that filmed history was accurate to the point, related in contemporary terms by Chadwick, that even though the Academy Award winning film, *Life Is Beautiful* tells audiences that the film is a "fable" most people who saw the film thought it was a true story. Chadwick makes the distinction that what they were seeing was "cinema history" as opposed to academic history.[8]

Historical films gravitated to genuine subject matter in a variety of guises to 'educate' the audiences. This ranged from travelogues and pseudo-documentary imagery to outright historical drama.[9] With the Spanish American War, the film, even in its very early stages, came to give audiences a version of live history that rivaled newspapers. The idea of a "visual newspaper" came to the fore, complete with powerful propagandistic and narrative elements.[10] Turn of the century battle films, and more accurately, reenactment films of famous or recent martial events proved to be both popular and "educational." Citing Richard Abel, Kristen Whissel quotes, that there wasn't much of a difference between "recording a current public event as it was happening and reconstructing a past (or even present) event in a studio."[11] Films based upon historical subject matter or historical fiction proved popular with audiences. In 1911, the Italian produced, *The Fall of Troy* was released by the Sales Company and was shown in conjunction with high school history courses in the Washington DC area.[12]

History on film is quite new in comparison to traditional written history. As Natalie Zemon Davis has written, "Film is only beginning to find its way as a medium for history."[13] Focusing on the biography and on an analysis of some small kernel of history—or "microhistory" is still the dominant approach.[14] More often than not, historical films still have a tendency to delve into the action adventure format in order to reach audiences. The adventure as history format intermingles fact and fiction and for the most part, never attempts to explain this convergence. If we label it as entertainment, it does not have that responsibility. Historical adventure films are not required to stand up to the scrupulous examination of professional historians.[15] The historical situations that were the fodder for the great adventure films of the 1920s to the 1970s were based more on what William McNeill calls "Mythistory" or popular history, than on rigorous analytic and objective history.[16] Attempts to film history "objectively" only started to influence filmed history since the late 1980s.

During the Second World War the visual industry matured—at least within the United States. According to Thomas Doherty's study of film

and American culture, this transition to "an impressionistic motion picture world" had been "percolating" since the days of early cinema. "In
1941–45," writes Doherty, "a linear, bookbound mentality was displaced
by a movie-mediated vision. Moving images became the new alphabet,
the hieroglyphics of meaning and memory for American culture."[17] What
is significant, as Doherty argues, is that film, used to entertain, to propa-
gandize and to explain a variety of issues, suddenly came to be seen as a
key historical transference point. During the war, the film entered the
American classroom as a surrogate for traditional forms of education.
Films could instruct and provide a window on a host of issues. The re-
liance on the visual now entered the classroom. As Doherty writes,

> In postwar America few high schools, commercial businesses, and civic or
> church groups were so backward as to be without a 16mm projector and a
> shelf of government-made educational films. Hollywood chalked up what it
> called "the celluloid blackboard" as one of its main wartime contributions.[18]

American mass culture has always been enormously powerful, affecting
not just native attitudes about history, culture, and society, but also, foreign viewers and their perceptions.[19] Hollywood had been particularly
aggressive in providing a multitude of takes on the past. Peter Rollins
suggests that "Hollywood's myths and symbols are permanent features
of America's historical consciousness."[20] For many who grew up watching film in the theatre or on TV, what constitutes historical information
has in fact come from the dream factories of Hollywood.

The merging of film and history was often, as has been stated, the result
of Hollywood and other entities marketing film as a form of education
about history. Many film makers and producers as well as writers chose
to define history through the visual nature of film. Roberto Rosellini was
quite overt in his intention to use film's didactic potential as a way to educate as many people as possible. Rosellini was conscious of the fact that
through historical film—*Louis XIV*, *The Age of Iron*—one could achieve the
often cited maxim of print history, that through an understanding of history one could understand the present.[21] In 1965, the Western, *Shenandoah*
was marketed as a true depiction of the real West. Classroom study
guides were mailed out to schools and the authenticity of the research that
went into the film was emphasized, attempting to legitimize the film as a
historical text.[22]

Yet, films that deal with history remain "interpretations."[23] They are either a Hollywood producer/director/writer's version of events or in the
case of many documentaries, professional historian's rendering. Although
more often than books, these works involve multiple people in their creation, they nonetheless originate in an attempt to put onto screen some-

one's particular interests, biases, and viewpoints. Like a book written by a single author the story in a film comes from a specific perspective that despite attempting to strive for objectivity, has a definite origin.

One can not simply dismiss film as fatuous especially given the hyper-visuality of today's society. Even if we have absolutely no intention of gleaning any information, of learning anything at all or of becoming informed, movies provide data and can function as some kind of pedagogic tool. According to bell hooks,

> Most of us go to movies to enter a world that is different from the one we know and are most comfortable with. And even though most folks will say that they go to movies to be entertained, if the truth be told, lots of us, myself included, go to learn stuff.[24]

This is especially and singularly applied to the past. As Robert A. Rosenstone has observed, "Today, the chief source of historical knowledge for the majority of the population—outside of the much despised textbook—must surely be the visual media, a set of institutions that lie almost wholly outside the control of us who devote our lives to history. Any reasonable extrapolation suggests that trend will continue."[25] Ian Jarvie though, finds film too deficient in content to convey the complexities of the past. He writes that "there is no way to do meaningful history on film."[26] Tom O'Brien, while respecting the place of film as an "agent of modernism" feels that films "foster visual appetite, limit attention span, and decrease the allure of books."[27] O'Brien goes further to lament the fact that within the United States, "'history'—once linked to prestige, tradition, authority—now mostly seems to suggest only an obituary."[28] Like many of the Cassandra's trashing visual history, O'Brien feels that it will lead to a *"China Syndrome* of intellectual meltdown."[29] Part of the problem in *accepting* film as an historical document begins with the adoption of a comparative frame of reference. According to John O'Connor and Martin Jackson, films should be seen as unique "cultural documents rather than comparing them with traditional records and archival manuscripts."[30] This constant comparison reflects the bias of traditional historians and at the same time, refuses to acknowledge the glaring fact that so much of history comes from film and other visual sources.

What makes this debate significantly problematic is the fact that in many instances, film has been used to define and display history. The fact that many historians are hostile to filmic representations of the past obscures the fact that films of historical events are often quite effective in conveying the essence of history. Peter Burke has noted that it was the British newsreels that were often used as "a source for the history of the Spanish Civil War" and perhaps more significant, the film "taken by the

British army at Belsen in April 1945 was used as evidence at the Nuremberg trials."[31]

If theatre as an antecedent of film, especially early film, had a tendency to exclude accuracy in historical presentation, movies that have strived for accuracy of detail historically speaking, should be commended. It used to be that within the theater; the dramatic presentation of history was almost irrelevant and was seen to detract from the enactment of the play. No thought whatsoever was paid to "historical exactitude." Yet today, the wide swaths of film products strive to recreate history with historical relevance and exactitude.[32] It is perhaps important to distinguish here from what Marcia Landy calls the "costume drama" from the historical film. Landy feels that the historical film, attempts to portray a particular historical person or epoch with accuracy while the costume drama is a genre that takes enormous liberties, historically speaking and is more about romance than actual history. The key distinction for Landy is that the historical film is at least concerned with the semblance of history while the costume drama focuses on the settings, costumes, and trappings of the past as mere window dressings. They are in essence, appendages that are used to convey a feeling rather than construct a historical focus.[33]

Movies can and should be considered forms of historical evidence, both for what they show and tell and from where they originate. As with so much else in history, historical films not only provide a visual record of the subject, but shed light upon the place and time from which they came.[34] Studying the Third Reich, for example, is far more effective when using Leni Refensthal's propaganda.[35]

The Vietnam War film is a useful example of this process. These films not only provide a sense of history but inform in the direction of the politics of the era. It took a number of years before Hollywood produced mainstream films about Vietnam. The war had been such a touchstone of divisiveness that a time-cushion was required before presenting any kind of visual narrative. As Michael Anderegg comments:

> Unlike World War II, during which Hollywood, in a sense created its own war that ran parallel to, but seldom could be mistaken for, the real war, the Vietnam films were produced with sufficient distance from the war that they could reasonably be considered mediations on and explications of America's military and political involvement in Indochina.[36]

This cinematic distance qualifies some of these films as history in the fact that they were produced after the event and not, as in the case of World War II, "contemporaneous to the war."[37] One could also speculate that the power of certain films has been derived precisely from this distance. The prominence of the historical catharsis of the Vietnam War film has reached such a level, that the bumper sticker, "Vietnam was a War, Not a Movie," suggests the power of cinematic representations in framing discussions of the past.

The presentation of the Vietnam War via film was often filtered through the eyes of the soldier or grunt and it was from that perspective that the audience saw the conflict. The main concern with the reduction of history to the individual is that it makes the conflict a personal drama rather than an historical panorama. Yet, in keeping with accepted narrative structure, this is quite effective. Whether it is seen from the viewpoint of the returning Veteran, as in *Coming Home* (1978) and *Born on The Fourth of July* (1990), or from the eyes of a combatant; *Apocalypse Now* (1979) *Platoon* (1986), and *Full Metal Jacket* (1987), or from the viewpoint of the insulted and emotionally drained soldier, as in *First Blood* (1982), and *Rambo* (1987)[38] a powerful way to present the conflict in terms acceptable to an audience is to focus on the individual, who in turn, is molded into a hero.

It should also be recognized that this visual perspective creates a deliberate distance which acts as a barrier between the often painful content and the viewer. Building on the ideas of Marita Sturken, A. Susan Owen makes the point that most of the Vietnam films, and especially those by Oliver Stone, intentionally employ this approach to bifurcate the screen. The distance created suggests that the viewer or audience is firmly in the camp of the civilian noncombatant and is thus distanced from the cinematic and perhaps actual concepts of the war. Owen intimates that in Steven Spielberg's *Saving Private Ryan*, the reverse is true. Unlike the Stone films and other groundbreaking Vietnam movies, Spielberg places the viewer directly into the "action." She writes, "Spielberg sutures viewers into his story visually, calling upon them to witness with the prophets. This sort of constructed immediacy is immensely powerful." The experience, she continues, even in visual form, becomes part of collective historical knowledge.[39]

The main reason for this treatment is to present the conflict in terms that are harmonious with the Hollywood narrative and which also serve to pose answers for many viewers. What most critics fail to recognize is that it is virtually impossible to present the enormous complexity of the war in filmic terms and thus it is necessary to resort to the hero-as-stand-in as a suitable substitute.[40] Snippets and angles can be presented and the films can be used as foundations for further inquiry, not as definitive history. So vital is this to keep in mind that missing this point is obviously going to bring into play numerous inconsistencies. As Pat Aufderheide has written,

the search for acceptable heroes is also the search for an acceptable vision of Vietnam, one that allows for the empathic union of character and audience. (The movie industry, after all, is in the business to sell tickets, not critical history.) So these films arrange reality to fit the Hollywood grunt's perspective.[41]

What critics of the filmed image of history constantly fail to recognize is that film is the major repository of history for most people in the West. Not to put too fine a point on it, Bruce Taylor suggests that the Vietnam War has been taught at the movies.[42] Over three million Americans served in that War, yet for most, it resides in the frames of film.

Not a year goes by when there are not at least a few major feature film releases that have an important historical basis. Either this is direct, as in *Schindler's List* or peripheral and social, as in *A League of Their Own*. For the summer 2000 season, there was *U-571*, *Gladiator*, *The Patriot*, and *Texas Rangers*.[43] There is no guarantee that a film with a historical theme will be a success at the box office. Studios are aware that even marketing a film as an historical document can backfire. If the advertising is overly didactic and comes across as too heavy-handed, the audience will stay away. When one studio decided to market the 1983 feature, *The Right Stuff* as "a patriotic history less rather than an action-adventure," ticket sales suffered.[44] The recent spate of films from the summer of 2007—such as Clint Eastwood's endeavors, also follows this pattern. Being forced to see a movie for the history it provides or for the patriotic message it conveys or in lieu of proper pedagogical offerings, changes the way the film is perceived.

The potency of the visual image should not and cannot be written off in today's society and for that matter, in the near future. Image-based history can, as Anton Kaes, has noted, "render the past ever-present." Kaes, in his analyses of history and film, ascertains that what is presented on film does in fact shape "our perspective on the past," functioning as a "technological memory bank" that "supercedes memory and experience."[45] The simple fact is that filmed history as popular or even collective history has more clout and more impact than traditional academic history, especially with high-school and college aged viewers. Whether it is a form of history based on a novel and then turned into a film or an original script, the influence of celluloid based history is vast.[46]

One can argue that film can make the past come alive in a much more visceral way than a book. This is not to say that it is fundamentally superior, but to suggest that film has the capacity to reach and affect students in ways that traditional forms of history cannot. John O'Connor uses films to grand effect in his classes. In particular, *The Return of Martin Guerre* (1982), based on the book by Natalie Zemon Davis, is, according to O'Connor, extraordinarily useful in getting a variety of historical elements across. What is important, writes O'Connor, is that by

> withholding key pieces of information until the very end, the film transforms history into an engaging mystery that never fails to capture students' atten-

tion. What is key, however, is less the entertainment value of the story than the historical context which is filled out so expertly.[47]

O'Connor and Davis, both recognize how history has come alive in the film, despite some concessions to a 1980s audience. The medieval flavor of the town, the "role of women" and the role of institutions such as the church, all stand out in ways that the same issues would not in a book. O'Connor feels that this is what the students take away, in essence, what they will remember.[48] The visual richness that can be created within a film often has the greatest effect on people and ultimately, enhances the learning process and gives the student something tangible in *their* language to take away. One must bear in mind that O'Connor utilizes film in conjunction with written texts—not as solitary visual objects.

One cannot and should not lose sight of the fact that the film can perpetuate distortions and even outright falsehoods. While printed texts can do the same, the audience is much smaller for history books and the multiplicity of viewpoints prevents the dominance of one perspective. The image of the American south, for example as Edward Campbell has noted, is primarily derived from the constant repetition of film mythology, which not only forms part of the "audience's education" but has the result of making the make-believe, believed.[49]

One of the many problems of historical knowledge presented on film is that, not everything worth knowing has been filmed. Not every nuance is on film and when using film to teach history there is, "a danger that reliance on exciting visuals may distort the curriculum."[50] The point made in the introduction about why we know so much about the American West—cowboys—is just such a problem. It was deemed or reworked to be exciting and thus, made excellent topics for 'historical' film. A significant illustration of this comes from the pervasiveness of war as a subject for film. No other genre has been so equated with history as the war film. There are numerous variations and many different manifestations. These run the gamut from *Wings* to *All Quiet on The Western Front* to *The Rules of the Game* to *Judgement at Nuremberg*, all the way up to *Saving Private Ryan and Three Kings*. While many of these movies serve as useful starting points for an analysis of historical themes and events, many also serve as wonderful recreations. War, has been a staple genre for many reasons. There is conflict, drama, action, and there is in general enough movement to capture the viewers' interests. It can be visceral or intellectual. But the war film, in virtually any manifestation, can erase distinctions between fiction and fact. The case of the documentary war film is even more telling. According to Alan Rosenthal, one reason, among many, that makes the war film, in this case, the documentary war film, such a popular offering is that "by showing human conflict at its most extreme," the result is a situation that is absolutely riveting for the audience. Even the documentary in this instance abides by the rules of drama.[51]

Before Ken Burns rose to prominence, Rosenthal edited a collection of essays on the state and future of documentary filmmaking. Rosenthal argued that there was a clear-cut reality with regard to the documentary: it was the main avenue for learning about the past in the visual age. In fact, he went so far as to write that the documentary is probably the "only serious access people have to history once they have left school."[52] Yet he was cautious not to laud the sanctity of the documentary too strongly, or at least, without recognizing its faults. In one interesting section he questioned how one was to handle subjects that did not have access to photographs or film? This was, in the pre-Ken Burns days. He listed the obvious: prints, reconstructions, sites, and location shooting, but was quick to warn that this requires an imaginative leap on behalf of the viewer that was not always successful.[53] But what was unique about Rosenthal's ponderings was his discussion of archival footage.

Rosenthal claimed that archival footage is the inspiration and elixir for the filmmaker. It is the essence of the film, the historical validation, but at the same time, when not used properly, "provided little insight into the deeper meaning of the events." And this improper use meant misuse and misappropriation. Stock archival footage that was of nebulous origin could be substituted for a variety of eras if it was close enough in resemblance. Another problem was the fact that this kind of "raw data" was often shot with a specific intention in mind and under a very specific set of circumstances. When appropriated and used by film—makers for other contexts, a great disservice is done. Recognizing this fact was a significant breakthrough.[54]

The rendering of history onto film is fraught with numerous problems. As the quote from Namier in an earlier chapter suggested, popular and entertaining history is often assumed to be erroneous, full of distortions and misrepresentations. In contrast, history that is too factual is often thought to be dull despite the fact that a tremendous amount of research and preparation goes into the production.[55] Even Hollywood history entails a substantial amount of research. The period films and the biopics produced by the studio system were often intensely researched. The same could be said for the British studio films. Libraries were consulted, (Warner Brothers' alone contained ten thousand volumes), costume experts brought in and of course, historians were solicited to give advice.[56] But it is vital to keep in mind, as Hayden White has argued, that the production of visual history is quite different from the production of traditional academic history. One is dealing, first and foremost, with a mass audience, not a few hundred undergraduates or half-dozen graduate students.[57] Accordingly those who are often going to be viewing visual history are not doing so in the same environment or often with the same set of expectations that have traditionally accompanied the presentation of history. As Jerry Kuehl writes, "they are not a captive audience in the sense that a university class or seminar is."[58] The obverse of this is that to many, history is found in film and shown on TV, not presented in a class-room.

The idea that film has the power to render history potent and real in a way that a book cannot is problematic. Ian Buruma suggests that a book simply does not have the impact and cannot reach the audience that a movie—especially a 'Hollywood movie'—can. He cites Iris Chang's work *The Rape of Nanking* and implies that there might be a bit of envy involved, when Chang wants "Steven Spielberg to do justice to that event as he did for the Holocaust with *Schindler's List*."[59] Like the Jewish genocide, the Rape of Nanking must be brought to a wider audience. Buruma, who has analyzed textbooks and studied their content for historical accuracy,[60] feels that Chang's comment is particularly "telling" with regard to the reference to Spielberg. As he writes, "the preferred way to experience historical suffering is at the movies. Hollywood makes history real."[61]

The films of Steven Spielberg, in particular *Schindler's List* but also, *Saving Private Ryan, The Color Purple* as well as others, reinforce the potency of the film as more than mere entertainment. Both *Schindler's List* and *Saving Private Ryan* have become cultural events in themselves. Further, they have stirred debate, discussion and thought about the events they portray as well as on the discourse of film and history. *Saving Private Ryan* has been marked as one of the most important American films of the last decade. It has taken the notion of the glamorous good war and turned it on its head. As Peter Ehrenhaus and Marouf Hasian, Jr. have pointed out, the film is spectacular in its portrayal of violence, yet displays tact and thought in showing the horrors of war. This approach comes out of the influence of the Vietnam War films produced in the 1980s.[62] *Schindler's List* became a definitive visual-historical statement on the Holocaust for a number of reasons. Primarily, the cause for this diffusion was that it was accessible to many people. In turn, many viewers saw it and see it as *The Story* of the Holocaust. It is important to keep in mind that as society in the West becomes more and more a society of seers and viewers, they may only choose one document/film to stand for an event.[63] Regardless of the problems associated with the film, it has become *that* visual record.

Films such as *Jefferson in Paris, Mrs. Parker and the Vicious Circle*, and *Malcolm X* take on a power that transcends entertainment. They become history yet are subjected to critiques and scrutiny that is often very hostile. Despite the acknowledgement of liberties being taken as an inherent part of dramatic license, they are still scanned for flaws rather than praised for presenting history in an accessible manner. The whole notion of accuracy seems clouded when filmed versions of history are presented. As Caryn James has written:

> History books are expected to provoke such wrangling; movies are unfairly expected to provide a phantom "truth" that doesn't exist. The reason has to do with the vast influence of films and television. No doubt, movies sometimes substitute for history that isn't being taught well in schools. But to expect filmmakers to become pedagogues is to throw up your hands at the idea that education can be improved.[64]

Another factor in the rising power of film to define or stand for a version of history is that by the 1970s, film was no longer what it originally was. In many cases, film had evolved into a form of art and certain films began to do what the best art often does—transcend beyond its original borders. Films thus became more than cultural events but in numerous instances evolved into intellectual touchstones. This gave the subject matter added resonance in provoking discussion beyond the mere entertainment realm.[65] By the 1970s, the Hollywood Studio System had changed and in its place came the rise of maverick film makers from a variety of diverse backgrounds. Whether Martin Scorsese or Francis Ford Coppola, they had a strong appreciation for film and, in particular, classic Hollywood film and European cinema. They set out to make epics and sweeping visual documents in a very conscientious way. At the same time, film schools were educating a generation of film scholars that appreciated what was going on and were only too willing to get into the debates and to write scholarly appreciations of this new generation. Finally, the influence of critics such as Pauline Kael and others elevated the viewing of film to new levels. All of these factors helped film and American film in general, become much more adept at placing visual ideas within the context of a much higher calling.

To suggest that film has no place as an historical barometer, that the cinema cannot convey historical resonance or that a movie is not capable of informing about the past is to be blind to the vast impact that the motion picture has had upon history, especially over the past few decades. This point is illustrated quite obviously in the work of Oliver Stone. Regardless of bias, politics or the machinations of entertainment, Stone's films have often become historical touchstones in the collective memory and the recovery of the past for western audiences. In some cases, they have become *the* key historical artifacts that people seek out when searching for information about a person, period, or subject. *Salvador*, released in 1981, shed light on the situation in Central America, but also provided insight into American involvement in El Salvador. *Platoon*, released in 1986, showed not only the horror of war, but the individualized reception from the point of view of the infantrymen. This film probably did more to reopen discussion about this contentious war than anything else. If one can use the photographs of Ben Shahn or Lewis Hine to try and understand what was going on in the lives of ordinary people during the depression, then Stone's films can also be used as similar benchmarks and blatant forms of historical documentation.

Stone's 1987 *Wall Street* is perhaps the best way to get an initial understanding of the greed and the grasping—the worst of capitalism, perhaps—that was a part of the excessive eighties. For an analysis into a significant feature of the American psyche, the seditious impact of the far right, there is *Talk Radio* (1988) and for the tabloid infected, violence addicted 1990s, Stone presented *Natural Born Killers* (1994). *Born on The Fourth of July* (1989), based on Ron Kovic's experiences in and with the Vietnam War, is, like *Platoon*, a way to reflect history back to people, free of the platitudes and ideological posturing that is often dished up. Even his biopics, such as *The Doors* (1991) and *Nixon* (1995) are grounded with historical sensibilities and a relevance to the past. The viewer/student gets a potent version of history from these two films. All the seminal events of the sixties and seventies, from Kent State to the moon landing and Martin Luther King are woven into the story. But, perhaps the best illustration of the potency of Stone's visual, historical record comes out in *JFK* (1991).[66]

Decades after the assassination of President John Fitzgerald Kennedy, the topic remains one of the most discussed and debated in post World War Two history. This could be because of the fact that the findings of the Warren Commission were either never satisfactorily conveyed to the American public or that the vast majority of the public never believed the findings. Perhaps the idea of conspiracy is too seductive and thus, a more interesting way to consider the president's death than the "lone gunman" theory. That J. F. K. was assassinated and the assassination was filmed by Abraham Zapruder makes the killing of a president all the more intriguing as well as horrifying. That the assassin was in turn assassinated himself, which was caught live for millions of viewers and still has shock impact. J. F. K.'s funeral and the period of mourning were seminal events of the sixties and had an enormous impact on people who experienced them. Kennedy's youth and vigor, his style and grace—the ushering in of the myth of "Camelot"—were also key factors that made him a president that fascinated. Stone's conclusions of a military conspiracy responsible for the president's death had the power to reopen the debate. Utilizing real people and sophisticated documentary tactics, the actual historical locations and archival footage as well as an earnest protagonist, the film succeeds in becoming a sincere historical document. When the film was released, it sparked a massive debate involving politicians, journalists and historians. Stone himself was highly visible in promoting the film, deflecting criticism, and defending his version of history.[67] When the *American Historical*

Review featured a picture of Stone and the movie's star, Kevin Costner, on the set of the film, on its April 1992 cover, the dialectic was complete. A significant part of the issue dealt with the study of history through film, which implied that the boundaries that had once been thought impenetrable, were now dissolved.[68] The film also demonstrated, yet again, how often filmmakers go to extremes to ensure an intellectual rigor on par with academics. As an illustration, according to Norman Kagan,

> Stone's research coordinator, Jane Rusconi, was hired straight out of Yale University, and read one or two hundred books, also becoming an expert with the subject files. An interview suggests the enormous research efforts made for *JFK*, not simply the recorded words and movements of those involved, but such matters as clothing worn, hairdos, [and] detailed appearances of all locations at the times of events.[69]

And similar to education tie-ins of the past, it was reported that Warners was involved in the financing of educational supplements that were mailed out to schools. A *JFK* study guide went out to high schools and college history departments.[70] For *Nixon*, a similar program of intensive research was also employed. Government documents, congressional-hearings transcripts, and memoirs were consulted. Interviews conducted and numerous books were read, from all political spectrums.[71] In essence, what Stone's body of work has resulted in, is that he has become the primary historian to many American people. Whether or not people—or academic historians in particular—agree with his versions of certain historical events is not the point. What is critical to consider is that his historical creations put otherwise marginal, controversial or possibly forgotten topics back in the spotlight.[72]

What culminated with Oliver Stone's *JFK* and what was in turn employed in films as disparate as *Forrest Gump* and *Schindler's List* is that there was an integration of historical event(s) and footage with what had traditionally been a purely fictive approach. The history of the cinema demonstrates that very soon after the invention of camera for motion pictures, audiences "rapidly became bored with babies eating breakfast, trains arriving at stations, and workers leaving factories." Thus, almost from its inception, the documentary format was challenged and the audiences craved what they were used to: the content of older media. This meant, according to Brian Winston, stories: "narratives with beginnings, middles, climaxes, denouements, and ends." The fine lines between fiction film and "objective" documentary have always tenuous.[73]

Films such as *Forrest Gump*, *Back to the Future*, *A League of Their Own*, *Blast from the Past* and *Pleasantville* deal with history, or rather versions of history in a very interesting manner. They employ the nostalgic versions of the past in a way that makes the past accessible, humorous and selective. Portraying a past that is based upon common referents and popular culture icons makes that past accessible which allows the audience to understand the eras reflected in these films. The use of period clothes, costumes, furniture, and consumer products, which range from cars and buses to signs and soft drinks, break down the barriers of complexity and become historical shorthand for making the point. In some ways this has been reduced to stereotypical assumptions about the past but those in fact are the ones that are the easiest to access, remember and comprehend. This is a parallel to the way certain television shows access the past by using heroic figures to stand for the era. Since the beginning of film, movies have tended to move in this direction, and in many cases, this was intentional. Borrowing heavily from the conventions of theatre and nascent popular cultural formats, early filmmakers wanted to reach audiences as quickly and efficiently as possible. Visual signals and abbreviations of all sorts were utilized in attempts to make the audience understand. By focusing too much on the most easily accepted signs, some films stand out today for their racist depictions and their marked tendency to neoromanticism.[74]

Given the fact that some tens of thousands of films have been made in the United States alone since 1930, a fair degree of specialization has resulted. Over the course of decades, a surprisingly large number of films have been about historical themes or historical personages. It is always easier to criticize rather than to praise and in the case of the culture of Hollywood, this is particularly gratifying. Regarding the quantity of historical content generated by Hollywood, it must be recognized, that on the whole, Hollywood, broadly defined, has done an admirable job. As George MacDonald Fraser writes, "What is overlooked is the astonishing amount of history Hollywood has got right and the immense unacknowledged debt we owe to the commercial cinema as an illuminator of the story of humankind."[75] In a way, Fraser's idea is buttressed by Mark C. Carnes in his introduction to the volume *Past Imperfect*, which contains essays by historians on historical films. Carnes writes that "Many of the authors of these essays acknowledge that movies were what attracted them to history as youngsters."[76] This has its corollary in the fact that cinematic history is itself self-perpetuating. Many people, and this is especially true of filmmakers, have been extraordinarily influenced by the long body of film that has been historically based. Their knowledge of history, as Gore Vidal and others have remarked, has in fact come from filmed versions of history as opposed to text studies of history.[77]

The biases against the problems and discrepancies of film remain firmly in place. One is forced to wonder if in fact there has never been an omission or mistake with the writing of a history book. Typical of this frame of mind—which is not to imply that this is incorrect—is the comment made by Bruce Chadwick: "Film has always been casual in its presentation of history. Driven by commercial considerations, the need for wide audience appeal, producers consistently distorted and sanitized the past."[78]

Chadwick's comments are on the one hand a bit extreme and on the other, rather dismissive of what film can and has done for history. One can suggest that filmed versions of history are firmly entertainment and that, consequently, are not intended to be substitutes for historical knowledge. But the power that film possesses to convey history is enormous. Films do replace the historical information that is no longer being taught in the grade schools, high schools and colleges. As a result, films are often unfairly picked upon. The three or four films that describe the space race and the Apollo missions have, arguably, replaced any other versions of the events.[79] *Apollo 13* for example, was lauded for its accuracy and its historical story. It is imperative to recognize how key the filmed version of history has become in contemporary society. The accessibility derived from the filmed perspective, the images and narratives that are used make film particularly visible; and consequently, digestible, to the point that they have become the history textbooks for most.

NOTES

1. Richard Schickel, *Intimate Strangers*, (New York: International Publishers, 1986), pp. 47–50, and Clive James, *Fame In the 20th Century*, (New York: Random House, 1993), pp. 30–35.

2. Robert Brent Toplin, *History By Hollywood: The Use and Abuse of the American Past*, (Urbana, IL: University of Illinois Press, 1996), p. 15.

3. Robert Brent Toplin, *History By Hollywood*, p. 20.

4. A. Gurr, *Playgoing in Shakespeare's London*, (Cambridge: Cambridge University Press, 1987), pp. 132, 135, 136, cited in Sir Peter Hall, *Cities in Civilization*, (New York: Pantheon, 1998), p. 151.

5. Leonard Quard and Albert Auster, *American Film and Society Since 1945*, Second Edition, (New York: Praeger, 1991), p. 2.

6. Alexander Stille, *The Future of The Past*, (New York: Farrar, Straus and Giroux, 2002), p. 329, writes that television has created a world of "an eternal present—in which everything, whether it is depicted in the present or the past, appears to be happening now. In historical representation, it is generally impossible to distinguish the fictional details from those based in historical fact, and past and present are often conflated and confused. When President Jimmy Carter was having trouble getting Congress to approve the return of the Panama Canal, the announcement that movie actor John Wayne approved of returning the canal to Panama suddenly turned the tide in the treaty's favor. Although Wayne had never fought in a foreign war and had no expertise in foreign policy, it was as if, in the public mind, he had become an amalgam of all the roles he ever played—as if he had re-

ally fought the Spanish at the Alamo, shot Indians at Fort Apache, defeated the Japanese on the sands of Iwo Jima, and been a Green Beret in Vietnam."

7. George F. Custen, *Bio/Pics: How Hollywood Constructed Public History*, (New Brunswick, NJ: Rutgers University Press, 1992), p. 2. Custen writes, p. 7, "Hollywood biography is to history what Caesar's Palace is to architectural history: an enormous, engaging distortion which after a time convinces us of its own authenticity."

8. Bruce Chadwick, *The Reel Civil War: Mythmaking in American Film*, (New York: Knopf, 2001), p. 11.

9. John Wyver, *The Moving Image: An International History of Film, Television and Video*, (Oxford: Basil/Blackwell, 1989), p. 25.

10. Charles Musser, *The Emergence of Cinema: The American Screen to 1907*, *History of the American Cinema, Volume 1*, (Berkeley, CA: University of California Press, 1994), p. 226.

11. Richard Abel, *The Cini Goes to Town: French Cinema 1896–1914*, (Berkeley, CA, 1998), p. 92, cited in Kristen Whissel, "Placing the Spectator on the Scene of History: The Battle Re-Enactment at the Turn of the Century, From Buffalo Bill's Wild West to the Early Cinema," *Historical Journal of Film, Radio and Television*, vol. 22, no. 2, 2002, p. 225.

12. Eileen Bowser, *The Transformation of Cinema: 1907–1915, History of the American Cinema, Volume 2*, (Berkeley, CA: University of California Press, 1994), p. 201.

13. Natalie Zemon Davis, *Slaves on Screen: Film and Historical Vision*, (Toronto: Vintage, 2000), p. 5.

14. Natalie Zemon Davis, *Slaves on Screen*, p. 6.

15. Brian Taves, *The Romance of Adventure: The Genre of Historical Adventure Movies*, (Jackson, MS: University Press of Mississippi, 1993), p. 95.

16. William H. McNeill, *Mythistory and Other Essays*, (Chicago: University of Chicago Press, 1986), pp. 3–22, and Brian Taves, *The Romance of Adventure*, p. 95.

17. Thomas Doherty, *Projections of War: Hollywood, American Culture, and World War II*, (New York: Columbia University Press, 1993), p. 6.

18. Thomas Doherty, *Projections of War*, p. 70.

19. John Tomlinson, *Cultural Imperialism*, (Baltimore: The Johns Hopkins University Press, 1991), and Richard Kuisel, *Seducing The French: The Dilemma of Americanization*, (Berkeley, CA: University of California Press, 1993).

20. Peter C. Rollins, ed., "Introduction," *Hollywood As Historian: American Film in A Cultural Context*, (Lexington, KY: The University Press of Kentucky, 1983), p. 1. Rollins continues, "Not satisfied with merely depicting the past, Hollywood has often attempted to influence history by turning out films consciously designed to change public attitudes toward matters of social or political importance."

21. Peter Burke, *Eyewitnessing: The Uses of Images as Historical Evidence*, (Ithaca, NY: Cornell University Press, 2001), p. 163.

22. Bruce Chadwick, *The Real Civil War*, p. 233.

23. Peter Burke, *Eyewitnessing: The Uses of Images as Historical Evidence*, p. 160.

24. bell hooks, "Making Movie Magic," in *The Crisis of Criticism*, ed., Maurice Berger, (New York: The New Press, 1998), p. 133.

25. Robert A. Rosenstone, "Reflections on the Possibility of Really Putting History onto Film," *American Historical Review* Forum: History in Images/History in Words, December 1988, vol. 93, no. 5, p. 1174.

26. Ian C. Jarvie, "Seeing through Movies," *Philosophy of the Social Sciences*, 8, 1978, p. 378, cited in Rosenstone, "Reflections," p. 1176.

27. Tom O'Brien, *The Screening of America: Movies and Value's from Rocky to Rain Man*, (New York: Continuum, 1990), p. 43.

28. Tom O'Brien, *The Screening of America*, p. 46.

29. Tom O'Brien, *The Screening of America*, p. 48.

30. John E. O'Connor and Martin A. Jackson, editors, "Introduction," *American History/American Film: Interpreting the Hollywood Image*, (New York: Ungar Publishing, 1988), p. xxi.

31. Peter Burke, *Eyewitnessing: The Uses of Images as Historical Evidence*, p. 155.

32. Richard Sennett, *The Fall of Public Man*, (New York: Vintage Books, 1978), p. 71.

33. Marcia Landy, *British Genres: Cinema and Society, 1930—1960*, (Princeton, NJ: Princeton University Press, 1991), p. 210.

34. Claudia Springer, "Vietnam: A Television History and the Equivocal Nature of Objectivity," *Wide Angle: A Film Quarterly*, vol. 7, no. 4, 1985, p. 60.

35. K. R. M. Short, "Introduction: Feature Films As History," in K. R. M. Short, ed., *Feature Films as History*, (London: Croom Helm, 1981), p. 16.

36. Michael Anderegg, "Introduction," in Michael Anderegg, ed., *Inventing Vietnam: The War in Film and Television*, (Philadelphia: Temple University Press, 1991), p. 3.

37. Michael Anderegg, "Introduction," in Michael Anderegg, ed., *Inventing Vietnam: The War in Film and Television*, p. 3.

38. Henry A. Giroux, *Disturbing Pleasures: Learning Popular Culture*, (New York: Routlege, 1994), p. 177.

39. A. Susan Owen, "Memory, War and American Identity: *Saving Private Ryan* as cinematic jeremiad," *Critical Studies in Mass Communication*, vol. 19, no. 3 (September 2002) p. 261.

40. Bruce Taylor, "The Vietnam War Movie," in D. Michael Shafer, ed., *The Legacy: The Vietnam War in the American Imagination*, (Boston: Beacon Press, 1990), pp. 196–97 writes, "Any literature about war is to some degree about *the people* (individually and collectively) who fought that war, the societies that involved themselves in it, the history that preceded it and that which will follow, as well as about the war itself, the actual hostilities, the killing and the dying." My emphasis.

41. Pat Aufderheide, "Vietnam: Good Soldiers," in Mark Crispin Miller, ed., *Seeing Through Movies*, (New York: Pantheon Books, 1990), p. 87.

42. Bruce Taylor, "The Vietnam War Movie," p. 186.

43. Susan Wloszcyna, "History is back in action," *USA Today*, April 21, 2000, p. 1E.

44. Thomas Doherty, *Teenagers & Teenpics: The Juvenalization of American Movies in the 1950s*, (Boston: Unwin Hyman, 1988), p. 5.

45. Anton Kaes, *From Hitler to Heimat: The Return of History as Film*, (Cambridge, MA: Harvard University Press, 1989), p. ix.

46. Jim Cullen, *The Civil War in Popular Culture: A Reusable Past*, (Washington, DC: Smithsonian Institution Press, 1995), pp. 2–3.

47. John E. O'Connor, "Reading, Writing and Critical Viewing: Coordinating Skill Development in History Learning," *The History Teacher*, vol. 34, no. 2, February 2001, p. 3, www.history.cooperative.org/journals/ht/34.2/oconnor.html.

48. John E. O'Connor, "Reading, Writing and Critical Viewing: Coordinating Skill Development in History Learning," p. 3.

49. Edward D. C. Campbell, Jr., *The Celluloid South: Hollywood and the Southern Myth*, (Knoxville, TN: The University of Tennessee Press, 1981), p. 28.

50. Diane Ravitch, "Technology and the Curriculum: Promise and Peril," in Mary Alice White, ed., *What Curriculum for the Information Age?*, (Hilldale, NJ: Lawrence Erlbaum Associates Publishers, 1987), p. 30.

51. Alan Rosenthal, "Introduction, Part IV—Documentary and History," in Alan Rosenthal, ed., *New Challenges for Documentary*, (Berkeley: University of California Press, 1988), p. 425.

52. Alan Rosenthal, "Introduction, Part IV—Documentary and History," in Alan Rosenthal, ed., *New Challenges for Documentary*, p. 426.

53. Alan Rosenthal, "Introduction, Part IV—Documentary and History," in Alan Rosenthal, ed., *New Challenges for Documentary*, p. 427.

54. Alan Rosenthal, "Introduction, Part IV—Documentary and History," in Alan Rosenthal, ed., *New Challenges for Documentary*, p. 427.

55. Donald Watt, "History on the Public Screen, I ," in Alan Rosenthal, ed., *New Challenges for Documentary*, pp. 435–36.

56. George F. Custen, *Bio/Pics* and George MacDonald Fraser, *The Hollywood History of the World*, (London: Curtis Brown, 1988).

57. Jerry Kuehl, "History on the Public Screen, II," in Alan Rosenthal, ed., *New Challenges for Documentary*, pp. 445–47.

58. Jerry Kuehl, "History on the Public Screen, II," in Alan Rosenthal, ed., *New Challenges for Documentary*, p. 448.

59. Ian Buruma, "History and Hollywood," *The Toronto Star*, May 2, 1999, p. D16.

60. Ian Buruma, *The Wages of Guilt: Memories of War in Germany and Japan*, (New York: Meridian/Penguin, 1995). In "History and Hollywood," p. D16, Buruma, echoing many historians, writes, "What I find alarming is not the attention we are asked to pay to the past. Without history, including its most painful episodes, we cannot understand who we are, or indeed who others are. There is a lack of historical perspective. Without perspective we flounder in the dark and will believe anything, no matter how vile."

61. Ian Buruma, "History and Hollywood," p. D16.

62. Marouf Hasian, Jr, "Nostalgic Longings, Memories of the 'Good War,' and Cinematic Representations in *Saving Private Ryan*," and Peter Ehrenhaus, "Why we Fought: Holocaust Memory in Spielberg's *Saving Private Ryan*," *Critical Studies in Media Communication*, September, 2001.

63. Omer Bartov, "Spielberg's Oskar: Hollywood Tries Evil," in *Spielberg's Holocaust: Critical Perspectives on Schindler's List*, ed. by Yosefa Loshitzky, (Bloomington, IN: Indiana University Press, 1997), p. 46.

64. Caryn James, "They're Movies, Not Schoolbooks," *The New York Times*, May 21, 1995, section 2, p. 18h.

65. Michael Anderegg, "Introduction," *Inventing Vietnam: The War in Film and Television*, p. 3.

66. Chris Salewicz, *Oliver Stone: The Making of His Movies*, (London: Orion Media, 1997) Norman Kagan, *The Cinema of Oliver Stone*, (New York: Continuum, 2000) and Susan Mackey-Kallis, *Oliver Stone's America*, (Boulder, CO: Westview Press, 1996).

67. Chris Salewicz, *Oliver Stone: The Making of His Movies* and Norman Kagan, *The Cinema of Oliver Stone*.

68. Michael Rogin, "Body and Soul Murder: *JFK*" in John Matlock and Rebecca L. Walkowitz, editors, *Media Spectacles*, (New York: Routledge, 1993), p. 3. Another very interesting development was that when the screenplay, by Stone and Zachary Sklar was published, it contained the definitive academic signifier: footnotes. This was done, according to Janet Staiger, to "substantiate every reenacted scene in the movie as reality, thus claiming to adhere to traditional standards of authenticating claims." Janet Staiger, "Cinematic Shots: The Narration of Violence," in Vivian Sobchack, ed., *The Persistence of History: Cinema, Television, And the Modern Event*, (New York: Routledge, 1996), p. 45.

69. Norman Kagan, *The Cinema of Oliver Stone*, p. 183.

70. Norman Kagan, *The Cinema of Oliver Stone*, p. 206.

71. Norman Kagan, *The Cinema of Oliver Stone*, p. 253.

72. Norman Kagan, *The Cinema of Oliver Stone*, p. 281.

73. Brian Winston, "Documentary: I Think We Are in Trouble," in Alan Rosenthal, ed., *New Challenges for Documentary*, (Berkeley: University of California Press, 1988), pp. 21–22.

74. Kenneth M. Cameron, *America On Film: Hollywood and American History*, (New York: Continuum, 1997), pp. 23–70. Commenting on the early features that were produced in the teens, Cameron writes that historical films were often produced in the same manner that one would teach children. "History," he writes, "was handed down from above, 'projected,' and its tone was didactic or celebratory. Its themes were mostly military, its heroes male, mature, white." p. 23.

75. George MacDonald Fraser, "Hollywood and World History," in Alan Rosenthal, ed., *Why Docudrama? Fact-Fiction on Film and TV*, (Carbondale, IL: Southern Illinois University Press, 1999), p. 13.

76. Mark C. Carnes, "Introduction," *Past Imperfect: History According to the Movies*, ed., Mark C. Carnes, (New York: Henry Holt, 1996), p. 9.

77. Bruce Chadwick, *The Reel Civil War*, pp. 11–12.

78. Bruce Chadwick, *The Reel Civil War*, p. 4.

79. Thomas Mallon, "Visions of the Future, Relics of the Past," *The New York Times*, June 25, 1995, p. 24.

6

Televising History

For good or ill, television seems to be providing students today with whatever common culture they possess.

—Paul A. Cantor, *Gilligan Unbound: Pop Culture in the Age of Globalization*, ix

Many people around the world who will never pick up a history book will derive most of their views about the past . . . from television programmes.

—Taylor Downing, "History on Television: The Making of *Cold War*, 1998," 331

The first quotation is not a surprising statement in any way or form. It reflects a fact of reality and describes an obvious station in human development. The accuracy of the statement is buttressed by many similar observations, and it is increasingly, harder to disprove. As the dominant form of communication and the "thing hundreds of millions of humans" have in common,[1] the impact of television is vast. Television, regardless of both concerns and criticisms, is the main facilitator of what is called "common knowledge." In essence, the role that television plays is as a mediator of knowledge, information and data is transmitted to a large group of people, which helps individuals form ideas and perspectives on a wide variety of beliefs, values and norms.[2] This has led to television garnering an enormous amount of influence, a power which often transcends the trivial attributes that are usually associated with the medium. The second comment, voiced by Taylor Downing suggests that television has much more to offer than simple entertainment. Whether one likes it or not, television has usurped the previous conveyors of history and remains the preeminent transporter of historical information. Television has ushered in a fundamentally novel way of perceiving and understanding reality which is significantly different from the culture of books and art in that it is "more relaxed, diffuse, multidimensional, and immediate."[3]

The mid-1950s saw television move into its role of mainstay in North American life. It was during the 1950s that American television in particular, adopted its traditional formats and found both its artistic and commercial potential. It was also during the 1950s that American television, albeit briefly, served as a key testing ground for complex social issues and heavy historical themes. During the late 1950s, teleplays grappled with key critical concepts and provided both a social and historical context that has rarely been imitated since.[4] In the years since, television has become the focal point of most discourse and can arguably be termed, "the epicentre of our existence."[5]

On average, in the United States (and Canada) the television set is on for about seven hours a day, although actual viewing could be around three hours. Children between the ages of two and eighteen, on average live in homes with 2.9 TVs and 1.8 VCRs. TV watching is the activity most engaged in by Americans.[6] Television is by far the dominant form of both entertainment and information access for Americans and Canadians. For most people, what constitutes history is both what they see on the news and what they are entertained with in televised drama.[7] If we subscribe to the fact that history is inextricably linked to memory and memory—individual, collective, social—is more and more a function of media, than what one sees on television—as history—is enormously potent as a conveyor of the past.

Television, as David Marc has observed, is "a throbbing public memory. It continuously delivers and creates history."[8] As alluded to earlier, most of what constitutes history is what was or is seen on television. All "historical" events are televised or are defined in someway by television.[9] Very quickly, this came to be understood as a key feature of television itself. By the late 1950s, and certainly by the early 1960s, history became equated with what was seen on television. In the words of Mary Ann Watson, "It is impossible to separate the major events of American history in the early 1960s from the development of American television. They are inextricably intertwined."[10] Such is the power of television that for many, history is synonymous with the "pseudo-events" or the "media-events" that become or in fact are history.[11] These 'events' include most of the major moments of history from the past fifty years.

The history that television delivers varies from instantaneous capturing of the past, to the recording of important events, to the portrayal and recasting of historical information in potent and in trivial ways. According to Jeffrey Scheuer, "television is in one sense quintessentially 'historical': it records the passage of time and space."[12] Although Scheuer argues that what is recorded is subject to interpretation, he does give television points for its ability to create "an imperfect (if often successful) marriage of information and entertainment."[13]

In the Western world, the ubiquitous nature of television is undisputed. Not since the printing press has there been a communications invention that has "transformed" virtually every aspect of society, from leisure to education, from religion to politics.[14] Television genres, be they news, drama, documentaries, historical docudramas, biographies, science fiction or westerns, and even comedies use history in numerous ways. The History Channel, and Arts and Entertainment, especially the show *Biography*, are just two examples of how important and popular televisual history is in today's society. As mentioned previously, television's versions of history should never be considered the "last word" on a particular subject, but rather, they should be considered a first step; often, an introduction to a particular historical moment.[15] As Gary Edgerton writes, televised history should be,

> viewed as a means by which unprecedentedly large audiences can become increasingly aware of and captivated by the stories and figures of the past, spurring some viewers to pursue their newfound historical interests beyond the screen and into other forms of popular and professional history.[16]

To compare history on television to traditional, academic history is both problematic and antiquated. The two kinds of history are in many ways, worlds apart. The logic of television dictates an entirely different approach and it is futile and erroneous to see the two as the same.[17] Televised history is not as comprehensive and as multifaceted as the history provided in a book format. It is meant to capture a large audience and very often, is oriented around "emotion."[18] The point of good television history is to provoke interest and dialogue in or order to foster further investigation. Television has appropriated and perfected the use of mythology as history, and has been able to consistently recycle its spectacles—as well as constantly transform them—in a way that directly links the mythology of the old with the mythology of the new.[19] Perhaps the best illustration of this approach comes from the work of Ken Burns.

In his study of the television films of Ken Burns, Gary Edgerton has suggested that the characteristic "impulses" that were a part of the work of Homer: "heroism, honour and nobility," are found embedded in collective historical memory and give focus to the "great men" portrayed in *The Civil War*. Whether solely directed at Lincoln, Douglas, or Lee, or down towards the common foot soldier, the viewer can understand the complexities because of this common collective notion. Historical view-points are in fact personalized and controlled, as Edgerton remarks, be-cause of the nature of the television narrative but also because of the re-liance on established popular historical conventions.[20] This process is applicable to a variety of national contexts—not only the American.

For *Canada: A People's History*, the massive CBC production, the intention of the producers was to capitalize on the conventions of popular narrative, as well as to fuse the best of journalism and narrative history. As the pro-ducer of the series explained in a memo, *A People's History* would be,

> a narrative history emphasizing the diaries and letters of farmers, explorers, traders and immigrants, rather than a diplomatic history. This is the core ap-proach of Shelby Foote's *A Narrative History of the Civil War* and Peter Watkin's *Culloden*. It is vibrant, story-driven and exciting. It is also very good historiography.[21]

The monumental Canadian series was designed from the beginning to be more than the average telehistorical representation. Mark Starowicz in-tended to consult historians and to go to extreme lengths to render the various episodes as accurately as possible. Most importantly this series was designed to be a "national event."[22] Conceived during the Quebec Referendum of the late 1990s, the motive was political but also, very con-sciously accessible to large groups of people. The producer was aware that the Americans had access to a vast array of visual sources that told their story. Nothing even remotely comparable existed in the Canadian case. As Starowicz wrote, "There is no current material that can show our audience the exciting and dramatic evolution of our country. . . . This is more than a pity, because of the excitement inherent in the story, this is a social and even political problem. This is a failure of cultural policy, and it is happening on our watch."[23]

A very significant role that television plays in defining, creating, and showing history is in the live broadcasting of seminal events. In numer-ous instances, as Daniel Dayan and Elihu Katz have suggested, these events become key "occasions" that "spotlight some central value or some aspect of collective memory," which is vital in defining modern society as well as national and international identity. These events, such as the Olympics, or a historic visit of one leader to another leader, or a state fu-neral are scripted in a way to a particular story. To some extent they are "hegemonic" when they are "proclaimed historic," but nonetheless, they are the distinct times when people gather around the television to literally, watch history.[24]

Current or news based events are one version of these scripted and structured historical occasions. Yet there have been a number of "fiction" based events that have generated the same set of audience responses. One repeated occurrence has been the broadcast of blockbuster television events that become more than just pure television, but that often stand as experiences in themselves. The broadcasting of *Holocaust*, in 1978, is one such historical occurrence. A definitive benchmark in televised history is the Persian Gulf War. In contrast to Vietnam, the Gulf War was about the ability of television to present history live.[25] As Mitchell Stephens puts it: "The members of my generation have gone on to live their lives with television. The history we experienced—from Dallas to Baghdad—most of us experienced most powerfully on television."[26] Since the 1960s, the transition from a current event to "packaged history" is much quicker.

The camera as both surrogate weapon and recorder of memory/history is as old as the invention of photography. The link between "vision and war" and the "weapon and the eye" have a long history, as Paul Virilio has asserted.[27] But with the Persian Gulf War, it was constant and "live." As Marita Sturken writes:

> These two roles of the camera—as a device for constructing cultural memory and history as a device for waging warfare—were inseparable in the production of images of the Persian Gulf War.[28]

Many critics found this dependency and reaction extremely problematic. In acknowledging the fact that television now provides the primary linkages to historical discourse and critical historical research, the "first draft of history," versions of the past were now conforming to the dictates of television's fundamentals. Douglas Kellner has observed that with this large audience for televised drama, there were several capitulations to the structure of television which provided a problematic view of history.[29] Kellner points out the close relationship of the major American media outlets to both the military and the defense industries. As well, he suggests that to openly critique U.S. policy was quickly deemed to be unpatriotic. This line of thinking forced the major media outlets to construct a live historical narrative that clearly demarcated the 'good' U.S. from the evil Saddam Hussein. Like traditional drama a clearly defined enemy is constructed and villainized while the hero is made to seem noble and benevolent.[30] Naturally, this fits in with the morally ambiguous constructs of popular culture. Kellner notes that "TV presented the Gulf war primarily as entertainment, complete with dramatic titles, graphics, and music."[31] CNN positioned itself at the forefront of coverage with its "Crisis in the Gulf" title and the other American networks quickly followed suit, complete with dramatic typography and bold music. But to Kellner, what seemed particularly problematic to the presentation of the news in this manner was the dependency on popular culture paradigms and rhetoric:

> In its presentation of the war, the TV networks used the codes of the war movie, Western, action/adventure, and miniseries to present the war as a dramatic conflict with exciting events, ups and downs, and threats and triumphs.[32]

Most reporting on war has the American news networks constantly framing the conflicts, in Northern Ireland, Israel, El Salvador, and virtually any other theatre, as a battle between the aggressors and the victims. Mark Crispin Miller, in "How TV Covers War" makes this point, which is fully compatible with the structure of both narrative drama and mythologized history.[33] This is not necessarily solely the preserve of the visual media. Television news and documentary came out of, among other things, the print traditions established *vis-à-vis* news in the nineteenth century. James Carey relates this to the reading of newspapers. Here, a particular world view is confirmed, but what is more relevant is the way the reader perceives the world in terms of drama and ritual. "As readers make their way through the paper," he writes, "they engage in a continual shift of roles or of dramatic focus."[34] Where the TV world view of history comes together with the newspaper variant is in the area of the generated dramatic action in which the reader/viewer "joins a world of contending forces as an observer at a play." News moves from information to the substance of drama.[35] To some extent, this negates the point that information can be gleaned about history via this format. Yet, just as a play or a novel can yield information and knowledge beyond entertainment, then so too can the presentation in this genre. The enormous popularity of *Time Magazine* stemmed from the fact that, at least originally, its features and stories were designed to merge the appeal of "fiction and reporting."[36]

This seeping of television characteristics into society at large has had a number of variations. As discussed in the introduction to this work, *USA Today* is often cited as the definitive example of a newspaper for television viewers. This characterization stems from the bias towards the visual, "what catches the eye more than what feeds the mind"—and what results are the trappings or vestiges of visual culture. These elements include more photographs, lots of color, bolder headlines, and many more graphs. In trying to appeal to the viewer through the seemingly inconsistent arena of text, some critics feel that you cannot have it both ways. This pandering might alienate the serious reader,[37] but may also capture a potential dormant reader. This graphic revolution has also revealed itself in other ways.

The graphics that have been a staple of television since the 1960s, and in particular, the graphic images and logos that are behind the head of the news anchor, act as primary icons in the visual shorthand of television news. As if people could not listen to a person talking for too long, a compressed visual icon is necessary to hammer the point home. As John Hockenberry writes,

> graphic images associated with television news stories, especially the biggest stories, can acquire a certain timelessness, lingering in memory like trademarks. Events beget television logos, which in turn beget a kind of historical record unique to our age. Sometimes the graphic for an event is dominated by a single still photograph, as in the Tiananmen Square disaster, defined by a man facing a tank. Other times the graphic is more abstract, as in CNN's "War in the Gulf" logo for its coverage of Operation Desert Storm. History is captured, encapsulated in a quick sketch and the occasional notes of canned music.[38]

As discussed earlier, the CBC produced, *Canada: A People's History* and the CRB Foundation's Heritage Minutes are two significant examples of the new way history is being produced for a fundamentally different audience. Both productions and their producers make no attempt to disguise the fact that these are new forms of historical presentation with specific goals that blatantly incorporate narrative structures—albeit in different ways—to make history exciting. *Canada: A People's History* employs pseudo-historical techniques, for example, primary sources and texts to ensure that the production's foundational assumptions are taken seriously. At the same time there is an emphasis on visuals, such as paintings and photographs which recognize the importance of these images in contemporary society, while giving the series a credible documentary flavor.[39]

In order to avoid the problems that can be a part of traditional documentary visual history, the production team behind *Canada: A People's History*, set out to literally combat the association that Canadian history is boring. Only the most sophisticated techniques, pioneered and used effectively by Ken Burns, could successfully prevent this dismissal. As the producer of the series stated, "We've got to capture people's imagination. All they hear are the three deadliest words in television: 'Canadian,' 'history,' and 'documentary.' Then we say 'sweeping' and they hear 'long and deadly.' Our problem is that Canadians think our history is a snore."[40]

Beyond news and documentary, history finds its way onto television in some very creative, bizarre and "subtle" ways. One of the obsessions in certain TV genres is to "play" with history in specific plot lines that allow history to be presented in an innocuous manner.[41] Steve Anderson feels that this is a common attribute of science fiction shows, with their focus on time-travel narratives. He mentions the ubiquitous rerun staple, the original *Star Trek* series and others, such as *Quantum Leap*, and the short-lived *Timecop*. *Star Trek* in particular, in its various manifestations has a tendency to use historical plotlines, many of them focusing on significant and popular features of western history.[42] Commenting on this same historical preoccupation, Paul A. Cantor writes: "Time and again, space travelers from earth journey to remote planets only to find themselves in ancient Greece or Rome."[43]

Unlike the *You Are There* format and other historical recreation shows, the science fiction/time-travel have no pretensions to being educational or historically accurate, but are fully designed as entertainment vehicles. Nonetheless, the historical metaphors, personalities, and components that these shows employ convey information of an historical nature and affect how history—in particular, American History—is processed and received.[44] This is not to say that fiction or science fiction and other genre television programming cannot aspire to lofty pedagogical aims. For the series, *Young Indiana Jones Chronicles*, a show bursting with historical tropes and analogies, an educational study guide was prepared by Lucasfilm for teachers. This series, revolved around the adventures of Indiana Jones and his historical encounters with "historic" personages ranging from Freud and Einstein to Roosevelt and Ataturk and contained, as most textbook accompaniments, information about the historical people as well as topics for research and ideas for discussion.[45]

The "TV Movie," and its cousin, the miniseries, are staples of primetime television and a constant offering on television is both unique in its easy access for the viewer and because of the fact that it is original to television. The TV movie is produced on a different scale than its larger relative on the big screen and can tackle historical subjects in a way that is "simpler" than mainstream films. Since its inception in the early 1970s, the TV movie has billed itself as a "socially important document" and one which was capable of dealing with serious social and historical topics.[46] It is often through this vehicle that much of television's emphasis on history is conveyed.

Roots, based on Alex Haley's book, had, according to Michael Kammen, a social and cultural impact that is "virtually incalculable.[47] Airing on ABC on consecutive nights, *Roots* was capable of generating and keeping a huge audience for over a week. The previous miniseries, *QB-VII* and *Rich Man, Poor Man*, which were aired in 1976, "paved the way for *Roots* by demonstrating that the miniseries form pioneered by British Television had genuine appeal for American audiences."[48] Haley's book had already been a best seller and the mix of his personal family story with the history of a controversial and divisive subject proved to be a very appealing saga. The allure on the small screen was just as vast and was aided by the "highly satisfying" "narrative structure," complete with "end-of-episode teasers."[49]

Holocaust, which aired on four consecutive nights in April of 1978, drew an audience of approximately 120 million American viewers. According to Jeffrey Shandler, it was a definitive historical moment in that it brought the enormity of the Shoah to a very large audience for the first time.[50] Shandler contends that the preceding thirty years had provided American audiences with glimpses of a variety of elements about the Holocaust. These included early television plays that were "landmarks of Holocaust drama" scripted by such luminaries as Rod Serling and Paddy Chayefsky.[51] Like *Roots*, *Holocaust* became an event, complete with a viewers' guide that was distributed to educators and initiated numerous forums, which opened up discussion on the Holocaust. Shandler makes the point that because it aired before the ubiquity of the VCR, *Holocaust* became an event that people came together to watch and discuss.[52] When the series aired, many criticized the attempt to tell a Holocaust story in the form of a soap opera. One of the most vocal critics of the television movie was Elie Wiesel, who denounced the program. Importantly, years later, Wiesel changed his assessment. He recognized that television could bring people together and make us aware of "our humanity." Significantly, he also stated that the medium "has the obligation to bear witness."[53]

Roots, *Holocaust*, *Winds of War*, and *The Blue and the Gray*, are all television movies that engaged wide-ranging debate and provoked interest in the analysis of history. As Elayne Rapping has observed, these movies were more than just entertainment fare, they became accepted documents in themselves as well as touchstones for discussion and analysis.[54] Like so much of mature or postmodern mass culture, they can be dismissed as lightweight tripe or combed for their contributions to popular perceptions of history. These movies do have more in common with genre fiction in their plot, presentation, style, and narrative features yet they are viewed by large numbers of people and thus must be considered as historical lightening rods. As Rapping states, they are the primary "forms through which history and politics are perceived and understood by most Americans," and thus, "they are a matter of serious concern."[55] It is the TV movie, or more accurately, the miniseries, that "has become, in some ways, the predominant discourse through which Americans, especially young Americans, are now "educated about our national history."[56] These series, for example, *Winds of War* and *The Blue and The Gray* are often shown in classrooms and come complete with study guides. As educational tools they are a form of necessary evil, for as Rapping suggests, watching history is one of the few ways students will learn about history.[57]

This notion, of receiving history from television, is only shocking to those steeped in the world of books. To most students in school today and to the generation in their twenties and early thirties, television as a purveyor of historical knowledge is accepted as undebatable. This "naturalization" of television as the main conveyor of history is their reality.[58] The anxieties that derive from this are put in place by those who have grown up, matured, and learned from a linear, print based bias. Very quickly, after its rapid acceptance into the home in the 1950s, television became the focal point of the family room; a place where everyone gathered together to watch.[59] Television networks as well as manufacturers equated watching television with watching history.[60]

The line between social issues and history is often a vague one. What is a pressing social issue today quickly evolves into an historical theme tomorrow. If what is going to be history is today, a current event, the way it is presented by television in virtually any format proves most interesting. News stories, documentaries, and of course TV movies can and do facilitate interest in a variety of key issues. In turn, these can and do provoke "interest" in the topics covered. Most often, though, the interest is greatest in the period immediately following the airing of the program.[61]

Since the 1950s, television has had the power to focus attention upon an idea, concept, or notion. The rise of popular perceptions of history corresponds to the time when television came on the air. It is no accident that Disneyland was dependent upon the visual nature of both film and television. Disney's *Davy Crockett* series sparked the modern heritage/history mania that caused much of the United States to begin to rethink popular history. It was, according to Steven Stark, the popularity of the series *Davy Crockett* that elevated the Alamo from a regional attraction to a "major tourist destination" and one to "alter traditional views of history."[62] This comes back to the postmodern interpretation of history as a spectacle dependent upon the appropriation of a variety of historical eclecticisms. As R. Hewison has remarked in his work on museums and the "heritage industry," history under this view becomes a "contemporary creation, more costume drama and reenactment than critical discourse."[63]

The relationship between television and this living world of museums and fantasy parks such as Disney World and Colonial Williamsburg is a consequential episode of the second half of the twentieth century. Although primarily an amusement park, Disney World and Disney culture in general seeks to deal with history in a variety of interesting and controversial ways. Not surprisingly, most of the work dealing with the impact of the Disney universe has been extraordinarily critical of the Magic Kingdom and in many cases, alarmist about what impact the Disney Corporation has had on culture and history. In Disneyland and Disney World, history is conveniently mythologized into archetypical shorthand. As well, new visions of the past are constantly being appropriated and standardized within the Disney universe. Critiques of the Disney universe have a tendency to resort to overkill in their focus on the selectivity, and vagueness of the presentation of history. But, as with the Vietnam War films, it must be recognized that this is a specific kind of history which is primarily meant to entertain rather than to educate. Yet, entertainment can educate, or at the very least, spark inquiry and rekindle curiosity about history.

The Disneyland/Disney World themed historicization can be broken down, according to Mike Wallace, into "Main Street," "Frontierland," "Adventureland," and the "Hall of Presidents."[64] This segmented and sanitized categorization of history is one man's (Walt's) and one corporation's take on the past. This perspective is meant to filter out the problems and messiness of real history and presents a version of the past that is based on some idea of historical reality but that is purged of the vagaries of "authentic" history. As Wallace discusses, this is done deliberately, guiltlessly, and even enthusiastically, because under the guise of entertainment, what Disney is attempting is to "recapture the *essence*," not replicate the actuality. Main Street, is a postmodern spectacle that becomes a "stage set that cultivated nostalgia for a fabricated past."[65]

What one must keep in mind is that this is exactly what occurs in the more highbrow domains of estate homes and museums. There is the same sweeping away of the ugly and conflict-torn documentation of the past in favor of a more palatable, and enticing portrait. History Museums pander to their audience's tastes and expectations in the same way that Disney World does. As Carol Duncan has written, "It has become possible to visit the museum, see a show, go shopping, and eat, and never once be reminded of the heritage of civilization."[66] People are visiting Disney World and other more accepted entertainment venues that present history for a variety of reasons. People watching and absorbing history are key motivations for making these pilgrimages. Linking the two is the desire to "get in touch with history" in a way that makes history real. There is burning desire to see historic sites and variations of history with one's own eyes. Seeing is the key feature to this kind of experience.[67]

The criticisms and complaints labeled against television are lengthy.[68] These of course include: that television panders to the lowest common denominator, television discourages thought, it stifles the imagination, it encourages passivity, it is anti-intellectual, it distorts reality, it encourages laziness and aggression, it perpetuates negative or false stereotypes etc.[69] Its very nature as both a business and as a primarily entertainment oriented medium, have dictated much of what television has become. The way television approaches virtually any facet of history is tailored to the needs of a commercial narrative dependent on advertising. Television is forced by its very nature to resort to numerous shorthand devices to achieve its desired effects. These involve a grand dependence on myth and heroic endeavor in order to create a loosely defined series of historical moments.

Television advertising in particular has a tendency to nostalgize selective examples of the past in much the same manner as television narratives and Disney culture does. Presentations and glorifications of, for example, small town life and all its associations by advertising on television have resulted in a form of mirage. Given farm foreclosure and jobs that have gone overseas, it just does not exist anymore, albeit in the world of Ford trucks, french-fried potatoes and Pepsi. Yet, this image is constantly invoked by television as one that generates the ideals and values of a time past; values of a mythic rural America, with its roots of friendship and security, of hard work and craftsmanship.[70]

The conciseness of a commercial leaves no room for contemplating more that what is there and what is immediately implied. In this sense, it can be stated that this kind of image and resulting emotional manipulation and the deep evocations that it triggers on many levels is a technique that has become pervasive in many media. What occurs in a variety of instances is a plea to emotional icons and references that most people are aware of, and a subsequent playing upon the viewers sentiments in order to convey a message. According to Richard Slotkin,

> Each of these mythic icons is in effect a poetic construction of tremendous economy compression and a mnemonic device capable of evoking a complex system of historical associations by a singe image or phrase. For an American, allusions to 'the Frontier,' or to events like 'Pearl Harbor,' 'The Alamo,' or 'Custer's Last Stand,' evoke an implicit understanding of the entire historical scenario that belongs to the event and of the complex interpretive tradition that has developed around it.[71]

Leo Marx has termed this a "cultural symbol" which has special meaning to those sharing the same culture.[72] Commenting on Marx's idea, Bruce Lohof suggests that this "transcendent form of advertising offers to consumers an image that will evoke a cluster of ideas and emotions which they hold in common with fellow Americans. Lohof maintains that this is "the merchandising of a metaphor that will speak to and be understood by the collective imagination of the culture."[73]

The repetitiveness and omnipresence of these cultural symbols in the media, and in television in particular, mobilizes short facts of history into a larger narrative. The brief historical snippets used by the CRB Foundation to tell the story of Canada in their heritage series, a collection of sixty-second historical narratives are a benchmark in this idea. Similar to the process of Haiku poetry or ideograms, which put one image or verbal bite with another, a powerful result is achieved. So potent are the layers of myth and the cultural symbols woven within them that they can be accessed easily. Politicians appearing on television and their speech writers are very aware of this.[74] Utilization of these symbols taps the historical or collective memory that people carry with them.

In George Lipsitz's *Time Passages*, this "collective memory" process is succinctly explained in his analysis of a Ronald Reagan speech. Reagan's speech, according to Lipsitz, incorporates a series of references to historical 'myths' that, the audience registers in an almost cued response. They trigger a whole series of assumptions, values, and images that compose a historicity which has been put into place by the media, popular heroic iconography and collective public mythology. The symbols invoked by Reagan, like those before him, appear before the mind's eye in harmony with references to the images.[75] These images, of "westward expansion, world war, and space exploration, activated," according to Lipsitz, "deep layers of sentiment and emotion shaped by endless narratives—dime novels, motion picture, television programs."[76] Like John F. Kennedy's "New Frontier" speech given in 1960, the historical signifiers employed by Reagan, were accessible to virtually everyone.[77] Both Kennedy and in particular, Reagan, make use of the Frontier concept and specifically, the cowboy idea. The cowboy myth or icon is central to American heroic history. In the words of James Oliver Robertson, "It is available to Americans: it comes to their minds easily, in many variations; it is rich in associated images and ideals; it grows from thousands of tellings and retellings—in stories, movies, television programs, history books, children's play—of cowboy stories which are part of life in America."[78] The symbolism or mythology of the west is a ripe trope in American history. Ronald Reagan, with his ranch, his western clothes, his rugged physical appearance, was successful in his attempt to capture this idea.[79] The attempt on his life was also reworked to convey this image. As James Comb's relates, "when he was shot, Reagan displayed the aplomb and fearlessness we associate with the Western hero who carries on despite his wounds."[80]

In the world of the television series, the western, in all its manifestations, has been one of the most consistent formats. In becoming an entertainment staple, it is harmonious with the popular and accepted versions of history that Americans, Canadians and others now accept as "fact." Intrinsic to all of this are the ideals that Reagan emphasized ad nauseam: the hero fighting, conquering or taming evil. Yet, the television Western has come a long way since *Gunsmoke* and *Bonanza*. The most recent spate of shows, which range from the short lived *The Young Riders'* to *Bordertown*, to *Dr. Quinn, Medicine Women*, and *Deadwood*, attempt to present the west in a more 'realistic' or accurate format. The reality of the west was very different than the traditional Hollywood presentations. This new generation of western shows tries to present the complexities. As Jonas McCord, executive producer of *The Young Riders'* states: "We want to get into the fact that most of the people who lived in the West spoke with foreign accents not with a western drawl. There were Swedes, Dutch, Chinese. You go to Boot Hill and under it is an old Jewish cemetery dating from those

days."[81] *Dr. Quinn, Medicine Woman*, boasts numerous characters and plotlines designed to redress the way the west has been portrayed. As in *The
Young Riders*, there are ground breaking ventures to include women—the
title character being the most obvious—as well as African Americans and
Native Americans in more than merely stereotypical roles.[82] Yet for all the
aspirations, there is still an attempt to recapture the essence of the western formula. This formula was set in an early version of American popular culture, Buffalo Bill Cody's Wild West Show:

> Buffalo Bill's [Wild West Show] formula consisted of a simplified presenta-
> tion of conflict between good and evil, between the forces of civilization and
> barbarism. The cowboy hero of the American Frontier became a mythic crea-
> ture of extraordinary virtue and skill with who the audience identified. The
> cowboy exemplified popular values: he stood above man-made law, but al-
> ways followed a higher law; he was close to nature, yet a foe of savagery; he
> was civilized and gentlemanly yet an enemy of contrivance and corruption.
> The inevitable triumph of nature's nobleman, after a series of predictable tri-
> als, provided ritualistic catharsis.[83]

This sample of early American, exported popular culture mythology
demonstrated that the American western formula had universal appeal.
Crowds throughout the world identified with the victors and loved it.[84]
As well, this contained all the proper elements of appeal to audiences; heroes and villains, triumph and fortune. This was mythic, popular history
at its best.

Whether it is the Wild West with its archetypical cowboy, or any other
variety of the mythic hero, there is a similarity of plot. From the cowboy
it is no great distance, in fact, of the same mould, to move throughout the
pantheon of heroes and their quests. The pioneering series *Star Trek* contains many of the themes found in western and action adventure series.
According to Jay Goulding, the appeal of *Star Trek* consists of a composite
of all the fundamental characteristics: the frontier spirit, the quest for
knowledge, identification with heroes and the taste for victory in battle.
Goulding goes on to state that "consistent with the frontier mentality, the
Federation occupies the center of its exploration territory and like a
wagon train, is surrounded by barbaric enemies which are buffered by a
neutral zone with Federation outpost colonies."[85] Even in space, there is
an historical, mythological familiarity. When Reagan, Bush, or George W.
make a speech and invoke terms like "the frontier," the viewer does not
have to reach too far to find the image being conveyed; it is in most genres, many histories, and all media.

Every country has myths which evolve into popular presentations of
history. It is what many people living in a country can relate to and what
gives them a sense of belonging. The fact that they are constantly re-

worked and retold through television gives them a particular potency.[86] The perpetuation of these myths as history, which the public readily devours and absorbs, is accomplished by presenting them in ways which people can relate to with far more access than traditional formats. Television has reshaped the existing established body of culture to meet its own needs.[87] According to Brian Rose, the television genres that continue to exist do so because they were already established on radio. In turn, these were ideally suited to the needs of the new medium: they

> were those which lent themselves to frequent interruptions, strong personality identification, mass audience involvement, and a conventional moral view unlikely to ruffle the sponsors. This meant that, by and large, broadcast formats rarely strayed from familiar situations and from the entertainment formulas already popularized by literature, theatre, and motion pictures.[88]

Again, the Kennedy years provide an instructive reference. Television was new and the ideal medium for reflecting the dynamism of the Kennedy era, especially in contrast to the blandness of the Eisenhower years.[89] The elections of 1960 provided a vehicle for television to prove itself. Aiding in this technological forum was the script that excited people in various ways. There was the handsome, photogenic, dignified east coast representative versus the plain and the ordinary Nixon. For months, the campaign was cast as a drama. This was a drama filled with "conflict and plot twists" and "leading to a cliff-hanger ending."[90] In essence, from this crucial point in time, the media and television in particular, dealt with politics and social history as if it was a narrative story. What is created is an 'endless narrative' of production, a ceaseless conveyor belt of culture. Individual viewers within this realm enjoy following the familiar. They relish in the adventures of others vicariously, as the recent wave of reality based shows have shown. There is a certain appeal of that mythic fellowship of the past; it is comforting in the nostalgic sense. Illustrated by icons, sweetened by the intimacy of familiarity, one seeks nothing new, with the exception of variations of a theme.

As Todd Gitlin, Guy Debord, and others have recognized, many within the television universe are consciously playing roles that previous actors in history have played—even if that version of history has been defined, interpreted and scripted by popular visual culture. The President of the United States is often conscious of his role as sheriff or "marshal" and must act accordingly, to defend his town.[91] Regardless if it is a nature documentary, a western or a news documentary, the conventions of drama play a role. Television's dependency on drama for a significant amount of what it transmits—in the form of dramatic foundations, is the most obvious reason why it is a dramatic medium.[92]

Historian Erick Barnouw relates the structure and setting in which the media are often viewed and produced. He writes that for many people, television viewing is akin to a "psychological refuge, a fortress." Most of television "confirmed the average man's view of the world." There is a marked tendency to carefully craft a past that is not threatening and does not tarnish heroic figures and often, one that does not disturb the most fundamental beliefs and desires. There is the search for the perfect product; the perfect vision of the past.[93]

When attempts to break away from this cycle are achieved, they are often hailed as critical works of art. Yet even the most noble of television's (and film's) attempts to portray accurate and substantial history (*Gandhi*) the residue of historical shorthand is too powerful and too necessary to fall back on. Part of the reason for this fallback position is no doubt because of the fact that people do not possess the emotional energy, time, or inclination to concentrate on the horrors of the past or to rework the embedded collected history; they prefer neat, exact, and seamless stories. To constantly battle pleasure and thrill, and substitute instead pain and remorse, would contradict human nature. Similar to the trip to Disney world, the viewer willingly suspends the perception of reality. Perhaps, to paraphrase Neil Postman, the viewer is "dying to be amused," in his or her designated leisure time.

In a famous *Harper's* "conversation" between Camile Paglia and Neil Postman, the discussion moved toward then President, Ronald Reagan as the quintessential image president. Postman stated that, "a nation as heterogeneous as ours gropes to find comprehensive symbols and icons to pull us together." He then mentions George Bush, Sr.'s resume, which contains many elements of what Americans historically find heroic in their leaders. "If you read Bush's resume," writes Postman, "it is one of the most macho documents of recent times . . . first baseman at Yale, youngest Navy pilot shot down in combat, head of the CIA."[94] Quite a list for the average American; all the characteristics of heroism and adventure. In this same piece, cultural critic Camille Paglia concludes that television is a consistent rerun—a "formulaic return to what we know." Paglia writes that television is made up of a constant recycling of the old into the new. "It is like mythology, like the Homeric epics, the oral tradition in which the listener hears passages, formulae, and epithets repeated over and over again."[95] Like a child asking to hear his or her favorite bedtime story over and over, Paglia suggests that that is what makes television so comforting and familiar. The viewer knows the ending; knows how it is going to work out! This televisual narrative replaces traditional history with history that is composed of meta-narratives: stories with myths and heroes that cement versions of what is meant by nations and their respective past.

This is not a new version of history but rather, in many elements, a return to the way the past was chronicled in oral or traditional cultures. The dominant stories and myths, told and retold, varied and explained with slight discretions, was the way the past was dealt with until the advent of print. They were tinged with authority and capable of collectively unifying the diverse members of society.[96] History on television, film or within the photograph, serves as a form of—or becomes—"collective nostalgia." What we understand to be history in this case is more or less an amalgamation of recognizable public symbols "from the past that under, proper conditions can trigger wave upon wave of nostalgic feeling in millions of persons at the same time." These triggers are predominantly media creations which ranged from old movies to "dated speech mannerisms."[97] Interestingly, they can also be reworked and modified to become part of a new language in a postmodern form. This is most often seen in shows that utilize older conventions in new formats. The western was remade as has been noted, in the guise of the police show.

The western enjoyed its heyday during the early years of television is currently reborn and shown anew. Of course, it lives on in reruns. When television utilizes historical settings—that is beyond the western, historical docudrama and the odd play, it has a tendency to employ collective or popular nostalgia. In prime time and in reruns, this results in *Happy Days* or *Laverne and Shirley*. There are also shows such as *Little House on the Prairie* and *Anne of Green Gables* which attempt to picture the past in popular ways. As an entertainment medium, television is handicapped, or was handicapped in its historical presentations that were not situation comedies or variations of soap operas. It is Robert J. Thompson's contention that comedy shows using the past—even the recent past as a backdrop were one of the few ways history snuck in. Most of the shows discussed in this chapter did not last long, because, according to Thompson, people were not willing to engage them with the level of serious attention that was required. In his discussion of prime time television, Thomson singles out *M*A*S*H* as being one of the few series able to deal with certain historical problems and issues. The show was successful because it was situated during the Korean War and not the divisive Vietnam War, which was thematically what it really was about. Both *Tour of Duty* and *China Beach* appeared in 1987, well after the Vietnam conflict was over. What had paved the way for the prime time fictional treatment of that war was the spate of movies that had acclimatized the audience to the story of the war. Unfortunately, what Thompson pinpoints, is that the movie versions were much better than the television shows. It was simply not possible to transfer the horror and graphic nature of the war onto the small screen. This was particularly so for *Tour of Duty*. *China Beach* broke new ground, historically speaking in a number of ways.[98] It shed light on the contribution of women and at the same time, allowed for a focus on a different aspect of that conflict. In contrast to *M*A*S*H* the focus was on women and their role as agents in one segment of history.[99]

What Ken Burns has done is to take all the popular elements of myth and epic that, at least for Americans, have served as or evolved into key notions of American history and refitted them into a format that is both appealing and instructive. Using allegory as refined by popular culture, Burns has succeeded in creating a body of historical work that is accessible to many people. By capturing the elements that the viewing public expects and ensuring that there is a significant level of accuracy, Burns has been able to push the boundaries of historical discourse to new levels. Increasingly, his significant body of work has been capable of standing alongside the more established formats of historical enquiry, on an equal level.[100]

Burns's body of work is harmonious with the process of "standard academic practice[s]." As Gary Edgerton writes,

> Preparing each historical documentary includes the disciplined rigours of thoroughly researching his subject, writing grant proposals, collaborating and debating with an assortment of scholarly advisors, composing multiple drafts of the off screen narration, as well as gathering and selecting the background readings and expert commentaries.[101]

This exactitude is somewhat tempered by the fact that Burns is especially responsive to the fact that his films *are* films, and that they will air on television. Given this very significant element of historical presentation, the "storytelling" or narrative aspect of his expressions looms large.

Although, according to Edgerton, he has admitted this in interviews, he is still taken to task for this approach. The notions of "emotion" and "sympathy" crop up in his work because of how he approaches history. This stylistic aptitude also allows for a multiplicity of perspectives, which is not always possible in more traditional historical formats.[102] What should be kept in mind with regard to the visual histories of Ken Burns is that they serve as both starting points for many people and at the same time, are often definitive examinations for the average viewer. They are not necessarily *the* "last word on any given subject, simply because of the unprecedented power of television as a medium." They can and should be introductions, but often serve as much more. At the minimum, the filmed histories of Ken Burns stand as "dramatic alternatives" to published history.[103]

NOTES

1. Robert Kubey and Mihaly Csikszentmihalyi, *Television and the Quality of Life: How Viewing Shapes are Everyday Experience*, (Hillsdale, NJ: Lawrence Erlbaum Associates, 1990), p. 24.

2. Jostein Gripsrud, "Television and Common Knowledge: An Introduction," in Jostein Gripsrud, ed., *Television and Common Knowledge*, (New York: Routledge, 1999), p. 2.

3. Martin Esslin, *The Age of Television*, (New York: W. Freeman, 1982), p. 4.

4. William Boddy, *Fifties Television: The Industry and Its Critics*, (Urbana, IL: University of Illinois Press, 1990), pp. 15, 85.

5. Lawrence K. Grossman, *The Electronic Republic: Reshaping Democracy in The Information Age*, (New York: Viking/Penguin, 1995), p. 77.

6. Todd Gitlin, *Media Unlimited: How the Torrent of Images and Sounds Overwhelms Our Lives*, (New York: Henry Holt/Metropolitan Books, 2001), pp. 15–17, and Lawrence K. Grossman, *The Electronic Republic*, p. 77.

7. Gary R. Edgerton, "Introduction: Television as Historian: A Different Kind of History Altogether," in Gary R. Edgerton and Peter C. Rollins, eds., *Television Histories: Shaping Collective Memory in the Media Age*, (Lexington, KY: The University Press of Kentucky, 2001), p. 1. In the introduction to *Media Spectacles*, (New York: Routledge, 1993), p. xiii, Marjorie Garber, John Matlock and Rebecca L. Walkowitz write: "In an era of global technology, instant news, infomercials, electronic town meetings, and made-for-TV "documentaries," the borderlines between news and analysis, news and entertainment, news and fiction are constantly shifting." One must add visual history and traditional history into the above mix.

8. David Marc, *Bonfire of The Humanities: Television, Subliteracy, And Long-Term Memory Loss*, (Syracuse, NY: Syracuse University Press, 1995), p. 59.

9. As Marita Sturken, "The Television Image and Collective Amnesia: Dis(re)membering the Persian Gulf War," in Peter d'Agostino and David Tafler, eds., *Transmission: Toward a Post-Television Culture*, 2nd Edition, (Thousand Oaks, CA.: Sage Publications, 1995), p. 145, writes, "As electronic images, the images of the Gulf War carry with them the problematic relationship of television to history. In its connotation of immediacy and instant information, the television image evokes the present rather than the past. However, since the early 1980s, many images of *history* have been created on television screens."

10. Mary Ann Watson, *The Expanding Vista: American Television in The Kennedy Years*, (New York: Oxford University Press, 1990), p. 3.

11. Daniel J. Boorstin, *The Image: A Guide to Pseudo-Events in America*, (New York: Atheneum, 1987), pp. 9–44, and Daniel Dayan and Elihu Katz, *Media Events: The Live Broadcasting of History*, (Cambridge, MA: Harvard University Press, 1992), pp. 1–24.

12. Jeffrey Scheuer, *The Sound Bite Society: Television and The American Mind* (New York: Four Walls Eight Windows, 1999), p. 35.

13. Jeffrey Scheuer, *The Sound Bite Society*, p. 108.

14. Lawrence K. Grossman, *The Electronic Republic*, p. 77.

15. Jeffrey Scheuer, *The Sound Bite Society*, p. 109.

16. Gary R. Edgerton, "Introduction: Television as Historian: A Different Kind of History Altogether," p. 9.

17. Gary R. Edgerton, "Introduction: Television as Historian: A Different Kind of History Altogether," p. 10. Edgerton writes: "Any constructive evaluation of "television as historian" also needs to start with the assumption that it is an entirely new and different kind of history altogether. Unlike written discourse, the

language of TV is highly stylized, elliptical (rather than linear) in structure, and associational or metaphoric in the ways in which it portrays images and ideas."

18. Robert Brent Toplin, "Plugged Into the Past," *The New York Times*, August 4, 1996, Section 2, p. 1.

19. Todd Gitlin, "Introduction: Looking Through the Screen," in Todd Gitlin, ed., *Watching Television*, (New York: Pantheon, 1986), p. 4.

20. Gary R. Edgerton, *Ken Burns's America*, (New York: Palgrave/St. Martin's Press, 2001, p. 9.

21. Mark Starowicz, *Making History*, (Toronto: McClelland & Stewart, 2003), pp. 28–29.

22. Mark Starowicz, *Making History*, p. 29.

23. Mark Starowicz, *Making History*, p. 28.

24. Daniel Dayan and Elihu Katz, *Media Events: The Live Broadcasting of History*, pp. viii–8.

25. Bruce Cummings, *War and Television*, (New York: Verso, 1992), p. 1. Cummings writes, "The Gulf War was a war fought in the interest of forgetting. It was, for President George Bush, a war to 'put Vietnam behind us.'" p. 2. Marita Sturken, "The Television Image and Collective Amnesia: Dis(re)membering the Persian Gulf War," p. 137, writes, "Phenomenologically, the Persian Gulf War was the first television war of the United States. While the Vietnam War is called the first "living room war," images of the Vietnam War were almost exclusively shot on film and hence subject to the delays the film developing process requires. There was always at least a 24-hour delay for images of the Vietnam War to reach the United States. The Persian Gulf War, on the other hand, took place in an era of satellite technology and highly portable video technology. It was technologically possible for the world to watch the Persian Gulf War live as it happened."

26. Mitchell Stephens, *The Rise of The Image, The Fall of the Word*, (New York: Oxford University Press, 1998), p. 27.

27. Paul Virilio, *War and Cinema: The Logistics of Perception* (1984), trans. Patrick Camiller, (New York: Verso, 1989), p. 20, cited in Rey Chow, "The Age of the World Target: On the Fiftieth Anniversary of the Dropping of the Atomic Bomb," in Peter Gibian, ed., *Mass Culture and Everyday Life*, (New York: Routledge, 1997), p. 94.

28. Marita Sturken, "The Television Image and Collective Amnesia: Dis(re)membering the Persian Gulf War," p. 137.

29. Douglas Kellner, *The Persian Gulf TV War*, (Boulder, CO: Westview Press, 1992), p. 4.

30. Douglas Kellner, *The Persian Gulf TV War*, pp. 64–65.

31. Douglas Kellner, *The Persian Gulf TV War*, p. 113.

32. Douglas Kellner, *The Persian Gulf TV War*, p. 114.

33. Mark Crispin Miller, "How TV Covers War," in Alan Rosenthal, editor, *New Challenges for Documentary*, (Berkeley, CA: University of California Press, 1988), p. 370

34. James W. Carey, *Communications as Culture: Essays on Media and Society*, (Boston: Unwin Hyman, 1989), p. 20.

35. James W. Carey, *Communications as Culture*, p. 22.

36. Robert Fulford, *The Triumph of Narrative: Storytelling in the Age of Mass Culture*, (Toronto: House of Anansi Press Limited, 1999), p. 80. Fulford writes: "Jour-

nalists may occasionally claim they are merely messengers, passing on the facts that come to them, but this pose won't withstand scrutiny. At their most accomplished, journalistic narratives may appear natural and inevitable, as if each story *had* to be told and could not have been told another way."

37. Knowlton Nash, *Trivia Pursuit: How Showbiz Values are Corrupting the News*, (Toronto: McClelland & Stewart, 1998), p. 158.

38. John Hockenberry, "Graphic News," *I.D. Magazine*, Sept./Oct. 1996, p. 63.

39. Emily West, "Selling Canada to Canadians: Collective memory, national identity, and popular culture," *Critical Studies in Media Communication*, June, 2002, p. 217.

40. Mark Starowicz, *Making History*, p. 61.

41. Steve Anderson, "History TV and Popular Memory," in Gary R. Edgerton and Peter C. Rollins, eds., *Television Histories: Shaping Collective Memory in the Media Age*, (Lexington, KY: The University Press of Kentucky, 2001), p. 25.

42. Steve Anderson, "History TV and Popular Memory," pp. 25, 30.

43. Paul A. Cantor, *Gilligan Unbound: Pop Culture in the Age of Globalization*, p. 58.

44. Steve Anderson, "History TV and Popular Memory," pp. 25, 30.

45. Mimi White, "Masculinity and Femininity in Television's Historical Fictions: *Young Indiana Jones Chronicles* and *Dr. Quinn, Medicine Woman*," in Gary R. Edgerton and Peter C. Rollins, eds., *Television Histories: Shaping Collective Memory in the Media Age*, p. 56.

46. Elayne Rapping, *The Movie of The Week: Private Stories, Public Events*, (Minneapolis, MN: University of Minnesota Press, 1992), pp. x, xi. Both David Marc, *Comic Visions: Television Comedy and American Culture*, (Boston: Unwin Hyman, 1989) and Alvin H. Marill, *Movies Made for Television* (New York: Da Capo, 1980) suggest that the two hour, socially, politically, and culturally relevant two hour television movie originated in the late sixties.

47. Michael Kammen, *Mystic Chords of Memory: The Transformation of Tradition in American Culture*, (New York: Knopf, 1991), p. 642.

48. Leslie Fishbein, "*Roots*: Docudrama and the Interpretation of History," in Alan Rosenthal, editor, *Why Docudrama? Fact-Fiction on Film and TV*, (Carbondale, IL: Southern Illinois University Press, 1999), p. 272.

49. Leslie Fishbein, "*Roots*: Docudrama and the Interpretation of History," p. 275.

50. Jeffrey Shandler, *While America Watches: Televising the Holocaust*, (New York: Oxford University Press, 1999), p. 155.

51. Jeffrey Shandler, *While America Watches: Televising the Holocaust*, pp. 41, 45.

52. Jeffrey Shandler, *While America Watches: Televising the Holocaust*, p. 163.

53. Jeffrey Shandler, *While America Watches: Televising the Holocaust*, p. 209.

54. Elayne Rapping, *The Movie of The Week*, pp. xi–xii.

55. Elayne Rapping, *The Movie of The Week*, p. 36.

56. Elayne Rapping, *The Movie of The Week*, p. 118.

57. Elayne Rapping, *The Movie of The Week*, p. 118.

58. Cecelia Tichi, *Electronic Hearth: Creating an American Televsion Culture*, (New York: Oxford University Press, 1991), p. 11.

59. Lynn Spigel, *Make Room For TV: Television and the Family Ideal in Postwar America*, (Chicago: University of Chicago Press, 1992), pp. 37–45, Cecilia Tichi, *Electronic Hearth*, pp. 42–61, and Karal Ann Marling, *As Seen on TV: The Visual Cul-*

ture of Everyday Life in the 1950s, (Cambridge, MA: Harvard University Press, 1994).

60. Cecilia Tichi, *Electronic Hearth*, p. 134.

61. Aletha C. Huston et al., *Big World, Small Screen: The Role of Television in American Society*, (Lincoln, NE: University of Nebraska Press, 1992), pp. 76–77.

62. Steven D. Stark, *Glued To The Set: The 60 Television Shows and Events That Made Us Who We Are Today*, (New York: The Free Press, 1997), p. 54.

63. R. Hewison, *The Heritage Industry*, (London: 1981), p. 135, cited in David Harvey, *The Condition of Postmodernity*, (Cambridge, MA: Blackwell, 1990/1995), pp. 62–63.

64. Mike Wallace, "Mickey Mouse History: Portraying the Past at Disney World," *Radical History Review*, 32, 1985, p. 33.

65. Mike Wallace, "Mickey Mouse History," p. 36.

66. Carol Duncan, *Civilizing Rituals: Inside Public Art Museums*, (New York: Routledge, 1995), p. 71.

67. Diane Barthel, *Historic Preservation: Collective Memory and Historical Identity*, (New Brunswick, NJ: Rutgers University Press, 1996), pp. 2–3, Susan Willis, "The Problem with Pleasure," The Project on Disney, *Inside the Mouse: Work and Play at Disney World*, (Durham: Duke University Press, 1995), pp. 1–11.

68. In *The Sound Bite Society: Television and The American Mind* (New York: Four Walls Eight Windows, 1999), Jeffrey Scheuer, p. 6, writes, "Television, though seldom directly fatal, has particularly complicated and ambivalent social functions. The medium's most obvious shortcomings are well-known, and we needn't belabor them. Commercial TV at once epitomizes and amplifies everything mediocre and excessive in a consumer society. In manipulates our emotions, numbs us with social stereotypes, saturates us with the trivial and the superficial. It is both a wunderkind of twentieth century technology (like the computer), with vast potential to inform and entertain, and a whore of profit."

69. Eric Barnouw, *Tube of Plenty* (New York: Oxford 1990), Bill McKibben, *The Age of Missing Information*, (New York: Random House, 1992), Neil Postman, *Amusing Ourselves To Death*, (New York: Penguin Books, 1985), Joshua Meyrowitz, *No Sense of Place: The Impact of Electronic Media on Social Behavior*, (New York: Oxford University Press, 1985), and Danny Schechter, *The More You Watch, The Less You Know*, (New York: Seven Stories Press, 1997).

70. In a review of David Plowden's photographic essay, *Small Town America* (New York: Abrams, 1994), Jim Doherty writes: "As the pictures reproduced here make clear, he has a passion for authenticity—the Coca-Cola signs on a grimy storefront, the trophies adorning a parlor wall. These unvarnished images are ambiguous. They remind us that many small towns are a far cry from the idealized versions we often see portrayed on television and in movies." "Maybe Small Towns aren't fancy, but at least they're real," *Smithsonian*, vol. 24, no. 12, March 1994, p. 42.

71. Richard Slotkin, *Gunfighter Nation: The Myth of the Frontier in Twentieth Century America*, (New York: Anteneum, 1992), p. 6.

72. Leo Marx, *Machine in The Garden*, p. 4, cited in Burce Lohof, "The Higher Meaning of Marlboro Cigarettes," in Christopher D. Geist and Jack Nachbar, eds., *The Popular Culture Reader*, third edition, (Bowling Green, OH: Bowling Green University Popular Press, 1983), p. 112.

73. Bruce Lohof, "The Higher Meaning of Marlboro Cigarettes," p. 112.

74. Lawrence K. Grossman, *The Electronic Republic: Reshaping Democracy in the Information Age*, (New York: Viking, 1995).

75. George Lipsitz, *Time Passages: Collective Memory and American Popular Culture*, (Minneapolis, MN: University of Minnesota Press, 1990), p. 33.

76. George Lipsitz, *Time Passages*, p. 33.

77. Richard Slotkin, *Gunfighter Nation*, p. 2. Slotkin writes: "For Kennedy and his advisors, the choice of the Frontier as symbol was not simply a device for trademarking the candidate. It was an authentic metaphor, descriptive of the way in which they hoped to use political power and the kinds of struggle in which they wished to engage. The 'Frontier' was for them a complexly resonant symbol, a vivid and memorable set of hero-tales—each a model of successful and morally justifying action on the stage of historical conflict."

78. James Oliver Robertson, *American Myth: American Reality*, (New York: Hill and Wang, 1980), p. 6. The truth though, is quite different. Robertson writes: "the real cowboy, or cowpoke, was a skilled technician hired to do the boring, and often dangerous business of working cows" for a large ranch corporation or railroad," p. 161.

79. Walter R. Fisher, "Romantic Democracy, Ronald Reagan, and Presidential Heroes," *Western Journal of Speech Communication*, 46, Summer 1982, p. 302, cited in James Combs, *The Reagan Range: The Nostalgic Myth in American Politics*, (Bowling Green, OH: Bowling Green State University Popular Press, 1993), p. 51.

80. James Combs, *The Reagan Range*, p. 51.

81. Pearl Sheffy Gefen, "A return to the Old West and 'simpler values,'" *The Globe and Mail*, August 30, 1990, p. C6.

82. Mimi White, "Masculinity and Femininity in Television's Historical Fictions," p. 47.

83. Emily S. Rosenberg, *Spreading the American Dream: American Economic and Cultural Expansion, 1890—1945*, (New York: Hill and Wang, 1989), p. 35.

84. Emily S. Rosenberg, *Spreading the American Dream*, p. 35.

85. Jay Goulding, *Empire, Aliens and Conquest: A Critique of American Ideology in Star Trek and Other Science Fiction Adventures*, (Toronto: Sisyphus Press, 1985), pp. vii, 15.

86. Jeffrey Richards, *Visions of Yesterday*, (London: Routledge and Kegan Paul, 1973), p. xv.

87. Brian Rose, "Preface" in Brian Rose, ed., *T.V. Genres: A Handbook and Reference Guide*, (Westport, CT: Greenwood Press, 1985), p. vii.

88. Brian Rose, "Preface," p. 6.

89. Mary Ann Watson, *The Expanding Vista*, p. 3.

90. Mary Ann Watson, *The Expanding Vista*, p. 10.

91. Daniel C. Hallin, "Network News: 'We Keep America on Top of the World.'" in Todd Gitlin, ed., *Watching Television*, p. 12.

92. Martin Esslin, *The Age of Television*, p. 7.

93. Erik Barnouw, *Tube of Plenty: The Evolution of American Television*, (New York: Oxford University Press, 1975), p. 403.

94. Neil Postman, "The Dinner Conversation?" *Harpers*, March 1991, p. 51.

95. Cited in Neil Postman, "The Dinner Conversation?" *Harpers*, March 1991, p. 51.

96. Warren I. Susman, *Culture As History: The Transformation of American Society in the Twentieth Century*, (New York: Pantheon Books, 1984), p. 8.

97. Robert J. Thompson, *Television's Second Golden Age*, (New York: Continuum, 1996), pp. 140–142.

98. Fred Davis, *Yearning For Yesterday: A Sociology of Nostalgia*, (New York: The Free Press, 1979), pp. 122–123, 125. Davis, p. 126, writes: "Because there is money to [be] made from nostalgia the media have come to devour their past creations at an ever increasing rate. A consequence has been that the time span between the "original appearance," as it were, and its nostalgic recycling has shrunk to a fraction of what it once was. Oddly the recent past is made to seem as a result more removed and historic than previous ways of subjectively relating to it would have made it appear." This fascinating development has a number of manifestations. These range from "classic" television stations that show reruns, to the myriad history television formats that show 'historical' footage as packaged entertainment.

99. Robert J. Thompson, *Television's Second Golden Age*, pp. 142–44.

100. Gary R. Edgerton, Ken Burns's America, p. vii.

101. Gary R. Edgerton, Ken Burns's America, p. 13.

102. Gary R. Edgerton, Ken Burns's America, pp. 14, 16.

103. Gary R. Edgerton, Ken Burns's America, p. 105.

7

The Process of Holocaust Commemoration in the Media Age

What I eventually had to accept was that for some survivors of the Holocaust, the only acceptable response to the tragedy they endured is commemoration—and its complement, commemorative history.

—Erna Paris, *Long Shadows: Truth, Lies and History*, 313 [1]

We live in a time when advances in technology have begun to affect the individual's surrounding awareness of society to such an extent that new forms of expression may be needed to address age-old ways of doing things. It is no secret that since the advent of the printing press, traditional notions of memory, study, learning, and reflection have been altered. With photography and soon after, the cinema, these faculties were further transformed. Modern culture and in fact, modernism as an "era" has created collections of technologies which force societies to perceive both the past and the present in fundamentally different ways. For example, information is now packaged in very specific ways; the screen, both on the computer and through television is perceived of as reality; memory has been altered by mass culture and finally, many more people have access to mass culture and garner so much knowledge from it that it is now a dominant information platform.

Mass culture or popular expositions of rigorous subjects have had a substantive influence in disseminating information on a variety of subjects, in particular, the Holocaust.[2] How we think about the past and, in particular, how memorialization is attempted, has to be considered within the framework of media and mass culture. This is especially relevant to young people. As one observer recently wrote,

As a twenty-something Canadian male living in Toronto I've always had a hard time coming to terms with the Holocaust. It's a world existing in shades of grey, experienced through black-and-white photos and grainy film footage.[3]

Television has perhaps had the most serious impact on the rigors of memory, observation, powers of contemplation, and assessment. Computers will no doubt accelerate and intensify what television has already set in motion.[4] Within this framework, it is also critical to keep in mind that the popular postmodern structuring of history and, by extension, memory, is oriented around narrative and drama. The Holocaust Museum in Washington is in fact charged with the mission to tell the story of the Holocaust. In this context, the changing nature of an individual's power to contemplate difficult and demanding issues, new ways to reach that individual— to tell the historical story—have to be devised. No area of enquiry is immune from this process. One must acknowledge as well that it would be tragic, shortsighted and dangerous not to recognize this point.

The process of Holocaust commemoration is one such area that faces a particularly daunting task. Popular culture and mass media have provided many opportunities to reflect on the severity of the Holocaust. Films such as *Sophie's Choice, Schindler's List,* and *A Beautiful Life,* books such as *The Diary of Anne Frank, Night, Maus,* and *The Periodic Table,* and television series such as *Holocaust* provide the reader and viewer with an easily digestible format with the necessary triggers to our emotions, the ones required to unlock the gravity of such a massive and tragic period in history. Thanks to efforts at popularization and aided by media savvy techniques, the whole conceptual apparatus of Holocaust commemoration has shifted to accommodate new approaches in thinking and memorialization. The ideas of public memory and collective history have been accelerated to such an extent, that any thinking about the Holocaust in an open forum, tends to gravitate towards nontraditional commemorative formats. No more is this felt as in structures like the United States Holocaust Museum in Washington, the Museum of Tolerance in Los Angeles, and in films such as *Schindler's List* and *A Beautiful Life.* These two embodiments of the Holocaust, museums, and movies, have come to stand as repositories of both memory and meaning regarding the Holocaust and have taken on lives of their own as far as the process of commemoration in the media age. Bridging the two are memorials, which derive much of their power from traditional notions of commemorization, yet have accommodated emerging notions of perception harmonious with a media world.

Commemoration most often means "to preserve in memory." Memory, whether collective, social, or personal, is related to learning and as such, is a central component of history. Memory is far more complex than the simple recollection of the past. It is a process of construction. People and institutions, documents and texts are part of the movement to constantly reshape, change, and modify aspects of the past in a continuous and on-going way.[5] Yet, the dominant factor in affecting memory and history to-day is the visual image. The impact of the visual image in today's society is unparalleled.[6] Its consequences spill over into numerous areas and it forces new challenges upon different audiences. Although this is a process that has been building since the advent of photography,[7] it was severely altered with the motion picture and accelerated greatly since television. Often, the dominant visual media 'fight' against both the book and indi-vidual memory for elbow room. The power of film to evoke emotion, to initiate discussion and to articulate history has been recognized for decades.[8] Films are forms of narrative with such power, that according to Anton Kaes, they "have begun to supersede memory and experience."[9] At the beginning of the second millennium, it is the image, that reigns supreme as a locus of meaning, and that all else must accommodate. In an image saturated environment and an information oriented society, the more outstanding the image, the more effective is its message.[10]

Up until the last few decades, the book and the footnoted article were the main sources of "the past." As our society becomes increasingly de-voted to sources of the past, other than the book, it is necessary to appre-ciate these new sources, to understand them, and to analyze them, rather than dismiss them as substandard or incomplete.[11] The dominance of vi-sual sources—photographs, films, television, CD-ROMs—is unques-tioned in comparison to "the book" in particular, when it comes to histor-ical interpretation.[12]

One of the hallmarks of postmodern culture is the atmosphere of speed in which western society finds itself caught.[13] Television sets a quick pace in both its time to convey information and the time audiences are ex-pected to absorb information. As viewers became accustomed to speed and came to expect it, their powers of contemplation were reduced. Even two generations ago, the powers of concentration for the average indi-vidual were much longer. Today, the immediacy and pace set by televi-sion mark a quantum leap in the ability of the average individual to process large quantities of information over substantial periods of time. Short bursts of scenes and quick changes in content are now the preferred methods.

Attempts to present a weighty topic with the seriousness of the Holo-caust grapple first with the possibility of representing terror and tragedy on such a massive scale. The popular media's paring down complex and serious historical subjects are problematic, fraught with the risk of trivial-ization, "emotional manipulation" and "vulgarization."[14] But there have also been extraordinarily powerful displays of Holocaust commemora-tion that borrow and expand on elements of popular culture. David

Levinthal's photographs of toys, in particular soldiers and other assorted figurines, are derived from a plethora of mass culture influences which range from play and television, to film and postwar consumer culture. Levinthal's photographs are extraordinarily powerful and one may suggest that their force is built on the contradictions of using seemingly trivial or even innocent counterpoints as illustrations. Regardless of how one sees these creations it must be understood that Levinthal is working from experiences that are or already have been "mediated." What elements in this past have come to Levinthal, are present from film, photographs and other media.[15] This is a fact present in much of the art produced to discuss or commemorate the Holocaust in the past few years.

The graphic novel, the offshoot of the comic book, has proven to be one of the most interesting publishing phenomena of the last few decades. These original and unique documents seem to straddle the traditional world of print and the postmodern, "mosaic" texture of the visual age. Art Spiegelman's *Maus*, a Pulitzer Prize winning adult comic book, is the story of Spiegelman's father's concentration camp experience. The story features the Jews as mice, the Germans as cats and the Poles as pigs. Rather than trivializing the holocaust, the work is effective in conveying the horror of something that is often beyond the scope of description.[16] What this work demonstrates is that beyond the traditional means of reaching an audience to both inform and commemorate, there can be methodologies that incorporate nontraditional practices which achieve a high degree of effectiveness. In an interview, restated by James Young, Spiegelman intimates that the visual and written impact of "commix," is much closer to "actual human thought," and is in fact, uniquely suited to convey a more powerful message "than either words or pictures alone."[17] *Maus* was put out in a CD-ROM version which goes even farther in getting the message across. This version includes interviews with Vladek Spiegelman, Art's father, as well as aerial photographs of concentration camps.[18] As long as the work does not trivialize, it can have an enormous impact especially upon those who gravitate to these newer forms of media.

At the same time, this is of particular concern as Holocaust deniers and revisionists do not lack platforms to spread their odious message. As the generation who experienced the horrors ages, and as we move farther and farther away from the events, Donald Schwartz feels that information about the Holocaust "grows more urgent and compelling as the Nazi nightmare dims in the collective consciousness."[19] Within the academy, horrors have become commonplace teaching subjects. Special care must be taken especially when the theme is emotional and so complex.[20] For many people the Holocaust remains beyond the scope of comprehension. The enormous quantities of documentation, physical evidence, and survivor testimony attempts to do justice but given the scale of destruction, the subject often remains unprocessed. Given this parameter, there is a strong need to keep the memory alive and a tendency to resort to methods of "informing" that some people feel are in questionable taste and which foster debatable practices. For example, concerns that arise with regard to pilgrimages to death camp sites and tours that focus on the Holocaust.[21]

Over the last number of years two significant fountainheads have been created where much of the debate around commemoration practices has coalesced. One is the inception of a number of museums to honor the dead, in particular, the United States Holocaust Museum. The other is a number of films on the Holocaust, specifically, Stephen Spielberg's film, *Schindler's List*. Given the forces transforming traditional notions of history and memory, it is useful to look at how the museum structure, memorials and movies have accommodated these changes.

Prior to the construction of the United States Holocaust Museum in Washington, the main repository of Holocaust memory was to be found in Jerusalem, at Yad Vashem. This is a place that serves as both a memorial and a museum. Created by an act of parliament in the early 1950s, Yad Vashem was a "commemorative" site designed to house "the collective memory of the Jewish people."[22] Yad Vashem was first and foremost a place to spark memory while at the same time, a living memorial to the six million Jews and others who perished. As a museum, it was also charged with the practical applications of defining history through the prism of objects and glass. Thus, like any form of history, choices had to be made in deciding what to show and how to tell the story.[23] For forty years, Yad Vashem stood alone, albeit with smaller versions in communities throughout the world, until a larger, more obvious, American version was built. In the ensuing decades, much has changed. Whereas Yad Vashem has all the solemnness of a funeral parlor, and evokes the reverence that one experiences in a place of worship, a fundamentally different set of characteristics affects the visitors to the Washington museum, which can effectively convey the serious and horrific consequences of the memorialized tragedy.[24]

Edward T. Linenthal's work on The United States Holocaust Museum suggests that visitors are made to feel a part of the Holocaust narrative upon entering the building.[25] Immediately, visitors are intentionally drawn into an environment which is meant to convey something of the enormity of the subject. Linenthal writes that visitors are "herded into intentionally ugly, dark grey metal elevators," where they are "crowded" together to watch U.S. G.I.'s first responses to the camps, and then they are "unloaded" at another floor to begin the actual tour, in a context "'visceral' enough so that visitors would gain no respite from the narrative." Linenthal suggests that the designers deliberately constricted the space on the third floor so that a feeling of darkness and claustrophobia would set in. They intended to literally take the visitors on a journey, as close as possible to the actual route the victims undertook. The use of identity cards which are given to each visitor propels this message even deeper. The visitor is bombarded with photographs of the victims in another exhibit, which are "shattering in their power" and "assault, challenge, accuse, and profoundly sadden visitors throughout the exhibition."[26]

From the outset, the United States Holocaust Memorial Museum, which opened in 1993, was meant to be different from any other museum in existence. It was designed to tell an account, to be a "narrative museum," which displayed the chronicle of the Holocaust.[27] As part of its mission, the Museum both shocks and stuns visitors in a way that makes it difficult to forget what one has seen inside.[28] The Hall of Witness, is specifically designed to invoke "an immediate emotional reaction."[29] Artifacts, both personal effects and instruments of torture, occupy a prominent position in the museum. Such objects are capable of providing, "the strongest historical evidence, stronger even than documentary photographs. They constitute a direct link to the events, which are embedded in them, as it were. Having been there, they have become silent witnesses."[30]

When the Imperial War Museum in London England mounted a Holocaust exhibition, the museum chose to include the Exhibition as part of the other exhibits depicting the horrors of World War II, rather than to keep the Holocaust exhibit separate. As with the Museum in Washington, the Imperial War Museum's exhibit displayed artifacts: toys, sewing machines, a marble dissecting table. Discussions of the exhibit raised the issue of "voyeuristic experience" and two opinions came to the fore. Historian David Cesarini felt that these objects would not only offend survivors but risk creating a "kind of prurient interest" in the viewer. The other opinion came from Martin Smith, who was involved with the museum in Washington and who suggested that playing down or "sanitizing the nature of the extermination process would do an injustice to the subject."[31] Artifacts, like much of material culture, carry weight and lend authority to narratives. They transcend being looked at and can stand for—or perhaps are—tangible elements of evidence.[32] The use of actual artifacts: suitcases, umbrellas, clothes, prisoner's jackets, Zyklon B cans, artificial limbs, and human hair, which were brought to the museum in Washington as a result of an agreement with the State Museum at Auschwitz, not only dramatically demonstrates the complete and thorough nature of the extermination process but also personalizes the story. Objections to the use of these artifacts oriented around similar concerns voiced by Cesarini, focused initially, on the fear of creating a "cabinet of horrible curiosities" and the potential of creating a "more ghoulish" response than a "sympathetic or painful memorial response."[33]

The artifacts, the employment of the tools of death (Zyklon B, freight cars), and a desire to recreate the vestiges of concentration camp life, in this and in other Holocaust museums, does lead to a form of emotional manipulation.[34] It is deliberate, overt, and necessary. Unlike more functional and traditional educational goals and museum motives, changes in society have allowed a kind of sensationalizing that "emotionally recreates the tragedy so that it remains a raw wound."[35] This is particularly effective in a society which almost glorifies violence or, at the very least, allows for immediate and constant horrific images via the mass media. Critics of this approach feel that by focussing on the sensational or gory aspects of the event, the emphasis on the actual tragedy is lost, and a focus on sensationalization and distorting vulgarity comes to the fore.[36] The fact that over the last fifty years, the mass media have initiated many changes in viewer's capacity to absorb information in particular ways, further compresses the ability of individuals to process historical data. Judith Miller, aware of the media-saturated environment, writes:

> This vulgarisation is a new form of historical titillation. And in a society like America's, where the public attention span is measured in seconds and minutes rather than years or decades, where fad is often confused with trend, where sentimentality replaces insight and empathy, it represents a considerable threat to dignified remembrance.[37]

Critics like Miller, feel that because of the nature of mediated communication, its anti-historical, noncontemplative agenda, and emphasis on sentimentality, it is impossible to deal with a subject like the Holocaust on the contemporary terms that have been established without threatening the seriousness of the subject matter. Yet others disagree. Rabbi Marvin Hier, Director of the Simon Wiesenthal Center and Museum in Los Angeles feels that one must employ techniques present in the media in order to get the message across. As long as the message gets out, that is all that matters.[38] Yet one can sympathize with Hier in the sense that he is forced to work with a subject matter that does not lend itself well to postmodern technology, advertising ideas, and marketing techniques.[39] But perhaps Hier is on to something. He is trying to reach out, as are others, towards individuals who normally would not be accessible in more conventional, text-based formats. And attempting to do this causes controversy. To add fuel to the fire, concepts such as universalization and Americanization get mixed into the attempts at getting the message out.

The first director of the Holocaust Museum in Washington, Michael Berenbaum, writes that one of the main tasks of the Holocaust Museum is to "tell the American public as clearly and comprehensively as possible what happened in that darkest chapter of human history."[40] Lawrence Langer, author of the important essay entitled "The Americanization of

the Holocaust on Stage and Screen," has written that the way the Holocaust has been presented to American audiences has, in fact been quite the
opposite of what Berenbaum has suggested. Langer suggests that the
prettified and romanticized images presented do not, by any stretch of the
imagination, "convey the terror and despair" that characterized the actual
Holocaust. But, according to Langer, the end result is still laudable. Despite the fact that this is the way the Holocaust is often framed by the popular media, information does reach people about this increasingly historically distant period. In fact, Langer implies that without this more
sanitized format, the event could have disappeared from the public eye.[41]

In a critical article on the Holocaust Museum in Washington, Philip
Gourevitch suggests that this process of Americanization is a hollow one,
for denouncing evil via the American political and social identity is a far
cry from doing good.[42] The nimble balancing act required between getting
the message across and informing in good taste is problematic for some.
If the bottom line is to inform, to educate, to teach, then criticism and controversy is seemingly inevitable.[43] An institution devoted to the uniqueness of the Holocaust simply cannot meet the expectations of every critic.
As such, the question of the role of a Holocaust museum comes to be
judged differently than the traditional museum, for it has, at its core, an
essence for being that is fundamentally more serious than its more casual
cousins.

This is made even more problematic fact that within the context of today's media environment, museums no longer hold the special and effective associations that they once held. Museums must compete with
other entertainment forums and activities.[44] As a consequence of the
competition, they must play by a set of rules that is not always acceptable to those who are uncomfortable with the marketing aspect of culture. As Philip Gourevitch has recognized, "however serious their subject
they are obliged to win and reward the attention of their audience."[45]
Marvin Hier and Michael Berenbaum have recognized this and have
gone forward in this direction. Holocaust museums—despite their subject matter—must play by the rules of appeal and popularity. They must
incorporate the latest technology and the most cutting edge techniques of
museumology in order to reach out and inform the greatest number of
people. The merging of entertainment and education, titillation and commemoration that result crosses a line that many people feel is disconcert-
ing. Hier, in attempting to reach out to people beyond the converted, justifies his attempts to move in this direction because he feels that he is
talking to them in terms and in a language that they can understand. This
"high-tech" approach means giving "them information about this period
and its moral lessons in a form that they are used to receiving it—the
tube."[46]

While fighting to get information about the Holocaust out, museums devoted to this task are torn between participating in a popularity contest, which may guarantee interest, and the difficult and solitary task of standing alone, out of line with the media age. It is almost a given imperative that new technology should be incorporated into the presentation of the Holocaust, with the hope that care and consideration are never sacrificed. While this process will only become more acceptable and hence, more sophisticated, eventually a balance will be found and reached that will combine cutting edge technology and high tech presentation with a palatable and serious dignity.

Holocaust museums are key components in the harnessing of a particularly ugly period of history, processing the complexities, and presenting the end result in a manner both accessible and effective to "audiences." This must be done both in the internal set-up of the exhibits and in any other way possible. As architects have known for thousands of years, the exterior quality of the building is often as important as the displays and message inside. The architectonic property of the building is necessary to make the governing philosophies of its construction and contents visible. As Herbert Muschamp has written:

> The Holocaust museums are grounded in the belief that buildings can establish a visibility on a permanent basis, as though their size, their placement in the context of daily life, and their capacity to house as well as depict events gives them a claim to reality—and to its meaning—beyond that exercised by other works of art.[47]

As well as the buildings, sculpture, or monuments become key factors in the commemoration/memory process. Monuments and memorials are reminders not to forget but also warn.[48] James Young feels that memorials take on added importance and become more "prominent" as the "events of World War II recede into time."[49] Public memory then is being molded by monuments and memorial structures. Implicit in the use of monuments is something more than just the idea of a "secular shrine" designed to trigger thought, for memorials are "temporal institutions reflecting changing public constituencies and distinctive political, social, and cultural contexts."[50] These monuments transmit the history, meaning, memory and the severity of the Holocaust, and consequently, like memory, they become bound to the culture of history.

Societies do not record their past as faithfully as one would expect and when they do, a process of reconstruction as far as memory is concerned, is undertaken. This is attempted with present-day concerns often jostling for attention and a place on the agenda. There is a reorientation of history in order to shape the needs of the contemporary society.[51] Examples of this abound and they range from Israeli discussions on resistance to the other extreme of Polish monuments, and concerns over Bitburg. On this, Sybil Milton has remarked that "the Holocaust has thus sometimes been presented in distorted exhibitions or sanitized sites."[52] Offending a new generation of Germans or risking an already touchy situation with the French are just two reasons why this molding of the historical agenda occurs.

When looking at monuments in the media age, unique problems arise. One main concern is the displacement of the message into a symbolic form that can either bury the intention or obfuscate the meaning in the highly abstract construction of the monument. Extended, the concern here is that this can alleviate the burden of remembering and in the same way, transfer this "obligation" from the individual to the structure.[53] The fact that there is such a diversity of styles and tastes, artistic ideas, and agendas in the decision to erect a monument problematizes the whole notion of symbolically sublimating memory towards a monument or a memorial. Any consensus reached may stem from the fact that these structures are similar to commemorative tombstones, which suggest a sacred function is at work. Yet, in contrast to national monuments commemorating the war dead—which often become pilgrimage sites and national expressions of patriotic sacrifice—the Holocaust monument must intimate that this is no ordinary form of commemoration. In fact, an aura of the fantastic must be harnessed in order to convey that something out of the ordinary happened. The danger here is that the site can become a place of shame, or a novel attraction which encourages the wrong emotions.[54] Still, in this media saturated age, monuments and memorials can be potent reminders and warning beacons.[55] "Throughout the world," writes Vivian Thompson, "memorials to the Holocaust have been built in an attempt to give form to an incomplete mourning process and to build markers to those who died."[56]

One could also suggest that straddling the fence between monuments and museums is the realm of pure art—photography, sculpture, painting—that is oriented around Holocaust themes and that takes as its foundation, a combination of complex messages. Like monuments and museums, but more refined, Holocaust art is used for the dual purpose of commemorization and historical touchstone. Tangible manifestations such as art photography and sculpture contribute to the material memory of evidence and round out what Thompson suggests is often an incomplete process. Andrea Liss suggests that these artifacts serve as "a bridge" to translate the horrors. It is often their abstract qualities, open to multiple interpretations, which serve to provoke thought in the face of trauma.[57] It is precisely this vagueness that gives them their power, in contrast to the more direct and pedagogic agenda of traditional resources.

In this age of unlimited media, monuments might be left untouched by the changes in perception. Monuments may resonate even more strongly in counterpoint to the flow and speed of the imagery of the mass media, which, unlike museums, has had to adapt. Monuments may become solitary reminders, ancient remnants, or quaint relics whose purpose is not to speak to large audiences, but to remind a select few. There is also the possibility that they will no longer serve as reminders to a society that cannot focus on or reflect upon sculpture because of the changes to the pace of contemplation. In place of the monument, the importance of the film as a remembrance tool and historical marker may supersede.

Film (and by extension television[58]), is still, the only medium capable of approximating real life in a format that is alive, full of movement, and that is credible. As Ray Browne has remarked,

> Pictures as history are exceptionally effective because although words lie flat and dormant to some readers (indeed to a certain extent 'all' readers) it is difficult to miss messages carried in a motion picture as it explains a historical period or event.[59]

Film, (and TV docudrama) both fiction and documentary, has become the medium that defines historical discourse for most in North America. As such, it plays a pivotal role in the dissemination of information about the Holocaust.

Filmed versions of the Holocaust, most specifically *Schindler's List*, but also peripheral offerings and television dramas, are uniquely suited to offering up a palatable version to audiences. Reined in by the structures of narrative and drama, the filmed version must present the story or the history in a way that does not alienate western viewers. To some extent, this is exactly what happened with the TV event of 1978, Gerald Greene's *Holocaust*. *Holocaust* was a watershed in the move towards "seeing history" because it was a highly watched compelling melodramatic version of the past that entranced viewers. This, as was previously mentioned, is part and parcel of the "universalization"/Americanization debate. As Alan Mintz observes,

> each time a new commercially successful treatment of the Holocaust would come on the scene, one position argued that the vulgarity of a given film or show was mitigated by its power to convey the "message" of the Holocaust to those who would otherwise be untouched by it. The other position argued that any vulgarization of the Holocaust cannot escape betraying the victims and desecrating the sacred mystery of the event.[60]

Like Hier and others who want to get the message out, who desire to inform on people's own terms, this debate is often resuscitated and as with *Schindler's List*, is always open. Interestingly, though, the popularisers seem to be winning out—albeit in a bizarre manner. Mintz (like Lawrence

Langer) goes on to remark that this television miniseries was so effective in informing people about the history and tragedy of the Holocaust that the Holocaust itself quickly evolved into the benchmark "referent for collective suffering."[61] In the end, Mintz concludes that the process of universalization is "a double-edged sword. It evades its subject on the one hand, yet on the other, it may, under certain conditions, represent the 'only' way to approach the subject."[62]

As Alan Mintz has argued, Annete Insdorf similarly suggests that the classic pre-*Schindler's List* example of this is the miniseries *Holocaust*. In order to reach the mass audience, to stimulate discussion and awaken historical knowledge the Hollywood product has to pander and manipulate. Insdorf suggests that *Holocaust* was the definitive example of the "benefits of exposure and the drawbacks of distortion. Its case illustrates the rewards and tendencies inherent in films made for mass audiences—from the power of sensitizing, to the danger of romanticizing and trivializing."[63] By making the film *Holocaust* deliberately bearable, its producers were criticized for altering history and making the characters stereotypically beautiful for a mass audience. Such manipulations are necessary however, to overcome the average viewer's guilt and "resistance" to the subject.[64]

The power of film is so vast, that it often goes unnoticed as the agent of historical ideas. The immense quantity of film and its relatively easy access, have, in the words of Anton Kaes, "rendered the past ever-present." Film, according to Kaes, is a supremely effective force of persuasion and information. "Cinematic representations," Kaes writes, "have influenced—indeed shaped—our perspective on the past; they function for us today as a technological memory bank."[65] From this vantage point, the importance of film as an historical document is paramount, yet along with this power comes a very significant responsibility to interpret or present aspects of the Holocaust with more sensitivity and more equanimity, lest the product or text degenerate to kitsch. This does not contradict the situation present with universalization but rather, accentuates it. Underestimating the power of film to convey an historical message can be negligent and short-sighted. "Films," according to David Lowenthal, "make history both intense and plausible; figures seen moving and speaking in locales redolent of the past seems more alive than ever." This may offend academic historians and their sense of distance and objectivity, but the fact remains that there is a potency to film that can inform or even affect change. This is particularly the case with documentary films, which play to larger audiences outside of North America. There is a "formidable power" within documentary cinema, one that does not seem to exist in most commercial feature films, that allows it to register historical events.[66] No more is this power as obvious as in the documentary *Shoah*.

The emphasis above is in reference to feature films, but there is an implication to refer to new technological visual formats and to documentary as well. Documentary films, such as Claude Lanzmann's *Shoah*, are often accepted as "fact" as being more real or at least more "truthful" than fiction, yet they are never far from the claims of hyper-subjectivity, controversy or inaccuracy. As definitive forms though they are supposed to work by utilizing evidence, objectivity, and rationality rather than the fiction-favored play to emotion.[67] One of the high points of documentary film as history has to be Lanzmann's *Shoah*. It is Ron Burnett's extravagant claim that this Holocaust documentary has "fully justified August Lumiere's early hopes for the cinema."[68] Burnett feels that the survivors and perpetrators testimony is in fact, history. By "making the past *"so alive"* *Shoah* transcends film and becomes something else—an historical text.[69] Florence Jacobowitz confirms Burnett's praise by stating that:

> viewing *Shoah* is like entering a site of memorialization; it is a monument to the murdered, and its tone is elegiac and mournful. It becomes a memorial space where the relationship between past and present is contemplated and, like memorials, it addresses not only what should be remembered but how, and the way a work of art can contribute to the inscription of historical testimony and public memory.[70]

Jacobowitz pinpoints the importance of testimony, which is given in a contemporary context, as a powerful factor in the historical weight behind the film. Like Burnett, she emphasizes Lanzman's focus on the possibility of "knowing the past" through testimony as a key reason why this documentary film is so potent. This evidentiary tactic flies in the face of the postmodern interpretation of historicity in that, one can get a cogent handle on the past by using fact as a foundation and experiential detail to solidify the process.[71] *Shoah* as distinguished from *Schindler's List* is art in the sense that it serves as both a form of history or as a history lesson but importantly, performs a secondary role in that it serves as a monument.[72]

This is not to say that the average film will not convey history or will not promote history or will not inspire historical knowledge—it most certainly does (as this work has attempted to show). What occurs with *Shoah* is that its subject matter, its length, its demands on the viewer move it into a realm that is closer to academic history than virtually any other comparable film—and certainly, in Burnett's and Jacobowitz's view, much more historically potent than *Schindler's List*.[73] Lanzmann prepared for the film by reading virtually everything on the Nazi era including archival material. This enormous preparation caused some soul searching within Lanzmann, in that he felt that this was not truly real.[74] According to Burnett:

> he wanted to experience history, experience the Holocaust and then crucially reconstruct both his experience and the event. He wanted to be part of a process that would join historical inquiry with reproduction, that would link

the past with the present and that would transform the past into a living event for the viewer.[75]

The focus for Lanzmann is the emphasis of transforming "the past into a living event for the viewer." Lanzmann, according to Burnett, defines historical relevance as something to be comprehended when brought to life.[76] This seems to be in counterpoint to most aspirations of established history, but it works with *Shoah*.

Steven Spielberg's *Schindler's List* has become the definitive visual historical document. The film, based on Thomas Keneally's novel, focuses on the heroism of the industrialist, Oskar Schindler, who saved over 1,100 Jews by employing them in his factory. Despite the controversies surrounding the film's place as an historical document, the style chosen by Spielberg jarred the viewer out of the placid sense put in place by the characteristics of universalization and Americanization. The more than three hour black- and white-documentary-style film, has been compared to *Shoah* and *The Sorrow and the Pity*.[77] Spielberg, known for his family oriented fantasies and fast paced adventures, faced considerable pressure in making this film, especially given the fact that his previous serious artistic endeavors, notably *The Color Purple*, were met with heavy criticism. He was also very much aware that his film could be perceived as trivializing the Holocaust. At the heart of this concern was the fact that he did "not want to make a film so graphic that audiences would avert their eyes from the screen."[78] What was at the core of the desire to make this film were two themes. Spielberg wanted "to make a contribution to the memory" of the Holocaust.[79] As well, he very much wished to rescue Schindler's reputation from being buried, and perhaps, more importantly, he desired to make a film that would reach an audience that would never see *Shoah*. This is a very salient point, for who better to inform about the Holocaust than someone who is practiced at reaching a mass audience. To a grand extent, Spielberg has been inordinately successful in achieving this goal. In contrast to some—in fact most—of the European products that have looked at the Holocaust, *Schindler*, a definitive Hollywood product has gained a huge following as a Holocaust document. One of the problems with the esoteric European fare has always been its failure to penetrate beyond the art house. Films such as *The Night Porter* and *The Damned* were never capable of moving beyond this fringe. As Yosefa Loshitzky rightly states,

> Their effect on global historical consciousness has therefore been limited. In contrast, *Schindler's List* has penetrated historical consciousness on a global scale and has transformed the image of the Holocaust as perceived by millions of people all over the world.[80]

What makes *Schindler's List* so important is that according to Maurice Yacower, "with compelling realism it represents a fading historical moment."[81] As with the impact of Spiegelman's *Maus*, this is especially relevant during a period that has seen the rise of historical revisionism about the Holocaust[82] and as well, the increasing distance of the event that makes it less likely to be discussed as historically significant. What this implies is that to a generation of children who know little about the Holocaust,[83] this film takes on added importance. It speaks to a generation that understands the structures of focusing on a hero and can relate to the good versus evil dichotomy setup within the film.[84]

Shortly after the film was released, and after the early positive reviews had passed, the notion that the film was "too entertaining" began to creep up. A significant amount of this criticism centered on Spielberg's personality as well as his previous body of cinematic work.[85] Critics of the film point to the fact that it does move into the realm of emotional manipulation and simplistic melodrama. One critic cited the fact that it does revert to the Manichean duality of good versus evil, but what he felt was particularly disturbing was the fact that it turned into "an allegory about the nature of the German soul, with its 'good' and 'evil' aspects embodied by Schindler and [Amon] Goeth, [the commandant,] functioning as each other's symbolic double."[86] By extension, the most often cited criticism of the film is that Schindler was not at all typical of Germans, or Poles for that matter, and that by focusing on this "exotic exception" in the words of Jason Epstein, one is allowed to take a kind of comfort in this "virtuous behavior." What Spielberg chose to focus on was, according to Epstein, a distortion of significant proportions.[87]

The fact that the narrative structure of mass culture has influenced young viewers to expect a certain story line has had a significant impact on how *Schindler* has been received. What Tim Cole suggests has happened is that in contrast to the "banality of evil" thesis, as exemplified by Adolf Eichmann and the bureaucracy of killing, we have come to expect perceptions of evil as truly villainous. Viewers today, and in particular students, can not relate to the fact, says Cole that "Eichmann never killed with his own hands." When discussing the history of the Holocaust, Cole reports that his students can not process this fact. Instead, he feels that perhaps he should show them *Schindler's List* and satisfy their expectations of what true screen villains are like. Importantly, Cole concludes "that it will be Amon Goeth—rather than Eichmann—who will stand—if he doesn't stand already—as *the* "Holocaust killer" in contemporary iconography."[88] Cole goes on to suggest that this narrative power has already made an impact upon the historical reception and perception of the Holocaust. It is, unquestionably, the way the Holocaust is now historically represented and more so, for many, the real thing, not just a film.[89]

If filmed versions of history are used as a starting point, a weigh-station for the viewer to either be informed or provoked into finding out more, the techniques Landzmann employs can be extended to serve the purpose of framing difficult to express feelings for the viewer. Whilst some may scoff at the supposedly trivial nature of film, its power, commemoratively and therapeutically speaking, can give shape to complex emotions. In the preface to her book *Indelible Shadows: Film and the Holocaust*, Annette Insdorf confirms this procedure. She states, eloquently, "If I, the only child of Holocaust survivors, needed a film to frame the horror and thus give it meaning, what about others? How great a role are films playing in determining contemporary awareness of the final solution?"[90]

The short answer to Insdorf's question is that, to a large degree, films play an inordinately significant role in determining awareness of history and in particular, of the Holocaust.[91] Judith E. Doneson suggests that because the Holocaust is not an indigenous American event, it enters the public record and social history through film as a "refugee event." Like the journeys covered by most refugees, Doneson remarks that this phenomenon evolved through specific American conventions in order to become something that was meaningful and understandable to the American public.[92] This returns the discussion to both notions of Americanization and universalization, for the American or Hollywood version is usually the most popular and thus, the most successful and very often, the least controversial or offensive to the majority of the viewing public. The bottom line is that Hollywood can get a message across despite both reductionist and stereotypical preferences.

There is a tendency in Hollywood cinema to let the "commercial imperative" reign and subsequently, to focus on the evocation of terror in contrast to European films, such as *Life is Beautiful*, which tend to be introspective and use the medium to probe responsibility.[93] This, one could generalize, has its parallel in the European monuments in contrast to American ones. One could suggest that this is a result of the war occurring overseas, on their soil.[94]

Regardless of the motives and the results, at the very minimum a residue of historical information leaks out. This in turn gives producers and directors great power in defining the historical agenda. These individuals are, "in effect mass educators, redefining the nature and perception of history for a large audience."[95] What Barbie Zelizer has called "the growing diversification of history-making" has had an enormous impact on transmission and understanding of the past. Popular culture manifestations of history have greatly aided in transmitting historical information more potently than the world of the ivory tower. The ability to offer historical detail in entertaining, compelling, or even controversial formats has made this form of history much more accessible. In sum though, "new spaces" have been created for the viewer to "associate oneself with the past."[96]

Memory is a perpetually constructive process. Films, sights, visuals, museum exhibits, all contribute to this process and become aspects of collective memory. "Historical knowledge," as William H. McNeil has written, "is no more and no less than carefully and critically constructed collective memory."[97] History is written, put down, filmed, recorded, and visualized in order to prevent the loss of memory. In the west, there has been a shift in focus, to a significant extent in the way history is distributed and learned. With the Holocaust, special care must be taken to preserve an accurate and adequate memory of the event. Mass mediated culture does not necessarily conspire against this process, but rather, provides new ways and creates new opportunities for remembering.

NOTES

1. Erna Paris, *Long Shadows: Truth, Lies and History*, (Toronto: Alfred A. Knopf, 2000), pp. 313–14. This comment was voiced after Paris gave a talk to a group of individuals, some of whom were survivors, on Daniel Goldhagen's *Hitler's Willing Executioners*.

2. Alan Mintz, *Popular Culture and the Shaping of Holocaust Memory in America*, (Seattle, WA: University of Washington Press, 2001), pp. 6–9.

3. Simon Watson, "Dachau Awakening," *Queen's Quarterly*, vol.114, no. 3 (Fall 2007) p. 433.

4. Among the numerous works that discuss this evolution, see Mitchell Stephens, *The Rise of the Image, The Fall of The Word*, (New York: Oxford University Press, 1998), David Marc, *Bonfire of the Humanities: Television, Subliteracy, and Long-Term Memory Loss*, (Syracuse, NY: Syracuse University Press, 1995), Neil Postman, *Amusing Ourselves To Death*, (New York: Penguin Books, 1985), Joshua Meyrowitz, *No Sense of Place: The Impact of Electronic Media on Social Behavior*, (New York: Oxford University Press, 1985), and Danny Schechter, *The More You Watch, The Less You Know*, (New York: Seven Stories Press, 1997).

5. David Thelen, "Memory and American History," *Journal of American History*, vol. 75, no. 4, March 1989, p. 1120, David Marc, *Bonfire of the Humanities: Television, Subliteracy, and Long-Term Memory Loss*, p. 48, David Lowenthal, *The Past is A Foreign Country*, (Cambridge: Cambridge University Press, 1985), p. xvi.

6. Mitchell Stephens, *The Rise of the Image, The Fall of The Word*, writes, "Although moving images are gaining responsibility for more and more of our communication, this is a suggestion most of us have great difficulty accepting." p. 5.

7. In *The Power of Photography: How Photographs Changed Our Lives*, (New York: Abbeville Publishing Groups, 1991), pp. 135–136, Vicki Goldberg makes the following astute observation about how photography has displaced the once seemingly implacable position of the monument: "Photographs have come to occupy this position more and more often, partially displacing the public monument. Where generals once rode bronze horses in public squares, Douglas MacArthur now wades ashore on the pages of a news magazine. Where once only a poem was more lasting than bronze, now the poem goes to a halftone reproduction on glossy paper. The photograph's unbreakable tie to the reality it represents nominates it to

the position of history's proxy; it stands for people as if they were present and for events as if they were still occurring."

8. See the well thought out discussion in Robert Brent Toplin's *History By Hollywood: The Use and Abuse of The American Past*, (Urbana, IL: University of Illinois Press, 1996), "preface" and introduction. Toplin is concerned primarily with analyzing films based on real events and real people. What he focuses on in the preface and the introduction is that historical interpretation via film, possesses many of the same characteristics as does historical interpretation via the book. Toplin writes: "Historical films help to shape the thinking of millions. Often the depictions seen on the screen influence the public's view of historical subjects much more than books do." p. vii.

9. Anton Kaes, *From Hitler to Heimat: The Return of History as Film*, (Cambridge, MA: Harvard University Press, 1989), p. ix.

10. Oliver Thompson, *Mass Persuasion in History*, (Edinburgh: Paul Harris Publishing, 1977), p. 42, and G. H. Jamieson, *Communication and Persuasion*, (London: Croom Helm, 1985), p. 28.

11. See the wide-ranging discussion by various historians, producers and filmmakers in Sean B. Dolon, ed., *Telling The Story: The Media, The Public, and American History*, (Boston: New England Foundation for the Humanities, 1994).

12. Robert Rosenstone, "History in Images/History in Words: Reflections on the Possibility of Really Putting History onto Film," *American Historical Review*, 'Forum,' December 1988, vol. 93, no. 5, p. 1174, John E. O'Connor, "Reflections on the Importance of Film and Television Study for an Understanding of the Past," in *Ibid.*, p. 1201, Ben Agger, *The Decline of Discourse: Reading, Writing and Resistance in Post Modern Capitalism*, (Philadelphia, PA: The Falmer Press, 1990), pp. 33–34.

13. James Gleick, *Faster: The Acceleration of Just About Everything*, (New York: Pantheon, 1999).

14. Henry Friedlander, "Postscript: Toward a Methodology of Teaching about the Holocaust," in *The Holocaust: Ideology, Bureaucracy and Genocide*, ed. by Henry Friedlander and Sybil Milton, (New York: Krauss Publishers, 1980), p. 325, Judith Miller, *One by One by One: Facing the Holocaust*, (New York: Simon and Schuster, 1990), p. 232, and Yossi Klein Halevi, "Who Owns the Memory?," *The Jerusalem Report*, February 25, 1993, p. 31.

15. James Young, *At Memory's Edge: After-Images of the Holocaust in Contemporary Art and Architecture*, (New Haven, CT: Yale University Press, 2000), p. 44.

16. Roger Sabin, *Adult Comics: An Introduction*, (New York: Routledge, 1993), pp. 90, 91.

17. Cited in James Young, *At Memory's Edge*, p. 18.

18. Sarah Lyall, "Are These Books, or What? CD-ROM and the Literary Industry," *The New York Times Book Review*, August 14, 1994, p. 20.

19. Donald Schwartz, "Who will tell them After we're Gone: Reflections on Teaching the Holocaust," *The History Teacher*, vol. 23, no. 2, February 1990, p. 98. Oral history projects such as Stephen Spielberg's and the Yale Archive, are perhaps the only means of preserving the testimony of experience in non-written formats. In contrast to writing a book, publishing a memoir, or even making a film, videos are accessible and relatively easy to produce. Many, as opposed to few, are possible. See Sara Kviat Bloch, "Highlights of the Holocaust: Survivors of the

Shoah Visual History Foundation," A Paper Presented at the 30th PCA Annual Conference, New Orleans, April 19–22, 2000, Martin Gilbert, "Unfinished Business," *The Jerusalem Post* (International Edition), May 12, 1990, p. 9, and Yossi Klein Halevi, "Who Owns the Memory?," p. 29.

20. Henry Friedlander, "Postscript," p. 325 and Robert Alter, "Deformations of the Holocaust," *Commentary*, February 1981, p. 50.

21. John Lennon and Malcolm Foley, *Dark Tourism: The Attraction of Death and Disaster*, (London: Thomson, 2004). On the visitation to concentration and death camp sites, the authors, p. 32, write: "The analysis of such dark tourism sites in terms of their selection, interpretation, use of media and the understanding of motivation for visitation is important to develop an understanding of human behavior and understanding events in the 'other past.' Such analysis is necessary for the appreciation of these sites. Yet, invariably, one is dealing with a subject so enormous that it threatens to overwhelm both media and language."

22. Erna Paris, *Long Shadows*, p. 320.

23. Erna Paris, *Long Shadows*, p. 322.

24. Tim Cole writes that when the Washington Museum opened in 1993, "the staff at Yad Vashem expressed fears that their authoritative position in exhibiting the Holocaust was seriously threatened." *Selling The Holocaust: From Auschwitz to Schindler—How History is Bought, Packaged, and Sold*, (New York: Routledge, 2000), p. 146.

25. The austerity and cathedral-like atmosphere of most museums, art and history, is in complete contrast to the way one is supposed to experience the Holocaust Museum in Washington. Although a feeling of reverence is immediately inspired, the overall impact is quite different from visiting a traditional museum.

26. Edward T. Linenthal, "The Boundaries of Memory: The United States Holocaust Memorial Museum," *American Quarterly*, vol. 46, no. 3, September 1994, pp. 406–18.

27. Jeshajahu Weinberg and Rina Elieli, *The Holocaust Museum In Washington*, (New York: Rizzoli, 1995), p. 17. The authors write, "By leading visitors through a narrative, the museum forces them to follow a preconceived circulation path. The visitors are not free to choose their own way through the museum, just as they are not free to choose their own way between the scenes of a play or film. This restriction, usually not imposed in collection-based museums or art galleries, is the price that has to be paid for having the museum exhibition based on a narrative." p. 50.

28. Alan Mintz, *Popular Culture and the Shaping of Holocaust Memory in America*, pp. 29–30, writes, "It was the threshold of the visitor's sensitivities that the museum planners had to gauge in designing the exhibits. How much horror could be tolerated? There was the concern that if the museum became known principally as a place where visitors were forced into a shocking exposure to atrocity that few would come and the opportunity for education would be lost. There were heated debates among the staff about how much of the horror should be withheld without compromising the story the museum was responsible for telling. A critical compromise involved the use of a privacy wall."

29. Jeshajahu Weinberg and Rina Elieli, *The Holocaust Museum In Washington*, (New York: Rizzoli, 1995), pp. 25, 56.

30. Weinberg and Elieli, *The Holocaust Museum In Washington*, (New York: Rizzoli, 1995), p. 67.

31. Suzanne Bardgett, "Exhibiting Hatred," *History Today*, June 2000, pp. 18–20.

32. Tim Cole, *Selling The Holocaust*, p. 160.

33. Edward T. Linenthal, "The Boundaries of Memory," pp. 421–22.

34. Yossi Klein Halevi, "Who Owns the Memory?," p. 31.

35. Halevi, "Who Owns the Memory?," p. 29.

36. Alter, "Deformations of the Holocaust," p. 49.

37. Judith Miller, *One by One*, p. 232.

38. Hier states, "If you want to keep the Holocaust a secret, you can set up a place that has all the solemnity of a Christian Science reading room. With 'revisionists' denying the Holocaust happened, we can't afford to keep a low profile. We're a modern educational center using modern techniques." Cited in Halevi, "Who Own's the Memory?," p. 31.

39. Robert Alter's comments on Hier in "Deformations of the Holocaust," p. 54. The whole notion of exploitation *vis-à-vis* a Holocaust industry is a new arena for debate.

40. Michael Berenbaum, *The World Must Know: The History of the Holocaust As Told In the United States Memorial Museum*, (Boston: Little Brown, 1993), p. xiv.

41. Lawrence L. Langer, "Introduction," to *Admitting the Holocaust: Collected Essays*, (New York: Oxford University Press, 1995), pp. 8–9.

42. Philip Gourevitch, "Behold Now Behemoth," *Harpers*, May 1993, pp. 55, 57.

43. Martin Gilbert, "Unfinished Business," p. 9.

44. Bruno Bettelheim, "Children and Museums," in *Freud's Vienna and Other Essays*, (New York: Vintage, 1991), p. 141, John Berger, *Ways of Seeing*, (London: BBC/Penguin, 1981), p. 24, Harold Rosenberg, "The 'Mona Lisa' Without a Moustache," in *Art and Other Serious Matters*, (Chicago: The University of Chicago Press, 1985), p. 9, and Philip Gourevitch, "Behold Now," p. 61.

45. Philip Gourevitch, "Behold Now," p. 61.

46. Cited in Judith Miller, pp. 242–243.

47. Herbert Muschamp, "How Buildings Remember," *The New Republic*, August 28, 1989, p. 28.

48. Charles L. Griswold, "The Vietnam Veterans Memorial and the Washington Mall: Philosophical Thoughts on Political Iconography," *Critical Inquiry*, 12 (Summer 1986) p. 691, and Arthur Danto, cited in James Young, *The Texture of Memory: Holocaust Memorials and Meaning*, (New Haven, CT: Yale University Press, 1993), p. 3.

49. James Young, *The Texture Of Memory*, p. 1.

50. Sybil Milton, *In Fitting Memory: The Art and Politics of Holocaust Memorials*, (Detroit, MI: Wayne State University Press, 1991), p. 1.

51. Michael Kammen, *Mystic Chords of Memory*, (New York: Knopf, 1991), p. 3.

52. Sybil Milton, *In Fitting Memory*, p. 1.

53. James Young, *The Texture of Memory*, pp. 5–6.

54. Sybil Milton, *In Fitting Memory*, p. 8, Donald Horne, *The Great Museum: The Representation of History*, (London: The Pluto Press, 1984), p. 18, and James M. Mayo, *War Memorials as Political Landscape: The American Experience and Beyond*, (New York: Praeger Publishers, 1988), pp. xvi, 8, 211.

55. The Twin Towers or World Trade Center in New York have, posthumously acquired this status. Ironically, there not "being there" gives them, through memory, images (such as photography and film) and symbolism, they have become monuments.

56. Vivian Alpert Thompson, *A Mission in Art: Recent Holocaust Works in American*, (Macon, GA: Mercer University Press, 1988), p. 49.

57. Andrea Liss, "Rituals of Mourning and Mimesis: Arie A. Galles's Fourteen Stations," in in *Image and Remembrance: Representation and the Holocaust*, eds., Shelley Hornstein and Florence Jacobowitz, (Bloomington, IN: Indiana University Press, 2003), p. 31.

58. On this conflation, see Michael Parenti, *Make Believe Media*, (New York: St. Martin's Press, 1991), pp. 9–10.

59. Ray B. Browne, "Forward" in Peter C. Rollings, editor, *Hollywood as Historian: American Film in a Cultural Context*, (Lexington: The University of Kentucky Press), p. vix.

60. Alan Mintz, *Popular Culture and the Shaping of Holocaust Memory in America*, pp. 24–25.

61. Alan Mintz, *Popular Culture and the Shaping of Holocaust Memory in America*, p. 26.

62. Alan Mintz, *Popular Culture and the Shaping of Holocaust Memory in America*, p. 100.

63. Annete Insdorf, *Indelible Shadows: Film and the Holocaust*, (Cambridge: Cambridge University Press, 1989), p. 4.

64. David Lowenthal, *The Past as a Foreign Country*, (Cambridge: Cambridge University Press, 1985), p. 347.

65. Anton Kaes, *From Hitler to Heimat: The Return of History as Film*, p. ix.

66. Ilan Avisar, *Screening the Holocaust: Cinema's Images of the Unimaginable*, (Bloomington, IN: Indiana University Press, 1988), p. 33.

67. Pierre Sorlin, *The Film in History: Restaging the Past*, (Oxford: Basil Blackwell, 1980), p. 4.

68. Ron Burnett, *Cultures of Vision: Images, Media and The Imaginary*, (Bloomington, IN: Indiana University Press, 1995), p. 160. Burnett continues, "*Shoah's* power as a representation of the Holocaust has been equated by commentators and viewers to the events of history itself."

69. Ron Burnett, *Cultures of Vision*, p. 160.

70. Florence Jacobowitz, "*Shoah* as Cinema," in *Image and Remembrance: Representation and the Holocaust*, p. 7.

71. Florence Jacobowitz, "*Shoah* as Cinema," p. 11.

72. Andrea Liss, "Rituals of Mourning and Mimesis: Arie A. Galles's Fourteen Stations," in *Image and Remembrance: Representation and the Holocaust*, p. 31.

73. Ron Burnett, *Cultures of Vision: Images, Media and The Imaginary*, p. 161.

74. Ron Burnett, *Cultures of Vision: Images, Media and The Imaginary*, p. 162.

75. Ron Burnett, *Cultures of Vision: Images, Media and The Imaginary*, pp. 163–64.

76. Ron Burnett, *Cultures of Vision: Images, Media and The Imaginary*, p. 166.

77. Bernard Weinraub, "Steven Spielberg Faces the Holocaust," *The New York Times*, December 12, 1993, Section 2, p. 1.

78. Bernard Weinraub, "Steven Spielberg Faces the Holocaust," p. 28.

79. Michel Pascal, Interview with Steven Spielberg, "Why I Made *Schindler's List*," *Queen's Quarterly*, 101/1, Spring 1994, p. 29.

80. Yosefa Loshitzky, "Introduction," *Spielberg's Holocaust: Critical Perspective on Schindler's List*, Edited by Yosefa Loshitzky, (Bloomington, IN: Indiana University Press, 1997), p. 2.

81. Maurice Yacower, "Schindler's Film," *Queen's Quarterly*, 101/1 (Spring 1994) p. 39.

82. In *Eyewitnessing: The Uses of Images as Historical Evidence*, (Ithaca, NY: Cornell University Press, 2001), p. 155, author Peter Burke writes, "At a time when the Holocaust is being denied in some quarters, the testimony of film is worth remembering." Burke is referring to documentary film but his comment can just as readily by applied to fiction film.

83. According to a Roper Poll cited shortly after the opening of the Holocaust Museum in Washington, "most American high school students know so little about the Holocaust that they are unfamiliar with the word." Cited in Harry F. Rosenthal, "Holocaust Museum assaults the human senses," *The Globe and Mail*, April 28, 1993, p. D7.

84. Maurice Yacower, "Schindler's Film," *Queen's Quarterly*, pp. 39–40.

85. Caryn James, "Seeing *Schindler* Plain," *The New York Times*, January 23, 1994, Arts and Leisure, p. 13

86. Michael Andre Bernstein, "The *Schindler's List* Effect," *The American Scholar*, Summer 1994, p. 429.

87. Jason Epstein, "A Dissent of *Schindler's List*," *The New York Review of Books*, April 21, 1994, p. 65.

88. Tim Cole, *Selling The Holocaust*, pp. 71–72.

89. Tim Cole, *Selling The Holocaust*, p. 75.

90. Annete Insdorf, *Indelible Shadows: Film and the Holocaust*, p. xiii.

91. Alan Mintz, *Popular Culture and the Shaping of Holocaust Memory in America*, p. 34.

92. Judith E. Doneson, *The Holocaust in American Film*, (New York: Jewish Publication Society, 1987), p. 6.

93. Marcia Landy, in *Italian Film*, (Cambridge: Cambridge University Press, 2000) pp. 118–120, raises some interesting ideas about the film in the tradition of comedy and the theme of family.

94. Annete Insdorf, *Indelible Shadows: Film and the Holocaust*, p. 23.

95. Eric Breitbart, "The Painted Mirror: Historical Re-creation from the Panorama to the Docudrama," in Susan Porter Benson, et. al, eds., *Presenting the Past: Essays on History and the Public*, (Philadelphia: Temple University Press, 1986), p. 111.

96. Barbie Zelizer, "Every Once in a While: *Schindler's List* and the Shaping of History," in Yosefa Loshitzky, ed., *Spielberg's Holocaust*, p. 20.

97. William H. MacNeill, Michael Kammen, Gordon Craig, "Why Study History? Three Historians Respond," in Paul Gagnon, ed., *Historical Literacy: The Case for History in American Education*, (Boston: Houghtlon Mifflin Co., 1991), p. 103.

8

Computer Technology and History

Visual technology holds the potential to supplement, expand, and even radically alter the evolutionary future of the human brain.

—Jane M. Healy, "Visual Technology: Vacuous or Visionary?," 14

Jane Healy's comment, stated above, suggests many things. It points to the fact that visual culture and technology must be taken into consideration and in fact reckoned with as a source of information and knowledge. It also warns that anyone who cares about the future of education and young people must pay close attention to the ramifications of all visual media. Healy states that the enormous authority of visual electronic systems of information holds both promise and peril for education but she is extraordinarily cautious about the adoption of computer technology. Computer technology is "highly engaging" and can have "constructive purposes in educational settings" especially in the realm of history.[1]

It is important to recognize as well, that as the whole world moves toward more computer technology and more of a dependence on electronic visual communication, education will not remain isolated. According to Paul Starr, "The new media, moreover, are becoming essential to intellectual and artistic expression and scientific work. As the entire world of communication and knowledge is transformed, it becomes inconceivable to leave education out."[2] As one colleague phrased it, "It's coming and it's here."

Since the late 1980s, the influence of the computer and all its manifestations has grown with every passing year.[3] Computer culture is something most young people in the West are immersed in from a very young age. Young adults are adept at using technologies and thrive in an environment that older generations find impossibly complex and even bizarre. This is particularly pronounced with regard to the ability to absorb and scan a multiplicity of test, image, and screen formats.[4] Young children and university students alike, carry with them the vestiges of the computer constantly. As sociologist Sherry Turkle has written, "Today's children are growing up in the computer culture; all the rest of us are at best its naturalized citizens."[5] Each year, discussion of the application of computer technologies seems to get louder especially with regard to students and the implementation of computer technology in the classroom.[6] Preschoolers and students are exposed to software that is designed to be educational, at younger and younger ages, and parents often experience anxiety if their children are not exposed to electronic information on the computer quickly enough.[7]

Computer technology has impacted both the idea and the study of history in a number of ways. The Internet has provided numerous websites for students to read, see, and look into for historical information. Historians, both professional and public, have also begun to utilize the computer in a variety of ways, both in academic terms as well as in leisure formats. Computer software packages have reoriented the way history can be presented. This in turn can be divided into two arenas: the first are CD-ROMs which offer a unique view of history—for example, Voyager company's pioneering products[8], or the *Where in the World is Carmen Sandiego* group of discs.[9] This also includes games that use history as a major point of departure and reference. The main example of this version is the *Civilization* series. The second main area is web sites that run the gamut from those maintained by academic institutions and governments to the plethora of sites designed by media outlets and heritage preservationists. Each of these avenues has come in for their share of criticism.

Most scholars, who come from the disciplines of English, the Humanities, or Education, are not necessary great supporters of computer technology as a mode of delivery for education. Theorists such as Robert Logan and Clifford Stoll, see the computer as a tool which is valued for its potential and understood for its limitations. Others, such as Douglas Noble view the computer either in the classroom or in virtually any pedagogic manner, nothing more than a form of marketing technology to school boards at great financial and human expense.[10] There are exceptions such as Lewis Perlman who see the computer as a panacea for all that ails education. The simple fact is that the computer and its technological offspring can accentuate teaching but never replace a good teacher. It must also be recognized that online learning is only successful a fraction of the time with students who are particularly driven and who are self-motivated learners.[11]

The above views can be further divided into those who feel we should leave the basic structure alone—and incorporate new technology as it is necessary and as it becomes a useful accompaniment to established practice, such as Peter C. Emberley, and those who bemoan the fact that our educational practices are simply archaic. The latter view is, to some extent voiced by Robert K. Logan. Logan feels that the educational system is one that is harmonious with the factory and not with the postcapitalist economy. In particular, Logan writes:

> Our schools are based on an industrial model with a delivery system patterned on the factory. Millions of school children are taught the same content in the same linear sequential order guided by a uniform curriculum dictated by a centralized bureaucracy at a municipal school board or state department (or provincial ministry) of education. Teachers continue to deliver an old style of book learning which does not take into account the nature of today's information-age economy or even some of the needs of day-to-day living. Students do not find enough relevancy in their schooling to take it seriously, which explains the high drop-out rate.[12]

There are no doubt, many other factors which may explain the high dropout rate—other than relevancy, but nonetheless, Logan does make a series of valid points. In particular, the fact that students are in essence dealing with a language—in the classroom—which is often very foreign to what they are accustomed to.

At this point in time it must be recognized that the computer cannot take the place of reality—of truly being in a different place or time. But, with some CD-ROMs and with some Web sites, it is the next best thing. No, it is not the same as going out and smelling the fauna in the forest, as Clifford Stoll has remarked, but it is convenient and feasible to look at a simulation in a classroom. To a great extent, that is what the best computer technology can do; offer a view, a glimpse, not the whole story. Like a movie or a photograph it can supplement and round out. It can give the student a viewpoint to start or to accentuate what she has learned. The use of computer hypertext or hypermedia does not and should not take the place of the teacher in the lecture hall. "Multimedia," writes Paul Starr, "permits an extraordinary flexibility in conveying concepts—through words, pictures, and sounds, as something that can be built or played as well as read or watched."[13]

The debate will continue and it is not the purpose of this chapter to get involved with a prolonged discussion about the merits of computers and technology in the classroom, but rather, to incorporate, briefly, the impact of technology in the learning environment, and specifically, to discuss the fact that history is presented in a variety of electronic formats and to students of history and that this in turn, has consequences for the visualization of the past.

As was mentioned earlier, technology has often been employed to enhance and accentuate traditional educational formats. With the coming of each new development, the technology of the day was touted as a way to supplement teaching. Yet, one consistent fact remains. As Larry Cuban has documented, everything from slides to projectors have been employed but inevitably, failed, overall, to reach the potential objectives first envisioned. Radio, television, and film have had numerous impacts on education and on history in particular, and if measured from the popular standpoint of history, can be said, as this whole work seeks to argue, a fair degree of success in conveying information about history to a fairly large audience. There may be problems or inaccuracies, but history has been successfully transmitted to a significant audience by audiovisual media. What Cuban and others fail to recognize is that the issue is not whether it is good or bad. We have already gone beyond that debate. This is a reality for young people in particular that cannot be ignored. Just as students may learn about history from fiction TV or a Spielberg film, they can learn from the CD-ROM or the Internet. Once again, this is not to suggest that this is a case of one being inferior over another format but that young people today gravitate towards these formats in a way that, as Sherry Turkle implies, is natural. In essence, the history they access on the computer is the way they are often exposed to history. There should be not be debate about this.[14]

One need not cite studies that state that computer software has little impact on increasing historical or geographic knowledge.[15] One could in fact cite just as many studies and surveys claiming the opposite. And this is not to suggest that this is simply irrelevant, but for the scope of concern here, not the focus. One should be aware, that the nonlinear, graphic-based world of computer images differs from the structure of the book, even more than a film differs from a book. It is "going to jump all over" and the historical game is going to have inconsistencies in chronology and errors in information just as a book could contain. More serious concerns such as a lack of contextuality should be recognized as endemic to the computer and the Internet, but one must be cognizant of the fact that this is part and parcel of the computerized universe.[16]

As a further qualification to the above, some theorists draw a distinction between devices such as projectors, the DVD and the computer. In particular, the interactivity aspect of the computer pushes it into a different category. If one subscribes to the notion that television watchers are "passive" or at least have a tendency to view in a more passive state, then one has to recognize that in dealing with a web site, searching the Internet, or interacting with a CD-ROM involves much more activity and perhaps, more cognitive stimulation.[17] If this is in fact the case, then at the very least one can conclude that something very different is happening on a cognitive level. One researcher has stated that in writing and deciphering the printed/written word, one kind of information processing is occurring; "linear, sequential, analytic, specialized, and logical." With electronic media, the kind of information-processing at work is "holistic or global, integrated, synthetic, generalist, and metaphorical."[18]

Why are people still surprised that these offerings are different from what is contained in a book? Is this a question or perhaps *the* question that should be considered? Of course the text is going to be subservient to the visual. That is the pattern and that is the essential characteristic of the computer mediated universe. Prolonged and exclusive use of this technology may stunt the imagination and affect reading and comprehension skills. The key though is to build upon this devotion and channel it towards more holistic approaches. One can bemoan the fact that students cannot read for as long as students did in the past and one can be hypercritical of the fact that too much information is being accessed by visual formats. Regardless though, one must move on, to a more productive acceptance and examine what can be done. There is hope in the fact that CD-ROMs and the Internet provide enormous potential, but this must be contextualized properly for without historical paradigms, societies can lose their way.[19] Too vast an array of choices in this regard fragments the already existing technologies and provides too many gimmicks. It is necessary to be open to new ideas and concepts but also, to make distinctions between fads and choices that too quickly date.

In an often cited article on CD-ROMs and history, Roy Rosenzweig, makes the point that technology has much to offer the discipline of history and has the capacity to "transform the way we research, analyze, teach, and present the past." Rosenzweig qualifies that statement by warning of the past hype that has been heaped on various new technologies and their failed impacts in furthering the cause of the humanities.[20] The technological sophistication of some CD-ROMs allows for access and freedom in a way that many books or traditional lectures do not. Many of the CD-ROM's available use the language of students and at the same time, quality CD-ROMs can enhance the research and the teaching process. Allowing the viewer/student access to a video clip of a famous speech, literally hits the point home, in a way that slides or audio tapes cannot. Given the fact that so much of twentieth century history has been recorded in visual formats, the usage of such documents is extremely valuable.[21] The ability to access musical performances, newsreels, broadcasts, and other forms of popular culture not only accentuates the awareness of historical knowledge, but deepens interest in the topic.

William G. Thomas, III, who has been at the forefront of utilizing technology to convey and impart history, believes that computer technology and electronic delivery systems have an important role to play in the dissemination of historical scholarship. In an article that cogently summarizes the state of this situation, Thomas writes that technology contributes much more than data collection and analysis, two staples of historical inquiry. Venues such as the Internet and the Web have, "presented new technologies to enable and create aesthetically appealing, multifaceted works that emphasize complexity, extensibility, and multiple viewpoints" of historical narratives. Thomas implies that technological information systems are now at a point where they could be harnessed to accentuate the process of historical enquiry and "allow historians to do better in their scholarship."[22] What Thomas cites as being particularly interesting is the appropriation and utilization of developments in literature, art, and criticism, but in particular, postmodern criticism, as barometers or maps for historians to follow. The concept of an open-ended textual narrative along with the possibilities of hyperlinks has been especially useful in this case, particularly among those historians subscribing to the narrative tradition of history.[23] While there have been many variations and much opposition to these approaches one must be impressed with some of the results.

Thomas's own work at the Virginia Centre for Digital History has yielded a number of offerings in electronic form, which allow for an open-ended dialogue as well as utilization of new, cutting edge formats. One version of this process "tries to structure the scholarly form of a historical journal article in such a way that it provides strikingly enhanced accessibility, readability, and connectivity without compromising the professional craft of historical narrative."[24] Referencing the work of Robert Darnton, who warns about the vast void of non-information in the cyberworld, Thomas stresses that accessing links and/or "hyperlinking" is a key attribute in the new forms of historical, digital scholarship. This is obvious both for practitioners and consumers of history. The ability to reference other sources and sites, to see and hear, and to move between websites, is something important because to Thomas—and others, it offers exciting possibilities. Most salient is the fact that "hypertext" is a new and excellent form of notation. With that in mind, historians such as Thomas, see themselves,

> as part of a continuum of scholarship, picking up some traditions from centuries ago, such as glosses, commentary, and footnotes; some neglected experiments of recent decades, such as social science history and narrative innovation; and some emergent technologies, such as an open and extensive markup language that permits a more powerful and flexible kind of linking

than we had in 1999—or 2000, for that matter. Ideally, historians will combine these tools to create a professional scholarship that is richer, more rigorous, and more useful than current practice permits.[25]

According to Thomas, it is an auspicious time for the furthering of historical scholarship within digital parameters.[26] Whether this involves the further exploration of linkages, or piggybacking on existing digital archives, both of which involve the harnessing of "manuscripts, maps, images, and other data," a form of standardization and elegant simplicity in interconnectivity could be reached. The merging of library techniques with hybrid forms of interactive museum-like exhibits is one possible result. All in all this might allow room for new comparative perspectives as well as levels of connectivity between disciplines that will facilitate new levels of dialogue and debate.[27] But until this point is reached, there will only be a gradual incorporation of technology into the heart of historiography.

One of the many significant issues surrounding the utilization of new technology in the presentation of a discipline such as history has been and continues to be the attachment to traditional modes of knowledge transmission. As Thomas has remarked, certain versions of hypertext linking are built upon the frameworks established by existing forms of annotation, developments in online library delivery systems and the postmodern incarnations of museumology. To some extent these are predictable variations, but they can also be cumbersome reminders and archaic weights, which hold back the full-fledged development and acceptability of newer versions. It is of course natural to utilize existing structures and in many cases; most new technological developments have in some ways begun by attempting to "build a better mousetrap."[28]

At this point in time, the full-fledged adoption of computer technology—what electronic/data worlds have to offer, has not been realized. As John Lutz has observed,

> We in history and the humanities have not yet figured out what the computer is really for. Of course we make use of the information technology. We put our diagrams and course outlines on the Internet when photocopying them would probably be more useful, and we setup online discussion groups which are poor substitutes for bringing people together. These are all conservative and sometimes misguided uses of the new technologies.[29]

Lutz implies that the way we use computers, primarily for historical discourse, is not significantly different from what is available with older technologies. A form of built-upon variation is what is happening which he suggests stems from the historical antipathy that many historians and scholars within the humanities have towards technology.[30] To counter balance this, Lutz posits a rebalancing of this equation by practitioners, to take control and harness what technology has to offer. In harmony with many who are, at the very least, quite comfortable engaging with technology, Lutz conjectures a strategy where the book version is not the final word. What is required is that within the rubric of what he calls "our critical intellectual responsibilities," there must be a move to react to or outrightly "embrace technologies beyond the book."[31] Unlike so many who glorify technological offerings without consideration of the consequences, Lutz, while excited about the options, is also careful and thoughtful. He proposes quite convincingly, that to graduate with a degree in the humanities should very importantly include the traditional curriculum requirements but as well, the ability to "analyse critically print, film, video, and other digital communication including the Internet. The alternative," he writes, "is to fail in our social responsibility and to lose our social support."[32] Given the increasing amount of history being presented in the formats listed above—beyond print—this is a wise recommendation. A significant way to reach this harmony is to not just think outside of the box, but to reinvent how we interact with new information technologies.[33] This is what the students are already doing as noted earlier by Sherry Turkle.

What does technology have to offer that will be useful in teaching and accessing history? One answer to this question asked by Lutz is that "it must improve how people think historically." This involves everything from having a foundation about a time before now to being able to follow an event through time, to weighing differing viewpoints, to an awareness of how not to engage in presentism. Lutz states that the resources available on the Internet are vast, but in teaching historical skills, there is not much out there. This is a result of the dependence on "old technological metaphors," which use the book, or the encyclopedia, as their models.[34] Lutz cites a number of very engaging sites, such as a simulated recreation of P. T. Barnum's American Museum, which have potential, but states quite severely that these examples are too closely book-based. In his words, the problem is that "they do not push beyond the book metaphor, where the student is the consumer of a history packaged, often creatively, with a choice of routes in the material, by an author or team of authors."[35] Even the vast storehouse of information available in digital formats such as the American National Digital Library or Early Canada Online, which on the one hand are clearly advances are still, according to Lutz, quite conservative. Despite this conservative format, they give the student of history a chance to be active participants in the creation of history.[36] This in turn, provides a stimulating historical experience, which attempts to harness the best of what is available. Although built upon an existing textual structure, these sites foreshadow the exciting possibilities to come. The most sophisticated versions of these Internet sites allow the student not only to hear and see aspects of history, but to engage in a dialogue which is a wonderful pedagogic experience. The use of photographs, letters, actor's voices, and maps greatly accentuate the historical experience for students comfortable with the interactivity and the fluidity of multimedia.

In Italy, there have been a number of progressive attempts to codify history on the Web and the Internet. There is *Eliohs—Electronic Library of Historiography* which provides a vast storehouse of obscure historical texts as well as *Reti Medievali* a medieval site which incorporates a resource archive, a digital library, and an electronic journal, a project put together by a university consortium. Given such examples, to simply dismiss the Web as an improper site for the transmission of historical data is like the dismissal of historical film—ludicrous. Digital archives in particular are key places of access. It is now possible to view documents hitherto buried and completely inaccessible. The Florentine State archives provide scholars, in digital formats, entry to the long and contentious history of that region. But not only scholars can use these materials. Virtually anyone can view these products which make the burdensome cost of travelling to the place they are kept, no longer an obstacle. An often overlooked advantage is that the digitized format allows for the complete preservation of documentation which in turn, "safeguards" these "texts" from further erosion. As long as this preservation is ongoing and continually updated, future generations will be able to access the wealth of this heritage.[37]

It is interesting that the one area that Lutz feels has pushed the envelope is in the realm of computer games. The most hardheaded traditionalist is naturally going to balk at the thought of using a game or simulation format to acquire historical knowledge but unless one has either tried the offering or seen students working within this format, one should suspend passing of judgment. Like much of what Hollywood offered as far as historical films and costume dramas, these historio-fantasy simulations are deeply researched and accurate historically. Lutz cites the *Age of Empires*, *Sim City* and *Deus Ex* as three examples. Lutz does not commit to saying that these current manifestations are "great teachers of history," but does confide that more of this kind of technology should be developed for the teaching of history. While budgetary constraints must be considered, the possibilities of putting students into "other places, other times," and to "give them the opportunity to interact with historical people," is the best way to get them to think historically.[38] One of the ways in which these games have been particularly effective is that they attract audiences that would not normally be drawn to such offerings. Video games are often action oriented and this is often in sync with the choices boys make in their reading. The propensity for boys to choose action over introspection in reading makes their attraction to the computer game format particularly strong and at the same time, something of an alternative to what is offered by the traditional school curriculum.[39] Like Japanese *Manga*, the speed and the action are quite enticing.[40]

Before one is too dismissive of video games and interactive historical quests, it is important to be cognizant of the element that makes certain disc-based and online formats relevant and challenging. Video games, especially violent ones such as *Halo 3*, have been singled out for criticism as unhealthy and detrimental to virtually every form of behavior. Yet the more challenging titles, such as *Civilization* and *SimCity*, require a fair amount of patience to master and also involve mastery of a variety of complex mental skill sets. In an interesting trend, it is these games that are not talked about with the same attention and devotion as the more thrilling and sinister ones. As journalist Steve Johnson writes in a recent book, "the most intellectually challenging titles are also the most popular."[41]

The Microsoft produced *Age of Empires* is a strategy game that involves a fair amount of technological maturation. In order for a society to move along in progress, it must amass territory but maintain a proper economic foundation. Proper development involves access to food and shelter, collecting weaponry, and other essentials for a society to thrive. Progress or advances are made by moving from one society such as The Dark Age to another, more sophisticated one. Simple villages must be expanded through trade and technology, as well as warfare. A "technology tree" will allow players to see things such as the capacity of an archer and his range or the ability of the militia. At the beginning of the Disc, there is a text-based history section, with fairly detailed, albeit brief, descriptions of the major peoples of the Medieval world. The entry on the Britons, for example, moves from approximately 500 to 1453 AD. It is every bit as good, as readable, as an encyclopedia entry. The text explains the origins of Roman/British culture, which the Celts were, and the beginnings of the Anglo-Saxons. There are also sentences on language and the invasions of the Danish Vikings. The Battle of Hastings is explained, as is the Hundred Years War, with emphasis given to the success of English longbow men. Similar entries can be found on the Byzantines, the Celts, the Japanese, and other medieval nationalities.

Computer video games, such as *Age of Empires*, have traditionally attracted a young male audience. It has been recognized for quite some time that they can serve as an introduction to certain aspects of education. Far from being a hidden-source of pedagogy, computer based video discs have increasingly come to be seen as a strong source of educational awareness especially in the realm of history.[42] This is especially pronounced in historically-based simulation games.

It is important to recognize that CD-ROM games of virtually any genre are often about choices. What the player decides to do in a given format is often selectively predetermined by what the creators have allowed. The simulation games that engage player, viewers, and students with history are, in fact, closely related in a number of ways to interactive CD-ROMs that educators and educational institutions have used.[43] The two meet in the way that an attempt to blur the technology comes into being. A player is supposed to become *one* with the virtual environment and to forget about the peripherals.[44] The computer game *Myst*, is for all intents and purposes a fantasy based game. Yet within the narrative structure, there is a refreshing and novel emphasis on the world of books. In contrast to many games, the tempo is slower, almost anti-hyper, in comparison to many other offerings. *Myst* excels for a variety of reasons and one could be its antitechnology bias. The focus on books and libraries seems to not only slow the game down, but highlights a world that does not necessarily glorify the speed and reflexes necessary for success.[45]

Like much that is on the Web, many video games, utilize reading in quite significant ways. *Age of Empires* and *Myst* are just two, but *Deus Ex* is also structured around "reading" in a number of ways. In order to successfully survive, or complete the game, a fair amount of print must be consumed. This includes accessing e-mail, diaries, and other forms of writing. The manuals or "booklets" that accompany these games can also be substantial. As well, "strategy guides" are produced to help the player find his or her way through the myriad of obstacles.[46] Players are required to read a lot to get through the game—just not traditional kinds of reading—and in doing so they acquire large quantities of information.

In discussing certain video games, the words "educator" and "educational institution" are employed because it has been the museums and libraries and their ancillary components rather than schools who have been at the forefront of this approach. The concept or impression of "real-life" and tactile accessibility is crucial in this respect. Research has demonstrated that students who have a foundation of knowledge will acquire new knowledge via computer assisted learning—under the right conditions. Another way of saying this is to suggest that if a student is curious and is supported, the CD-ROM versions of history will greatly enhance their ability to absorb another level of knowledge. Further, if information is presented in formats that mirror student comfort levels, rates of knowledge acquisition are also increased.[47]

Often, the above phenomenon occurs on an individual learning curve. Most teachers, who utilize technology in the classroom, do not use it as a substitute for traditional instruction but rather, as a supplement.[48] The most often cited reason for this use has to do with the fact that there is little time to find the right software.[49] The technical capacities required to master the technology that could deliver historical information visually is also a daunting obstacle. As well, the weighty bias against these forms of delivery remains. Yet for every teacher of history who may resist, there are many who are interested.

Beyond the lack of time, it is essential to be aware of the fact that arguably for the first time, teachers and professors have familiarity with the new technology in ways that previous generations of educators did not. Those currently teaching in the schools and colleges have grown accustomed to the visual nature of information and knowledge dissemination. This has a number of interesting effects. According to Chris Lanz one of the main problems facing information/knowledge that is conveyed in a visual format, and one that has been alluded to throughout this work, is simply, the bias against the visual. The impartation of information in visual format has traditionally been dismissed as light-weight and not scholarly when compared to traditional delivery systems. Lanz writes: "Visuals are often so strongly associated with entertainment that they are considered incapable of stimulating or organizing thought toward cognitive objectives."[50] But quite to the contrary, visual forms of knowledge dissemination are loaded with information and require forms of analysis that can be as rigorous to master as reading is.[51]

David J. Staley echoes Lanz's concerns. Staley suggests that simply put, the bias against the visual is overwhelming. The image is viewed as inferior to the word. Subsequently, what is considered serious, acceptable academic history is not what is projected in visual formats. Staley uses an illustration from William McNeill's *The Rise of the West* to get this point across. It is, according to Staley more than an illustration. The "visualization" (of an historical period in Japanese society) is significant for today's audience because it is capable of conveying information in a particularly unique fashion. "The visualization," writes Staley, "allows one to perceive simultaneously the whole and the individual parts in a manner reminiscent of a map or the periodic table." Staley makes the salient point that this kind of visualization is not a mere accoutrement to the written word—it is not "designed to break up or enliven" the text, but rather, "it can stand alone as a vehicle of historical thought and scholarly communication."[52] This in turn leads to two key arenas: one is the idea of media/visual literacy and the second is multiple intelligences.

At the heart of the argument for visual (media) literacy is the concept that virtually no emphasis is put on teaching students/people to decipher the plethora of visuals that bombard us in continuous fashion. As Paul Messaris puts it, "images, like language, are a distinct means of making sense of reality and that visual education will give students an alternative, but equally valuable form of access to knowledge and understanding."[53] In Howard Gardner's research, most notably, *Frames of Mind: The Theory of Multiple Intelligences*, (1983), the Harvard psychologist suggests that there are various types of intellectual capacities which when combined, or measured independently, define mental ability. Gardner feels that it is possible to measure intelligence not solely by traditional methods, but by a variety—in actuality seven forms—of measurements.[54] If Gardner is correct, than the part of the brain that deals with visual forms of information cannot be dismissed as less vital than the part which deals with mathe-matical or other forms of information.

The idea of visual education is most certainly, not a new one. Within a decade of film's inception, educators, or as a group, visual educators were very quick to push film as an educational avenue and to cite its pedagogic virtues. [55] Before film's use as a pedagogic passageway, there was pho-tography. Photographs of places and people had been employed as edu-cational texts since 1839. In the settling of the western region of the United States and in the counterpart to this, the anthropological documentation of the demise of the Native American, photographs told the story. These travel pictures and visual documentation projects, such as those by Ed-ward Weston provided a model for the travelogues later produced by mo-tion picture companies.[56]

What was recognized in the 1920s are many of the same concerns voiced by contemporary visual/media literacy advocates. One of the points of consternation that was carefully negotiated was the importance of the teacher as well as the traditional text. Key as well was the fact that visuals had to be interpreted and in turn, that students had to be taught to interpret. Elizabeth Wiatr points out that this was an especially pro-nounced concern in the years after the propaganda filled Great War. Edu-cational films were produced in the thousands—Eastman Kodak made al-most two hundred between 1927 and 1931—and in order to ensure that they would be accepted as pedagogic tools of instruction a variety of "reality-effect" devices were incorporated. These included maps and dia-grams, as well as accompanying print literature. To some extent, what be-came obvious was that the film could not go it alone. Educational visuals required the accompaniment of the printed word.[57]

The above point is made in the context of a society still heavily inclined in favor of the printed word. This is the world that Gore Vidal has remi-nisced about and one in which the visual sophistication of the image had yet to mature to a point of superseding the printed text. What is occurring today has little in common with the visual world of the late nineteen twenties and early nineteen thirties. While the tools that were then avail-able to students from educational film houses should not be forgotten, they cannot really be compared to the offerings available today. It must be recognized that the Web and the Internet are reorienting every aspect of knowledge acquisition. It must also be recognized that the process of learning from technology is often fundamentally different from learning in the traditional lecture format. To compare the two, as is often done with distance education versus the traditional classroom, is the most inaccu-rate method of equivalence. It must be recognized and acknowledged that the Internet and its ancillary devices are altering how history is being pre-sented and, as well, that numerous methodologies are necessary to filter and hone the enormous quantities of data out there.[58] This in itself poses a significant problem. Over the last ten years, millions of historical documents have been placed on the Web. It is estimated that more "than a million Web pages were being added to the Internet each day."[59] Access as well as volume has increased.[60] Digital information of all kinds is proliferating at an alarming rate.

Democratization of knowledge brought by the Internet is a double-edged sword. Spurious and silly information, as well as erroneous and mistake-ridden data occupies the same space as enormously valuable documents, well-researched essays and creative and mind-expanding Web sites. As the authors of a current book put it, "After all, thirteen hundred words of gibberish and the Declaration of Independence are digitally equivalent."[61] Sorting out what is relevant—in essence filtering out the problematic content from legitimate information—remains a huge concern. One way to get around this obstacle has been to employ a rating system which attempts to classify and to advise both students and researchers on acceptability.[62]

When students are encouraged to explore multimedia pathways for historical discourse some interesting, but not surprising, results can occur. In a project of multimedia development for a history seminar, students were instructed to develop web-based/multimedia essays. According to an article on the assignment, the project was overwhelmingly successful. What occurred though was the preference for viewing the images rather than reading the written text. According to Professor Daniel Ringrose,

> At the public open house it quickly became evident that few visitors, if any, started by reading this or any of the project texts beyond the initial introductory page. Instead, the vast majority preferred to explore the maps, listen to the annotations, and only occasionally (and often accidentally) follow links from the visual materials back to the body of the paper.[63]

The obstacle to overcome, according to Ringrose, is to get the "reader" to balance the linear with the other "entry points." What Ringrose means is that the "intensely visual nature of multimedia" automatically privileges the visual over the textual. "One well-known consequence," he writes, "is that most people avoid reading lengthy texts on screen." Maps and other elements of visual "iconography" were often the first choice over the written texts.[64]

One result of the entry of computers in the rubric of historical discourse is that students become active agents in the discovery of the history process. As students are encouraged to become more active in the pedagogy of learning, via the computer, there is more emphasis on student-centered learning. This is one of the most contentious aspects of the digital divide. With the employment of "computer-based technologies," there is a shift towards student centered learning in a manner that is marked and noticeable.[65] According to Historian Linda Pomerantz, "The student's active learning is facilitated in that the computer-using student is in a better position to direct his or her own access to information through the Internet." Pomerantz feels that as more computer-based technology is incorporated into the classroom, the role of the instructor will no doubt be altered. In particular, she implies that the current "master of the classroom" status will evolve into more of a "guide or facilitator," a very disturbing and controversial situation, especially to traditionalists. [66]

Digital history, beyond making history accessible, allows the student to play a role in the deciphering of history. Echoing Linda Pomerantz, John K. Lee writes, "In the digital genre of history, students stand side by side with professional historians generating an infinite number of interpretations from the electronic archives of the Web. Digital history encourages a view of the past that is tentative and process orientated."[67] This is very similar to Mimi White's analysis of television's relationship to history. White speaks of a "peculiar relationship" which is brought on with time conflations, which in turn causes a form of "hyperhistory." History presented in this kind of visual medium, is not bound to traditional orderly presentations, but rather, and is present as "fragmentary" and "multiple." History gets conflated and can be both present and past, not necessarily closed and final.[68]

An inherent problem in getting the full-fledged adoption of the new technology curriculum is the simple resistance to reading lengthy documents on the computer screen. Research at Carnegie Mellon University in Pittsburgh supports this concern. One of the authors of a survey of history and the Web puts it like this: "students have a deep-rooted aversion to reading these documents from their computer screens, which may result in lowered levels of assignment completion, decreased comprehension, or other unintended consequences."[69] This somewhat undermines the successes that have been attributed to computer based-education. Yet as a coda to this, one must bear in mind that "asynchronous Internet transmissions," as a form of communication do have a higher rate of engagement and often do result in better quality student-teacher interaction.[70] This though, is not the same as reading on the computer.

At the University of Southern California, a more sophisticated multimedia project is underway. Students in dozens of courses are now expected to hand in interactive media presentations in lieu of traditional research papers. The significant difference in this case is that the educational institution backs up this expectation with a full support system. Students get all the help that they need. At the behest of one of the university's most famous graduates, George Lucas, an Institute for Multimedia Literacy was created in order to facilitate the production and creation of this kind of assignment. The purpose, according to Michel Marriott, is to "demystify" multimedia and make it accessible to all.[71] The Institute's executive director, Stephanie Barish states:

> We believe a shift is under way in which text, the prime communications medium for centuries, is giving way to a new mode of expression, one that fuses sound, moving and still images, databases and interactivity, to create a 'language of screens.'[72]

This project has been so successful if judged by the thousands of works and students involved, because of the support structure. Inspired by George Lucas and his comments to the Dean of the School of Cinema-Television, the university has put in play numerous support and training procedures that facilitate such high caliber work. The recognition of how vital this is, as a form of literacy, hit the point home. Lucas remarked to the Dean, "If students are not taught the language of sound and images, should they not be considered as illiterate as if they left college without being able to read or write?"[73] Essential here is this full-fledged training in the intricacies of the multimedia world. The Institute and others involved in the university recognized that this process is not simply about moving directly from print to the visual realm. A whole new grammar has to be acquired. And that is why the products (that can be seen on the Annenberg School's Web site) are so effective.

One of the richest examples of how the Internet and the Web can be employed to teach history, and more importantly, to do it well, is to look at the work being done with the French Revolution. One could argue that more sites and digital archives are being directed to the study of France, 1789–1815 than virtually any other era. One reason for this has to do with the fact that so much historical data that remains vis-à-vis the Revolution, has a foundation in the visual.[74] The numerous visual icons on and about the French Revolution have opened up a new world to students of that era. They can now access a variety of texts, images such as engravings and caricatures, songs, and other historical paraphernalia devoted to the Revolution. Like other Web-based offerings, exposure to primary source materials is of particular pedagogic appeal. On the one hand, like many visual sources these many sites serve as a starting point but increasingly, they can also stand alone.[75] As David Trask has suggested, the situation for the historian today, can be challenging. Trask writes,

> We must find effective ways to introduce the study of history, an academic discipline embedded in the conventions and understandings of print media, to students whose facility with the printed word is limited. It is electronic media with which they are most familiar.[76]

Trask is adamant in insisting that it is the electronic world that the students live in and subsequently, it is this world that "shapes" their understanding of what constitutes history. Historians must reach out to students in that language.[77] A very successful digital web archive that speaks to Trask's concerns but that also accomplishes many other—traditional—objectives, is the Library of Congress's American Memory Project, which employs numerous novel offerings.[78] The fluidity and accessibility of digital historical resources is one of the main ways they are both different and unique—in comparison to traditional sources. John Lee suggests that "the Web's hypertextuality encourages alternative narrative forms" which goes a long way to speak to the disposition of contemporary students.[79]

The use of Web-based resources usually has two major drawbacks. The first is the plagiarism problem that results from students downloading material and simply not citing it. The problem of plagiarism is not a new one. One significant difference is that in physically copying a page, a process of analyses was, at the very minimum, occurring. Simply cutting and pasting does not even allow for that primary focus.[80] The second problem arises with many uninformed students running a search on an engine and getting hits that they cannot make sense of. For example, the inability of students to sift through vast quantities of material can lead to them writing a paper on the Holocaust which cites information from Holocaust denial sites.[81] This in turn necessitates the importance of some kind of historical and critical literacy skills that students are going to need. Students at virtually all levels must be able to decipher where the information has come from and to determine not just its source but its legitimacy. Also, filters of some kind, possibly editorial notes such as those put in place by publishers of scholarly journals—some in existence already—will have to be applied.[82] Established historical entities such as research foundations, magazines, museums and educational institutes are often at the forefront of these checks. Librarians working in conjunction with faculty members can preview sites which in turn can be posted on Web pages for specific courses.

Most people gravitate towards ideas and outlets with which they are comfortable. In some cases this is what they have grown up with while in other instances it reinforces a belief system of some kind. For historians and for teachers of history, the dominance of the written word is the "natural" and expected form of expression. This omnipresence has been absolute. David Staley makes the following observation:

> The written word, the central idiom of communication in the practice of history, surrounds us like an atmosphere. Perhaps because of its ubiquity, however, we rarely notice writings effects on our discipline, how it shapes our thoughts, interpretations, and assumptions.[83]

Staley points to Hayden White's idea that written history is as much a "constructed artifact" as, say, film or other forms of predominantly visual history. White, according to Staley, contends that written history is about "condensation, displacement, symbolization, and qualification" and so is filmed history. What constitutes the difference is the medium, not "the way messages are produced."[84]

Perhaps then, this is the essential issue to explore. It is no secret that computer technology and the Internet will influence and affect historical discourse. It is happening already. One may also ask what role instructors will play. It is vital that they are "confident" in their role and comfortable with the technology or else they will remain isolated from the benefits it offers and unaware of the dangers it poses. If this is in fact the essence of the situation, then one must assume that in order for the deliverers of history to be effective they must go down that path with a fair amount of confidence and a willingness not just to be involved but to be active participants.[85]

D. Antonio Cantu and Wilson J. Warren have written that the most important educational transmutation to occur in the last one hundred years may have been the "introduction of computers and the Internet into the class room."[86] The impact of this change has yet to be truly felt. Yet, one significant result is emerging. This has to do with the fact that students at both the high school and the college level are coming to the classroom or lecture hall with a computer/visual framework firmly in place. One could even say that this is even more pronounced than the generation raised on *Sesame Street*. As a number of writers—James Glieck, J. C. Hertz, and Douglas Rushkoff—have suggested there has been a subsequent expectation of similarity in the temples of learning. Consequently, Cantu and Warren state, that "a growing number of students are no longer content to have history fed to them through means of a didactic lecture. Instead they demand that history teachers integrate the wealth of digital historical resources available on the Internet into their curriculum."[87] At the same time, this involves presentation skills that incorporate PowerPoint and WebQuest. And once again, these authors put the responsibility in the hands of the teachers. It is, they imply, up to the instructors to utilize the technology at hand and to deliver. When successful, they are careful to remark, these predominantly visual delivery systems have the power to provide a "conceptual hook that most students find quite appealing and engaging."[88]

Despite Clifford Stoll's remark that learning is not fun and should be hard work, the appeal of visual technology to students and the autonomy granted to them can be harnessed for very productive and positive educational purposes. As Michel Marriott detailed, regarding the University of Southern California, it is important, if not vital, to allow students the opportunities to learn to access this ever changing media culture and to present and view history in these formats. "As electronic communication grows by way of desktop computers, camcorders, the Internet and more, the way people express, educate, and entertain themselves is fast evolving."[89]

NOTES

1. Jane M. Healy, "Visual Technology: Vacuous or Visionary?" pp. 14, 20.

2. Paul Starr, "Computing Our Way to Educational Reform," *The American Prospect*, July/August, 1996, p. 50.

3. Larry Cuban, *Oversold and Underused: Computers in the Classroom*, (Cambridge, MA: Harvard University Press, 2001), p. 104.

4. John Seely Brown, "Growing Up Digital: How the Web Changes Work, Education, and the Ways People Learn," *USDLA Journal*, vol. 16, no. 2, February 2002, p. 6, 23.

5. Sherry Turkle, *Life on the Screen: Identity in the Age of the Internet*, (New York: Simon & Schuster, 1995), p. 77.

6. For the most comprehensive survey of this see Todd Oppenheimer, *The Flickering Mind: The False Promise of Technology in the Classroom and How Learning Can be Saved*, (New York: Random House, 2003). Oppenheimer suggests that large corporations and government funded educational bureaucrats repeatedly jump on the technology bandwagon without thinking through the data or the consequences.

7. Jane M. Healy, *Failure to Connect: How Computers Affect Our Children's Minds—For Better and Worse*, (New York: Simon & Schuster, 1998), pp. 19–21.

8. The 1996–1997 catalog from Voyager is now ten years old. Yet, it contains a wealth of innovative and progressive products which range from "Who Built America" to Art Spiegelman's "The Complete Maus." Both offerings contain intensive interactive historical data including maps, interviews, photographs and film footage. They were pioneering interactive historical media ten years ago and still retain a fair amount of impressive historical information.

9. Jane Healy writes that the most common media forms remove children from social interaction and free play. When they do engage in activities on the computer, such as *Carmen Sandiego*, they seem to be simply focused not on learning, but rather, on getting to "the finish as quickly as possible. They learned," writes Healy, "what worked and didn't work in that particular game, but little about reflective problem solving or the general concepts involved." "Visual Technology: Vacuous or Visionary?," p. 16.

10. Douglas Noble, *The Classroom Arsenal: Military Research, Information Technology and Public Education*, (Philadelphia, PA: The Falmer Press, 1991).

11. For an articulate anti-computer diatribe see Todd Oppenheimer, "The Computer Delusion," *The Atlantic Monthly*, July 1997, pp. 45–62. This article prefigured the ideas that were to be expanded upon in his 2003 book.

12. Robert K. Logan, *The Fifth Language: Learning a Living in the Computer Age*, (Toronto: Stoddart Publishing, 1995), p. 7.

13. Paul Starr, "Computing Our Way to Educational Reform," p. 53.

14. The concern that can't be overlooked is the enormous amount of money spent on computers, and software and the expense of teachers, librarians, and books. Once these purchases become obsolete or require maintenance the institution is left back where they started. On the other hand, the right technology in the right place can be invigorating as far as libraries go. Peter C. Emberley, *Zero Tolerance: Hot Button Politics in Canada's Universities*, (Toronto: Penguin, 1996), p. 186.

15. James H. Wiebe and Nancy J. Martin, "The Impact of a Computer-Based Adventure Game on Achievement and Attitudes in Geography," *Journal of Computing in Childhhod Education*, vol. 5, no. 1, 1994, cited in Alison Armstrong and Charles Casement, *The Child and The Machine: Why Computer's May Put Our Children's Education at Risk*, (Toronto: Key Porter Books, Limited, 1998), pp. 80–81.

16. Alison Armstrong and Charles Casement, *The Child and The Machine: Why Computer's May Put Our Children's Education at Risk*, pp. 80–85.

17. Robert K. Logan, *The Fifth Language*, p. 168.

18. Robert K. Logan, *The Fifth Language*, p. 169.

19. Alexander Stille, *The Future of The Past*, (New York: Farrar, Straus and Giroux, 2002), p. xiv.

20. Roy Rosenzweig, "'So, What's Next for Clio?' CD-ROM and Historians," *The Journal of American History*, March 1995, vol. 81, no. 4, p. 1622.

21. Roy Rosenzweig, "'So, What's Next for Clio?' CD-ROM and Historians," p. 1624.

22. William G. Thomas, III, "Blazing Trails Toward Digital History Scholarship," Round Table, *Histoire social/Social History*, vol. XXXIV, no. 68, November 2001, p. 416.

23. William G. Thomas, III, "Blazing Trails Toward Digital History Scholarship," pp. 416–417. Robert K. Logan, in *The Fifth Language*, pp. 275–76, writes that linked pages which use hypertext, are in turn, very related to oral traditions of storytellers. As alluded to earlier, the Greeks often slanted a version to appeal to a particular audience. Like Jazz, there is an improvisational quality. A further parallel is found in discussion groups which remind Logan of the classic Symposium dialogues.

24. William G. Thomas, III, "Blazing Trails Toward Digital History Scholarship," p. 419.

25. William G. Thomas, III, "Blazing Trails Toward Digital History Scholarship," p. 420.

26. William G. Thomas, III, "Blazing Trails Toward Digital History Scholarship," p. 421.

27. William G. Thomas, III, "Blazing Trails Toward Digital History Scholarship," pp. 422–23.

28. John Lutz, "Riding the Horseless Carriage to the Computer Revolution: Teaching History in the Twenty-first Century," Round Table, *Histoire sociale/Social History*, vol. XXXIV, no. 68, November 2001, pp. 427–28.

29. John Lutz, "Riding the Horseless Carriage to the Computer Revolution: Teaching History in the Twenty-first Century," p. 428.

30. John Lutz, "Riding the Horseless Carriage to the Computer Revolution: Teaching History in the Twenty-first Century," p. 428.

31. John Lutz, "Riding the Horseless Carriage to the Computer Revolution: Teaching History in the Twenty-first Century," p. 429.

32. John Lutz, "Riding the Horseless Carriage to the Computer Revolution: Teaching History in the Twenty-first Century," p. 429.

33. John Lutz, "Riding the Horseless Carriage to the Computer Revolution: Teaching History in the Twenty-first Century," p. 429.

34. John Lutz, "Riding the Horseless Carriage to the Computer Revolution: Teaching History in the Twenty-first Century," pp. 429–30.

35. John Lutz, "Riding the Horseless Carriage to the Computer Revolution: Teaching History in the Twenty-first Century," p. 430.

36. John Lutz, "Riding the Horseless Carriage to the Computer Revolution: Teaching History in the Twenty-first Century," p. 431.

37. Guido Abbattista and Filippo Chiocchetti, "An Outline Survey of Italian Historiography In the World Wide Web," *History and Computing*, vol. 12, no. 3, 2000, pp. 292–93.

38. John Lutz, "Riding the Horseless Carriage to the Computer Revolution: Teaching History in the Twenty-first Century, pp. 433–34.

39. Thomas Newkirk, *Misreading Masculinity: Boys, Literacy, and Popular Culture*, (Portsmouth, NH: Heinemann, 2002), p. 70.

40. On this point see Geoffrey O'Brien, *Castaways of the Image Planet*, (Washington, DC: Counterpoint, 2002), p. 32. Although there are grand differences, there are also interesting similarities with mediated visual culture. O'Brien writes: "Whether swirling or galloping or exploding, the page layouts are designed to sustain a relentless flow of energy. One does not so much read a manga as submit to it, entering a state of total absorption in which the book seems to read itself. Manga contain far fewer words than the average American or European comic, so that the reader's eyes race from frame to frame and his hands turn the page without any awareness of conscious intent. The layouts encourage a lightning-swift reading process."

41. Steven Johnson, *Everything Bad is Good For You: How Today's Popular Culture is Actually Making Us Smarter*, (New York: Riverhead Books/Penguin, 2005), p. 136.

42. Stephen Kline, Nick Dyer-Witheford and Greig De Peuter, *Digital Play: The Interaction of Technology, Culture, and Marketing*, (Montreal: McGill-Queen's University Press, 2003), p. 13.

43. One of the problems that the first generation of CD-ROM games contained is their dependence on simple "decision-trees" which necessitated a yes or no answer. Roy Rosenzweig writes that this caused a problem for historians who are "fans of 'maybe,' 'perhaps,' and 'partially,'" as ways to deal with the "ambiguity" and "nuance" of historical analysis. See Roy Rosenzweig, "'So, What's Next for Clio?' CD-ROM and Historians," p. 1626.

44. Stephen Kline, Nick Dyer-Witheford and Greig De Peuter, *Digital Play: The Interaction of Technology, Culture, and Marketing*, pp. 19–20.

45. Stephen Kline, Nick Dyer-Witheford and Greig De Peuter, *Digital Play: The Interaction of Technology, Culture, and Marketing*, p. 148.

46. James Paul Gee, *What Video Games Have To Teach Us About Learning and Literacy*, (New York: Palgrave MacMillan, 2003), pp. 101–02.

47. Michael J. Albright, "Teaching in the Information Age: A New Look," *New Directions for Teaching and Learning,* 80, Winter 1999, pp. 91–98.

48. Daniel M. Ringrose, "Beyond Amusement: Reflections on Multimedia, Pedagogy, and Digital Literacy in the History Seminar," *The History Teacher,* vol. 34, no. 2, February 2001, p. 1. www.historycooperative.org/journals/ht/34.2/ringrose.html.

49. Larry Cuban, *Oversold and Underused,* p. 97. On page 138, Cuban writes, "In classrooms where the new equipment was used, some teachers found that particular films or television programs motivated students to read the textbook, complete worksheets during the day, and do classroom assignments. Other teachers used the audiovisual equipment to give themselves a tiny break from the tough grind of constant interactions with students over a six-hour school day. In most cases, teachers used the new technology to maintain existing practices."

50. Chris J. Lantz, "Realistic Visuals and Instruction," *College Quarterly* (Summer 1995). p. 2.

51. Chris J. Lantz, "Realistic Visuals and Instruction," p. 3.

52. David J. Staley, *Computers, Visualization, and History: How New Technology Will Transform Our Understanding of the Past,* (Armonk, NY: M. E. Sharpe, 2003), p. 5.

53. Paul Messaris, *Visual Literacy: Image, Mind, & Reality,* (Boulder: Westview Press, 1994), p. 21.

54. Cited in Paul Messaris, *Visual Literacy: Image, Mind, & Reality,* p. 27.

55. Elizabeth Wiatr, "Between Word, Image, and the Machine: Visual Education and Films of Industrial Process," *Historical Journal of Film, Radio and Television,* vol. 22, no. 3, 2002, p. 336.

56. Elizabeth Wiatr, "Between Word, Image, and the Machine: Visual Education and Films of Industrial Process," p. 342.

57. Elizabeth Wiatr, "Between Word, Image, and the Machine: Visual Education and Films of Industrial Process," pp. 342, 345, 347.

58. Howard M. Wach, "How I Arrived on the Web: A History Teacher's Tale," *The History Teacher,* vol. 36, o. 1, November 2002, www.historycoop.org/journals/ht/36.1 /wach.html.

59. Todd Openheimer, *The Flickering Mind,* p. 155. Oppenheimer writes that many websites either disappear or linger in cyberspace which further complicates the problem.

60. John K. Lee, "Digital History in the History/Social Studies Classroom," *The History Teacher,* vol. 35, no. 4, August 2002, p. 504.

61. John Seely Brown and Paul Duguid, *The Social Life of Information,* (Boston: Harvard Business School Press, 2002), p. xiii.

62. Mark Tebeau, "Pursuing E-Opportunities in the History Classroom," *The Journal of American History,* March 2003, vol. 89, no. 4, p. 1490.

63. Daniel M. Ringrose, "Beyond Amusement: Reflections on Multimedia, Pedagogy, and Digital Literacy in the History Seminar," *The History Teacher,* vol. 34, no. 2, February 2001, p. 5. www.historycooperative.org/journals/ht/34.2/ringrose.html.

64. Daniel M. Ringrose, "Beyond Amusement," p. 12.

65. John K. Lee, "Digital History in the History/Social Studies Classroom," p. 504.

66. Linda Pomerantz, "Bridging the Digital Divide: Reflections on 'Teaching and Learning in the Digital Age,'" *The History Teacher*, vol. 34, no. 4 (August 2001) p. 1–10. www.historycoop.org/journals/ht/34.4/pomerantz.html.

67. John K. Lee, "Digital History in the History/Social Studies Classroom,' p. 508.

68. Mimi White, "Television: A Narrative—A History," *Cultural Studies*, vol. 3, no. 3, October 1989, pp. 282–84.

69. James Longhurst, "World History on the World Wide Web: A Student Satisfaction Survey and a Blinding Flash of the Obvious," *The History Teacher*, vol. 36, no. 3, May 2003, p. 1. www.historycoop.org/journals/ht/36.3/longhurst .html.

70. Linda Pomerantz, "Bridging the Digital Divide: Reflections on 'Teaching and Learning in the Digital Age,'" p. 10.

71. Michel Marriott, "It's a Multi-Multimedia World," *Education Life, The New York Times*, November 9, 2003, p. 17.

72. Michel Marriott, "It's a Multi-Multimedia World," p. 17.

73. Michel Marriott, "It's a Multi-Multimedia World," p. 17.

74. Gregory S. Brown, "The Coming of the French Revolution in Multi-Media," *The History Teacher*, vol. 34, no. 2, February 2001, p. 4. www.historycooperative.org/journals/ht/34.2/brown.html.

75. See the list provided in Gregory S. Brown, "The Coming of the French Revolution in Multi-Media."

76. David Trask, "Did the Sans-Coulottes Wear Nikes? The Impact of Electronic Media on the Understanding and Teaching of History," *The History Teacher*, vol. 35, no. 4, August 2002, p. 473.

77. David Trask, "Did the Sans-Coulottes Wear Nikes? The Impact of Electronic Media on the Understanding and Teaching of History," p. 473.

78. John K. Lee, "Digital History in the History/Social Studies Classroom," p. 505.

79. John K. Lee, "Digital History in the History/Social Studies Classroom," p. 508.

80. Lauren Picker, "The Web As Homework Helper," *Newsweek/Score* 2000 Edition, p. 56.

81. Stephen Kneeshaw, "Bring the Internet and World Wide Web into the History Classroom," in Dennis A. Trinkle and Scott A. Merriman, Editors, *History.edu: Essays on Teaching with Technology*, (Armonk, NY: M. E. Sharpe, 2001), p. 154.

82. Lauren Picker, "The Web As Homework Helper," p. 56.

83. David J. Staley, *Computers, Visualization, and History: How New Technology Will Transform Our Understanding of the Past*, p. 14.

84. Hayden White, cited in David J. Staley, *Computers, Visualization, and History: How New Technology Will Transform Our Understanding of the Past*, pp. 16–17.

85. D. Antonio Cantu and Wilson J. Warren, *Teaching History in the Digital Classroom*, (Armonk, New York: M. E. Sharpe, 2003), pp. x–xi, xiii.

86. D. Antonio Cantu and Wilson J. Warren, *Teaching History in the Digital Classroom*, p. 49.

87. D. Antonio Cantu and Wilson J. Warren, *Teaching History in the Digital Classroom*, p. 49.

88. D. Antonio Cantu and Wilson J. Warren, *Teaching History in the Digital Classroom*, p. 49.

89. Michel Marriott, "It's a Multi-Multimedia World," p. 17.

Conclusion

Screens surround us; they envelop us; and increasingly, they serve as our primary conduits of information delivery. Their presence in our lives is ubiquitous, seamless, endless.

—Jessica Helfand, *Screen: Essays on Graphic Design,*
New Media, and Visual Culture, xiii

What am I seeing? From time to time in the history of visual technologies, viewers look at a new medium so startling that it evokes the primal response of an infant opening its eyes. Viewers of the first photographs had no means of comparison that would allow them to comprehend the automatic, unrelenting detail of the daguerreotype. When the Lumiere brothers' black-and-white, silent image of a train appeared at the beginning of cinema, audiences ducked beneath their seats. Early in the days of television, Edward R. Murrow sat at his anchor desk playing with the transcontinental television long lines. Before us was the Golden Gate Bridge and the New York skyline, not as reproductions but in real time, replacing each other at Murrow's command. For an instant, there was a sense that mediation had vanished. The screen had become a window.

—Seth Feldman, "Our Regularly Scheduled
Paradigm Shift," 211

The possibilities to access history are perhaps the greatest ever in the present time. Individuals and in particular students, have avenues to historical presentations and historical offerings in enormous quantity and unique diversity. As has been argued throughout this work, the vitality and prominence of visual forms of history in conveying ideas about what the past is should be undisputed. "Cinematic representation," writes Michael Anderegg, "in short, seem to have supplanted even so-called factual analyses as *the* discourse."[1] This is not to say that defining the past is wholly dependent upon the visual image but rather to recognize that a substantial amount and a dominant form of historical discourse is the visual image. In the case of new technologies—computer mediated communication—the enormous content now available on the Web/Internet is a force to be reckoned with. The more quality information and scholarly knowledge available and accessible the more impact upon traditional notions of history. This necessitated a major shift in textbook publishing and an increased respect for what can be accessed.[2]

The success of *Canada: A People's History*, as well as Ken Burns's work, point in a direction that will only be accentuated in the near future. The fact that these works are highly popular in schools suggests that their roles in education are quite pronounced. For the average Canadian or American, the access provided by these seminal series and the opportunities to view history on television also reinforce the notion that visual history has come of age.[3]

Since early in this century, the "visual" has been able to capture the story in such a potent way that it has displaced other forms or traditional forms of historical evidence. What has been deemed significant as far as the discipline of history has often been determined, captured, and accessed by some form of visual technology.[4] Regardless of the subject matter, the image almost fully determines the historical interpretation. To cite one often played out historical example, war, for individuals who have not experienced it, is understood by the images transmitted.[5]

The importance of media literacy is often discussed in relation to the preeminent position of electronic media delivery systems in contemporary society. In his pioneering study, Len Masterman listed reasons why media education was an urgent priority in the media age. Underlying these reasons was the fact that communication systems and information flow were inextricably linked to virtually all levels of society. Masterman writes of "The increasing importance of visual communication and information in all areas."[6] As each year has passed since the publication of Masterman's book, this seems to increase in importance. To a great extent, the more we understand of the visual world, the more we will be able to appreciate the artistry of the visual universe and understand the "implications" of visual data.[7]

Perhaps it is even necessary to talk about expanding the notion of what literacy now means, as so many commentators have suggested. Perhaps it should mean visual and traditional, both print and non-print.[8] This is especially pronounced for two reasons. The first, which has been discussed, is the fact that print as literacy is under siege from television and other visual media as literacy.[9] The second reason is that the child today—the adolescent—possesses literacy and capabilities in the realms of visual and computer technology which may count as new forms of knowledge. This is especially pronounced when juxtaposed with those who lack that new knowledge. This has in turn caused a rupturing of traditional forms of assessment. As Donna E. Alvermann writes:

> By embracing a rapidly changing digital world, the so-called millennial adolescent is proving quite adept at breaking down century-old distinctions between age groups, among disciplines, between high-and-low brow media culture, and within print and digitized text types.[10]

The youngest members of society, armed with these tools, are at the forefront of massive change. Yet the demise of the traditional delivery systems of history does not entail the obsolescence of the instructor in the classroom or the text book. One of the major strengths of the computer is in sorting and classifying information, making it accessible to a wide audience of people. In the realm of reference material as well as the archived primary source material, the Internet and the Web have proven to be extremely valuable for historical documentation and research. From dictionaries to directories, encyclopedias to almanacs, the accessibility of online versions is increasingly recognized as a key entry point, challenging the supremacy of traditional bound text-based formats.[11] When surveyed, as many as two thirds of students say that they utilize the Internet as their main source for research reports.[12] Books and print texts, and possibly teachers and professors will not have as much of an impact as they once did. The professor/instructor may serve more in the role of interpreter than ever before. The importance of reading to higher education, in particular, will remain eminent.[13] It is also significant to state, as Robert Logan has observed, that the reason people print long documents off the computer, rather than read them in that format, is that when we read on the screen, it is "unnatural" in that "reading is a left-brain activity, whereas viewing video is a right-brain one." This "conflict" is a major reason why the book will survive, especially for longer and more literary creations.[14]

In the introduction to this work, the ideas of J. C. Hertz and James Gleick provided evidence which highlights the postmodern condition affecting young people. To Hertz and Gleick, one can add the concepts of Douglas Rushkoff, especially his work, *Playing the Future*. Rushkoff, like Hertz, identifies a subculture or even a culture among contemporary youth. This subculture of young people does not view the world in the traditional, linear sense and in many cases, rebels against these ways of perception and understanding. These "screenagers" are comfortable in the visual universe and are adept at moving around in a way that is antithetical to the structures of organized academic thought.[15] The point is that they are comfortable with nonlinearity and do not necessarily see jumping between time frames, sources, and disciplines as problematic.

The more accessible visual sources of history become—regardless of the formats—whether on CD-ROMs, video tapes, DVDs, photographic databases, Internet search engines, or digital archives, the more historical "evidence" and resources there are available. The problems with using screens, with preservation and with veracity are still going to be present, but access will greatly augment the discourse of history. The quantity of information on the Internet may be overwhelming but with pinpoint searching tools and technology, the ability to find what one desires will rise as the speed of access increases. Roy Rosenzweig discusses the necessity of future historians to be well versed in the ability to mine and retrieve information from an enormous array of offerings and from old computer formats.[16] These new abilities do not preclude "old fashioned skills" because they will only be useful if historians and others know what they are in fact looking for.

Technology, in its many forms can contribute, enhance, and supplement traditional forms of learning, provided certain fundamental qualities are in place. Jane Healy lists a number of prerequisites which include sufficient cognitive skills, a well-planned curriculum, arts programs, parental involvement, traditional teaching priorities, and overall, a foundation grounded in fundamentals.[17] In essence then, technology can be used and should be used, if all the "essentials" are in place. The problem is that in too many instances these important foundations are not in place and for a variety of reasons can no longer be counted on to provide the necessary preconditions. To think otherwise is, according to some, utopian.

The bias against the visual and the popular has been echoed for many years by scholars uncomfortable with the accessibility guaranteed to nontraditional formats. In some cases, the prejudice acts as a wall to prevent nontraditionalists from gaining access to the rarified and legitimate history. Joseph Ellis has called this "pastism" while Robert Sklar has coined the term "historian-cop" which means that historians have the right to apply their standards across the board to nontraditional visual history.[18] The backlash against this exclusivity is well under way, despite attempts to keep history firmly with in academia. As has been alluded throughout this work, historical discourse has gone beyond the bounds of its traditional guardians, whether they like it or not. In the past decade historians themselves have seen a variety of ruptures in their work. From plagiarism and politics to infighting and political correctness,[19] the divisiveness within the historical community has inadvertently given a green light to more nimble and provocative approaches to history. While bickering and unaware, and without their approval, many historians have let opportunities for collaboration slip by. In a provocative article on the enormous appeal of public and popular history, Raphael Samuel comments on the fact that access and popularity do not necessarily mean that responses and interpretations must be frivolous:

> Education and entertainment need not be opposites; pleasure is not by definition mindless. There is no reason to assume that people are always more passive when looking at old photographs or film footage, handling a museum exhibit, following a local history trail, or even buying a historical souvenir, than when reading a book. People do not simply "consume" images in the way in which, say, they buy chocolate. As in any reading, they assimilate them as best they can to preexisting images and narratives. The pleasures of the gaze are different in kind from those of the written word but not necessarily less taxing on historical reflection and thought.[20]

As with Lewis Namier's observations, Samuel recognizes, in a more progressive way, the vitality and importance of popular history and its reliance on visual history. It is no longer possible to dismiss the impact of visual history and one must be aware of this as a pedagogic fact. This is especially the case in countries like the United States and Canada where pluralism and diversity make it more difficult to establish a traditional consensus-based history. When history is structured in ways that make it penetrating, relevant, and accessible, it reaches a wide audience. In works like *Canada: A People's History*, producer Mark Starowicz successfully combines "this audience need for narrative" with a credible foundation also designed to entertain. Increasingly this is what people want.[21]

NOTES

1. Michael Anderegg, "Introduction," in Michael Anderegg, ed., *Inventing Vietnam: The War in Film and Television*, (Philadelphia, PA: Temple University Press, 1991), p. 1. Italics in the original. Anderegg is talking about filmed versions of the Vietnam War.

2. Mark Tebeau, "Pursuing E-Opportunities in the History Classroom," *The Journal of American History*, March 2003, vol. 89, no. 4, p. 1489.

3. David Glassberg, *Sense of History: The Place of the Past in American Life*, (Amherst, MA: University of Massachusetts Press, 2001), p. 14.

4. Eduardo Cadava, *Words of Light: Theses on The Philosophy of History*, (Princeton, NJ: Princeton University Press, 1997), p. xxiii.

5. Susan Sontag, "Looking at War: Photography's View of Devastation and Death," *The New Yorker*, December 9, 2002, p. 87.

6. Len Masterman, *Teaching The Media*, (New York: Routledge, 1985/1990), pp. 1–2.

7. Paul Messaris, *Visual Literacy: Images, Mind & Reality*, (Boulder, CO: Westview Press, 1994), p. 165.

8. Donna E. Alvermann, "Preface," to *Adolescents and Literacies in a Digital World*, ed., Donna E. Alvermann, (New York: Peter Lang, 2002), p. viii.

9. Thomas Newkirk, *Misreading Masculinity: Boys, Literacy, and Popular Culture*, (Portsmouth, NH: Heinemann, 2002), p. 42.

10. Donna E. Alvermann, "Preface," to *Adolescents and Literacies in a Digital World*, pp. viii–ix.

11. Brian Plane, "Computer-Generated Graphics and the Demise of the History Textbook," in Dennis A. Trinkle and Scott A. Merriman, eds., *History.edu: Essays on Teaching with Technology*, (Armonk, NY: M. E. Sharpe, 2001), p. 72.

12. Bertram C. Bruce, "Diversity and Critical Social Engagement: How Changing Technologies Enable New Modes of Literacy in Changing Circumstances", in Donna E. Alvermann, ed., *Adolescents and Literacies in a Digital World*, p. 3.

13. In *Zero Tolerance: Hot Button Politics In Canada's Universities*, (Toronto: Penguin, 1996), p. 39, Peter C. Emberley writes, "The oldest tradition of the university is that of reading. The awakening, cultivation, and maturation of a student's needs, passions, and longings happens largely through teachers fostering a communion between their students and books. As in other literate cultures, books in the Western world serve as the main medium for self-interpretation and exploration of meaning. They offer us the opportunity to enter a great dialogue spanning millennia and continents. It is a distinctive characteristic of our culture that it is defined by a pedigree of books, a continuous lineage that runs parallel to, and that has shaped, the history of our institutions and social practices. The scholarly culture is an artifice that is an organized remembrance of this lineage."

14. Robert K. Logan, *The Fifth Language: Learning a Living in the Computer Age*, (Toronto: Stoddart Publishing, 1995), p. 278.

15. Douglas Rushkoff, *Playing the Future: How Kids' Culture Can Teach Us to Thrive in an Age of Chaos*, (New York: HarperCollins, 1996).

16. Roy Rosenzweig, "Scarcity or Abundance? Preserving the Past in a Digital Era," *The American Historical Review*, vol. 108, issue, 3, p. 14. www.historycoop.org/journals/ahr /108.3/rosenzweig.html.

17. Jane Healy, *Failure to Connect: How Computers Affect Our Children's Minds—for Better and Worse*, (New York: Simon & Schuster, 1998), p. 245.

18. Joseph Ellis, *American Sphinx; The Character of Thomas Jefferson*, (New York: Knopf, 1997), p. 22 and Robert Sklar's observations, both cited in Gary R. Edgerton, *Ken Burns's America*, (New York: Palgrave/St. Martin's Press, 2001), p. 153.

19. Peter Charles Hoffer, *Past Imperfect*, (New York: Public Affairs, 2004).

20. Raphael Samuel, "Theme Parks—Why Not?" in Malcolm Miles, Tim Hall, Iain Borden, eds., *City Cultures Reader*, (New York: Routledge: 2000), p. 107.

21. Kerry Abel, "Visual History Reviews: Canada: A People's History," *Canadian Historical Review*, December 2001, vol. 82, no. 4, p. 747.

Bibliography

BOOKS

Adelson, Roger. *Speaking of History: Conversations With Historians*. East Lansing, MI: Michigan State University Press, 1997.

Agger, Ben. *The Decline of Discourse: Reading, Writing and Resistance in Postmodern Capitalism*. Philadelphia, PA: The Falmer Press, 1990.

Anderson, Benedict. *Imagined Communities*. London: Verso, 1991.

Arato, Andrew, et al. *The Essential Frankfurt School Reader*. New York: Urizen Books, 1978.

Armstrong, Alison and Charles Casement. *The Child and The Machine: Why Computers Put Our Children's Education at Risk*. Toronto: Key Porter Books Limited, 1998.

Auge, Marc. *Non-Places: Introduction to an Anthropology of Supermodernity*. Translated by John Howe. London: Verso, 1995.

Auster, Paul. *Hand to Mouth: A Chronicle of Early Failure*. New York: Henry Holt, 1997.

Avisar, Ilan. *Screening the Holocaust: Cinema's Images of the Unimaginable*. Bloomington, IN: Indiana University Press, 1988.

Barber, Benjamin. *Jihad Vs. McWorld*. New York: Times Books/Random House, 1995.

Barnouw, Erik. *Tube of Plenty*. New York: Oxford University Press, 1990.

Baron, Naomi S. *Alphabet to Email: How Written English Evolved and Where It's Heading*. New York: Routledge, 2000.

Baron, Robert A., Bruce Earhard, Marcia Ozier. *Psychology*. Scarborough, ON: Allyn & Bacon Canada, 1995.

Barth, Gunther. *City People: The Rise of Modern City Culture in Nineteenth-Century America*. New York: Oxford University Press, 1980.

Barthel, Diane. *Historic Preservation: Collective Memory and Historical Identity*. New Brunswick, NJ: Rutgers University Press, 1996.

Barzun, Jacques. *From Dawn to Decadence: 1500 to the Present*. New York: Harper Collins, 2000.

Bazine, Andre. *What is Cinema?* Selected and Translated by Hugh Gray. Berkeley, CA: University of California Press, 1967.

Bell, Daniel. *The Cultural Contradictions of Capitalism*. New York: Basic Books, 1976.

Benjamin, Walter. *Illuminations*. Edited with and Introduction by Hannah Arendt. Translated by Harry Zohn. New York: Schocken Books, 1968.

Berenbaum, Michael. *The World Must Know: The History of the Holocaust As Told in the United States Memorial Museum*. Boston: Little Brown, 1993.

Berger, John. *Ways of Seeing*. London: Penguin/BBC, 1972.

———. *About Looking*. New York: Pantheon, 1980.

Bettelheim, Bruno. *Freud's Vienna and Other Essays*. New York: Vintage, 1991.

Birkerts, Sven. *The Gutenberg Elegies: The Fate of Reading in An Electronic Age*. Boston: Faber and Faber, 1994.

Biskind, Peter. *Seeing Is Believing: How Hollywood Taught Us To Stop Worrying and Love the Fifties*. New York: Pantheon Books, 1983.

Blom, Philipp. *Encyclopedie: The Triumph of Reason in an Unreasonable Age*. London: Fourth Estate, 2004.

Boddy, William. *Fifties Television: The Industry and Its Critics*. Urbana, IL: University of Illinois Press, 1990.

Bolter, Jay David. *Writing Spaces: The Computer, Hypertext, and the History of Writing*. Hillsdale, NJ: Lawrence Erlbaum, 1991.

Boorstin, Daniel J. *The Image: A Guide to Psuedo-Events in America*. New York: Antheneum, 1961/1987.

———. *The Seekers*. New York: Random House, 1998.

Borgman, Christine L. *From Gutenberg To The Global Information Infrastructure: Access to Information In the Networked World*. Cambridge, MA: MIT Press, 2000.

Bowra, C. M. *The Greek Experience*. London: Weidenfeld and Nicolson, 1957.

Bowser, Eileen. *The Transformation of Cinema: 1907–1915, History of the American Cinema*. vol. 2. Berkeley, CA: University of California Press, 1994.

Braudy, Leo. *The World In a Frame: What We See in Films*. Chicago: The University of Chicago Press, 1984.

Briggs, Asa and Peter Burke. *A Social History of the Media: From Gutenberg to the Internet*. Cambridge, MA: Polity Press, 2002.

Brown, John Seely, and Paul Duguid. *The Social Life of Information*. Boston: Harvard Business School Press, 2002.

Burgoyne, Robert. *Film Nation: Hollywood Looks at U.S. History*. Minneapolis, MN: University of Minnesota Press, 1997.

Burke, James and Richard Ornstein. *The Axemaker's Gift*. New York: Grosset/Putnam, 1995.

Burke, Peter. *Eyewitnessing: The Uses of Images as Historical Evidence*. Ithaca, NY: Cornell University Press, 2001.

Burnett, Ron. *Cultures of Vision: Images, Media and The Imaginary*. Bloomington, IN: Indiana University Press, 1995.

Burns, Eric. *The Joy of Books: Confession of a Lifelong Reader*. Amherst, NY: Prometheus Books, 1995.

Buruma, Ian. *The Wages of Guilt: Memories of War in Germany and Japan*. New York: Meridian/Penguin, 1995.

Cadava, Eduardo. *Words of Light: Theses on The Philosophy of History*. Princeton, NJ: Princeton University Press, 1997.

Cameron, Kenneth M. *America On Film: Hollywood and American History*. New York: Continuum, 1997.

Campbell, Edward D. C. *The Celluloid South: Hollywood and the Southern Myth*. Knoxville, TN: The University of Tennessee Press, 1981.

Cantor, Norman. *The American Century: Varieties of Culture in Modern Times*. New York: HarperCollins Publishers, 1997.

Cantor, Paul. *Gilligan Unbound: Pop Culture in the Age of Globalization*. Lanham, MD: Rowman and Littlefield Publishers, Inc., 2001.

Cantu, D. Antonio and Wilson J. Warren. *Teaching History in the Digital Classroom*. Armonk, NY: M. E. Sharpe, 2003.

Carey, James W. *Communication as Culture: Essays on Media and Society*. Boston: Unwin Hyman, 1989.

Carr, E. H. *What is History?* London: Penguin (1961)1990.

Chadwick, Bruce. *The Reel Civil War: Mythmaking in American Film*. New York: Knopf, 2001.

Chapnick, Howard. *Truth Needs No Ally: Inside Photojournalism*. Columbia, MO: University of Missouri Press, 1994.

Clark, Kenneth. *Civilization: A Personal View*. New York: Harper & Row, 1969.

Clarke, Graham. *The Photograph*. New York: Oxford University Press, 1997.

Cohen, Leah Hager. *Glass, Paper, Beans: Revelations on the Nature and Value of Ordinary Things*. New York: Doubleday/Currency, 1997.

Cole, Tim. *Selling The Holocaust: From Auschwitz to Schindler—How History is Bought, Packaged, and Sold*. New York: Routledge, 2000.

Combs, James. *The Reagan Range: The Nostalgic Myth in American Politics*. Bowling Green, OH: Bowling Green State University Popular Press, 1993.

Crary, Jonathan. *Techniques of the Observer: On Vision and Modernity in the Nineteenth Century*. Cambridge, MA: MIT Press, 1992.

———. *Suspensions of Perception: Attention, Spectacle and Modern Culture*. Cambridge, MA: MIT Press, 1999.

Cuban, Larry. *Teachers and Machines: The Classroom Use of Technology*. New York: The Teachers College Press, 1986.

———. *Oversold and Underused: Computers in the Classroom*. Cambridge, MA: Harvard University Press, 2001.

Cullen, Jim. *The Civil War in Popular Culture: A Reusable Past*. Washington, DC: Smithsonian Institution Press, 1995.

Cummings, Bruce. *War and Television*. London: Verso, 1992.

Custen, George F. *Bio/Pics: How Hollywood Constructed Public History*. New Brunswick, NJ: Rutgers University Press, 1992.

Daval, Jean-Luc. *Photography: History of An Art*. New York: Rizzoli International Publications, 1982.

Davidson, Cathy. *Revolution and the Word: The Rise of the Novel in America*. New York: Oxford University Press, 1996.

Davies, Norman. *Europe: A History*. New York: Oxford University Press, 1996.

Davis, Bob. *Whatever Happened to High School History? Burying The Political Memory of Youth: Ontario: 1945–1995*. Toronto: OS/OS/James Lorimer & Co., 1995.

Davis, Fred. *Yearning For Yesterday: A Sociology of Nostalgia*. New York: The Free Press, 1979.

Davis, Natalie Zemon. *Slaves on Screen: Film and Historical Vision*. Toronto: Vintage, 2000.

Dayan, Daniel and Elihu Katz. *Media Events: The Live Broadcasting of History*. Cambridge, MA: Harvard University Press, 1992.

De Kerckhove, Derrick. *The Skin of Culture: Investigating the New Electronic Reality*. Ed. by Christopher Dewdney. Toronto: Sommerville House Publishing, 1995.

Doherty, Thomas. *Teenagers & Teenpics: The Juvenalization of American Movies in the 1950s*. Boston: Unwin Hyman, 1988.

———. *Projections of War: Hollywood, American Culture, and World War II*. New York: Columbia University Press, 1993.

Doneson, Judith E. *The Holocaust in American Film*. New York: Jewish Publication Society, 1987.

Douglas, Susan J. *Where The Girls Are: Growing Up Female With the Mass Media*. New York: Random House, 1994.

Duncan, Carol. *Civilizing Rituals: Inside Public Art Museums*. New York: Routledge, 1995.

Dunne, Michael. *Metapop: Self-Referentiality in Contemporary American Popular Culture*. Jackson, MS: University Press of Mississippi, 1992.

Dyer, Geoff. *Ways of Telling*. London: Pluto Press, 1986.

Eco, Umberto. *Travels in Hyperreality*. New York: HBJ, 1986.

Edgerton, Gary R. *Ken Burns's America*. New York: Palgrave/St. Martin's Press, 2001.

Eisenstein, Elizabeth. *The Printing Revolution in Early Modern Europe*. Cambridge: Cambridge University Press, 1993.

Emberley, Peter, C. *Zero Tolerance: Hot Button Politics in Canada's Universities*. Toronto: Penguin, 1996.

Epstein, Jason. *Book Business: Publishing, Past, Present and Future*. New York: W. W. Norton and Co., 2001.

Esslin, Martin. *The Age of Television*. New York: W. Freeman, 1982.

Ewen, Elizabeth and Stewart Ewen. *Channels of Desire*. New York: McGraw-Hill, 1979.

Ewen, Stuart. *All Consuming Images: The Politics of Style in Contemporary Culture*. New York: Basic Books, Inc., 1988.

Febvre, Lucien and Henri-Jean Martin. *The Coming of The Book: The Impact of Printing, 1450–1800*. London: Verso, 1976.

Ferro, Mark. *Cinema and History*. Translated by Naomi Green. Detroit, MI: Wayne State University Press, 1988.

Finley, Moses I. *The World of Odysseus*. Revised Edition. London: Penguin, 1979.

Fitzgerald, Frances. *American Revised: History Schoolbooks in the Twentieth Century*. Boston: Little Brown, 1979.

Freund, Gisele. *Photography and Society*. Boston: David R. Godine, Publishers, 1980.

Fulford, Robert. *The Triumph of Narrative: Storytelling in the Age of Mass Culture*. Toronto: House of Anansi Press, Limited, 1999.

Furet, F. and M. Ozouf. *Reading and Writing: Literacy in France From Calvin to Jules Ferry*. New York: Cambridge University Press, 1982.

Gabler, Neil. *Life: The Movie—How Entertainment Conquered Reality*. New York: Vintage Books, 1998.

Gans, Herbert J. *Popular Culture and High Culture*. New York: Basic Books, 1974.

Garraty, John and Peter Gay. Editors. *The Columbia History of the World*. New York: Harper & Row/Dorsett, 1985.

Gee, James Paul. *What Video Games Have To Teach Us About Learning and Literacy*. New York: Palgrave MacMillan, 2003.

Giroux, Henry A. *Disturbing Pleasures: Learning Popular Culture*. New York: Routledge, 1994.

Gitlin, Todd. *Media Unlimited: How the Torrent of Images and Sounds Overwhelms Our Lives*. New York: Henry Holt/Metropolitan Books, 2001.

Glassberg, David. *Sense of History: The Place of the Past in American Life*. Amherst, MA: University of Massachusetts Press, 2001.

Gleick, James. *Faster: The Acceleration of Just About Everything*. New York: Harper-Collins, 1997.

Golby, J. M. and A. W. Purdue. *The Civilization of the Crowd: Popular Culture in England, 1750–1900*. London: Batsford, 1984.

Goldberg, Vicki. *The Power of Photography: How Photographs Changed Our Lives*. New York: Abbeville Publishing Group, 1991.

Golding, Jay. *Empire, Aliens and Conquest: A Critique of American Ideology in Star Trek and Other Science Fiction Adventures*. Toronto: Sisyphus Press, 1985.

Gombrich, E. H. *Art and Illusion: A Study in the Psychology of Pictorial Representations*. Princeton, NJ: Princeton University Press, (1969) 1984.

Gomez, Jeff. *Print is Dead: Books in Our Digital Age*. New York: Macmillan, 2008.

Gottdiener, Mark. *The Theming of America: Dreams, Visions and Commercial Spaces*. Boulder, CO: Westview Press, 1997.

Graff, Harvey J. Editor. *The Labyrinths of Literacy: Reflections on Literacy Past and Present*. Pittsburgh, PA: University of Pittsburgh Press, 1995.

Granatstein, Jack L. *Who Killed Canadian History*. Toronto: HarperCollins, 1998.

Grindon, Leger. *Shadows of the Past: Studies in the Historical Fiction Film*. Philadelphia, PA: Temple University Press, 1994.

Grossberg, Lawrence, Ellen Wartella, and D. Charles Whitney, *MediaMaking: Mass Media In A Popular Culture*. Thousand Oaks, NJ: Sage Publications, 1998.

Grossman, Lawrence, K. *The Electronic Republic: Reshaping Democracy in The Information Age*. New York: Viking/Penguin, 1995.

Gumpert, Gary. *Talking Tombstones & Other Tales of the Media Age*. New York: Oxford University Press, 1987.

Halbwachs, Maurice. *The Collective Memory*. New York: Harper Colophon Books, 1980.

Hale, John. *The Civilization of Europe in the Renaissance*. New York: Antheneum, 1994.

Hall, Peter. *Cities in Civilization*. New York: Pantheon, 1998.

Harris, Francis Jacobson. *I Found It on the Internet: Coming of Age Online*. Chicago: American Library Association, 2005.

Harvey, David. *The Condition of Postmodernity*. Cambridge, MA: Blackwell, 1990/1995.

Healy, Jane. *Failure to Connect: How Computers Affect Our Children's Minds—For Better and Worse*. New York: Simon & Schuster, 1998.

Heinich, Robert, Michael Molenda, James D. Russell, Sharon E. Smaldino. *Instructional Media and Technologies for Learning*. Seventh Edition. New Jersey: Merrill/Prentice Hall, 2002.

Heinze, Andrew R. *Adapting to Abundance: Jewish Immigrants, Mass Consumption, and the Search for American Identity*. New York: Columbia University Press, 1990.

Helfand, Jessica. *Screen: Essays on Graphic Design, New Media, and Visual Culture*. Princeton, NJ: Princeton Architectural Press, 2001.

Henighan, Tom. *The Presumption of Culture: Structure, Strategy, and Survival in the Canadian Cultural Landscape*. Vancouver, BC: Raincoast Books, 1996.

Hertz, J. C. *Joystick Nation: How Videogames Ate Our Quarters, Won Our Hearts and Rewired Our Minds*. Boston: Little Brown & Co., 1997.

Heskett, John. *Toothpicks & Logos: Design in Everyday Life*. New York: Oxford University Press, 2002.

Hof, Ulrich Im. *The Enlightenment*. Oxford: Basil Blackwell, 1994.

Hoffer, Peter Charles. *Past Imperfect*. New York: PublicAffairs, 2004.

Hollander, Anne. *Moving Pictures*. New York: Alfred Knopf, 1989.

Horkheimer, Max. *Critique of Instrumental Reason*. New York: Continuum, 1974.

Horkheimer, Max and Theodore Adorno. *Dialectic of Enlightenment*. New York: Continuum, 1972.

Hughes, Robert. *The Shock of The New*. New York: Knopf, 1981.

Huston, Aletha C., et al. *Big World, Small Screen: The Role of Television in American Society*. Lincoln, NE: University of Nebraska Press, 1992.

Ignatieff, Michael. *Virtual War: Kosovo and Beyond*. Toronto: Viking, 2000.

Insdorf, Annete. *Indelible Shadows: Film and the Holocaust*. Cambridge: Cambridge University Press, 1989.

James, Clive. *Fame In the 20th Century*. New York: Random House, 1993.

Jameson, Frederick. *Postmodernism or The Cultural Logic of Late Capitalism*. Durham, NC: Duke University Press, 1991.

Jamieson, G. H. *Communication and Persuasion*. London: Croom Helm, 1985.

Jardine, Lisa. *Worldly Goods: A New History of the Renaissance*. New York: Nan A. Talese/Doubleday, 1996.

Jay, Martin. *The Dialectical Imagination*. Boston: Little Brown and Co., 1973.

———. *Adorno*. Cambridge, MA: Harvard University Press, 1984.

———. *Downcast Eyes: The Denigration of Vision in Twentieth-Century French Thought*. Berkeley, CA: University of California Press, 1994.

Jeanneney, Jean-Noel. *Google and The Myth of Universal Knowledge*. Chicago: University of Chicago Press, 2006.

Jenkins, Henry. *Convergence Culture: Where Old and New Media Collide*. New York: New York University Press, 2007.

Jenks, Chris. Editor. *Visual Culture*. New York: Routledge, 1995.

Johnson, Pauline. *Marxist Aesthetics*. London: Routledge and Kegan Paul, 1984.

Johnson, Steven. *Everything Bad is Good For You: How Today's Popular Culture is Actually Making Us Smarter*. New York: Riverhead Books/Penguin, 2005.

Jowett, Garth and James M. Linton. *Movies as Mass Communication*. Beverly Hills, CA: Sage Publications, 1980.

Kaes, Anton. *From Hitler to Heimat: The Return of History as Film*. Cambridge, MA: Harvard University Press, 1995.

Kaestle, Carl F., et al. *Literacy in the United States: Readers and Reading Since 1880*. New Haven, CT: Yale University Press, 1991.

Kagan, Norman. *The Cinema of Oliver Stone*. New York: Continuum, 2000.

Kammen, Michael. *Mystic Chords of Memory: The Transformation of Tradition in American Culture*. New York: Knopf, 1991.

———. *American Culture American Tastes: Social Change and the 20th Century*. New York: Knopf, 1999.

Kay, Harvey J. *The Powers of the Past: Reflection on the Crises and the Promise of History*. London: Harvester Wheatsheaf, 1991.

Kebric, Robert B. *Greek People*. Mountain View, CA: Mayfield Publishing, 1989.

Kellner, Douglas. *The Persian Gulf TV War*. Boulder, CO: Westview Press, 1992.

Kernan, Alvin. *The Death of Literature*. New Haven, CT: Yale University Press, 1990.

Kline, Stephen, Nick Dyer-Witheford and Greig De Peuter. *Digital Play: The Interaction of Technology, Culture, and Marketing*. Montreal: McGill-Queen's University Press, 2003.

Kubey, Robert and Mihaly Csikszentmihlyi. *Television and the Quality of Life: How Viewing Shapes are Everyday Experience*. Hillsdale, NJ: Lawrence Erlbaum Associates, 1990.

Kuisel, Richard. *Seducing The French: The Dilemma of Americanization*. Berkeley, CA: University of California Press, 1993.

Kurtz, Howard. *Media Circus: The Trouble With America's Newspapers*. New York: Times Books, 1993.

Ladurie, Emmanuel Le Roy. *The Ancien Regime: A History of France 1610–1774*. Cambridge, MA: Basil Blackwell, 1996.

Landy, Marcia. *British Genres: Cinema and Society, 1930–1960*. Princeton, NJ: Princeton University Press, 1991.

———. *Italian Film*. Cambridge: Cambridge University Press, 2000.

Langer, Lawrence, L. *Admitting the Holocaust: Collected Essays*. New York: Oxford University Press, 1995.

Langford, Michael. *The Story of Photography*. London: Focal Press, 1980.

Lanham, Richard A. *The Electronic World: Democracy, Technology and the Arts*. Chicago: University of Chicago Press, 1993.

Lennon, John and Malcolm Foley. *Dark Tourism: The Attraction of Death and Disaster*. London: Thompson, 2004.

Lerner, Fred. *The Story of Libraries: From the Invention of Writing to The Computer Age*. New York: Continuum, 1999.

Lester, Paul Martin. *Visual Communication: Images with Messages*. Second Edition. Belmont, CA: Wadsworth/Thomson Learning, 2000.

Levine, Lawrence W. *The Unpredictable Past: Explorations in American Cultural History*. New York: Oxford University Press, 1993.

Levy, David M. *Scrolling Forward: Making Sense of Documents in The Digital Age*. New York: Arcade Publishing, 2001.

Levy, Steven. *The Perfect Thing: How the iPOD Shuffles Commerce, Culture, and Coolness*. New York: Simon & Schuster, 2006.

Lippmann, Walter. *Public Opinion*. New York: The Free Press (1922), 1965.

Lipsitz, George. *Time Passages: Collective Memory and American Popular Culture.* Minneapolis, MN: University of Minnesota Press, 1990.

Logan, Robert K. *The Fifth Language: Learning A Living in the Computer Age.* Toronto: Stoddart Publishing, 1995.

Lowenthal, David. *The Past is a Foreign Country.* Cambridge: Cambridge University Press, 1985.

Lowenthal, Leo. *Literature, Popular Culture and Society.* Palo Alto, CA: Pacific Books, 1968.

Lubar, Steven. *InfoCulture.* Boston: Houghton Mifflin and Company, 1993.

Lukacs, John. *Historical Consciousness: The Remembered Past.* New Brunswick, NJ: Transaction Publishers, (1968) 1985.

Mackey-Kallis, Susan. *Oliver Stone's America.* Boulder, CO: Westview Press, 1996.

Man, John. *The Gutenberg Revolution.* London: Review, 2002.

Manguel, Alberto. *A History of Reading.* Toronto: Alfred A. Knopf, 1996.

Marc, David. *Comic Visions: Television Comedy and American Culture.* Boston: Unwin Hyman, 1989.

———. *Bonfire of The Humanities: Television, Subliteracy, And Long-Term Memory Loss.* Syracuse, NY: Syracuse University Press, 1995.

Marchand, Phillip. *Marshall McLuhan: The Medium and the Messenger.* Toronto: Random House, 1989.

Marchand, Roland. *Advertising the American Dream: Making Way for Modernity, 1920–1940.* Berkeley: University of California Press, 1986.

Marill, Alvin H. *Movies Made for Television.* New York: De Capo, 1980.

Marling, Karal Ann. *As Seen On TV: The Visual Culture of Everyday Life in the 1950s.* Cambridge, MA: Harvard University Press, 1994.

Marwick, Arthur. *The Nature of History.* Third Edition. London: Macmillan, 1989.

Masterman, Len. *Teaching the Media.* New York: Routledge, 1985/1990.

May, Larry. *Screening Out The Past: The Birth of Mass Culture and The Motion Picture Industry.* Chicago: University of Chicago Press, 1983.

Mayo, James M. *War Memorials as Political Landscape: The American Experience and Beyond.* New York: Praeger Publishers, 1988.

McLuhan, Marshall. *The Gutenberg Galaxy.* Toronto: University of Toronto Press, 1986.

———. *Understanding Media: The Extensions of Man.* Cambridge, MA: MIT Press, 1998.

McNeill, William H. *Mythistory and Other Essays.* Chicago: University of Chicago Press, 1986.

Meier, Christian. *From Athens to Auschwitz: The Uses of History.* Translated by Deborah Lucas Schneider. Cambridge, MA: Harvard University Press, 2005.

Mendelsohn, Daniel. *The Lost: A Search for Six of Six Million.* New York: HarperCollins, 2006.

Merriman, J. *A History of Modern Europe: From the Renaissance to the Age of Napoleon.* New York: W. W. Norton, 1996.

Messaris, Paul. *Visual Literacy: Image, Mind & Reality.* Boulder, CO: Westview Press, 1994.

Meyrowitz, Joshua. *No Sense of Place: The Impact of Electronic Media on Social Behavior.* New York: Oxford University Press, 1985.

Miller, Judith. *One by One by One: Facing the Holocaust.* New York: Simon and Schuster, 1990.

Milton, Sybil. *In Fitting Memory: The Art and Politics of Holocaust Memorials*. Detroit, MI: Wayne State University Press, 1991.

Mindich, David T. Z. *Tuned Out: Why Americans Under 40 Don't Follow the News*. New York: Oxford University Press, 2005.

Mintz, Alan. *Popular Culture and the Shaping of Holocaust Memory in America*. Seattle, WA: University of Washington Press, 2001.

Mirzoeff, Nicholas. *An Introduction to Visual Culture*. New York: Routledge, 1999.

Morris, Wright. *Time Pieces: Photographs, Writing and Memory*. New York: Aperture Foundation, Inc., 1989.

Moss, Mark. *Manliness and Militarism: Educating Young Boys in Ontario for War*. Toronto: Oxford University Press, 2001.

Mukerji, Chandra and Michael Schudson. Editors. *Rethinking Popular Culture: Contemporary Perspectives in Cultural Studies*. Berkeley, CA: University of California Press, 1991.

Mumford, Lewis. *Technics and Civilization*. New York: Harcourt, Brace & World, 1963.

Musser, Charles. *The Emergence of Cinema: The American Screen to 1907, History of the American Cinema*. Volume 1. Berkeley, CA: University of California Press, 1994.

Nash, Knowlton. *Trivia Pursuit: How Showbiz Values are Corrupting the News*. Toronto: McClelland & Stewart, 1998.

Nauert, Charles. *Humanism and the Culture of the Renaissance*. Cambridge: Cambridge University Press, 1995.

Negroponte, Nicholas. *Being Digital*. New York: Alfred Knopf, 1995.

Neuman, Johanna. *Lights, Camera, War: Is Media Technology Driving International Politics*. New York: St. Martin's Press, 1996.

Newkirk, Thomas. *Misreading Masculinity: Boys, Literacy, and Popular Culture*. Portsmouth, NH: Heinemann, 2002.

Newman, Robert D. *Transgressions of Reading: Narrative Engagement as Exile and Return*. Durham, NC: Duke University Press, 1993.

Noble, Douglas. *The Classroom Arsenal: Military Research, Information Technology and Public Education*. Philadelphia, PA: The Falmer Press, 1991.

Novick, Peter. *That Noble Dream: The "Objectivity Question" and the American Historical Profession*. Cambridge: Cambridge University Press, (1988)1999.

Novitz, David. *Pictures and Their Use in Communication*. The Hague, Netherlands: Martinus Nijhoff, 1977.

O'Brien, Geoffrey. *Castaways of the Image Planet*. Washington, DC: Counterpoint, 2002.

O'Brien, Tom. *The Screening of America: Movies and Value's from Rocky to Rain Man*. New York: Continuum, 1990.

Olson, David. *The World on Paper*. Cambridge: Cambridge University Press, 1994.

Ong, Walter J. *Orality and Literacy: The Technologizing of the Word*. London: Methuen, 1986.

Oppenheimer, Todd. *The Flickering Mind: The False Promise of Technology in the Classroom and How Learning Can be Saved*. New York: Random House, 2003.

Osborne, Ken. *In Defense of History: Teaching The Past and the Meaning of Democratic Citizenship*. Toronto: Our Schools/Our Selves Educational Foundation, 1995.

Parenti, Michael. *Make Believe Media*. New York: St. Martin's Press, 1991.

Paris, Erna. *Long Shadows: Truth, Lies and History*. Toronto: Alfred A. Knopf, 2000.

Pocklington, Tom and Allan Tupper. *No Place To Learn: Why Universities Aren't Working*. Vancouver, BC: University of British Columbia Press, 2002.

Poole, Robert M. *Explorers House: National Geographic and the World it Made*. New York: Penguin, 2004.

Postman, Neil. *Amusing Ourselves to Death*. New York: Penguin, 1985.

———. *Technopoly: The Surrender of Culture to Technology*. New York: Knopf, 1993.

———. *The End of Education: Redefining the Value of School*. New York: Knopf, 1995.

———. *Building a Bridge to the Eighteenth Century: How the Past Can Improve the Future*. New York: Knopf, 1999.

Quard, Leonard and Albert Auster. *American Film and Society Since 1945*. Second Edition. Westport, CT: Praeger, 1991.

Quitavalle, Arturo Carlo. *Fratelli Alinari, Photographers In Florence: 150 Years of Picturing the World, 1852/2002*. Guide to the Exhibition. Florence: 2002.

Rapping, Elayne. *The Movie of the Week: Private Stories, Public Events*. Minneapolis, MN: University of Minnesota Press, 1992.

Richards, Jeffrey. *Visions of Yesterday*. London: Routledge and Kegan Paul, 1973.

Ridless, Robin. *Ideology and Art*. New York: Peter Lang, 1984.

Robertson, Heather-Jane. *No More Teachers, No More Books: The Commercialization of Canada's Schools*. Toronto, ON: McClelland and Stewart, 1998.

Robertson, James Oliver. *American Myth: American Reality*. New York: Hill and Wang, 1980.

Rosen, Jonathan. *The Talmud and the Internet: A Journey Between Worlds*. New York: Farrar, Straus and Giroux, 2000.

Rosenberg, Emily S. *Spreading the American Dream: American Economic and Cultural Expansion, 1890–1945*. New York: Hill and Wang, 1989.

Rosenberg, Harold. *Art & Other Serious Matters*. Chicago: University of Chicago Press, 1985.

Rushkoff, Douglas. *Playing the Future: How Kids' Culture Can Teach Us to Thrive in an Age of Chaos*. New York: HarperCollins, 1996.

Rutter, N. Keith and Brian A. Sparkes. Editors. *Word and Image in Ancient Greece*. Edinburgh: Edinburgh University Press, 2000.

Sabin, Roger. *Adult Comics: An Introduction*. New York: Routledge, 1993.

Salewicz, Chris. *Oliver Stone: The Making of His Movies*. London: Orion Media, 1997.

Saul, John Ralston. *The Unconscious Civilization*. Toronto, ON: House of Anansi Press, 1995.

Scheuer, Jeffrey. *The Sound Bite Society: Television and The American Mind*. New York: Four Walls Eight Windows, 1999.

Schickel, Richard. *Intimate Strangers: The Culture of Celebrity*. New York: International Publishers, 1986.

Schudson, Michael. *Watergate in American Memory: How We Remember, Forget, and Reconstruct the Past*. New York: Basic Books, 1992.

Seabrook, John. *Nobrow: The Culture of Marketing, The Marketing of Culture*. London: Methuen, 2000.

Sennett, Richard. *The Fall of Public Man*. New York: Vintage Books, 1978.

Shandler, Jeffrey. *While America Watches: Televising the Holocaust*. New York: Oxford University Press, 1999.

Shapin, Steve. *The Scientific Revolution*. Chicago: University of Chicago Press, 1996.

Shenk, David. *Data Smog: Surviving The Information Glut*. New York: Harper-Collins, 1997.

Shlain, Leonard. *The Alphabet Versus The Goddess: The Conflict Between Word and Image*. New York: Viking, 1998.

Slotkin, Richard. *Gunfighter Nation: The Myth of the Frontier in Twentieth Century America*. New York: Antheneum, 1992.

Soley, Lawrence C. *Leasing The Ivory Tower: The Corporate Takeover of Academia*. Boston: South End Press, 1995.

Sontag, Susan. *On Photography*. New York: Farrar, Straus and Giroux, 1978.

Sorlin, Pierre. *The Film in History: Restaging the Past*. Oxford: Basil Blackwell, 1980.

Speilvogel, Jackson L. *Western Civilization*. New York: Thomson/Wadsworth, 1999.

Spender, Dale. *Nattering on the Net: Women, Power and Cyberspace*. Toronto, ON: Garamond Press, 1995.

Spigel, Lynn. *Make Room For TV: Television and the Family Ideal in Postwar America*. Chicago: University of Chicago Press, 1992.

Spitz, Ellen Handler. *Inside Picture Books*. New Haven, CT: Yale University Press, 1999.

Staley, David J. *Computers, Visualization, and History: How New Technology Will Transform Our Understanding of the Past*. Armonk, NY: M. E. Sharp, 2003.

Stark, Steven D. *Glued To The Set: The 60 Television Shows and Events that Made Us Who We Are Today*. New York: The Free Press, 1997.

Starowicz, Mark. *Making History*. Toronto, ON: McClelland & Stewart, 2003.

Steinberg, S. H. *Five Hundred Years of Printing*. London: Penguin, 1961.

Stephens, Mitchell. *The Rise of The Image: The Fall of The Word*. New York: Oxford University Press, 1998.

Stewart, Susan. *On Longing: Narratives of the Miniature, the Gigantic, the Souvenir, the Collection*. Durham, NC: Duke University Press, 1993.

Stille, Alexander. *The Future of the Past*. New York: Farrar, Straus and Giroux, 2002.

Stoll, Clifford. *Silicon Snake Oil: Second Thoughts on The Information Highway*. New York: Doubleday, 1995.

———. *HighTech Heretic*. New York: Doubleday, 1999.

Sturken, Marita. *Tangled Memories: The Vietnam War, The Aids Epidemic, and The Politics of Remembering*. Berkeley, CA: University of California Press, 1997.

Sturken, Marita and Lisa Cartwright. *Practices of Looking: An Introduction to Visual Culture*. New York: Oxford University Press, 2005.

Susman, Warren. *Culture as History*. New York: Pantheon, 1984.

Tavis, Brian. *The Romance of Adventure: The Genre of Historical Adventure Movies*. Jackson, MS: University Press of Mississippi, 1993.

Taylor, Gary. *Cultural Selection: Why Some Achievements Survive the Test of Time—And Others Don't*. New York: Basic Books, 1996.

Taylor, John. *War Photography: Realism in The British Press*. New York: Routledge, 1991.

Thompson, John B. *Books in the Digital Age*. Cambridge: Polity Press, 2005.

Thompson, Oliver. *Mass Persuasion in History*. Edinburgh: Paul Harris Publishing, 1977.

Thompson, Robert, J. *Television's Second Golden Age*. New York: Continuum, 1996.

Thompson, Vivian Alpert. *A Mission in Art: Recent Holocaust Works in America*. Macon, GA: Mercer University Press, 1988.

Tichi, Cecelia. *Electronic Hearth: Creating an American Television Culture*. New York, Oxford University Press, 1991.

Toffler, Alvin. *The Third Wave*. New York: Bantam Books, 1981.

Tomlinson, John. *Cultural Imperialism*. Baltimore: The Johns Hopkins University Press, 1991.

Toplin, Robert Brent. *History By Hollywood: The Use and Abuse of the American Past*. Urbana, IL: University of Illinois Press, 1996.

Trachtenberg, Alan. *Reading American Photographs: Images as History—Mathew Brady to Walker Evans*. New York: Hill and Wang/FSG, 1989.

Turkle, Sherry. *Life on the Screen: Identity in the age of the Internet*. New York: Simon and Schuster, 1995.

Twitchell, James B. *Carnival Culture: The Trashing of Taste in America*. New York: Columbia University Press, 1992.

———. *Lead Us Into Temptation: The Triumph of American Materialism*. New York: Oxford University Press, 1999.

Tyner, Kathleen. *Literacy In A Digital World: Teaching and Learning in the Age of Information*. Philadelphia, PA: Lawrence Erlbaum Associates, 1998.

Vidal, Gore. *Screening History*. Cambridge, MA: Harvard University Press, 1992.

Vincent, David. *Bread, Knowledge and Freedom: A Study of Nineteenth-Century Working Class Autobiography*. London: Europa Publications Limited, 1981.

Volti, Rudi. *Society and Technological Change*. Third Edition. New York: St. Martin's Press, 1995.

Walker, John. *Art in the Age of Mass Media*. London: Pluto Press, 1983.

Watson, Mary Ann. *The Expanding Vista: American Television in The Kennedy Years*. New York: Oxford University Press, 1990.

Weinberg, Jeshajahu, and Rina Elieli. *The Holocaust Museum in Washington*. New York: Rizzoli, 1995.

White, Hayden. *Tropics of Discourse*. Baltimore, MD: The Johns Hopkins University Press, 1978.

———. *The Content of the Form: Narrative Discourse and Historical Representation*. Baltimore: The Johns Hopkins University Press, 1987.

Whitfield, Stephen J. *The Culture of the Cold War*. Baltimore, MD: The Johns Hopkins University Press, 1991.

Wolin, Richard. *An Aesthetic of Redemption*. New York: Columbia University Press, 1984.

Wyver, John. *The Moving Image: An International History of Film, Television and Video*. Oxford: Basil/Blackwell, 1989.

Young, James. *The Texture of Memory: Holocaust Memorials and Meaning*. New Haven, CT: Yale University Press, 1993.

———. *At Memory's Edge: After-Images of the Holocaust in Contemporary Art and Architecture*. New Haven, CT: Yale University Press, 2000.

Zelizer, Barbie, and Stuart Allen, Editors. *Journalism After September 11*. New York: Routledge, 2002.

Zenderland, Leila, Editor. *Recycling The Past: Popular Uses of American History*. Philadelphia, PA: University Press, 1978.

ARTICLES AND ESSAYS

Abbattista, Guido and Filippo Chiocchetti. "An Outline Survey of Italian Historiography in the World Wide Web." *History and Computing*. Vol. 12, No. 3, 2000.

Abel, Kerry. "Visual History Reviews: Canada: A People's History." *The Canadian Historical Review*. *82*(4), 746–48, 200.

Abrash, Barbara and Daniel J. Walkowitz. "Sub/versions of History: A Mediation on Film and Historical Narrative." *History Workshop Journal*. Issue 38, 1994.

Albright, Michael J. "Teaching in the Information Age: A New Look." *New Directions for Teaching and Learning*. Vol. 80, Winter 1999.

Alter, Robert. "Deformations of the Holocaust." *Commentary*, February, 1981.

Alvermann, Donna E. "Preface." *Adolescents and Literacies in a Digital World*. Edited by Donna E. Alvermann. New York: Peter Lang 2002.

Amelunxen, Hubertus von. "The Century's Memorial: Photography and the Recording of History." *A New History of Photography*. Edited by Michel Frizot. Cologne, Germany: Konemann, 1998.

American Photo. Vol. II, No. 5. September/October 1991.

Anderegg, Michael. "Introduction." *Inventing Vietnam: The War in Film and Television*. Edited by Michael Anderegg. Philadelphia, PA: Temple University Press, 1991.

Anderson, Steve. "History TV and Popular Memory." *Television Histories: Shaping Collective Memory in the Media Age*. Edited by Gary R. Edgerton and Peter C. Rollins. Lexington, KY: The University of Kentucky Press, 2001.

Appleby, Joyce, Lynn Hunt, Margaret Jacob. "Telling the Truth About History." *The Postmodern History Reader*. Edited by Keith Jenkins. London/New York: Routledge, 1997.

Aufderheide, Pat. "Vietnam: Good Soldiers." *Seeing Through Movies*. Edited by Mark Crispin Miller. New York: Pantheon, 1990.

Axworthy, Tom. "Memories Shape the Way We See Ourselves." *The Toronto Star*. September 26, 1997.

Ayers, Edward L. "History in the Air." *Magazine of History*. Vol. 18, No. 4, July 2004.

Bardgett, Suzanne. "Exhibiting Hatred." *History Today*. June 2000.

Bartov, Omer. "Spielberg's Oskar: Hollywood Tries Evil." *Spielberg's Holocaust: Critical Perspectives on Schindler's List*. Edited by Yosefa Loshitzky. Bloomington, IN: Indiana University Press, 1997.

Barzun, Jacques. "The Future of Reading." *Books In Our Future*. Edited by John Y. Cole. Washington, DC: Library of Congress, 1987.

Benson, Susan Porter, Stephen Brier and Roy Rosenzweig. "Introduction." *Presenting the Past: Essays on History and The Public*. Edited by Susan Porter Benson, Stephen Brier and Roy Rosenzweig. Philadelphia, PA: Temple University Press, 1986.

Berger, John. "Problems in Socialist Art." *Radical Perspectives in the Arts*. Edited by Lee Baxandall. London: Penguin, 1972.

Bernstein, Michael Andre. "The *Schindler's List* Effect." *The American Scholar*. Summer 1994.

Bernt, Joseph and Phyllis Bernt. "World Wide Web, E-Commerce, and the Rise of the Book: Survey of Online Booksellers Indicates Increasing Value of Used Books." A Paper Presented to the Electronic Communication & Culture Area,

Popular Culture Association Conference, New Orleans, Louisiana, April 20, 2000.

Bloch, Sara Kviat. "Highlights of the Holocaust; Survivors of the Shoah Visual History Foundation." A Paper Presented at the 30th Popular Culture Association Conference, New Orleans, LA, April 19–22, 2000.

Bolter, Jay David. "Ekphrasis, Virtual Reality, and the Future of Writing." *The Future of the Book.* Edited by Geoffrey Nunberg. Berkeley, CA: University of California Press, 1996.

Bolton, Richard. "Introduction: The Contest of Meaning: Critical Histories of Photography." *The Contest of Meaning: Critical Histories of Photography.* Edited by Richard Bolton. Boston: MIT Press, 1993.

Breitbart, Eric. "The Painted Mirror: Historical Re-creation from the Panorama to the Docudrama." *Presenting the Past: Essays on History and the Public.* Edited by Susan Porter Benson, et al. Philadelphia, PA: Temple University Press, 1986.

Brown, Gregory S. "The Coming of the French Revolution in Multi-Media." *The History Teacher.* Vol. 34, No. 2, February 2001: www.historycooperative.org/journals/ht/34.2 /brown.html

Brown, John Seely. "Growing Up Digital: How the Web Changes Work, Education, and the Ways People Learn." *USDLA Journal,* Vol. 16, No. 2, February 2002.

Brown, Ray, B. "Forward." *Hollywood as Historian: American Film in a Cultural Context.* Edited by Peter C. Rollins. Lexington, KY: The University of Kentucky Press, 1983.

Bruce, Bertram, C. "Diversity and Critical Social Engagement: How Changing Technologies Enable New Modes of Literacy in Changing Circumstances." *Adolescents and Literacies in a Digital World.* Donna E. Alvermann, Editor. New York: Peter Lang Publishing, 2002.

Bruner, Jerome. "The Narrative Construction of Reality." *Critical Inquiry.* Vol. 18, No. 1, Autumn, 1991.

Buck-Morss, Susan. "Benjamin's Passagen-Werk: Redeeming Mass Culture for the Revolution." *New German Critique.* 29, 1983.

Buruma, Ian. "History and Hollywood." *The Toronto Star,* May 2, 1999.

Bush, Vannevar. "As We May Think." *Electronic Culture: Technology and Visual Representation.* Edited by Timothy Druckrey. New York: Aperture, 1996.

Cameron, Euan. "The Power of the Word: Renaissance and Reformation." *Early Modern Europe: An Oxford History.* Edited by Euan Cameron. London: Oxford University Press, 1999.

Carlson, Scott. "Do Libraries Really Need Books?" *The Chronicle of Higher Education.* July 12, 2002.

Carnes, Mark C. "Introduction." *Past Imperfect: History According to the Movies.* Edited by Mark C. Carnes. New York: Henry Holt, 1996.

Chalfen, Richard. "Home Movies as Cultural Documents." *Film/Culture: Explorations of Cinema in Its Social Context.* Edited by Sari Thomas. Lanham, MD: The Scarecrow Press, 1982.

Chapnick, Howard. "Forward." *Eyes of Time: Photojournalism in America.* By Marianne Fulton. Boston: Little Brown and Company, 1988.

Chartier, Roger. "Libraries Without Walls." *Representations.* 42, Spring 1993.

Chow, Rey. "The Age of the World Target: On the Fiftieth Anniversary of the Dropping of the Atomic Bomb." *Mass Culture and Everyday Life.* Edited by Peter Gibian. New York: Routledge, 1997.

Collins, Jim. "No (Popular) Place Like Home?" *High-Pop: Making Culture into Popular Entertainment.* Edited by Jim Collins. Boston: Blackwell Publishers, 2002.

Comolli, Jean-Louis. "Machines of the Visible." *Electronic Culture: Technology and Visual Representation.* Edited by Timothy Druckrey. New York: Aperture, 1996.

Conrad, Margaret. "My Canada Includes the Atlantic Provinces." *Histoire sociale/Social History.* Vol. XXXIV, No. 68, November 2001.

Cook, John R. "History-Makers." Review Essay. *Historical Journal of Film, Radio and Television.* Vol. 22, No. 3, 2002.

Coupland, Douglas. "J.F.K. Remembered, Even for Those Who Don't." *The New York Times,* November 14, 1993.

Crain, Caleb. "Twilight of the Books." *The New Yorker.* December 24, 31, 2007.

Custen, George F. "Clio in Hollywood." *Why Docudrama? Fact-Fiction on Film and TV.* Edited by Alan Rosenthal. Carbondale, IL: Southern Illinois University Press, 1999.

Davis, Natalie Zemon. "'Any Resemblance to Persons Living or Dead': Film and the Challenge of Authenticity." *Historical Journal of Film, Radio and Television.* Vol. 8, No. 3, 1988.

Davis, Susan G. "'Set Your Mood To Patriotic': History as Televised Special Event." *Radical History Review,* 42, 1988.

Doherty, Jim. "Maybe Small Towns Aren't Fancy, But at Least They're Real." *Smithsonian,* Vol. 24, No. 12, March 1994.

Downing, Taylor. "History on Television: The Making of *Cold War,* 1998." *Historical Journal of Film, Radio and Television.* Vol. 18, No. 3, August 1998.

Duren, Brad L. "NBC's The 60s: Incense, Politics and the Power of Nostalgia." A Paper Presented at the AC/PCA Conference, 2000, New Orleans, LA.

Edgerton, Gary R. "Introduction: Television as Historian: A Different Kind of History Altogether." *Television Histories: Shaping Collective Memory in the Media Age.* Edited by Gary R. Edgerton and Peter C. Rollins. Lexington, KY: The University of Kentucky Press, 2001.

Ehrenhaus, Peter. "Why We Fought: Holocaust Memory in Spielberg's *Saving Private Ryan.*" *Critical Studies in Media Communication,* September, 2001.

Elsaesser, Thomas. "Subject Positions, Speaking Positions: From *Holocaust, Our Hitler* and *Heimat* to *Shoah* and *Schindler's List.*" *The Persistence of History: Cinema, Television and the Modern Event.* Edited by Vivian Sobchack. New York: Routledge, 1996.

Epstein, Jason. "A Dissent of *Schindler's List.*" *The New York Review of Books.* April 21, 1984.

Featherstone, Mike. "Archiving Cultures." *British Journal of Sociology.* Vol. 51, No. 1, January 2000.

Feldman, Seth. "Our Regularly Scheduled Paradigm Shift." *Queen's Quarterly.* Vol. 104, No. 2 (Summer 1997).

Fishbein, Leslie. "*Roots*: Docudrama and the Interpretation of History." *Why Docudrama? Fact-Fiction on Film and TV.* Edited by Alan Rosenthal. Carbondale, IL: Southern Illinois University Press, 1999.

Frand, Jason L. "The Information-Age Mindset: Changes in Students and Implications for Higher Education." *EDUCAUSE Review,* September/October, 2000.

Franklin, John Hope. "Foreword." *The Past Before Us: Contemporary Historical Writing in the United States.* Edited by Michael Kammen. Ithaca, NY: Cornell University Press, 1980.

Franklin, Nancy. "Band of Brothers." *The New Yorker*. September 17, 2001.

Fraser, George MacDonald. "Hollywood and World History." *Why Docudrama? Fact-Fiction on Film and TV*. Edited by Alan Rosenthal. Carbondale, IL: Southern Illinois University Press, 1999.

Friedlander, Henry. "Postscript: Toward a Methodology of Teaching about the Holocaust." *The Holocaust: Ideology, Bureaucracy and Genocide*. Edited by Henry Friedlander and Sybil Milton. New York: Krauss Publishers, 1980.

Frisch, Michael. "The Memory of History." *Presenting The Past: Essays on History and The Public*. Edited by Susan Porter Benson, Stephen Brier and Roy Rosenzweig. Philadelphia, PA: Temple University Press, 1986.

———. "American History and the Structures of Collective Memory: A Modest Exercise in Empirical Iconography." *The Journal of American History*. Vol. 75, No. 4, March 1989.

Fulford, Robert. "The Ideology of the Book." *Queen's Quarterly*. Vol. 101, No. 3, Winter 1994.

Fulton, Marianne. "Changing Focus: The 1950s to the 1980s." *Eyes of Time*. Edited by Marianne Fulton.

Gandhi, Subash. "E-Books" The Future of Reading and Ultimate Books Publishing." *Journal of Educational Technological Systems*. Vol. 29, No. 1, 2000–2001.

Garber, Marjorie, John Matlock and Rebecca L. Walkowitz. "Introduction." *Media Spectacles*. Edited by John Matlock and Rebecca L. Walkowitz. New York: Taylor & Francis, 1993.

Gass, William H. "In Defense of The Book." *Harper's*. November 1999.

Gefen, Pearl Sheffy. "A Return to the Old West and 'Simpler Values.'" *The Globe and Mail*. Thursday, August 30, 1990.

Gibson, Stephanie B. "Literacy, Paradigm, and Paradox: An Introduction." *The Emerging Cyberculture: Literacy, Paradigm, and Paradox*. Edited by Stephanie B. Gibson and Ollie O. Oviedo. Cresskill, NJ: Hampton Press, Inc., 2000.

Gierstberg, Frits and Warna Oosterbaan. "Introduction: The Image Society." *The Image Society: Essays on Visual Culture*. Edited by Frits Gierstberg and Warna Oosterbaan. Rotterdam, The Netherlands: Nederlands Foto Institut, Nai Publishers, 2002.

Gilbert, Martin. "Unfinished Business." *The Jerusalem Post*, (International Edition), May 12, 1990.

Gitlin, Todd. "Introduction: Looking Through the Screen." *Watching Television*. Edited by Todd Gitlin. New York: Pantheon, 1986.

Godfrey, Donald G. "Broadcast Archives for Historical Research: Revisiting the Historical Method." *Journal of Broadcasting and Electronic Media*. Vol. 46, No. 3, September 2002.

Gourevitch, Phillip. "Behold Now Behemoth." *Harpers*. May 1993.

Griffin, Michael. "The Great War Photographs: Constructing Myths of History and Photojournalism." *Picturing the Past: Media, History and Photography*. Edited by Bonnie Brennen and Hanno Hardt. Urbana, IL: University of Illinois Press, 1999.

Gripsrud, Jostein. "Television and Common Knowledge: An Introduction." *Television and Common Knowledge*. Edited by Jostein Gripsrud. New York: Routledge, 1999.

Griswold, Charles, L. "The Vietnam Veterans Memorial and the Washington Mall: Philosophical Thoughts on Political Iconography." *Critical Inquiry*, No. 12 (Summer 1986).

Gross, Larry, John Stuart Katz, and Jay Ruby. "Introduction: Image Ethics in the Digital Age." *Image Ethics in the Digital Age*. Edited by Larry Gross, John Stuart Katz, and Jay Ruby. Minneapolis, MN: University of Minnesota Press, 2003.

Halevi, Yossi Klein. "Who Owns the Memory?" *The Jerusalem Report*. February 25, 1993.

Hallin, Daniel C. "Network News: 'We Keep American on Top of the World.'" *Watching Television*. Edited by Tod Gitlin. New York: Pantheon, 1986.

Hanke, Robert. "Quantum Leap: The Postmodern Challenge of Television as History." *Television Histories: Shaping Collective Memory in the Media Age*. Edited by Gary R. Edgerton and Peter C. Rollins. Lexington, KY: The University of Kentucky Press, 2001.

Hardt, Hanno and Bonnie Brennen. "Introduction." *Picturing the Past: Media, History and Photography*. Edited by Bonnie Brennen and Hanno Hardt. Urbana, IL: University of Illinois Press, 1999.

———. "Newswork, History, And Photographic Evidence: A Visual Analysis of a 1930s Newsroom." *Picturing the Past: Media, History and Photography*. Urbana, IL: University of Illinois Press, 1999.

Hasian, Jr., Marouf. "Nostalgic Longings, Memories of the 'Good War,' and Cinematic Representations in *Saving Private Ryan*." *Critical Studies in Media Communication*, September, 2001.

Healy, Jane M. "Visual Technology: Vacuous or Visionary?" *Holistic Education Review*. Vol. 6, No. 2 (Summer 1993).

Heidegger, Martin. "The Age of the World Picture." *The Question Concerning Technology and Other Essays*, translated and with an introduction by William Lovitt. New York: Harper Colophon Books, 1977.

Hockenberry, John. "Graphic News." *I.D. Magazine*. September/October 1996.

Hooks, Bell. "Making Movie Magic." *The Crisis of Criticism*. Edited by Maurice Berger. New York: The New Press, 1998.

Hoskins, Andrew. "New Memory: Mediating History." *Historical Journal of Film, Radio and Television*. Vol. 21, No. 4, 2001.

Jackson, Kenneth T. and Barbara B. Jackson. "Why the Time is Right to Reform the History Curriculum." *Historical Literacy: The Case for History in American Education*. Edited by Paul Gagnon. Boston: Houghton Mifflin, 1989.

Jacobowitz, Florence. "*Shoah* as Cinema." *Image and Remembrance: Representation and the Holocaust*. Edited by Shelley Hornstein and Florence Jacobowitz. Bloomington, IN: Indiana University Press, 2003.

James, Caryn. "Seeing *Schindler* Plain." *The New York Times*. January 23, 1994.

———. "They're Movies, Not Schoolbooks." *The New York Times*. Sunday, May 21, 1995, Section 2.

Jussim, Estelle. "'The Tyranny of the Pictorial': American Photojournalism from 1880 to 1920." *Eyes of Time: Photojournalism in America*. Edited by Marianne Fulton. Boston: Little, Brown & Company, 1988.

Kammen, Michael. "Some Patterns and Meanings of Memory Distortion in American History." *Memory Distortion: How Minds, Brains, and Societies Reconstruct the*

Past. Edited by Daniel L. Schacter. Cambridge, MA: Harvard University Press, 1995.

Kaplan, Nancy. "Literacy Beyond Books: Reading When All the World's a Web." *The World Wide Web and Contemporary Cultural Theory.* Edited by Andrew Herman and Thomas Swiss. New York: Routledge, 2000.

Kennedy, Janice. "Take-Out History: Canada's Past Served Up with Big Mac." *The Calgary Herald.* February 16, 1997.

Kneeshaw, Stephen. "Bring the Internet and World Wide Web into the History Classroom." *History.edu: Essays on Teaching with Technology.* Edited by Dennis A. Trinkle and Scott A. Merriman. Armonk, New York: M. E. Sharpe, 2001.

Kozol, Wendy. "'Good Americans': Nationalism and Domesticity in *LIFE* Magazine, 1945–1960." *Bonds of Affection: Americans Define Their Patriotism.* Edited by John Bodnar. Princeton, NJ: Princeton University Press, 1996.

Kuehl, Jerry. "History on the Public Screen, II." *New Challenges for Documentary.* Edited by Alan Rosenthal. Berkeley, CA: University of California Press, 1988.

Lacy, Dan. "Reading in an Audiovisual and Electronic Era." *Books in Our Future: Perspectives and Proposals.* Washington, DC: Library of Congress, 1987.

Lamm, Donald S. "Libraries and Publishers: A Partnerships at Risk." *DAEDALUS: Books, Bricks and Bytes.* Vol. 125, No. 4 (Fall 1996).

Landsberg, Alison. "Prosthetic Memory: *Total Recall* and *Blade Runner*." *Body and Society,* Vol. 1, Nos. 3–4, 1995.

Lantz, Chris J. "Realistic Visuals and Instruction." *College Quarterly.* Summer 1995.

Laville, Christian. "Historical Consciousness and Historical Education: What to Expect from the First for the Second." In Peter Seixas, Editor, *Theorizing Historical Consciousness.* Toronto: University of Toronto Press, 2005.

Lee, John K. "Digital History in the History/Social Studies Classroom." *The History Teacher.* Vol. 35, No. 4, August 2002.

Leith, James. "Ephemera: Civic Education Through Images." *Revolution in Print: The Press in France, 1775–1800.* Edited by Robert Darnton and Daniel Roche. Berkeley, CA: University of California Press, 1989.

Levine, Lawrence. "William Shakespeare and the American People: A Study in Cultural Transformation." *Rethinking Popular Culture: Contemporary Perspectives in Cultural Studies.* Edited by Chandra Mukeji and Michael Schudson. Berkeley, CA: University of California Press, 1991.

Linenthal, Edward T. "The Boundaries of Memory: The United States Holocaust Memorial Museum." *American Quarterly,* Vol. 46, No. 3, September 1994.

Liss, Andrea. "Rituals of Mourning and Mimesis: Arie A. Galles's Fourteen Stations." *Image and Remembrance: Representations and the Holocaust.* Edited by Shelley Hornstein and Florence Jacobowitz. Bloomington, IN: Indiana University Press, 2003.

Lister, Martin. "Introductory Essay." *The Photographic Image in Digital Culture.* Edited by Martin Lister. New York: Routledge, 1995.

Lohof, Bruce. "The Higher Meaning of Marlboro Cigarettes." *The Popular Culture Reader.* Third Edition. Edited by Christopher D. Geist and Jack Nachbar. Bowling Green, OH: Bowling Green University Popular Press, 1983.

Longhurst, James. "World History on the World Wide Web: A Student Satisfaction Survey and a Blinding Flash of the Obvious." *The History Teacher.* Vol. 36, No. 3, May 2003: www.historycoop.org/journals/ht/36.3.longurst.html

Loshitzky, Yosefa. "Introduction." *Spielberg's Holocaust: Critical Perspectives on Schindler's List*. Edited by Yosefa Loshitzky. Bloomington, IN: Indiana University Press, 1997.

Lutz, John. "Riding the Horseless Carriage to the Computer Revolution: Teaching History in the Twenty-First Century." Round Table. *Histoire sociale/Social History*. Vol. XXXIV, No. 68. November 2001.

Lyall, Sarah. "Are These Books, or What? CD-ROM and the Literary Industry." *The New York Times Book Review*. August 14, 1994.

Lyman, Peter. "What is a Digital Library? Technology, Intellectual Property, and the Public Interest." *DAEDALUS: Books, Bricks and Bytes*. Vol. 125, No. 4 (Fall 1996).

Macdonald, Dwight. "A Theory of Mass Culture." *Mass Culture*. Edited by B. Rosenberg and D. Manning White. London: Collier-Macmillan, 1957.

MacNeill, William H., Michael Kammen and Gordon Craig. "Why Study History? Three Historians Respond." *Historical Literacy: The Case for History in American Education*. Edited by Paul Gagnon. Boston: Houghton Mifflin Co., 1991.

Mallon, Thomas. "Visions of the Future, Relics of the Past." *The New York Times*. June 25, 1995.

Mallory, JoAnna Baldwin. "Introduction." *Telling The Story: The Media, The Public, and American History*. Edited by Sean B. Dolon. Boston: New England Foundation for the Humanities, 1994.

Mansbridge, Peter. "2004 Canada Post Lecture: Do the Media Reflect Canada's History?" *Tabaret: The Magazine of the University of Ottawa*. Spring 2005.

Marcus, Daniel. "Profiles in Courage: Televisual History on the New Frontier." *Television Histories: Shaping Collective Memory in the Media Age*. Lexington, KY: The University of Kentucky Press, 2001.

Marriot, Michel. "It's a Multi-Multimedia World." *Education Life, The New York Times*. November 9, 2003.

Marwil, Jonathan. "Photography at War." *History Today*. Vol. 50, No. 6, June 2000.

Mason, Marilyn Gell. "The Yin and Yang of Knowing." *DAEDALUS—Books, Bricks and Bytes*. Vol. 125, No. 4 (Fall 1996).

Mattheisen, Donald J. "Filming U.S. History During the 1920s: The Chronicles of America Photoplays." *The Historian*. Vol. 54, No. 4 (Summer 1992).

Mattson, Kevin. "Movies as History." *The Common Review*. Vol. 6, No. 1 (Summer 2007).

Miller, Mark Crispin. "How TV Covers War." *New Challenges for Documentary*. Edited by Alan Rosenthal. Manchester, UK: Manchester University Press, 2005.

Morgan, Konrad, Madeleine Morgan and John Hall. "Psychological Developments in High Technology Teaching and Learning Environments." *British Journal of Educational Technology*. Vol. 31, No. 1, January 2000.

Morton, Desmond. "A Shared Past is a Nation's Compass." *The Toronto Star*. September 26, 1997.

Moss, Mark. "Dressing History: Nostalgia and Class in the Worlds of Ralph Lauren." *Popular Culture Review*. Vol. XIV, No. 2 (Summer 2003).

Muschamp, Herbert. "How Buildings Remember." *The New Republic*. August 28, 1989.

Namier, Lewis. "History and Political Culture." *The Varieties of History: From Voltaire to the Present*. Edited by Fritz Stern. New York: Vintage Books, 1973.

Nehamas, Alexander. "Serious Watching." *The South Atlantic Quarterly*. Vol. 89, No. 1 (Winter 1990).

Newell, Margaret E. "Subterranean Electronic Blues; or, How a Former Technophobe Learned to Stop Worrying and Love Multimedia." *The Journal of American History*. Vol. 83, No. 4 (March 1997).

Nunberg, Geoffrey. "The Places of Books in the Age of Electronic Reproduction." *Representations* 42, (Spring 1993).

O'Connor, John E. "Reflections on the Importance of Film and Television Study for an Understanding of the Past." *American Historical Review*. "Forum." Vol. 93, No. 5, December 1988.

———. "Reading, Writing and Critical Viewing: Coordinating Skill Development in History Learning." *The History Teacher*. Vol. 34, No. 2, February 2001: www.history.cooperative.org/journals/ht/34.2/oconnor.html

O'Connor, John E. and Martin A. Jackson. "Introduction." *American History/American Film: Interpreting the Hollywood Image*. Edited by John E. O'Connor and Martin A. Jackson. New York: Ungar Publishing, 1988.

Oppenheimer, Todd. "The Computer Delusion." *The Atlantic Monthly*. July 1997.

Orcutt, William Dana. "Aldus Manutius." *A Passion for Books*. Edited by Harold Rabinowitz and Rob Kaplan. New York: Three Rivers Press, 1999.

Osborne, Ken. "Teaching Heritage in the Classroom." *The Place of History: Commemorating Canada's Past*. Edited by Thomas H. B. Symons. Proceedings of the National Symposium held on the Occasion of the 75th Anniversary of the Historic Sites and Monuments Board of Canada. November 26–28, 1994. The Royal Society of Canada, 1997.

Osman, Colin and Sandra S. Phillips. "European Visions: Magazine Photography in Europe Between the Wars." *Eyes of Time: Photojournalism in America*. Edited by Marianne Fulton. Boston: Little, Brown & Company, 1988.

Owen, A. Susan. "Memory, War and American Identity: *Saving Private Ryan* as Cinematic Jeremiad." *Critical Studies in Mass Communication*. Vol. 19, No. 3, September 2002.

Pascal, Michel. "Interview with Steven Spielberg: 'Why I Made *Schindler's List*.'" *Queen's Quarterly*, Vol. 191, No. 1 (Spring 1994).

Perlmutter, David D. "The Internet: Big Pictures and Interactors." *Image Ethics in the Digital Age*. Larry Gross, John Stuart Katz, and Jay Ruby, Editors. Minneapolis, MN: University of Minnesota Press, 2003.

Picker, Lauren. "The Web As Homework Helper." *Newsweek/Score*. 2000 Edition.

Plane, Brian. "Computer-Generated Graphics and the Demise of the History Textbook." In Dennis A. Trinkle and Scott A. Merriman, Editors. *History.edu: Essays on Teaching with Technology*. Armonk, NY: M. E. Sharpe, 2001.

Pomerantz, Linda. "Bridging the Digital Divide: Reflections on 'Teaching and Learning in the Digital Age.'" *The History Teacher*. Vol. 34, No. 4, August 2001: www.historycoop.org/journals/ht/34.4/pomerantz.html.

Postman, Neil. "The Dinner Conversation." *Harpers*, March 1991.

Price, Derrick and Liz Wells. "Thinking About Photography." *Photography: A Critical Introduction*, Second Edition. Edited by Liz Wells. New York: Routledge, 2000.

Qureshi, Afsun. "One Moment, Lasting Forever." *The Saturday Post*. December 29, 2001.

Ravitch, Diane. "Technology and the Curriculum: Promise and Peril." *What Curriculum for the Information Age?* Edited by Mary Alice White. Hilldale, NJ: Lawrence Erlbaum Associates, 1987.

Ringrose, Daniel. 'Beyond Amusement: Reflections on Multimedia, Pedagogy, and Digital Literacy in the History Seminar." *The History Teacher.* Vol. 34, No. 2, February 2001: www.historycooperative.or/journals/ht/34.2ringrose.html

Ritchin, Fred. "Close Witnesses: The Involvement of the Photojournalist." *A New History of Photography.* Edited by Michel Frizot. Cologne, Germany: Konemann, 1999.

Rivers, Dyanne. "Why Don't You Read Something Worthwhile?" *Home & School,* January 1995.

Rogin, Michael. "Body and Soul Murder: JFK." *Media Spectacles.* Edited by John Matlock and Rebecca Walkowitz. New York: Routledge, 1993.

Rollins, Peter C. "Introduction." *Hollywood As Historian: American Film In A Cultural Context.* Edited by Peter C. Rollins. Lexington, KY: The University Press of Kentucky, 1983.

Rose, Brian. "Preface." *T.V. Genres: A Handbook and Reference Guide.* Edited by Brian Rose. Westport, CT: Greenwood Press, 1985.

Rosenthal, Alan. "Introduction: Part I." *New Challenges for Documentary.* Edited by Alan Rosenthal. Berkeley, CA: University of California Press, 1988.

Rosenthal, Harry, F. "Holocaust Museum Assaults Human Senses." *The Globe and Mail.* April 28, 1993.

Rosenstone, Robert. "History in Images/History in Worlds: Reflections on the Possibility of Really Putting History onto Film." *American Historical Review.* Forum. Vol. 93, No. 5, December 1988.

———. "Historians and Their Audience." *Telling The Story: The Media, The Public, and American History.* Edited by Sean B. Dolon. Boston: New England Foundation for the Humanities, 1994.

———. "JFK: Historical Fact/Historical Film." *Why Docudrama? Fact-Fiction on Film and TV.* Edited by Alan Rosenthal. Carbondale, IL: University of Illinois Press, 1999.

Rosenzweig, Roy. "Scarcity or Abundance? Preserving the Past in a Digital Era." The *American Historical Review.* Vol. 108, No. 3, July 2003: www.historycoop.org/journals/ahr/108.3rsosenzweig.html

———. "'So, What's Next for Clio?' CD-ROM and Historians." *The Journal of American History.* Vol. 81, No. 4, March 1995.

Ross, Rachel. "E-mail at 30." *The Toronto Star.* October 8, 2001.

Ruby, Jay. "The Ethics of Imagemaking." *New Challenges for Documentary.* Edited by Alan Rosenthal. Manchester, UK: Manchester University Press, 2005.

Safire, William. "Standing History Still: A Prolegomenon." *Pictures of the Times: A Century of Photography from The New York Times.* Edited by Peter Galassi and Susan Kismaric. New York: The Museum of Modern Art/Harry N. Abrams, Inc., 1986.

Samuel, Raphael. "Theme Parks—Why Not?" *City Cultures Reader.* Edited by Malcolm Miles, Tim Hall, Iain Borden. New York: Routledge, 2000.

Schick, James B. M. "What Do Students Really Think of History?" *The History Teacher.* Vol. 24, No. 3, May 1991.

Schwartz, Barry, Yael Zerubavel, Bernice Barnett. "The Recovery of Masada: A Study in Collective Memory." *The Sociological Quarterly*. Vol. 27, No. 2, 1986.

Schwartz, Donald. "Who Will Tell Them After We're Gone: Reflections on Teaching the Holocaust." *The History Teacher*. Vol. 23, No. 2, February 1990.

Scully, Robert. "Heritage Sound Bites." *The Place of History: Commemorating Canada's Past*. Edited by Thomas H. B. Symons. Proceedings of the National Symposium held on the Occasion of the 75th Anniversary of the Historic Sites and Monuments Board of Canada. November 26–28, 1994. The Royal Society of Canada, 1997.

Seixas, Peter. "Introduction." *Theorizing Historical Consciousness*. Edited by Peter Seixas. Toronto: University of Toronto Press, 2006.

Short, K. R. M. "Introduction: Feature Films As History." *Feature Films as History*. Edited by K. R. M. Short. London: Croom Helm, 1981.

Sicher, Efraim. "The Future of the Past: Countermemory and Postmemory in Contemporary American Post-Holocaust Narratives." *History and Memory*. Vol. 12, No. 2 (Fall 2000).

Simon, Roger I. "Forms of Insurgency In the Production of Popular Memories: The Columbus Quincenteneray and the Pedagogy of Counter-Commemoration." Draft Chapter.

Smith, Michael L. "Selling The Moon: The U.S. Manned Space Program and the Triumph of Commodity Scientism." *The Culture of Consumption: Critical Essays in American History, 1880–1980*. Edited by Richard Wrightman Fox and T. J. Jackson Lears. New York: Pantheon Books, 1983.

Snyder, Joel. "Benjamin on Reproducibility and Aura." *The Philosophical Forum*. Vol. XV, Nos. 101–02 (Fall/Winter, 1983–1984).

Sontag, Susan. "Looking at War: Photography's View of Devastation and Death." *The New Yorker*. December 9, 2002.

Springer, Claudia. "Vietnam: A Television History and the Equivocal Nature of Objectivity." *Wide Angle: A Film Quarterly*, Vol. 7, No. 4, 1985.

Staiger, Janet. "Cinematic Shots: The Narrative of Violence." *The Persistence of History: Cinema, Television and the Modern Event*. Edited by Vivian Sobchack. New York: Taylor & Francis, 1995.

Stapp, William. "'Subjects of Strange . . . And of Fearful Interest': Photojournalism From Its Beginnings in 1839." *Eyes of Time: Photojournalism in America*. Edited by Marianne Fulton. Boston: Little, Brown & Company, 1988.

Starr, Paul. "Computing Our Way to Educational Reform." *The American Prospect*. July/August 1996.

Stater, Don. "Photography and Modern Vision: The Spectacles of 'Natural Magic.'" *Visual Culture*. Edited by Chris Jenks. New York: Routledge, 1995.

Stern, Fritz. "Introduction." *The Varieties of History: From Voltaire to the Present*. Edited by Fritz Stern. New York: Vintage Books, 1973.

Stoffman, Judy. "Taking fancy to fantasy: How Harry Potter changed children's literature forever." *The Toronto Star*. November 9, 2002.

Stone, Oliver and Mark Carnes. "A Conversation Between Mark Carnes and Oliver Stone." *Past Imperfect: History According to the Movies*. Edited by Mark Carnes. New York: Henry Holt, 1996.

Stricker, Frank. "Why History? Thinking About the Uses of the Past." *The History Teacher*. Vol. 25, No. 3, May 1992.

Sturken, Marita. "The Television Image and Collective Amnesia: Dis(re)membering the Persian Gulf War." *Transmission: Toward a Post-Television Culture*. Edited by Peter d'Agostino and David Tafler. Thousand Oaks, CA.: Sage Publications, 1995.

Tabeau, Mark. "Pursuing E-Opportunities in the History Classroom." *The Journal of American History*. Vol. 89, No. 4, March 2003.

Talbot, David. "Forward." *Afterwards: Stories and Reports from 9/11 and Beyond*. Compiled by the Editors of Salon.com. New York: Washington Square Press, 2002.

Taylor, Bruce. "The Vietnam War Movie." *The Legacy: The Vietnam War in the American Imagination*. Edited by D. Michael Shafer. Boston: Beacon Press, 1990.

Taylor, J. C. "The Art Museum in the United States." *Understanding Art Museums*. Edited by Sherman Lee. Upper Saddle River, NJ: Prentice Hall, 1975.

Thelen, David. "Memory and American History." *The Journal of American History*. Vol. 75, No. 4. March 1989.

Thomas, Marcel. "Manuscripts." *The Coming of The Book: The Impact of Printing, 1450–1800*. By Lucien Febvre and Henri-Jean Martin. London: Verso, 1976.

Thomas, William G., III. "Blazing Trails Toward Digital History Scholarship." Round Table. *Histoire social/Social History*. Vol. XXXIV, No. 68, November 2001.

Tisdale, Sally. "Silence Please: The Public Library as Entertainment Center." *Harper's*. March 1997.

Todd, Jennifer. "Production, Reception, Criticism: Walter Benjamin and the Problem of Meaning in Art." *The Philosophical Forum*. Vol. XV, Nos. 101–02 (Fall/Winter, 1983–1984).

Tomasulo, Frank P. "'I'll See It When I Believe It: Rodney King and the Prison-House of Video." *The Persistence of History: Cinema, Television and the Modern Event*. Edited by Vivian Sobchack. New York: Taylor & Francis, 1995.

Toplin, Robert Brent. "Plugged Into the Past." *The New York Times*. August 4, 1996, Section 2.

Trask, David. "Did the Sans-Coulottes Wear Nikes? The Impact of Electronic Media on the Understanding and Teaching of History." *The History Teacher*. Vol. 35, No. 4, August 2002.

Wach, Howard M. "'How I Arrived on the Web': A History Teacher's Tale." *The History Teacher*. Vol. 36, No. 1, November 2002: www.historycoop.org/journals/ht/36.1/wach.html

Wagar, W. Warren. "Past and Future." *American Behavioral Scientist*. Vol. 42, No. 3, November/December, 1998.

Waldrep, Shelton. "Story Time." *Inside The Mouse: Work and Play at Disney World*. The Project on Disney. Durham, NC: Duke University Press, 1995.

Wallace, Mike. "Mickey Mouse History: Portraying the Past at Disney World." *Radical History Review*. 32, 1985.

Watson, Simon. "Dachau Awakening." *Queen's Quarterly*. Vol. 114, No. 3 (Fall 2007).

Watt, Donald. "History on the Public Screen, I." *New Challenges for Documentary*. Edited by Alan Rosenthal. Manchester, UK: Manchester University Press, 2005.

Weinraub, Bernard. "Steven Spielberg Faces the Holocaust." *The New York Times.* Sunday, December, 12, 1993.

Weisberg, Jacob. "The Good E-Book." *The New York Times Magazine.* June 4, 2000.

West, Emily. "Selling Canada to Canadians: Collective Memory, National Identity and Popular Culture." *Critical Studies in Media Communication,* June 2002.

Whissel, Kristen, "Placing the Spectator on the Scene of History: The Battle Re-Enactment at the Turn of the Century, From Buffalo Bill's Wild West to the Early Cinema." *Historical Journal of Film, Radio and Television.* Vol. 22, No. 2, 2002.

White, Hayden. "Historiography and Historiophoty." *American Historical Review.* Forum. Vol. 93, No. 5, December 1988.

———. "The Modernist Event." *The Persistence of History: Cinema, Television and the Modern Event.* Edited by Vivian Sobchack. New York: Taylor & Francis, 1995.

White, Mimi. "Television: A Narrative—A History." *Cultural Studies.* Vol. 3, No. 3, October 1989.

———. "Masculinity and Femininity in Television's Historical Fictions: *Young Indiana Jones Chronicles* and *Dr. Quinn, Medicine Woman.*" *Television Histories: Shaping Collective Memory in the Media Age.* Lexington, KY: University Press of Kentucky, 2001.

Wiatr, Elizabeth. "Between Word, Image and the Machine: Visual Education and Films of Industrial Process." *Historical Journal of Film, Radio and Television.* Vol. 22, No. 3, 2002.

Williams, Raymond. "Drama in a Dramatised Society." *Raymond Williams on Television.* Edited by Allen O'Connor. Toronto: Between The Lines Press, 1989.

Willis, Susan. "The Problem With Pleasure." The Project on Disney. *Inside the Mouse: Work and Play at Disney World.* Durham, NC: Duke University Press, 1995.

Wilson, Michael L. "Visual Culture: A Useful Category of Historical Analysis?" *The Nineteenth-Century Visual Culture Reader.* Edited by Vanessa R. Schwartz and Jeannene M. Przyblysk. New York: Routledge, 2004.

Wind, Edgar. "The Revolution of History Painting." *Readings in Art History: The Renaissance to the Present.* Second Edition, Vol. 2. Edited by Harold Spencer. New York: Scribners, 1976.

Winston, Brian. "Documentary: I Think We Are in Trouble." *New Challenges for Documentary.* Edited by Alan Rosenthal. Manchester, UK: Manchester University Press, 2005.

Wloszcyna, Susan. "History is Back in Action." *USA Today.* April 21, 2000.

Yacower, Maurice. "Schindler's Film." *Queen's Quarterly.* Vol. 101, No. 1. Spring 1994.

Zelizer, Barbie. "Every Once in a While: *Schindler's List* and the Shaping of History." *Spielberg's Holocaust.* Edited by Yosefa Loshitzky. Bloomington, IN: Indiana University Press, 1997.

———. "From the Image of Record to the Image of Memory: Holocaust Photography, Then and Now." *Picturing the Past: Media, History and Photography.* Edited by Bonnie Brennen and Hanno Hardt. Urbana, IL: University of Illinois Press, 1999.

———. "Photography, Journalism and Trauma." *Journalism After September 11.* Edited by Barbie Zelizer and Stuart Allen. New York: Routledge, 2002.

Zevin, Ben D. "The Bible Through The Ages." *Passion for Books.* Edited by Harold Rabinowitz and Rob Kaplan. New York: Crown Publishing Group, 2001.

Index

About the Author

Mark Moss was educated at York University and the Ontario Institute for Studies in Education at the University of Toronto, where he obtained a doctorate in history of education. He is Chair of the Liberal Arts program at Seneca College in Toronto, Ontario. Author of *Manliness and Militarism* and *Shopping as an Entertainment Experience* (Lexington Books), his current scholarly focus is divided between completing a book on contemporary masculinity and research on the interplay between technology and the humanities.

VSW P 96 .H55 M68 2008

Moss, Mark Howard, 1962-

Toward the visualization of
history